Rick Steves®

BEST OF IRELAND

Rick Steves & Pat O'Connor

Contents

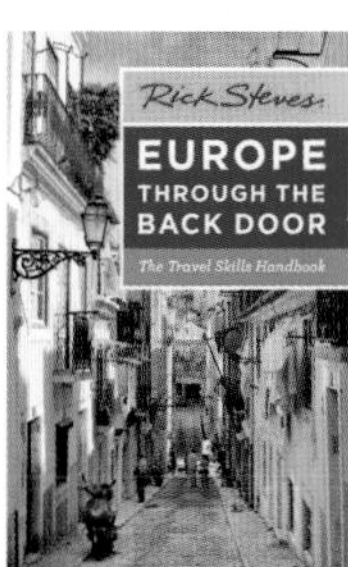

POCKET GUIDES

Compact, full color city guides with the essentials for shorter trips

Amsterdam
Athens
Barcelona
Florence
Italy's Cinque Terre
London
Munich & Salzburg
Paris
Prague
Rome
Venice
Vienna

SNAPSHOT GUIDES

Focused single-destination coverage

Basque Country: Spain & France
Copenhagen & the Best of Denmark
Dublin
Dubrovnik
Edinburgh
Hill Towns of Central Italy
Krakow, Warsaw & Gdansk
Lisbon
Loire Valley
Madrid & Toledo
Milan & the Italian Lakes District
Naples & the Amalfi Coast
Nice & the French Riviera
Normandy
Northern Ireland
Norway
Reykjavík
Rothenburg & the Rhine
Sevilla, Granada & Southern Spain
St. Petersburg, Helsinki & Tallinn
Stockholm

Rick Steves books are available from your favorite bookseller. Many guides are available as ebooks.

CRUISE PORTS GUIDES

Reference for cruise ports of call

Mediterranean Cruise Ports
Scandinavian & Northern European Cruise Ports

Complete your library with...

TRAVEL SKILLS & CULTURE

Europe 101
Europe Through the Back Door
European Christmas
European Easter
European Festivals
Europe's Top 100 Masterpieces
For the Love of Europe
Postcards from Europe
Travel as a Political Act

PHRASE BOOKS & DICTIONARIES

French
French, Italian & German
German
Italian
Portuguese
Spanish

PLANNING MAPS

Britain, Ireland & London
Europe
France & Paris
Germany, Austria & Switzerland
Iceland
Ireland
Italy
Spain & Portugal

ACKNOWLEDGEMENTS

Thank you to Risa Laib for her 25-plus years of dedication to the Rick Steves guidebook series.

PHOTO CREDITS

Front Cover: (top, left to right) Clonmacnoise Cross © Daniel M. Cisilino/Dreamstime.com, Temple Bar, Dublin © Daniel Serrano/Dreamstime.com, Titanic Belfast © VanderWolfImages/Dreamstime.com, Cliffs of Moher © Stefano Valeri/Dreamstime.com

Back Cover: (top, left to right) Parliament street, Kilkenny © Daniel M. Cisilino/Dreamstime.com, Rock of Cashel © Pierre Leclerc/Dreamstime.com, Pint of Guinness © Joaquin Ossorio Castillo/Dreamstime.com

Title Page: (top, left to right) Celtic Cross © Dominic Arizona Bonuccelli, Pub in Belfast © Dominic Arizona Bonuccelli, Cobh City © Madrugadaverde/Dreamstime.com, Ireland Coast © Gbphoto27/Dreamstime.com

Alamy: 16 (middle right) imageBROKER, 63 Rik Hamilton

Dreamstime: 13 (bottom left) © Arsty, 14 (middle right) © Pajda83, 14 (bottom) © Cmfotoworks, 15 (top right) © Gunold, 19 (top left) © VanderWolf Images, 21 (top left and right) © Andrews71, 21 (middle) © Tonybrindley, 25 (top) © Bred2k8, 25 (bottom) © Pajda83, 34 © Gunold, 36 © Iwhitwo, 60 (right) © Trondur, 70 © Andrews71, 71 (left) © Spanishjohnny72, 72 (left) © Gunold, 81 (right) © Madrugadaverde, 97 © Stbernardstudio, 100 © Juliusc, 102 © Gnup, 103 © Eireanna, 107 © Bjoernalberts, 110 © Pascalou95, 114 © Littleny, 115 © Wayfarer, 117 (right) © Krylon80, 118 © Peteleclerc, 122 (right) © Marcviln, 135 © Arsty, 142 © Andyperiam, 153 © Imagoinsulae, 154 (top) © Jmci, 201 © Matthi, 238 © Igabriela, 239 © Mustang79, 243 (right) © Powerspectrum, 244 © Albertoloyo, 275 (top) © Arsty, 287 © Surangaw, 292 © Zastavkin, 300 © Pkphotography, 302 © Nagalski, 312 © Juliamidd, 318 © Hecke01, 321 © Hecke01, 322 (top) © Hecke01, 322 (bottom) © Andrews71, 326 (right) © Andrews71, 328 © Wayneduguay

Public Domain via Wikimedia Commons: 11 (bottom left), 65 (left), 68, 73 (bottom)

Additional Photography: Dominic Arizona Bonuccelli, Robin Clewley, Rich Earl, Mike Neelley, Pat O'Connor, Rhonda Pelikan, Jessica Shaw, Rick Steves. Photos are used by permission and are the property of the original copyright owners.

Avalon Travel
Hachette Book Group
1700 Fourth Street
Berkeley, CA 94710

Printed in China
Third Edition. First printing November 2020.
ISBN 978-1-64171-271-2

For the latest on Rick's talks, guidebooks, tours, public television series, and public radio show, contact Rick Steves' Europe, 130 Fourth Avenue North, Edmonds, WA 98020, 425/771-8303, RickSteves.com, rick@ricksteves.com.

The publisher is not responsible for websites (or their content) that are not owned by the publisher.

RICK STEVES' EUROPE
Managing Editor: Jennifer Madison Davis
Assistant Managing Editor: Cathy Lu
Editors: Glenn Eriksen, Suzanne Kotz, Rosie Leutzinger, Teresa Nemeth, Jessica Shaw, Carrie Shepherd, Meg Sneeringer
Editorial & Production Assistant: Megan Simms
Graphic Content Director: Sandra Hundacker
Maps & Graphics: David C. Hoerlein, Lauren Mills, Mary Rostad
Digital Asset Coordinator: Orin Dubrow

AVALON TRAVEL
Editorial Director: Kevin McLain
Senior Editor and Series Manager: Madhu Prasher
Associate Managing Editors: Jamie Andrade, Sierra Machado
Copy Editor: Kelly Lydick
Indexer: Stephen Callahan
Interior Design: McGuire Barber Design
Interior Layout: Rue Flaherty, Tabitha Lahr, Ravina Schneider
Cover Design: Kimberly Glyder Design
Maps & Graphics: Kat Bennett, Kathryn Osgood

Let's Keep on Travelin'

Your trip doesn't need to end.

Follow Rick on social media!

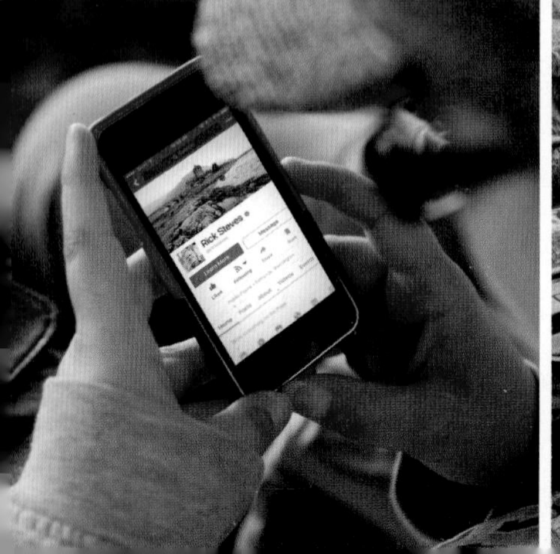

Post-Pandemic Travels: Expect a Warm Welcome...and a Few Changes

Research for this guidebook was limited by the COVID-19 outbreak, and the long-term impact of the crisis on our recommended destinations is unclear. Some details in this book will change for post-pandemic travelers. Now more than ever, it's smart to reconfirm specifics as you plan and travel. As always, you can find major updates at RickSteves.com/update.

LEGEND
A-4 Motorway
Major Roads
Major Rail Line
Airport
National Park or Natural Wonder
Gaeltacht (Irish-speaking Regions)
Ruin, Museum, Other Point of Interest
Castle/Monument/Palace
50 Kilometers
50 Miles
Bloody Foreland
Bunbeg
Dungloe
Glencolumbkille
Cliffs of Bunglass
Donegal
Ballyshannon
N-15
DRUMCLIFF (YEATS' GRAVE)
Belleek
Sligo
N-16
Lough Gill
SLIGO
Erris Head
Belmullet
Ballina
N-59
Achill Island
MAYO
Lough Conn
N-17
N-5
Clare Island
Clew Bay
Westport
Castlebar
Louisburgh
CROAGH PATRICK
Knock
Carrick-on-Shannon
Strokestown
Leenane
CONNEMARA
KYLEMORE ABBEY
N-59
Ballinrobe
Neale
Clifden
ASHFORD
Cong
N-17
Longford
Recess
Roscommon
Lough Ree
Roundstone
N-59
Lough Corrib
Tuam
Ross
N-84
Atlantic Ocean
REPU
Rossaveal
Galway
Athenry
Salthill
Athlone
DUN AENGUS
Kilronan
Galway Bay
M-6
O
Aran Islands
DUNGUAIRE
CLONMACNOISE
Ballyvaughan
Kinvarra
Doolin
Lisdoonvarna
Portumna
Cliffs of Moher
THE BURREN
Gort
IREL
Lahinch
Corrofin
M-18
Lough Derg
Birr
CLARE
Ennis
BUNRATTY CASTLE & FOLK PARK
Roscrea
Kilkee
N-67
N-68
Shannon
M-7
Loop Head
Killimer
Shannon
TIPPERARY
Limerick
Tarbert
Adare
M-8
DINGLE PENINSULA
N-69
Limerick Junction
N-24
GALLARUS ORATORY
N-21
ROCK OF CASHEL
Slea Head
Tralee
Cashel
Dingle
KERRY
N-86
N-20
Tipperary
Blasket Islands
MINARD CASTLE
Kerry
Caher
Clonmel
Inch Strand
N-72
Valentia Island
N-70
Lough Leane
Killarney
Mallow
RING OF KERRY
MUCKROSS HOUSE
N-72
Portmagee
WATER
Sneem
Kenmare
BLARNEY CASTLE
M-8
Dungarvan
Skellig Michael
DERRYNANE HOUSE
N-71
Macroom
N-22
Blarney
Midleton
Lee
Youghal
N-25
BEARA
Glengarriff
Cork
Adrigole
CORK
Cork
Cobh
Ardmore
Bantry Bay
Bantry
Kinsale
Skull
R-600
CHARLES FORT
N-71
Skibbereen
DROMBEG STONE CIRCLE
Mizen Head
To Roscoff, France

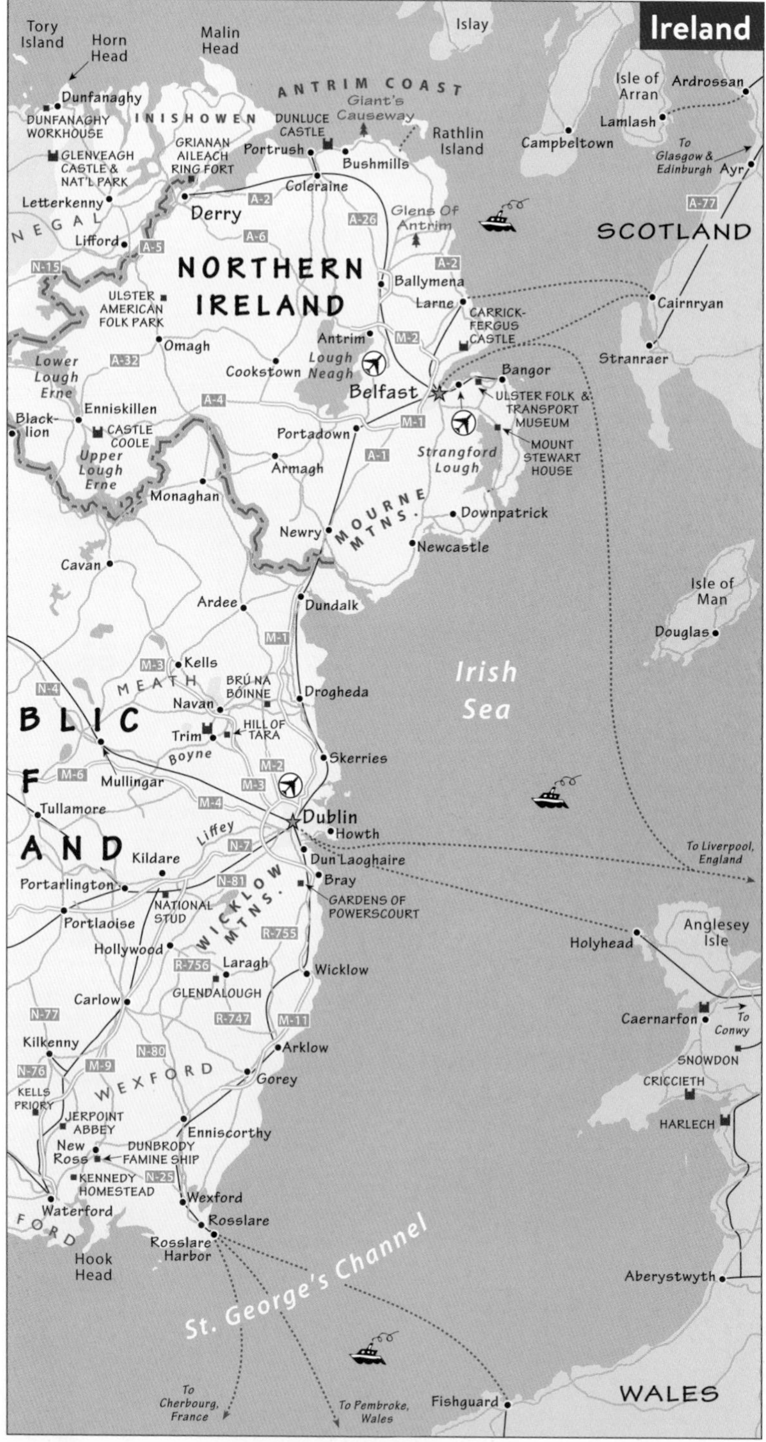
Ireland
Tory Island
Horn Head
Malin Head
Islay
ANTRIM COAST
Giant's Causeway
Isle of Arran
Ardrossan
Dunfanaghy
DUNFANAGHY WORKHOUSE
INISHOWEN
DUNLUCE CASTLE
Rathlin Island
Lamlash
Campbeltown
GLENVEAGH CASTLE & NAT'L PARK
GRIANAN AILEACH RING FORT
Portrush
Bushmills
To Glasgow & Edinburgh
Ayr
Letterkenny
Coleraine
Derry
Glens Of Antrim
SCOTLAND
DONEGAL
Lifford
NORTHERN IRELAND
Ballymena
ULSTER AMERICAN FOLK PARK
Larne
Cairnryan
CARRICK-FERGUS CASTLE
Antrim
Stranraer
Omagh
Lough Neagh
Lower Lough Erne
Cookstown
Bangor
Belfast
ULSTER FOLK & TRANSPORT MUSEUM
Enniskillen
Blacklion
CASTLE COOLE
Portadown
MOUNT STEWART HOUSE
Upper Lough Erne
Strangford Lough
Armagh
Monaghan
MOURNE MTNS.
Downpatrick
Newry
Newcastle
Cavan
Isle of Man
Ardee
Dundalk
Douglas
Kells
MEATH
BRÚ NA BÓINNE
Irish Sea
Navan
Drogheda
Trim
HILL OF TARA
Boyne
Skerries
Mullingar
Tullamore
Dublin
Howth
Liffey
Kildare
Dun Laoghaire
To Liverpool, England
Portarlington
Bray
GARDENS OF POWERSCOURT
NATIONAL STUD
WICKLOW MTNS.
Portlaoise
Anglesey Isle
Holyhead
Hollywood
Laragh
Wicklow
GLENDALOUGH
Carlow
Caernarfon
To Conwy
Kilkenny
Arklow
SNOWDON
WEXFORD
Gorey
CRICCIETH
KELLS PRIORY
JERPOINT ABBEY
HARLECH
Enniscorthy
New Ross
DUNBRODY FAMINE SHIP
KENNEDY HOMESTEAD
Wexford
Waterford
Rosslare
Rosslare Harbor
Hook Head
St. George's Channel
Aberystwyth
To Cherbourg, France
To Pembroke, Wales
Fishguard
WALES
A-2
A-26
A-6
A-5
N-15
A-32
A-4
M-1
M-2
A-1
A-77
M-3
N-4
M-6
M-4
N-7
N-81
R-755
R-756
R-747
M-11
N-77
N-80
M-9
N-76
N-25

Introduction

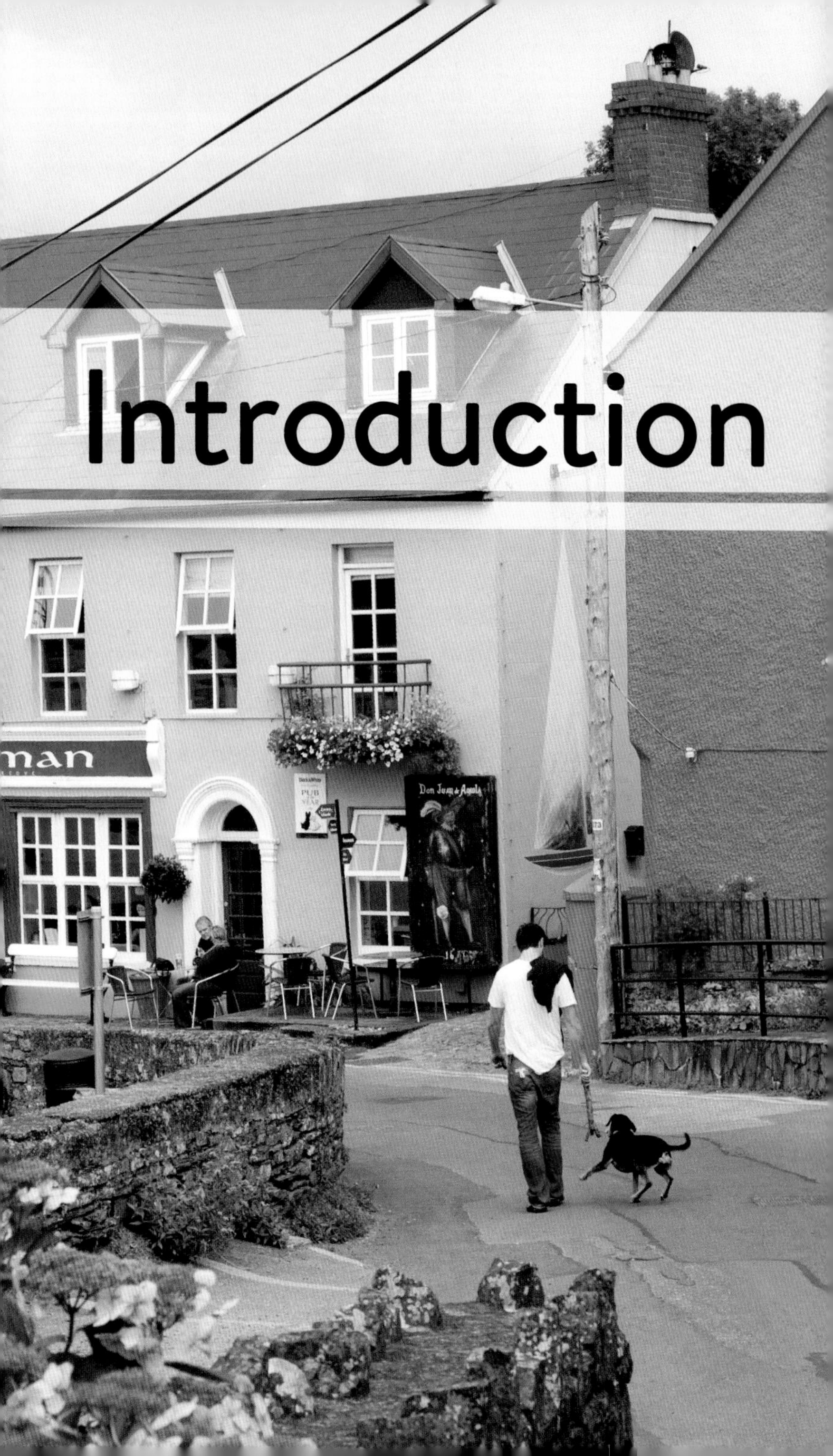

Flung onto the foggy fringe of the Atlantic pond like a mossy millstone, Ireland drips with mystery, drawing you in for a closer look. You won't find the proverbial pot of gold, but you will treasure the engaging and feisty Irish people. Irish culture—with its unique language, intricate art, and mesmerizing music—is as intoxicating as the famous Irish brew, Guinness.

The Irish revere their past and love their proverbs (such as "When God made time, he made a lot of it"). Ireland is dusted with prehistoric stone circles, beehive huts, and standing stones—some older than the pyramids. While much of Europe has buried older cultures under new, Ireland still reveals its cultural bedrock.

Today's Ireland is vibrant, cosmopolitan, and complex. The small island (about the size of Maine) holds two distinctly different Irelands: the Republic of Ireland (an independent nation that's mainly Catholic) and Northern Ireland (part of the United Kingdom, roughly half Protestant and half Catholic). No visit is complete without a look at both.

Want to really get to know Ireland? Belly up to the bar in a neighborhood pub and engage a local in conversation. The Irish have a worldwide reputation as talkative, musical, moody romantics with a quick laugh and a ready smile. Come join them.

THE BEST OF IRELAND

In this selective book, I recommend Ireland's top destinations—a mix of lively cities, cozy towns, and natural wonders—along with the best sights and experiences they have to offer.

The biggie on everyone's list is Dublin, the energetic, friendly capital of the Republic of Ireland. But there's so much more to see. The island is dotted with Celtic and Christian ruins, cliffside fortresses, and prehistoric sites. Brú na Bóinne's burial mounds are older than Stonehenge. There's the proud town of Kilkenny, the historic Rock of Cashel, colorful Kinsale, and two peninsula loops: the famous Ring of Kerry and the more intimate Slea Head Loop near Dingle. Youthful Galway is a good launchpad for dramatic scenery: the sheer Cliffs of Moher (in County Clare) and craggy Aran Islands.

In Northern Ireland, historic Belfast sheds light on the political Troubles that once bitterly divided this country. The lush Antrim Coast delights visitors, with fun-loving Portrush serving as a handy home base.

Beyond the major destinations, I cover the Best of the Rest—great destinations that don't quite make my top cut, but are worth seeing if you have more time: the region of Connemara and the town of Derry. When interesting sights or towns

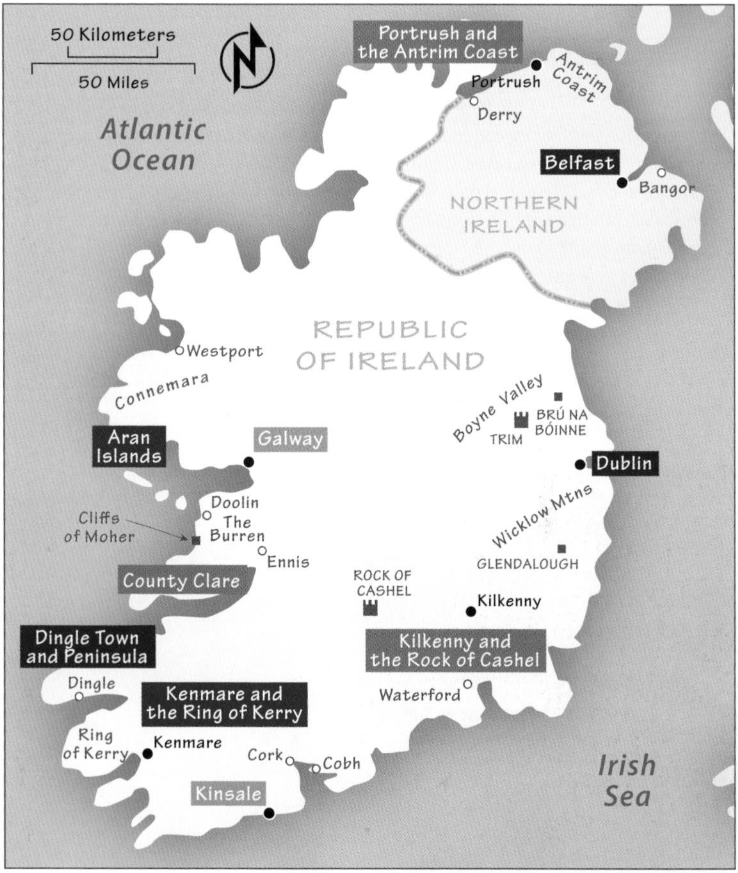

50 Kilometers
50 Miles
N
Atlantic Ocean
Portrush and the Antrim Coast
Portrush
Antrim Coast
Derry
Belfast
Bangor
NORTHERN IRELAND
REPUBLIC OF IRELAND
Westport
Connemara
Boyne Valley
BRÚ NA BÓINNE
TRIM
Aran Islands
Galway
Dublin
Doolin
The Burren
Cliffs of Moher
Ennis
Wicklow Mtns
GLENDALOUGH
County Clare
ROCK OF CASHEL
Kilkenny
Dingle Town and Peninsula
Kilkenny and the Rock of Cashel
Dingle
Kenmare and the Ring of Kerry
Waterford
Ring of Kerry
Kenmare
Cork
Cobh
Irish Sea
Kinsale

are near my recommended destinations, I cover them briefly, to help you enjoyably fill out a free day or a longer stay.

To help you link the top sights, I've designed a two-week itinerary (on page 24), with tips for tailoring it to your interests.

THE BEST OF DUBLIN

The bustling capital of the Republic of Ireland is a fascinating concoction of treasured Dark Age gospels, Celtic artifacts, and rambunctious pubs. It shows its heart in its sights—from the Kilmainham Gaol (where the English imprisoned Irish rebels and paupers) to the Guinness Storehouse, which deifies the national beer. Its musical tradition and writers' heritage fuel "trad" and literary pub crawls. While its greatest sight is the medieval Book of Kells, the best thing about Dublin is its people.

❶ ***Christ Church Cathedral*** *sits atop Norman crypts and anchors the historic heart of Dublin.*

❷ *The friendly pulse of this vibrant city is best felt in its many* ***traditional pubs.***

❸ *The* ***Ha' Penny Bridge,*** *just beyond the inn, replaced ferries and charged locals a half-penny toll.*

❹ *Turreted* ***Dublin Castle*** *was the center of dominant English control in Ireland for almost eight centuries.*

❺ *The popular* ***Musical Pub Crawl*** *introduces Irish traditional sessions to tune-loving travelers.*

❻ *Monastic scribes copying scriptures painstakingly created the* ***Book of Kells*** *during the Dark Ages.*

❼ ***Grafton Street*** *is a pedestrian shopping mecca, inviting for a stroll on a sunny day.*

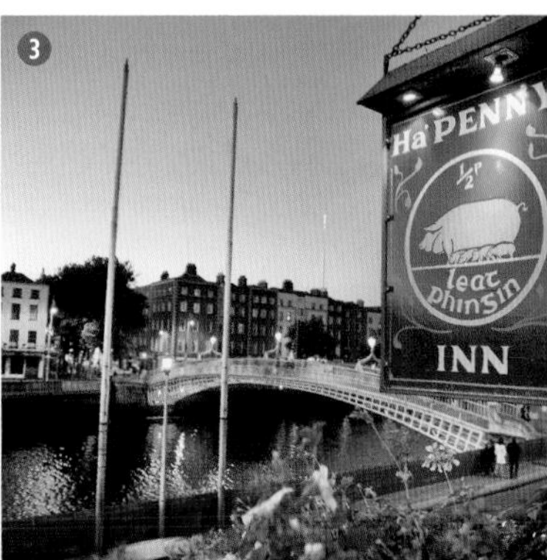
3
Ha'PENNY
INN

4

5
GUINNESS
GUINNESS
TUESDAYS

6

7

THE BEST OF KILKENNY AND THE ROCK OF CASHEL

Two fine stops between Dublin and Dingle are medieval Kilkenny and the massive Rock of Cashel. Kilkenny is a sturdy, hardworking town, with a castle, cathedral, and atmospheric pubs featuring live traditional folk music.

The evocative Rock of Cashel has majestic hill-topping ruins worth exploring and pondering. South of Kilkenny, you can make excursions to an old abbey, a replica of a famine ship, and the birthplace of Waterford crystal.

❶ *The ruins of the* ***Rock of Cashel*** *are the most evocative sight in Ireland's interior.*

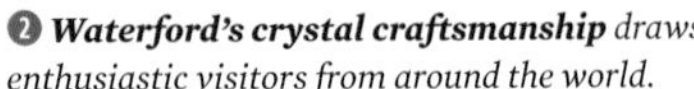

❷ ***Waterford's crystal craftsmanship*** *draws enthusiastic visitors from around the world.*

❸ *Colorful shop fronts and unpretentious pubs line the medieval streets of* ***Kilkenny.***

THE BEST OF KINSALE

Quaint Kinsale has served as a port since prehistoric times. Stroll the pedestrian-friendly medieval quarter and take the excellent walking tour that makes the town's history come alive. The squat Charles Fort on the harbor offers great bay views and an engrossing museum that covers rugged British military life. Kinsale is also Ireland's gourmet capital; try to fit in three meals. Nearby, the historic town of Cobh has a special appeal for visitors with Irish roots.

❶ ***Kinsale,*** *long a historic port, has a fun, fresh look.*

❷ ***Cobh****'s docks once creaked with* Titanic *passengers and US-bound emigrants.*

❸ ***Walking tours*** *transform Kinsale's back lanes with tales of former maritime glory.*

THE BEST OF KENMARE AND THE RING OF KERRY

The colorful town of Kenmare, known for tidiness and lacework, is a good base for side-stepping the throngs flocking to Ireland's famous scenic loop. Allow a full day to tour the 120-mile Ring of Kerry, exploring ancient ring forts, peaceful towns with names like Sneem and Portmagee, and dramatic islands. Time it right and drive clockwise around the peninsula to avoid the parade of tour buses going in the opposite direction.

❶ *Serene* ***Staigue Fort,*** *dating from the Iron Age, lies 10 minutes' drive off the Ring of Kerry.*

❷ *Visitors to* ***sheep ranches*** *can observe shearing and shepherd-dog training.*

❸ ***Muckross House*** *hosted Queen Elizabeth I and attracts garden lovers today.*

❹ ***Kenmare*** *offers a respite from crowds and a base for exploring the Ring of Kerry.*

THE BEST OF DINGLE TOWN AND PENINSULA

My favorite Gaelic village—Dingle—welcomes you to my favorite Irish peninsula. Wander the town's charming lanes, check out the stained-glass windows in the chapel, look for the resident dolphin in the harbor, and sound out the Gaelic signs. You're in a Gaeltacht, a region where the traditional Irish language and ways are prized. The 30-mile loop around Slea Head is awash with beehive huts, prehistoric stone pillars, and ancient ring forts. Look up to see the rugged hills; look down to see the surging waves. And slow down...to take it all in.

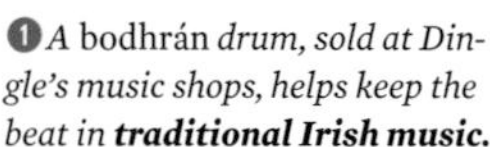

❶ *A* bodhrán *drum, sold at Dingle's music shops, helps keep the beat in* ***traditional Irish music.***

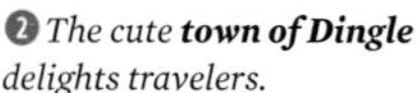

❷ *The cute* ***town of Dingle*** *delights travelers.*

❸ ***Fungie the dolphin*** *is a playful ambassador for boat tours around Dingle harbor.*

❹ *Early Christians gathered on the peninsula at holy places like the* ***Gallarus Oratory.***

❺ *Art Nouveau stained-glass artistry adorns Dingle's convent* ***chapel of Díseart.***

THE BEST OF COUNTY CLARE

This county on the rugged western coast offers the thrilling Cliffs of Moher, prehistoric structures in the wildflower wonderland of the Burren, and several musical towns. Little Doolin attracts music lovers with a trio of trad pubs, while Kinvarra hosts a medieval banquet for the lord or lady in you.

❶ *The 650-foot-high* ***Cliffs of Moher*** *drop dramatically into the Atlantic.*

❷ ***Dunguaire Castle,*** *standing sentry beside Galway Bay, offers memorable castle banquets.*

❸ *The little crossroads of* ***Doolin*** *sports lively* ***trad music sessions*** *in steamy pubs.*

❹ *In* ***the Burren,*** *the* ***Poulnabrone Dolmen*** *is a tomb built 5,000 years ago.*

THE BEST OF GALWAY

Galway is a youthful university town with a great street scene and lively nightlife, punctuated by pubs and street musicians. It's also a springboard to the Cliffs of Moher and the Burren to the south, the Aran Islands offshore, and the region of Connemara to the north.

❶ *Banners for the original 14 Norman founding "tribes" of Galway grace* ***Eyre Square.***

❷ *Picnickers along the River Corrib soak up sun and ambience.*

❸ *A youthful international college population energizes Galway's* ***pedestrian corridor.***

❹ *Proud Irish step dancing is fun to watch in Galway's* ***music pubs.***

THE BEST OF THE ARAN ISLANDS

The windswept Aran Islands have a stark and rugged beauty. From Galway, make a memorable crossing to Inishmore by ferry or flight. The island has simple towns, hiking trails, and a slew of early churches, but all roads lead to Dun Aengus, an Iron Age fort at the edge of a high cliff. The smaller island of Inisheer, with a hilltop castle, church ruins, and an evocative shipwreck, makes a fine excursion from Doolin.

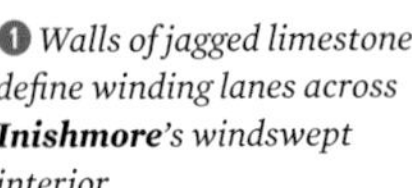

❶ *Walls of jagged limestone define winding lanes across **Inishmore**'s windswept interior.*

❷ *Islander-owned **minivans** greet travelers at the dock and scoot them efficiently around Inishmore.*

❸ *About 1,200 years ago, devoted pilgrims flocked to Inishmore and rest now near the **Seven Churches.***

❹ *The small isle of **Inisheer** sees fewer visitors and offers peaceful solitude to modern hermits.*

THE BEST OF BELFAST

Once the center of the Troubles, the no-nonsense capital of Northern Ireland has come a long way. Political murals depict its fractured past, but today's Belfast has a hopeful future, with bustling pedestrian zones, a cosmopolitan restaurant scene, and a bold, shiny *Titanic* museum that draws crowds.

❶ *The high-tech Titanic* ***exhibition*** *tells one of history's most famous stories.*

❷ *The stately* ***Victorian grandeur*** *of City Hall hints at former Industrial Revolution wealth.*

❸ *The historic* ***Crown Liquor Saloon*** *offers private snugs in which to enjoy your mellow pint.*

❹ *Rural craftsmanship is kept alive in simple village dwellings at* ***Cultra Folk Park.***

THE BEST OF PORTRUSH AND THE ANTRIM COAST

With old-time amusement arcades and waterfront dining, the small-town beach resort of Portrush is the gateway to the wonders of the lovely Antrim Coast. Explore the stunning basalt Giant's Causeway, stroll the ruins of Dunluce Castle, and test your nerve crossing the Carrick-a-Rede Rope Bridge, suspended high over a watery channel below.

❶ *Pleasant* ***Portrush*** *thrives on summer crowds exploring the scenic Antrim Coast.*

❷ *Hikers and birdwatchers thrill to the lofty* ***Carrick-a-Rede Rope Bridge.***

❸ ***Dunluce Castle*** *perches on a sea stack accessed by a strategic bridge.*

THE BEST OF THE REST

With extra time or interest, splice the following destinations into your trip. The region of Connemara has abbey ruins, a lakeside mansion, a pilgrimage mountain, and the genteel town of Westport. Derry is a revitalized Northern Ireland town that's come to terms with the Troubles.

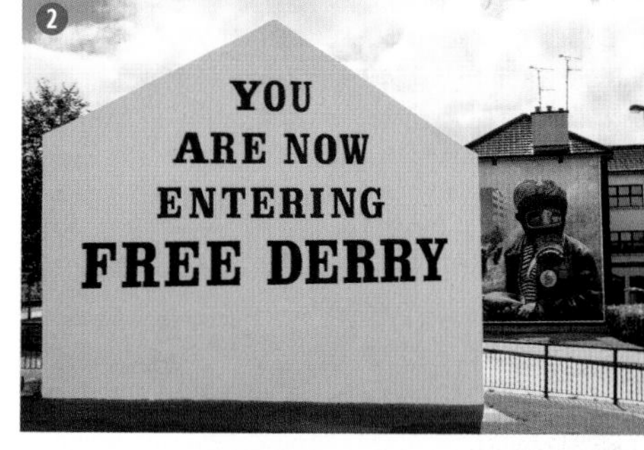

❶ *Colorful and passionate (often political) murals decorate* ***Derry's*** *buildings.*

❷ *During the Troubles, this* ***sign*** *marked a popular gathering point for speakers to address crowds.*

❸ ***Connemara****'s rugged vistas attract painters, naturalists, hikers, and photographers.*

❹ *Prim* ***Westport*** *makes a good stop or a home base when exploring Connemara.*

TRAVEL SMART

Approach Ireland like a veteran traveler, even if it's your first trip. Design your itinerary, get a handle on your budget, make advance arrangements, and follow my travel strategies on the road. For my best advice on sightseeing, accommodations, restaurants, and transportation, see the Practicalities chapter.

Designing Your Itinerary

Decide when to go. Travelers in "shoulder season" (April, May, Sept, and Oct) experience smaller crowds, mild weather, and the full range of sights and fun. Peak season, June through August, offers longer days and better weather, but larger crowds (especially in the cruise ports towns of Dublin, the Cobh region, and Belfast). Prices, crowds, and temperatures drop off-season (Nov through March); city sightseeing is generally fine, though in towns, some sights have shorter hours or shut down.

No matter when you go, expect rain. Just keep on traveling and take full advantage of "bright spells."

Choose your top destinations. My itinerary (on page 24) gives you an idea of how much you can reasonably see in 14 days, but you can adapt it to fit your own interests and time frame. Bustling, rollicking Dublin is a must for its museums, street scene, and nightlife. Music lovers follow their ear to pubs playing live traditional music. The top musical towns are—in this order—Dingle, Doolin, Galway, Westport, and Dublin. Foodies favor Kinsale, but won't go hungry elsewhere.

Historians choose among sights prehistoric (such as the Boyne Valley, the Burren, and the Dun Aengus cliff-edge fortress), medieval (Rock of Cashel and Glendalough), and modern (from the independence movement in Dublin to the Troubles in Belfast). Seekers of nonstop beauty visit the Republic's rugged west coast—the Dingle Peninsula, Ring of Kerry, Cliffs of Moher, and Aran Islands—and Northern Ireland's scenic Antrim Coast. Photographers want to go everywhere.

If you have time to explore only one idyllic peninsula, choose the Dingle Peninsula over the more famous Ring of Kerry. If you want to include both, this book will help you do it efficiently and enjoyably.

Draft a rough itinerary. Figure out how many destinations you can comfortably fit in the time you have. Don't overdo it—few travelers wish they'd hurried more. Allow enough days per stop: Figure on at least one to two days for major destinations.

Staying in a home base—like Galway or Dublin—and making day trips can be more time-efficient than changing locations and hotels. Minimize one-night stands, especially consecutive ones; it can be worth taking a late-afternoon train ride or drive to get settled into a town for two nights.

Connect the dots. Link your destinations into a logical route. Determine which cities you'll fly into and out of; begin your search for transatlantic flights at Kayak.com. All direct flights from the US to Ireland land in Dublin, low-key Shannon (good for cautious drivers), or Belfast.

Decide if you'll travel by car, take public transportation, or use a combination. For the efficiency and freedom, I recommend driving. You won't need a car in big cities (park it), but it's ideal for exploring the countryside, stopping wherever you like.

If relying on public transit, these destinations are easiest—Dublin, Dingle, Galway, Aran Islands, and Belfast—using a combination of trains, buses, taxis, and minibus tours, plus a flight or boat to the islands. Trains don't cover the entire island, and bus travel is slow due to multiple connections and/or frequent stops.

Allot sufficient time for transportation in your itinerary. Whether you travel by train, bus, or car, it'll take a half-day to get between most destinations.

To determine approximate transportation times between your destinations, study the driving chart (on page 353) or check Google Maps. To look at train and bus schedules in advance, go online (www.discoverireland.ie, select "Getting Around"). If your trip extends beyond Ireland, check Skyscanner.com for intra-European flights.

Give yourself some slack. Every trip, and every traveler, needs downtime for doing laundry, picnic shopping, relaxing, people-watching, and so on. Pace yourself. Assume you will return.

Ready, set... You've designed the perfect itinerary for the trip of a lifetime.

Trip Costs

Run a reality check on your dream trip. You'll have major transportation costs in addition to daily expenses.

Flight: A round-trip flight from the US to Dublin costs about $900-1,500, depending on where you fly from and when.

Car Rental: Allow roughly $250 per week, not including tolls, gas, parking, and insurance. Rentals are cheapest if arranged from the US.

Public Transportation: For a two-week trip, allow about $250 per person for buses and trains. Because Ireland's train system has gaps, a rail pass probably won't save you money, but buying train tickets online in advance can save as much as 50 percent.

Budget Tips: Cut your daily expenses by taking advantage of the deals you'll find throughout Ireland and mentioned in this book.

Transit passes (for multiple rides or all-day use) in bigger cities decrease

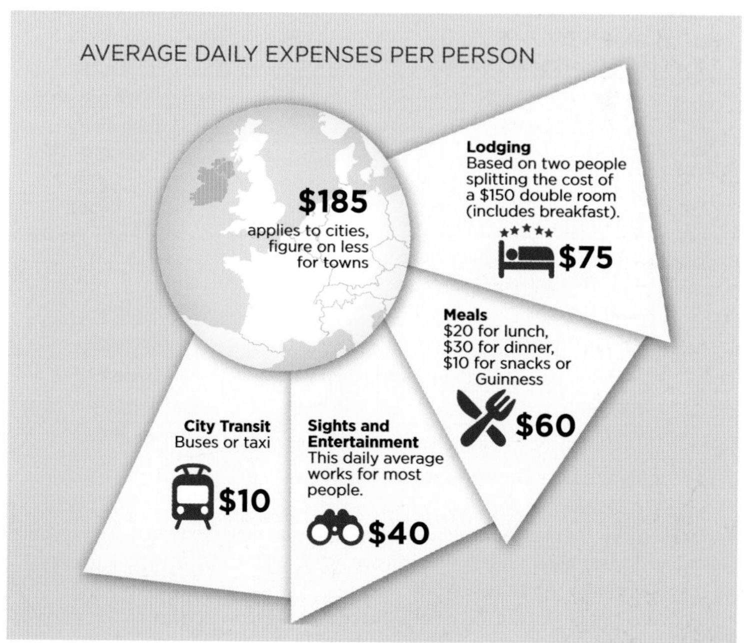

THE BEST OF IRELAND IN 2 WEEKS

This unforgettable trip will show you the very best Ireland has to offer.

DAY	PLAN	SLEEP
	Arrive in Dublin	Dublin
1	Sightsee Dublin	Dublin
2	Dublin	Dublin
3	Rent a car at Dublin Airport, drive to Kilkenny for lunch, visit the Rock of Cashel, and end in Kinsale	Kinsale
4	Kinsale	Kinsale
5	Drive to Kenmare for lunch, then visit a sheep farm and Muckross House, and end in Dingle town	Dingle
6	Dingle town	Dingle
7	Drive the Slea Head Loop	Dingle
8	Drive to the Cliffs of Moher, then through the Burren, ending in Galway	Galway
9	Day-trip by plane or boat to Inishmore (Aran Islands)	Galway
10	Drive to Portrush. (Or add another day to explore—and overnight in—Connemara or Derry en route to Portrush.)	Portrush
11	Antrim Coast	Portrush
12	More Antrim Coast, then drive to Belfast	Belfast
13	Belfast	Belfast
14	Drive to Boyne Valley to visit Brú na Bóinne	Trim
	Return car at Dublin Airport and fly home	

Notes: Even if you fly into Dublin, you don't need to start there; you can rent a car at the airport and drive to small-town Trim for an overnight, tour Ireland, then drop the car at the airport and enjoy Dublin as your trip finale.

To add the Ring of Kerry to this itinerary, spend the night in Kenmare on Day 5 and do the Ring on Day 6, ending in Dingle Town that night.

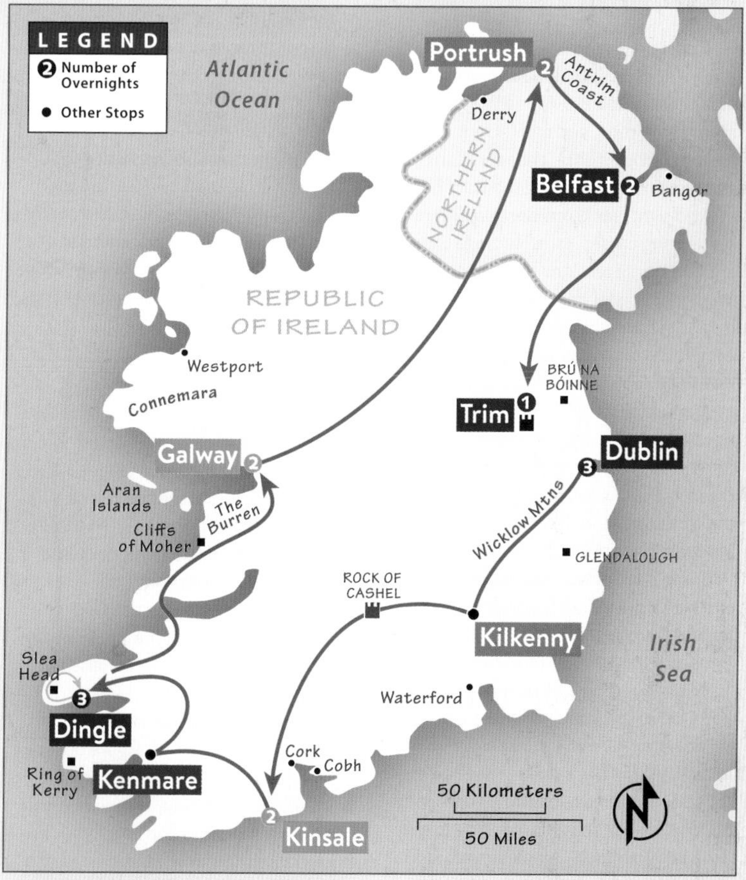

LEGEND

❷ Number of Overnights

● Other Stops

Atlantic Ocean

Portrush 2

Antrim Coast

Derry

NORTHERN IRELAND

Belfast 2

Bangor

REPUBLIC OF IRELAND

Westport

Connemara

BRÚ NA BÓINNE

Trim 1

Galway 2

Dublin 3

Aran Islands

The Burren

Cliffs of Moher

Wicklow Mtns

GLENDALOUGH

ROCK OF CASHEL

Kilkenny

Irish Sea

Slea Head

Dingle 3

Waterford

Cork

Cobh

Ring of Kerry

Kenmare

Kinsale 2

50 Kilometers

50 Miles

your cost per ride. In Dublin and Belfast, using a hop-on, hop-off bus to get around isn't cheap, but it provides a live guide, a city introduction, and an efficient way to reach far-flung sights (cheaper than taxis and less time-consuming than city buses).

Avid sightseers consider two different sightseeing passes—the Heritage Card and the Heritage Island Visitor Attraction Map—that cover dozens of sights across Ireland (see "Sightseeing" in the Practicalities chapter). On a smaller scale, some cities offer combo-tickets or passes that cover multiple museums, though you'll need to sightsee briskly to make them pay off. If a town doesn't offer deals, visit only the sights you most want to see, and seek out free sights and experiences (people-watching counts).

Some businesses—especially hotels and walking-tour companies—offer discounts to my readers (look for the RS% symbol in the listings in this book).

Book your rooms directly with the hotel via email or phone for the best rates. Some hotels give you a discount if you pay in cash and/or stay three or more nights (check online or ask). Rooms cost less outside of peak season (roughly November through March). And even seniors can sleep cheap in hostels (some have double rooms) for about $30 per person. Or check Airbnb-type sites for deals.

It's no hardship to eat inexpensively in Ireland. You can get hearty, affordable meals at pubs and early-bird dinner deals at nicer restaurants. Cultivate the art of picnicking in atmospheric settings.

When you splurge, choose an experience you'll always remember, such as the Dunguaire Castle medieval banquet or a flight to the Aran Islands. Minimize souvenir shopping; focus instead on collecting wonderful memories.

Before You Go

You'll have a smoother trip if you tackle a few things ahead of time. For more info on these topics, see the Practicalities chapter and check RickSteves.com, which has helpful travel tips and talks.

Make sure your travel documents are valid. If your passport is due to expire within six months of your ticketed date of return, you need to renew it. Allow up to six weeks to renew or get a passport (www.travel.state.gov).

Arrange your transportation. Book your international flights. Figure out your main form of transportation within Ireland: You can rent a car, or buy train and bus tickets (either as you go, or you can book train tickets in advance online at a discount). Younger and older drivers may face age restrictions; see page 353.

Book rooms well in advance.

Travel light and happy.

Rick's Free Video Clips and Audio Tours

Rick Steves Classroom Europe, a powerful tool for teachers, is also useful for travelers. This video library contains more than 400 short clips excerpted from my public television series. Enjoy these videos as you sort through options for your trip and to better understand what you'll see in Europe. Check it out at Classroom.RickSteves.com (just enter a topic to find everything I've filmed on a subject).

Rick Steves Audio Europe, a free app, makes it easy to download and listen to my audio tours offline as you travel. For this book, my two-part Dublin City Walk audio tour (look for the 🎧) covers sights and neighborhoods in central Dublin. The app also offers insightful interviews from my public radio show with experts from Europe and around the globe. Find it in your app store or at RickSteves.com/AudioEurope.

Book rooms well in advance, especially if your trip falls during peak season or any major holidays or festivals.

Reserve or buy tickets in advance for major sights. It's smart to book online for Dublin's Book of Kells, Guinness Storehouse, and Kilmainham Gaol (where reservations are required); Brú na Bóinne (near Dublin); Carrick-a-Rede Rope Bridge on the Antrim Coast; and the Titanic Belfast museum. Boat trips to Skellig Michael can sell out months in advance—reserve ahead.

Consider travel insurance. Compare the cost of the insurance to the cost of your potential loss. Check whether your existing insurance (health, homeowners, or renters) covers you and your possessions overseas.

Call your bank. Tell them you'll be using your debit and credit cards in Europe. Ask about transaction fees, and get the PIN number for your credit card. You won't need to bring along euros (for the Republic of Ireland) or pounds (for Northern Ireland); you can withdraw currency from cash machines while traveling.

Use your smartphone smartly. Sign up for an international service plan to reduce your costs, or rely on Wi-Fi in Europe instead. Download any apps you'll want on the road, such as maps, transit schedules, and Rick Steves Audio Europe (see sidebar).

Pack light. You'll walk with your luggage more than you think. Bring a single carry-on bag and a daypack. Use the packing checklist in the Practicalities chapter as a guide.

Travel Strategies on the Road

If you have a positive attitude, equip yourself with good information, and expect to travel smart, you will.

Read—and reread—this book. To have an "A" trip, be an "A" student. Study up on sights, and note opening hours, closed days, crowd-beating tips, and whether reservations are required or advisable. Check the latest at RickSteves.com/update.

Be your own tour guide. As you travel, get up-to-date info on sights, reserve tickets and tours, reconfirm hotels and travel arrangements, and check transit connections. Find out the latest from

tourist-information offices (TIs), your hoteliers, checking online, or phoning ahead. Upon arrival in a new town, lay the groundwork for a smooth departure; confirm the road, train, or bus you'll take when you leave.

Give local tours a spin. Your appreciation of a city or region and its history can increase dramatically if you take a walking tour in any big city or even hire a private guide. If you want to learn more about any aspect of Ireland, you're in the right place, with experts happy to teach you.

Plan for rain. No matter when you go, the weather can change several times in a day. Bring a jacket and dress in layers. A spell of rain is the perfect excuse to go into a pub and meet a new friend.

Outsmart thieves. Although pickpocketing isn't a major problem outside of Dublin, it's still smart to keep your cash, cards, and passport secure in a money belt tucked under your clothes. Carry only a day's spending money in your front pocket. Don't set valuable items down on counters or café tabletops, where they can be quickly stolen or easily forgotten.

Minimize potential loss. Keep expensive gear to a minimum. Bring photocopies or take photos of important documents (passport and cards) to aid in replacement if they're lost or stolen. Back up your digital photos and files frequently.

Guard your time and energy. Taking a taxi can be a good value if it saves you a long wait for a cheap bus or an exhausting walk across town. To avoid long lines, take advantage of my crowd-beating tips (such as making advance reservations, or sightseeing early or late).

Be flexible. Even if you have a well-planned itinerary, expect changes, closures, sore feet, rainy days, and so on. Your Plan B could turn out to be even better.

Connect with the culture. Interacting with locals carbonates your experience. Enjoy the friendliness of the Irish people. Most exchanges are accompanied by fun banter, especially at pubs, where lively conversations fueled by beer are called *craic* (crack). Ask questions—most locals are happy to point you in their idea of the right direction. Set up your own quest for the best pub, traditional music, or ruined castle. When an unexpected opportunity pops up, say "yes."

Hear the fiddler playing? Taste the Guinness? Your next stop...Ireland!

Welcome to Rick Steves' Europe

Travel is intensified living—maximum thrills per minute and one of the last great sources of legal adventure. Travel is freedom. It's recess, and we need it.

I discovered a passion for European travel as a teen and have been sharing it ever since—through my bus tours, public television and radio shows, and travel guidebooks. Over the years, I've taught millions of travelers how to best enjoy Europe's blockbuster sights—and experience "Back Door" discoveries that most tourists miss.

Written with my talented co-author, Pat O'Connor, this book covers the highlights of the entire island, offering a balanced mix of exciting cities and great-to-be-alive-in small towns. And it's selective—there are plenty of music-loving villages, but we recommend only the best ones. Our self-guided museum tours and city walks give insight into the country's vibrant history and today's living, breathing culture.

We advocate traveling simply and smartly. Take advantage of our money- and time-saving tips on sightseeing, transportation, and more. Try local, characteristic alternatives to expensive hotels and restaurants. In many ways, spending more money only builds a thicker wall between you and what you traveled so far to see.

We visit Ireland to experience it—to become temporary locals. Thoughtful travel engages us with the world, as we learn to appreciate other cultures and new ways to measure quality of life.

Judging from positive feedback from readers, this book will help you enjoy a fun, affordable, and rewarding vacation—whether it's your first trip or your tenth.

Taisteal sásta! Happy travels!

Rick Steves

Republic

The modern Irish state has existed since 1922, but its inhabitants proudly claim their nation to be the only contemporary independent state to sprout from purely Celtic roots (sprinkled with a few Vikings and shipwrecked Spanish Armada sailors to spice up the gene pool). The Romans never bothered to come over and organize the wild Irish. Through the persuasive and culturally enlightened approach of early missionaries such as St. Patrick, Ireland is one of the very few countries to have initially converted to Christianity without much bloodshed. The religious carnage came a thousand years later, with the Reformation. Irish culture absorbed the influences of Viking raiders and Norman soldiers of fortune, eventually enduring the 750-year shadow of English domination (1169-1922).

For most of the 20th century, Ireland was an isolated, agricultural economic backwater that had largely missed out on the Industrial Revolution. Things began to turn around when Ireland joined the European Community (precursor to the EU) in 1973, and really took off during the "Celtic Tiger" boom years (1995-2007), when American corporations saw big tax and labor advantages in locating here. Ireland's "Silicon Bog" became the European home to such big names as IBM, Intel, Microsoft, Apple, Facebook, and Google.

Today, the Republic of Ireland attracts both expatriates

# of Ireland

returning to their homeland and new foreign investment. As the only officially English-speaking country to have adopted the euro currency, Ireland makes an efficient base from which to access the European marketplace. About a third of the Irish population is under 25 years old, leading many high-tech and pharmaceutical firms to locate here, taking advantage of this young, well-educated labor force.

Until recently, Ireland was one of the most ethnically homogenous nations on earth, but the Celtic Tiger economy changed all that. A recent census found that more than 10 percent of Ireland's population was born elsewhere.

Everyone here speaks English, though you'll encounter Irish Gaelic (commonly referred to as "Irish") if you venture to the western fringe of the country. The Irish love of conversation shines through wherever you go. All that conversation is helped along by the nebulous concept of Irish time, which never seems to be in short supply. Small shops post their hours as "9:00ish 'til 5:00ish." The local bus usually makes a stop at "10:30ish." A healthy disdain for being a slave to the clock seems to be part of being Irish. And the warm welcome you'll receive has its roots in ancient Celtic laws of hospitality toward stranded strangers. You'll see the phrase "Céad míle fáilte" in tourism brochures and postcards throughout Ireland—it translates as "a hundred thousand welcomes."

Republic of Ireland Almanac

Official Name: The Republic of Ireland (a.k.a. "Ireland" or, in Irish, Éire).

Size: 27,000 square miles—half the size of New York State—it occupies the southern 80 percent of the island of Ireland. The country is small enough that radio broadcasts cover traffic snarls nationwide.

Population: 5 million people (about the same as Alabama).

Geography: The isle is mostly flat, ringed by a hilly coastline. The climate is moderate, with cloudy skies about every other day.

Latitude and Longitude: 53°N and 8°W. The latitude is equivalent to Alberta, Canada.

Biggest Cities: The capital of Dublin (550,000 people) is the only big city; about two in five Irish live in the greater Dublin area (2 million). Cork has about 125,000 people, Limerick 94,000, Galway 80,000, and Waterford 53,000.

Economy: The Gross Domestic Product is $353 billion, and the GDP per capita is $75,200—one of Europe's highest. Major moneymakers include tourism and exports (especially to the US and UK) of machines, medicine, Guinness, glassware, crystal ware, and software. Traditional agriculture (potatoes and other root vegetables) is fading fast, but dairy still does well.

Government: The elected president, Michael Higgins, appoints the Taoiseach (TEE-shock) or prime minister (youthful Leo Varadkar), who is nominated by Parliament. The Parliament consists of the 60-seat Senate, chosen by an electoral college, and the House of Representatives, with 166 seats apportioned after the people vote for a party. Major parties include Fianna Fáil, Fine Gael, and Sinn Féin—the political arm of the (fading) Irish Republican Army. Ireland is divided into 28 administrative counties (including Kerry, Clare, Cork, Limerick, and so on).

The Average Irish: A typical Irish person is 5'7", 37 years old, has 1-2 kids, and will live to be 81. An Irish citizen consumes nearly 5 pounds of tea per year and spends $5 on alcohol each day. He or she speaks English, though Irish Gaelic is spoken in pockets along the country's west coast. Nearly eight in 10 are nominally Catholic (a sharp decline in the last few years), though only one in three attends church.

The flag of the Republic of Ireland

Republic of Ireland

Over time, relations between Ireland and her former colonial master Britain have improved. In 2011, Queen Elizabeth II became the first British monarch to visit the Republic of Ireland since Ireland's 1921 split from the United Kingdom, which occurred during her grandfather's reign. Her four-night visit (to Dublin, Cashel, and Cork) unexpectedly charmed the Irish people and did much to repair old wounds between the two countries, establishing them, in the words of the Queen, as "firm friends and equal partners."

The big question now is how "Brexit" (Britain's exit from the EU) could complicate Ireland's easy trading relationship with its UK neighbors. Although the UK as a whole voted to leave the EU, the citizens of Northern Ireland voted to remain (recognizing the advantage of their soft border with the Republic). A "hardening" of this border is generally seen as a step backwards that both countries want to avoid.

At first glance, Ireland's landscape seems unspectacular, with few mountains higher than 3,000 feet and an interior consisting of grazing pastures and peat bogs. But its seductive beauty slowly grows on you. The gentle rainfall, called "soft weather" by the locals, really does create 40 shades of green—and quite a few rainbows as well. Ancient, moss-covered ring forts crouch in lush valleys, while stone-strewn monastic ruins and lone castle turrets brave the wind on nearby hilltops. Charming fishing villages dot the coast near rugged, wave-battered cliffs.

RTE: The Voice of Ireland

Many a long drive or rainy evening has been saved by the engaging programs I've happened upon on RTE: Raidió Teilifís Éireann. What the BBC is to Britain, RTE is to Ireland: This government-owned company and national public broadcaster produces a wide range of programs on television, radio, and online. Look for it as you travel (via RTE's apps, on the radio, or on TV).

First hitting the airwaves on New Year's Eve 1961, today's RTE TV broadcasts are all digital and in English on RTE channels 1 and 2. But don't shy away from channel 4 (TG4), with Irish language TV shows subtitled in English—it's a great way to get a feel for the sound of the language. You couldn't find a richer or more accessible introduction to Irish culture.

The resilient Irish character was born of dark humor, historical reverence, and a scrappy, "we'll get 'em next time" rebel spirit. The influence of the Catholic Church is less apparent these days, as 30 percent of Irish weddings are now civil ceremonies. But the Church still plays a part in Irish life. The average Irish family spends almost €500 on celebrations for the First Holy Communion of each child. And the national radio and TV station, RTE, pauses for 30 seconds at noon and at 18:00 to broadcast the chimes of the Angelus bells—signaling the start of Catholic devotional prayers. The Irish say that if you're phoning heaven, it's a long-distance call from the rest of the world, but a local call from Ireland.

Dublin's Leinster House is the seat of Irish government.

Dingle Peninsula

give
here

Dublin

With reminders of its stirring history and rich culture on every corner, Ireland's capital and largest city is a sightseer's delight. Dublin punches above its weight in arts, entertainment, food, and fun.

As the seat of English rule in Ireland for more than 700 years, Dublin was the heart of the "civilized" Anglo-Irish area (eastern Ireland) known as "the Pale." Anything "beyond the Pale" was considered uncultured and almost barbaric...purely Irish. The Golden Age of English Dublin was the 18th century. The British Empire was on a roll, and the city was right there with it. Largely rebuilt during this Georgian era (1714-1830), Dublin became elegant and cultured.

But the 19th century saw Ireland endure the Great Potato Famine, and tension with the British culminated in the Easter Rising of 1916, followed by a successful guerilla war of independence and Ireland's tragic civil war that left many of Dublin's grand streets in ruins.

While bullet-pocked buildings and dramatic statues keep memories of Ireland's struggle for independence alive, today's Dublin is lively, easy, and extremely accessible. The city's economy is on the upswing, with a forest of cranes sweeping over booming construction blocks and expanding light-rail infrastructure. Dubliners are energetic and helpful, and visitors enjoy a big-town cultural scene wrapped in a small-town smile.

DUBLIN IN 2 DAYS

While you could easily spend much longer here, for most Ireland vacations, Dublin merits three nights and two days. Here's how I would fill two days in Dublin:

Day 1: Follow my "Dublin City Walk" through the center of town, with stops at City Hall (Story of the Capital exhibit) and Temple Bar. After lunch, visit EPIC: The Irish Emigration Museum.

On any evening: Enjoy an early-bird dinner deal at one of my recommended restaurants, do the Traditional Irish Musical Pub Crawl (ends at 22:00), or attend a storytelling dinner (O'Sheas Pub, book in advance, ends at 21:30), the Literary Pub Crawl, or a play.

Day 2: See the Book of Kells exhibit at Trinity College (book in advance), then tour the Trinity campus with a college student, followed by a visit to the National Museum of Archaeology. Grab a pub lunch, then visit Kilmainham Gaol (book in advance).

ORIENTATION

Greater Dublin sprawls with about 2 million people—more than a third of the country's population. But the center of

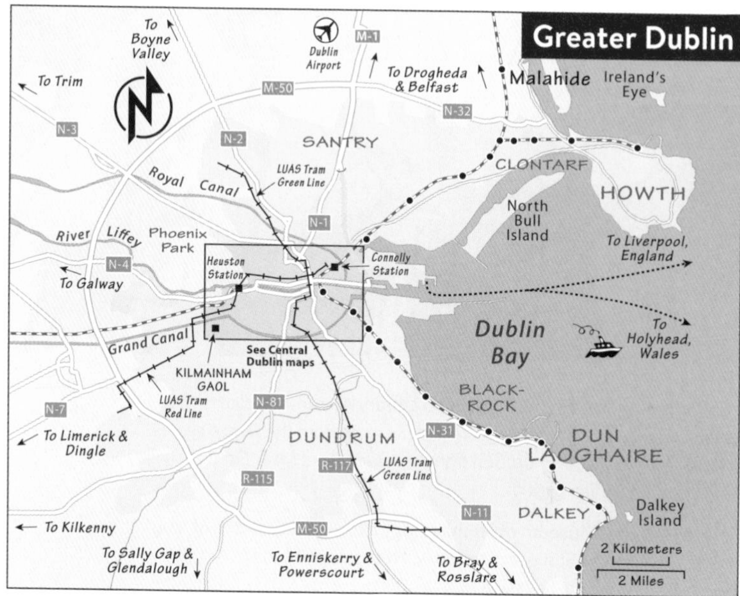

tourist interest is a tight triangle between O'Connell Bridge, St. Stephen's Green, and Christ Church Cathedral. Within or near this triangle, you'll find Trinity College (Book of Kells), a cluster of major museums (including the National Museum of Archaeology), touristy and pedestrianized Grafton Street, Temple Bar (touristy nightlife center), Dublin Castle, and the hub of most city tours and buses. Only two major sights are beyond easy walking distance from this central zone: Kilmainham Gaol and the Guinness Storehouse.

The River Liffey cuts the town in two, and most of your sightseeing will take place on its south bank. As you explore, be aware that many long Dublin streets change names every few blocks, including the wide main axis that cuts north/south through the tourist center. North from the O'Connell Bridge, it's called O'Connell Street; south of the bridge, it becomes Westmoreland, passes Trinity College, and becomes the pedestrian-only Grafton Street to St. Stephen's Green.

Tourist Information

Dublin's busy main TI has lots of info on Dublin and all of Ireland (Mon-Sat 9:00-17:30, Sun 10:30-15:00, a block off Grafton Street at 25 Suffolk Street, tel. 01/884-7700, www.visitdublin.com). A smaller TI is just past the stainless-steel sculpture

DUBLIN AT A GLANCE

▲▲▲**Book of Kells in the Trinity Old Library** An exquisite illuminated manuscript, Ireland's most important piece of art from the Dark Ages. **Hours:** Mon-Sat 8:30-17:00, Sun from 9:30; Oct-April Mon-Sat 9:30-17:00, Sun 12:00-16:30. See page 57.

▲▲▲**National Museum of Archaeology** Excellent collection of Irish treasures from the Stone Age to today. **Hours:** Sun-Mon 13:00-17:00, Tue-Sat 10:00-17:00. See page 60.

▲▲▲**Kilmainham Gaol** Historic jail used by the British as a political prison—today a museum that tells a moving story of the suffering of the Irish people. **Hours:** Guided tours daily June-Aug 9:00-19:00, April-May and Sept until 18:00, Oct-March 9:30-17:30. See page 76.

▲▲**Historical Walking Tour of Dublin** This group tour is your best introduction to Dublin. **Hours:** May-Sept daily at 11:00 and 15:00, April and Oct daily at 11:00, Nov-March Fri-Sun at 11:00. See page 44.

▲▲**Traditional Irish Musical Pub Crawl** A fascinating, practical, and enjoyable primer on traditional Irish music. **Hours:** April-Oct daily at 19:30, Nov and Jan-March Thu-Sat only. See page 44.

▲▲**Trinity College Campus Tour** Ireland's most famous school, best visited with a 30-minute student-led tour. **Hours:** Daily 9:15-16:00, off-season weekends only, no tours Dec-Jan. See page 57.

▲▲**Chester Beatty Library** American expatriate's sumptuous collection of literary and religious treasures from Islam, Asia, and medieval Europe. **Hours:** Mon-Fri 10:00-17:00, Sat from 11:00, Sun from 13:00. See page 66.

▲▲**Temple Bar** Dublin's rowdiest neighborhood, with shops, cafés, theaters, galleries, pubs, and restaurants—a great spot for live (but touristy) traditional music. See page 56.

▲▲**O'Connell Street** Dublin's grandest promenade and main drag, packed with history and ideal for a stroll. See page 71.

▲▲**EPIC: The Irish Emigration Museum** Creative displays about the Irish diaspora highlight the impact emigrants make on their new homelands. **Hours:** Daily 10:00-18:45. See page 71.

▲▲**14 Henrietta Street** A time capsule of urban Dublin life, following the 150-year decline of an aristocratic Georgian townhouse into tenement slum. **Hours:** Guided tours Wed-Sat 10:00-17:00, Sun from 12:00, closed Mon-Tue. See page 75.

▲**National Gallery of Ireland** Fine collection of top Irish painters and European masters. **Hours:** Sun-Mon 11:00-17:30, Tue-Sat 9:15-17:30, Thu until 20:30. See page 64.

▲**Dublin Castle** Once the city's historic 700-year-old castle, now a Georgian palace, featuring ornate English state apartments. **Hours:** Daily 9:45-16:45. See page 65.

▲**Christ Church Cathedral** Neo-Gothic cathedral on the site of an 11th-century Viking church. **Hours:** Mon-Sat 9:30-17:00, Sun 12:00-14:30. See page 69.

▲**Dublinia** A fun, kid-friendly look at Dublin's Viking and medieval past with a side order of archaeology and a cool town model. **Hours:** Daily 10:00-18:30, Oct-Feb until 17:30. See page 69.

▲**St. Patrick's Cathedral** The holy site of legend where St. Patrick first baptized Irish converts. **Hours:** Mon-Fri 9:30-17:00, Sat-Sun 9:00-18:00 except during Sun services. See page 70.

▲***Jeanie Johnston*** **Tall Ship and Famine Museum** Floating exhibit on the River Liffey explaining the Famine period that prompted desperate transatlantic crossings (by tour only). **Hours:** Daily 10:00-16:00, Oct-March 11:00-15:00. See page 72.

▲**Dublin Writers Museum** Collection of authorial bric-a-brac. **Hours:** Mon-Sat 9:45-17:00, Sun from 11:00, closed Mon Dec-March. See page 72.

▲**GPO Witness History Exhibit** Immersive presentation on the 1916 Easter Rising and its impact on Irish history, situated in the General Post Office building that served as rebel headquarters. **Hours:** Mon-Sat 10:00-17:30, Sun from 12:00. See page 73.

▲**Guinness Storehouse** The home of Ireland's national beer, with a museum of beer-making, a gallery of clever ads, and Gravity Bar with panoramic city views. **Hours:** Daily 9:30-19:00, July-Aug 9:00-20:00. See page 78.

▲**National Museum of Decorative Arts and History** Shows off Irish dress, furniture, silver, and weaponry with a special focus on the 1916 rebellion, fight for independence, and civil war. **Hours:** Tue-Sat 10:00-17:00, Sun and Mon from 13:00. See page 78.

▲**Gaelic Athletic Association Museum** High-tech museum of traditional Gaelic sports (hurling and Irish football). **Hours:** Mon-Sat 9:30-17:00, June-Aug until 18:00, Sun 10:30-17:00 year-round. On game Sundays, it's open to ticket holders only. See page 79.

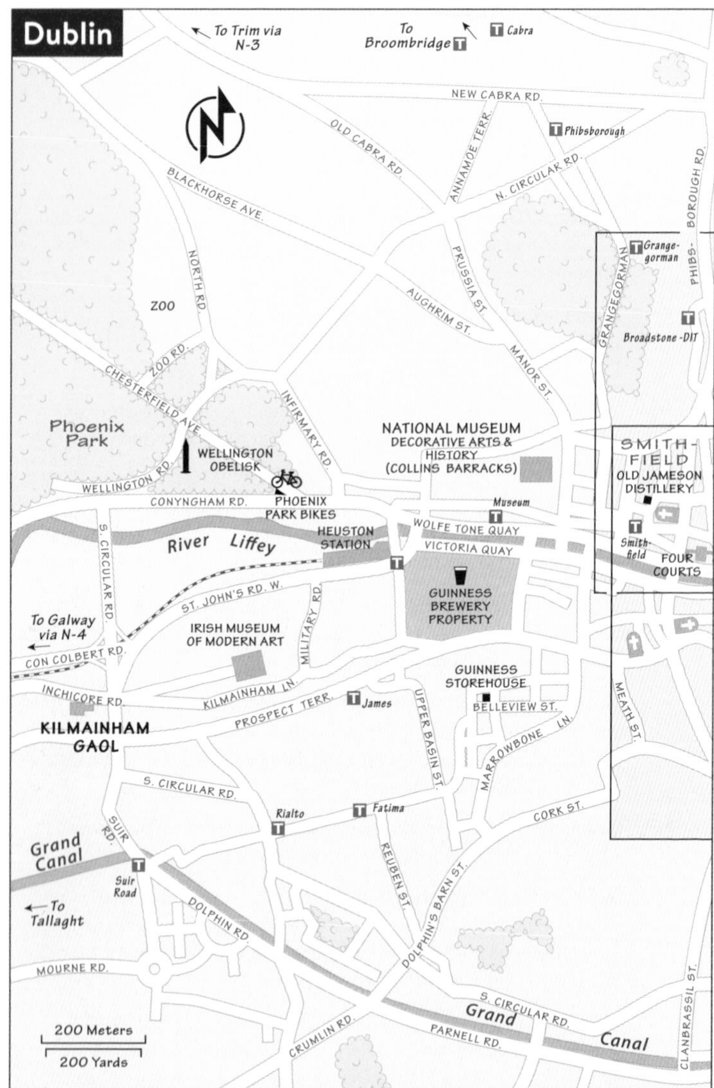

known as the Spire, on the east side of O'Connell Street (Mon-Sat 9:00-17:00, closed Sun). Beware of other shops claiming to be "Tourist Information" points, especially on O'Connell Street. Their advice is biased, aiming to sell you tours and collect commissions.

Dublin Pass: This sightseeing pass covers more than 30 sights and landmarks and hop-on, hop-off buses, and offers discounts on other attractions and the Aircoach airport bus (€62/1 day, multiday options available, purchase online, collect at TI or use the app, www.dublinpass.ie). Skip the pass if you already have the Heritage Card (see the Practicalities chapter)—it covers two big Dublin sights (Kilmainham Gaol and Dublin Castle).

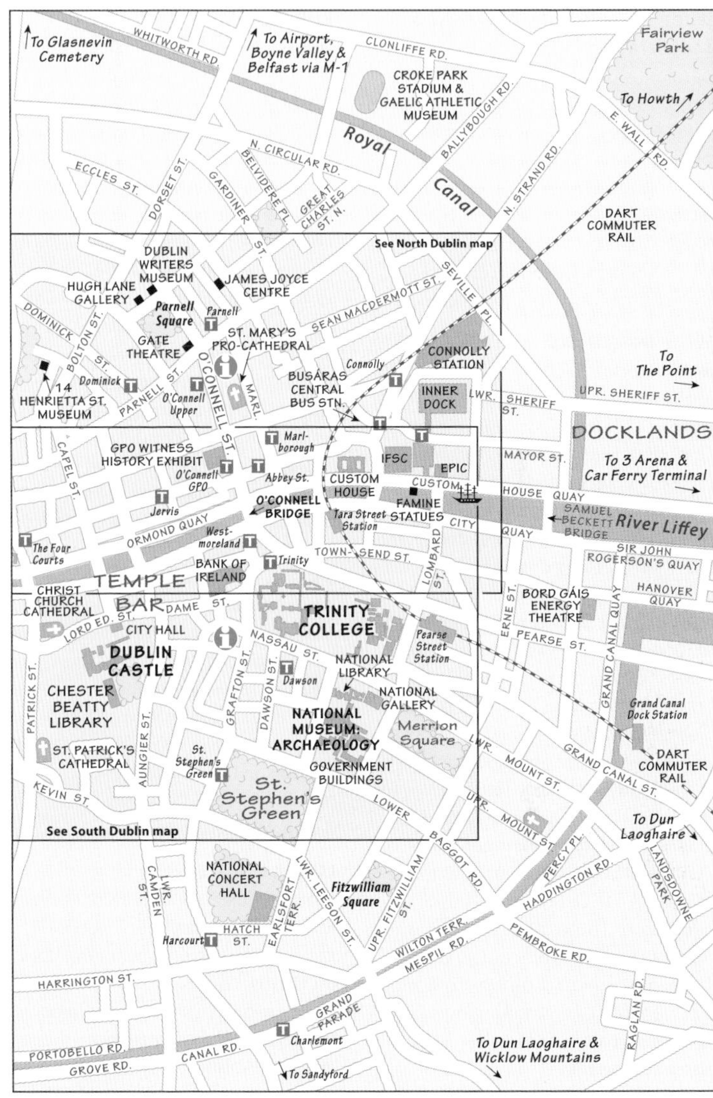

Helpful Hints

Sightseeing Tips: With rising popularity and more cruise ships than ever, Dublin can be crowded. Book in advance for the Book of Kells at Trinity College, the Guinness Storehouse, and Kilmainham Gaol (reservations are mandatory for Kilmainham Gaol). And, if you are set on any evening activity, tour, or fine meal, reservations are a must.

Rick's Tip: *Dublin is not immune to pickpocketing. Be on guard—***wear a money belt** *or carefully zip things up.*

Laundry: Krystal Launderette, a block southwest of Jurys Inn Christ Church on Patrick Street, offers same-day full service (Mon-Sat 8:00-20:00, Sun 12:00-17:00, tel. 01/454-6864). The **All-American Launderette** offers self- and full-service options (Mon-Sat 8:30-19:00, Sun 10:00-18:00, 40 South Great George's Street, tel. 01/677-2779). For locations, see the map on page 82.

Tours

Some tour companies offer a discount when you show this book (indicated in these listings with the abbreviation RS%).

WALKING TOURS

▲▲**Historical Walking Tours of Dublin,** led by history grads, is your best introduction to Dublin's basic historic strip (including Trinity College, Parliament House, Dublin Castle, Christ Church Cathedral, Grafton Street, and St. Stephen's Green). You'll get the story of the city, from its Viking origins to the present (May-Sept daily at 11:00 and 15:00, April and Oct daily at 11:00, Nov-March Fri-Sun at 11:00; €14, RS%—ask when booking, free for kids under 14, can book ahead online, departs from front gate of Trinity College, private tours available, mobile 087-688-9412, www.historicalinsights.ie).

Pat Liddy's Walking Tours, run by top local historian Pat Liddy, has a crew of guides who lead an assortment of informal 2.5-hour walks of Dublin (€14, RS%—save €2; April-Oct daily at 11:00; no tours Sun, Tue, or Thu in off-season; meet in front of Dublin Bus office at 59 Upper O'Connell Street, tel. 01/832-9406, mobile 087-905-2480, www.walkingtours.ie). While it's smart to book online, you can also just show up.

Rick's Tip: *Sign up in advance for the free* **City of a Thousand Welcomes** *service, which brings together Dubliner volunteers and first-time visitors. You'll meet an "ambassador," head for a nearby tearoom or pub, and enjoy a drink (paid for by the city) and a friendly, informal conversation (meet at Little Museum of Dublin, www.cityofathousandwelcomes.com).*

PUB CRAWLS

▲▲**Traditional Irish Musical Pub Crawl** visits the upstairs rooms of three pubs where you'll listen to two musicians talk about, play, and sing traditional Irish music. The evening—though touristy—provides a real education in traditional Irish music. It's easy to reserve ahead online (€16, RS%—use code "RSIRISH" online, beer extra, April-Oct daily at 19:30, Nov and Jan-March Thu-Sat only, no shows in Dec, maximum 65 people, meet upstairs at Gogarty's Pub at the corner of Fleet and Anglesea in the Temple Bar area, tel. 01/475-3313, www.musicalpubcrawl.com).

Dublin Literary Pub Crawl is led by two actors who take 40 or so tourists on two-hour walk punctuated with four 20-minute pub breaks (free time to drink and socialize). This is an easygoing excuse to drink beer in busy pubs, meet other travelers, and get a dose of witty Irish lit (€14, April-Oct daily at 19:30, Nov-March Thu-Sun only; reserve ahead July-Aug when it can fill up, otherwise just show up; meet upstairs in the Duke Pub—off Grafton on Duke Street, tel. 01/670-5602, mobile 087-263-0270, www.dublinpubcrawl.com).

LOCAL GUIDES

Suzanne Cole is good guide, both charming and smart (€120/2.5 hours, mobile 087-225-1262, suza.cole@gmail.com); **Dara McCarthy** will proudly show you around his hometown (€120/2.5 hours, mobile 087-291-6798, dara@daramccarthy.com); and **Jack Walsh** is a local actor who's both high-minded and soft-spoken (€180/half-day, mobile 087-228-1570, walshjack135@gmail.com).

▲HOP-ON, HOP-OFF BUS TOURS

Dublin works well for a hop-on, hop-off bus tour, which is an excellent way to orient yourself on arrival. Two companies with roofless double-deckers do similar 1.5-hour circuits of the city (up to 30 stops, buses circle every 10-15 minutes daily 9:00-17:00, usually until 19:00 in summer). Stops include the far-flung Guinness Storehouse and Kilmainham Gaol (**Do Dublin**—green buses, ticket includes free entry to the Little Museum of Dublin and a free walking tour from Pat Liddy's Walking Tours, €20/24 hours, €25/48 hours, tel. 01/844-4265, www.dublinsightseeing.ie; **Big Bus Tours**—red buses, €20/24 hours, €25/48 hours, tel. 01/531-1711, www.bigbustours.com, also offer a one-hour panoramic night tour).

DUBLIN CITY WALK

This walk covers the basic sights in the center of town on the south side of the River Liffey. It can be done as a light, fast-paced overview in under two hours. Or you can use it to lace together many of the city's top sights. Take this walk at the beginning of your Dublin visit to get the lay of the land—physically, culturally, and historically. As several of the stops and passageways along the route are closed after dark, this walk is best during normal business hours. For background on some of the historical events and personalities introduced, refer to the "Modern Ireland's Turbulent Birth" sidebar, later.

This walk is covered by part 1 of my free Dublin City Walk audio tour.

Self-Guided Walk

• *Start at the southernmost end of Grafton Street, where the city's thriving pedestrian boulevard meets its most beloved park. Stand before the big arch.*

1 *St. Stephen's Green*

This city park, worth ▲, was originally a medieval commons—a space for grazing livestock. The park got its start in 1664, when the city leased some of the land as building lots—and each tenant was obligated to plant six trees. Gradually the green was surrounded with fine Georgian buildings and access was limited to these affluent residents ("Georgian" is British for Neoclassical...named for the period from 1714 to 1830 when four consecutive King Georges occupied the British throne). Those were the glory days, when Dublin, both wealthy and powerful, was the number-two city in Britain, and squares and boulevards built in the

St. Stephen's Green

Georgian style gave the city an air of grandeur. In 1880, the park was opened to the public, and today it provides a grassy refuge for all Dubliners.

The gateway before you is the **Fusiliers Arch.** It commemorates Irishmen who died fighting in the British Army in the Boer War (against Dutch settlers in South Africa from 1899-1902). In Dublin's crushingly impoverished tenements of the time, one of the few ways for a young man without means to improve his lot would be to join the army (regular meals, proper clothing, and a chance to "see the world"). You can read a little of the Irish struggle into the names: Captains were Protestant elites with English names, and grunts were Catholic with Catholic names. Many more grunts died.

Two decades later, Ireland was embroiled in its own war against Britain (the Irish War of Independence, 1919-1921), and sentiments had evolved. With Irishmen fighting to end their own centuries of English domination, locals considered the Fusiliers Arch a memorial to those who fought for Britain—and began referring to it as "Traitors Arch." A key Dublin battleground during that war was in and around this park. Step around to the left of the arch and look up. **Bullet marks** scarring the side of the memorial are reminders of the 1919 Easter Rising.

During that short-lived revolt, a group of passionate Irish rebels—a mishmash of romantic poets, teachers, aristocratic ladies, and slum dwellers—dug trenches in the park, believing they were creating fortified positions. They hadn't figured on veteran British troops placing snipers atop the nearby Shelbourne Hotel (with a bird's-eye view into the trenches). The park is dotted with reminders of that struggle, like the **memorial stone** honoring Irish rebel O'Donovan Rossa a few steps into the park past the arch. An oration at his funeral in 1915 was a catalyst that helped galvanize the rebels who would rise in 1916.

Take a quick walk into the park, strolling a couple hundred yards around the lake counterclockwise, where you'll see a monument to **W. B. Yeats** (by Henry Moore) and a wonderful **central garden.**

• *Continue circling, then exit through the big arch. You're facing busy, pedestrianized Grafton Street (we'll go down it later). First we'll make a swing around the block to the right: Cross the street, dodging Dublin's new and popular tram line, and head right to the first corner, then go left, down Dawson Street.*

You can just make out the ***"tiniest pub in Dublin"*** *(on the left at #25). Next door (#27), the* ***Celtic Whiskey Shop*** *is a reminder that in recent years Ireland has exported more whiskey than Scotland. To find out why, and maybe score a free sample, drop in. The big white Georgian building across the street is the...*

Fusiliers Arch

Mansion House

John Kehoe pub

Phil Lynott statue

❷ *Mansion House*

Built in 1710, this is where Dublin's Lord Mayor lives. The building played roles in both of Ireland's wars.

In 1918 Ireland elected its representatives to the British Parliament—and chose mostly separatist members of the Sinn Féin ("Ourselves") party. The Sinn Fein parliamentarians refused to take their seats at Westminster in London. Instead, in January 1919, they created their own Irish Parliament (the Dáil Éireann) and met in an annex behind the Mansion House. The establishment of this rogue parliament in defiance of British rule kicked off the Irish War of Independence.

Three years later, they'd thrown off British rule, but found themselves at odds over the terms of the Anglo-Irish Treaty to end the war. Unable to agree, those opposed to ratification—led by Dáil Éireann president Éamon de Valera—marched out of parliament in protest. Within a few months, their festering disagreements ignited into the tragic Irish Civil War, eventually won by the pro-treaty forces of Michael Collins.

• *Continue down Dawson Street. The large neo-Romanesque (late 19th century) church ahead of you is the Anglican* **St. Ann's Church,** *where Irish author Oscar Wilde was baptized and Bram Stoker (of Dracula fame) was married. Turn left onto Anne Street South and walk two blocks toward Grafton Street, past a line of busy independent retailers and a popular pub,* **John Kehoe.** *This legacy pub is part of the Dublin landscape: Dubliners often refer to landmark pubs rather than street names when giving directions.*

Stop and enjoy the scene when you reach the busy, pedestrian boulevard.

❸ *Grafton Street*

Grafton Street is Dublin's most desirable retail address. It was pedestrianized in 1983, much to the consternation of local retailers—who were soon pleased to discover that business improved without all the traffic. Ireland's "Celtic Tiger" economic boom (2000-2008) gave the country Europe's hottest economy and a thriving tech sector. Business was so good that retail rents skyrocketed, which drove away small shops. Today Grafton Street is filled with mostly international retailers and a surging torrent of shoppers.

We'll stroll the boulevard to the right in a moment. But first, go directly across Grafton to Harry Street: A half-block up you'll find a hairy rock star. This life-sized bronze statue with bass guitar, picks wedged behind the strings as fan tributes, is **Phil Lynott,** Ireland's first hard-rock star. He lived a short, fast life and is remembered for his band Thin Lizzy (of

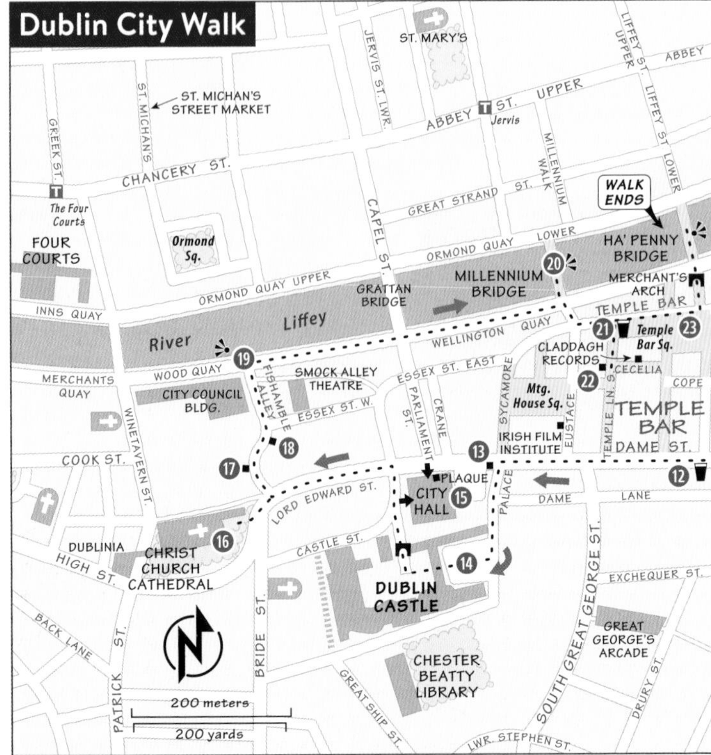

1. St. Stephen's Green
2. Mansion House
3. Grafton Street
4. Bewley's Oriental Café
5. St. Teresa's Catholic Church
6. Ulysses Plaque
7. Trinity College's Old Library
8. Trinity College
9. Parliament House & a Grand Boulevard
10. Irish House of Lords
11. Molly Malone Statue
12. The Bank Bar
13. Green Post Box
14. Dublin Castle
15. Dublin City Hall
16. Christ Church Cathedral
17. Viking Dublin
18. Handel's Hotel
19. River Liffey & View of the Four Courts
20. Millennium Bridge
21. Temple Bar
22. Wall of Fame & Irish Pop Music
23. Temple Bar Square

"The Boys Are Back in Town" fame).

• *Return to Grafton Street, take a left, and join the river of pedestrians. Stop 50 yards down at the venerable café on the left...*

❹ *Bewley's Oriental Café*

Bewley's is a Dublin tradition that your Irish great-grandfather would remember for its well-priced comfort food. The facade is done in an ornate neo-Egyptian, Art Deco style (built after the excitement of the discovery of King Tut's tomb in 1922). Approach it as if visiting an art gallery filled with people eating. Walk to the very back of the ground floor to view its famous stained-glass windows by artist Harry Clarke (1881-

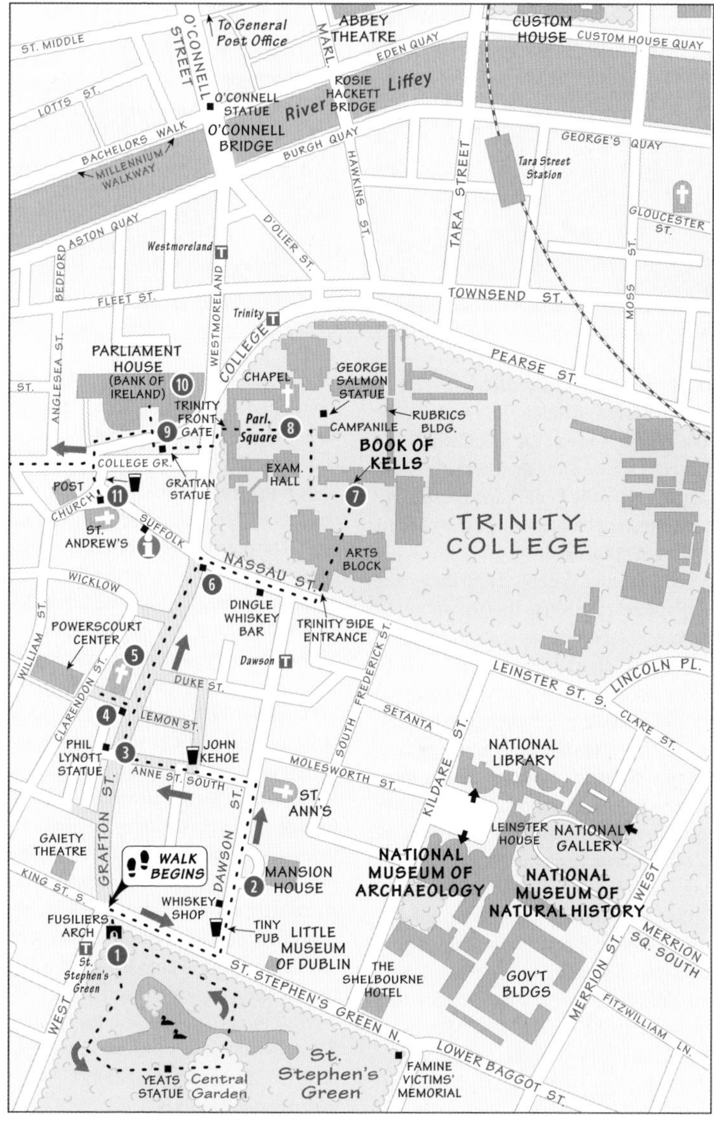

1931). For Clarke, famous for decorating churches with his exquisite windows, this is a rare secular subject—celebrating the four classical orders of column design. A fine Irish craftsman/artist, Clarke first learned his trade from his father, a stained-glass painter, and was part of the Irish Arts and Crafts movement. You're free to wander upstairs for more Bewley art. (For more about the restaurant, see the listing under "Eating.")

• *A couple of steps farther down Grafton, turn left on the narrow lane called Johnson's Court. About 50 feet down, through the ornate archway, find a peaceful church.*

Bewley's Oriental Café

St. Teresa's Church

❺ St. Teresa's Catholic Church

Tucked away as if hiding, St. Teresa's was built in 1792—one of the first Catholic churches allowed in Ireland after the gradual relaxing of the Penal Laws passed by the Protestant parliament (1691-1760) to regulate Catholics.

For a century, Catholics and their clergy were forced to practice their religion secretly, celebrating Mass at hidden rural "Mass rock" altars. But by the 1790s, the British government felt secure enough to allow some Catholic churches to be built again. They also wanted to appease the Irish—who could have been getting ideas as they observed Catholic France beheading its monarchs. Catholics were allowed to worship in actual churches as long as they kept a low profile.

Daniel O'Connell (b. 1775), an enlightened member of parliament, campaigned for Catholic equality and held political meetings at St. Teresa's. He brought down the last of those Penal Laws in 1829 by championing the Catholic right to vote.

• *Now stroll down Grafton Street. Step out of the flow of humanity to glance up the side streets. Commercial as this street is, it has standards—notice that the arches are not golden at McDonald's. At the end of the pedestrianized section of Grafton Street, at the right corner, find a brass plaque in the pavement.*

❻ Ulysses Plaque

The little brass plaque on the ground, rubbed shiny by foot traffic, marks a spot mentioned in James Joyce's most famous novel, *Ulysses.* Passionate Irish-lit fans know Joyce's challenging, stream-of-consciousness work, which unfolds as a single day in the life of Leopold Bloom—June 16, 1904. The date is celebrated every year in Dublin as "Bloomsday," with scholars and enthusiasts dressing in period Edwardian garb and quoting passages from Joyce.

• *Turn right and go a block on busy Nassau Street, passing the recommended* ***Dingle Whiskey Bar*** *(on the right, with 180 whiskeys on its shelves—an art form in itself). At the next corner, on the opposite (leafy) side of Nassau Street, is a side entrance to* ***Trinity College.*** *Follow the stream of students into the modern bunker-like Arts Building (note that the campus may be closed Sat-Sun after 18:00. In that case, walk left to the university's front door.) If you need a ticket to see the Book of Kells, two ATM-like machines in this hall can sell you one, quick and easy.*

Walk through the hall, exit the building down the ramp, and survey the grassy courtyard. The grand, gray three-story building with a line of tourists is...

❼ Trinity College's Old Library

The college's Old Library houses the **Book of Kells,** a medieval masterpiece of calligraphy and illustration. The ground floor contains the actual 1,200-year-old book (containing the gospels of Matthew, Mark, Luke, and John); the top floor is a venerable world of varnished wooden shelves

Old Library at Trinity College

George Salmon statue

giving a dignified home to a precious collection of reference books and artifacts, including an original copy of the 1916 Proclamation of the Irish Republic, which announced Ireland's dramatic split with Britain (for more on touring the library, see the listing under "Sights," later).

• *Go around to the left of the Old Library to enter a larger and grander square. Walk to the center, where the smooth paths intersect, and face the* ***Campanile*** *(bell tower).*

❽ *Trinity College*

You're standing on Parliament Square, in the heart of Ireland's oldest seat of learning, founded in 1592 by Queen Elizabeth to set the ill-disciplined Irish on the straight and righteous path to Protestant learning. These cobblestones were trod by Trinity graduates like Jonathan Swift, Oscar Wilde, Bram Stoker, and Samuel Beckett. (You're surrounded by dorms and administration. The actual classrooms are mostly elsewhere.)

Behind the graceful Campanile are the red-brick **Rubrics,** the oldest remaining buildings on campus (c. 1712). Their facades sport a faintly Dutch look, due to their construction soon after the reign of Dutch-born King William III of Orange. He took the British throne jointly with his English wife/cousin Mary II, bringing Dutch architecture into vogue for a generation.

Fifty feet to the left of the Campanile is a white-marble statue of **George Salmon,** a mathematician, theologian, and provost in the late 1890s, who said women would enter Trinity over his dead body. Coincidentally, days after he died in 1904, the first women were admitted to Trinity College.

Now turn 180 degrees to face the front gate of the college. To your right and left stand two identically majestic buildings, each with four Corinthian columns. To your right is the college chapel and to the left is the examination hall, respectively nicknamed "heaven and hell."

Directly ahead, at the front gate, you'll often spot a talkative college kid wearing an academic gown staffing a small kiosk and selling tickets for the fun Trinity College campus tours (see listing under "Sights," later).

• *Exit the campus through the front gatehouse and enter one of the most chaotic intersections in Dublin. Cross the street carefully to the traffic island at the bottom of the busy boulevard and stand before a statue of the guy who first cooked potatoes au Grattan (or an 18th-century member of the Irish House of Commons—you decide).*

❾ *Parliament House and a Grand Boulevard*

The long street stretching straight in front of you is College Green, which becomes Dame Street, and then Lord Edward Street as it reaches Christ Church Cathedral, a half-mile away (and we're about to walk the entire thing). For simplicity, I'll just refer to it as "the boulevard."

Roughly 250 years ago, this spot marked the start of Dublin's version of a "Royal Mile," where the parliament, castle, university, and big banks all intersected in full glory. Logically, this spot in front of parliament was also where serious protests took place.

The grand building with a rounded colonnade is the **Parliament House** (and now home to the Bank of Ireland). The Irish House of Commons and House of Lords met here until the 1801 Act of Union abolished the Irish parliament, moving its members to Westminster in London. Thus began Dublin's slow, century-long decay, from important British hub to largely impoverished, tenement-ridden backwater.

• *The original* ⑩ ***Irish House of Lords*** *survives in the bank, and is free to visit (open Mon-Fri 10:00-16:00). Follow the signs and pop in—you'll see a fireplace carved of Irish oak, tapestries celebrating Protestant victories over the indigenous and Catholic Irish, and busts of British kings and admirals.*

Leaving the bank, walk a block up the boulevard and take your first left (cross over at Ulster Bank), onto Church Lane. Go one block to an old church with a statue out front of a buxom maiden pushing a cart of wicker baskets.

⑪ *Molly Malone Statue*

You've probably heard Dublin's unofficial theme song "Molly Malone"—now let's meet the woman commemorated in the tune. The area around the Molly Malone statue (from 1988) is a popular hangout for street musicians—and for tourists wanting a photo with the iconic gal of Irish sing-along fame. She pauses cooperatively "in Dublin's fair city, where the girls are so pretty," to offer you "cockles and mussels, alive, alive-o" from her cart.

Across the street is **O'Neill's,** recommended for pub grub. Just for fun, enter on the right and work your way through its labyrinthine interior, eventually exiting on the left. The O'Neill family has had a pub at this intersection for over 300 years.

Molly Malone statue

• *Return to the main boulevard, turn left, and continue a few doors to a very fancy bank (on the left with a red sandstone facade, brass details, and showy banners) that's now a very fancy pub. Step just inside for a dazzling view.*

⑫ *The Bank Bar*

Built in 1894, The Bank Bar staggers visitors with its Victorian opulence. Back then, banks had to dazzle elite clients to assure them the bank was financially solid. Today, Dublin's banks have vacated such palaces for modern offices, and many ornate former bank interiors—like this one—now dazzle diners.

Even if you're not eating here, you're welcome to stand just inside the door for a look. The stained-glass ceiling still sparkles. The many mirrors make the space seem larger, and the ornate floor tiles and crow's nest balcony catch the eye. A stately painting of the Custom House (surrounded by the ships so vital to Dublin's economy) fills the wall on the left. And on the right is a painting of Parliament House. The paintings face each other as pillars of society: commerce and governance. In the back-right corner are seven male busts: the seven patriot signers of the 1916 Proclamation of Irish Independence, martyrs for the Irish Republic—all executed at Kilmainham Gaol.

• *Exit the bar, turn left, and walk a couple of minutes (2 long blocks) until you see a green post box.*

⓭ Green Post Box

An innocent-looking, round green postal box stands sentry in a small sidewalk plaza. Like all Irish post boxes, it's Irish green. But look closely at the elaborate monogram at knee height. It's an ornate "E" for "Edward," woven with "R" for "Rex" (Latin for "king")—indicating that this box dates from just before World War I, during the reign of King Edward VII (son of Victoria)—who reigned over Ireland as part of the United Kingdom of Great Britain and Ireland. Once royal red, after Ireland won its independence it was more practical to just paint the post poxes Irish green and call it good, than replace them. In 1922, this box, with its high-profile location at the entry to the grounds of Dublin Castle, was the first to be painted green. If a Royalist were to scratch the paint to show some underlying red, it would be repainted green before you could say Guy Fawkes.

• *Ahead is City Hall. But first we'll take a short detour, looping left and then right through the grounds of Dublin Castle before emerging just beyond City Hall.*

⓮ Dublin Castle

While Dublin Castle today shows only scant remains of its medieval architecture, it was the center of English power for 700 years, from its initial construction in 1204 (under bad King John of Magna Carta fame) until Britain handed the reins back to the Irish in 1922. Today, it's a prime example of a Georgian palace and the location for ceremonial affairs of state. The castle's grand state rooms are open to the public (for details, see the listing under "Sights," later).

Ⓐ *Parliament House*

Ⓑ *Green postboxes symbolize Ireland's independence.*

Ⓒ *The Bank Bar*

Ⓓ *Dublin Castle*

• *Leave the castle grounds through the gate at the top of the courtyard. On your right, facing the busy boulevard, is the...*

⑮ *Dublin City Hall*

Dublin's impressive City Hall, worth ▲, started in 1779 as the Royal Exchange, where Irish and British currencies were exchanged and where merchants gathered to discuss trading affairs. It's a splendid example of the Georgian style.

It became City Hall in 1852 and was the site of the first fatalities of the 1916 Easter Rising, when Irish rebels occupied it to control the main gate to Dublin Castle. Step inside (it's free) to feel the prosperity and confidence of Dublin in her glory days. The dramatic main-floor rotunda—with its grand Caesar-like statue of the great orator Daniel O'Connell (the city's first Catholic mayor, 1841)—was inspired by the Pantheon in Rome. A cycle of heroic paintings tells the city's history in a rare example of Arts and Crafts artwork from 1919. It was here, under the rotunda, that the body of modern Irish rebel leader Michael Collins lay in state after his assassination in 1922.

Downstairs, the fine and free little **Story of the Capital** exhibit does a good job of telling the city's history, including the stirring and heartbreaking events of 1916, the War of Independence, and the Irish Civil War (Mon-Sat 10:00-17:15, closed Sun, www.dublincity.ie/dublincityhall).

• *Leave City Hall through the Dame Street exit, and take the stairs on your right. Turn left and continue uphill on the big boulevard to the church tower in the distance.*

⑯ *Christ Church Cathedral*

The cathedral in front of you, worth ▲, is one of the oldest places of worship in Dublin. What you see today is an extensively renovated neo-Gothic structure dating from the 1870s, but its underground crypt goes back to 1172. An even earlier Viking-era church stood here back in the 1030s. Just beyond the *Homeless Jesus* bench/statue, an excavation contains the low-lying ruins of a small 12th-century church building. The stones you see on the exterior of the southern transept (above the excavation site) are 12th-century Romanesque—one of the few original features not disturbed by later restorations (for more on the church, see the listing under "Sights," later).

• *Leave the churchyard as you entered, turn left, and walk a few steps down Fishamble Street to the blocky concrete sign reading Dublin City Council. At your feet in the pavement is a marker celebrating some ancient history.*

⑰ *Viking Dublin*

You're standing on the site of Dublin's first Viking settlement, established over 1,200 years ago, with Fishamble Street as its fish market. When the foundations for the huge bunker-like modern offices of the Dublin City Council were dug in 1978, an intact Viking settlement was exposed. A treasure trove of artifacts was uncovered, carefully excavated, and catalogued by eager archaeologists. More than a million objects were found (the best are in the National Museum of Archaeology). Even so, researchers were allowed only a short time to dig before the office building that stands here now was erected, effectively burying the rest of the settlement under the pavement. Public protests were vehement and vocal, but to no avail. In an ironic twist, Dublin's citizens must come here to get planning permission to build. Sidewalk plaques (there are 18) based on photos from the dig remind all who pass of what was found—and lost.

• *Walk farther downhill, passing* ***Darkey Kelly's,*** *a good pub with music nightly. At the end of the block, you'll see* ⑱ ***Handel's Hotel,*** *named for the composer of the "Messiah" (with its beloved "Hallelujah Chorus"). The first public performance of this iconic oratorio took place in 1742 in a nearby music hall. Peek through the gate to the left of the hotel to see a statue of Handel standing like a pillar saint atop organ pipes.*

Continue walking down Fishamble all the way to the river.

⓳ *River Liffey and View of the Four Courts*

Look left. Across the river in the distance is a grand building with a green domed roof. This is the **Four Courts,** finished in 1802 and housing Ireland's Supreme Court. It was once the archive for irreplaceable birth and land records. When the Irish Civil War broke out in 1922, Irish nationalists opposed to British dominion occupied the building. Forces supporting the 1921 Anglo-Irish Treaty—led by Michael Collins—were left no alternative but to root them out with British-supplied artillery (the first shots of that tragic brother-against-brother conflict). The artillery onslaught resulted in the accidental detonation of rebel ammo in the Four Courts, sparking an intense fire that destroyed seven centuries of genealogical and historical records.

• *Turn right and walk downstream to the second bridge, the pedestrian-only Millennium Bridge. Walk halfway out to survey the scene.*

⓴ *Millennium Bridge*

From here the Liffey flows three miles to empty into the Irish Sea. Today the river is empty of vessels and contained by its concrete embankments, but it was once wider, with muddy banks, wooden piers, and sailing ships. After Vikings sailed their longboats down the Liffey in the ninth century, they built a ship harbor here, and for centuries afterward, the riverfront was the pumping heart of Dublin's commerce. The Liffey is a salty river, with high and low tides. Before the 1600s, boats could come this far upriver to the medieval port area. But with more bridges and bigger ships, the port moved farther and farther downstream. Today it's at the mouth of the river, three miles away.

Look downstream at the next bridge, the pedestrian-only **Ha' Penny Bridge,** a Dublin landmark since 1816. It's officially

Ⓐ *Dublin City Hall*

Ⓑ *Viking settlement site*

Ⓒ *Ha' Penny Bridge*

the "Wellington Bridge," named for Arthur Wellesley, the first duke of Wellington, who was born in Ireland, beat Napoleon at Waterloo, and became a British prime minister. It got its nickname because people paid half a penny ("Ha' penny") to cross the bridge rather than ride a ferry across the river—the only other option in the early 1800s.

• *Go a block inland from the river. At East Essex Street (and the Norsemen Pub), wander left into the heart of Dublin's infamous party district, known as...*

21 *Temple Bar*

Inspired by thriving bohemian cultural centers such as Paris' Left Bank and New York City's Greenwich Village, in 1991 Dublin scuttled a plan to demolish this neighborhood (filled with drugs, prostitutes, and decay) to build a bus station. Instead, the city imported quaint cobbles, gave tax breaks to entertainment businesses, and created a raucous party zone. The resulting tourist crowds and inflated beer prices drove away the locals long ago. (For more on Temple Bar, see pages 70 and 81.) On the first corner slouches a pub called **The Temple Bar.** While it looks venerable, it's only 25 years old, built to cash in on the district's rising popularity as a night spot. It encapsulates the commercialism of the tourists' Temple Bar. Venture in and sample the scene.

• *From The Temple Bar pub, side-trip right a block, up Temple Lane South, and stop at the corner of Cecelia Street.*

22 *Wall of Fame and Irish Pop Music*

The windows of the three-story, red "Wall of Fame" on your right are filled with photos of contemporary Irish musicians (Bob Geldof, Phil Lynott, Sinead O'Connor, U2, The Cranberries, and others). It marks the location of the **Irish Rock 'n' Roll Museum** (worth a visit for rock fans interested in seeing studio space and vintage mixing boards used by famous acts, visit by €16 guided tour only, daily 11:00-17:30, www.irishrocknrollmuseum.com).

Behind you, a couple doors up Cecelia Street, is **Claddagh Records,** a fine little Irish traditional music shop (closed Sun, www.claddaghrecords.com). This hole-in-the-wall shop is staffed by informed folks who love turning visitors on to Irish tunes. Above it, the modest third floor once held studios where U2 did some of its earliest recording.

• *Return to the main street and turn right into...*

23 *Temple Bar Square*

This square is the geographic heart of the Temple Bar district and a favorite haunt of street musicians. The quaint-looking pubs that front it are re-creations built in the early 2000s, when the area became so popular that pubs could sell the most expensive pints in town. Stand here on a Saturday night and you'll see how this party zone got its reputation for rowdy noise and drunken antics.

• *Walk along the square, then turn left up the narrow lane called Merchant's Arch, toward the river and* ***Ha' Penny Bridge.*** *Walk to the midway point of the bridge and celebrate the end of your walk.*

To continue from here to O'Connell Street and sights to the north of the River Liffey, continue across the river, turn right, and walk to the O'Connell Bridge via the wooden riverside Millennial Walkway.

Wall of Fame

SIGHTS

South of the River Liffey

Trinity College

▲▲TRINITY COLLEGE CAMPUS TOUR

Founded in 1592 by Queen Elizabeth I to establish a Protestant way of thinking about God, Trinity has long been Ireland's most prestigious college. Originally, the student body was limited to rich Protestant men. Women were admitted in 1903, and Catholics—though allowed entrance to the school much earlier—were given formal permission by the Catholic Church to study at Trinity in the 1970s. Today, half of Trinity's 12,500 students are women, and 70 percent are culturally Catholic.

Trinity students lead 30-minute tours of their campus (look just inside the college gate for posted departure times and students selling tickets). You'll get a rundown of the mostly Georgian architecture, a peek at student life past and present, and the enjoyable company of your guide—a witty college kid.

Cost and Hours: €6—or €4 if you have a Book of Kells ticket, purchase tour tickets on the spot at campus gate off Dame Street; tours run daily 9:15-16:00, off-season weekends only, no tours Dec-Jan; tours depart roughly every 30 minutes, weather permitting, www.tcd.ie/visitors/tours.

▲▲▲BOOK OF KELLS IN THE TRINITY OLD LIBRARY

The Book of Kells—a 1,200-year-old manuscript of the four gospels—was elaborately inked and meticulously illustrated by faithful monks. Combining Christian symbols and pagan styles, it's a snapshot of medieval Ireland in transition. Arguably the finest piece of art from what is generally called the Dark Ages, the Book of Kells shows that monastic life in this far fringe of Europe was far from dark.

Cost and Hours: €14, buy timed-entry ticket online in advance to avoid the line; Mon-Sat 8:30-17:00, Sun from 9:30; Oct-April Mon-Sat 9:30-17:00, Sun 12:00-16:30; audioguide-€5, tel. 01/896-2320, www.tcd.ie/visitors/book-of-kells.

Crowd Control: Without an advance ticket you'll likely wait in a long ticket-buying line (worst midday, roughly 10:00-15:00—especially when cruise ships are in). Skip it by heading to the Nassau Street/Arts Building entry to campus, where it's easy to book tickets—even same day, if available—from a pair of ticket machines in the lobby hallway.

➲ SELF-GUIDED TOUR

Your visit has three stages: 1) an exhibit on the making of the Book of Kells, including poster-sized reproductions of its pages (your best look at the book's detail); 2) the Treasury, a darkened room containing the Book of Kells itself and other, less ornate contemporaneous volumes; and, upstairs, 3) the Old Library (called the Long Room), containing a precious collection of 16th- to 18th-century books and historical objects.

Background: The Book of Kells was a labor of love created by dedicated Irish monks cloistered on the remote Scottish island of Iona. They slaughtered 185 calves, soaked the skins in lime, scraped off the hair, and dried the skins into a cream-colored writing surface called vellum. Only

Tour at Trinity College

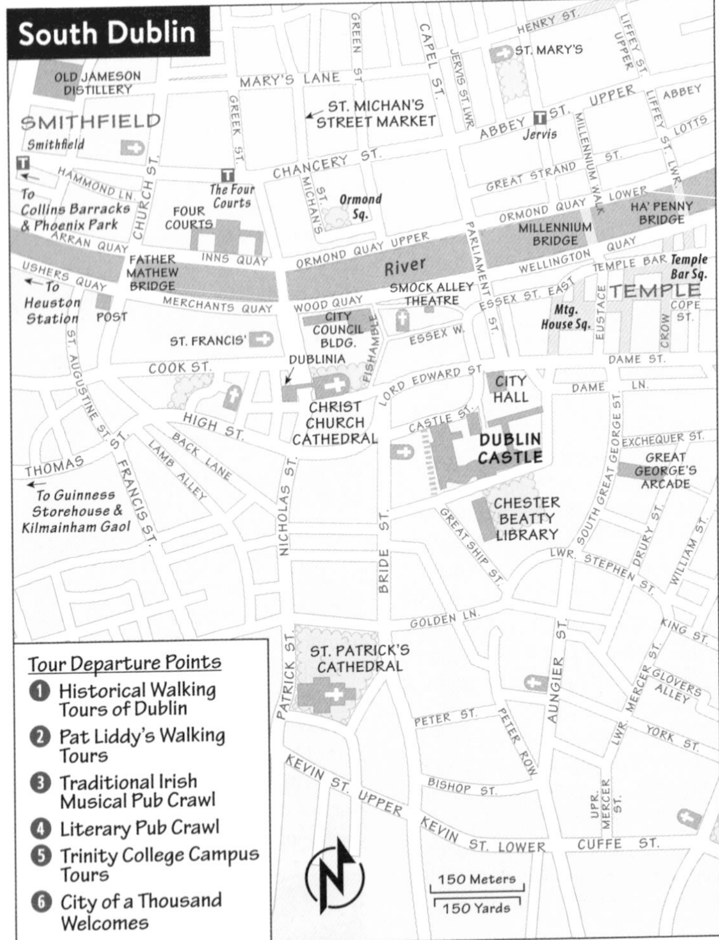

then could the tonsured monks pick up their swan-quill pens and get to work.

The project may have been underway in 806 when Vikings savagely pillaged and burned Iona, killing 68 monks. The survivors fled to the Abbey of Kells (near Dublin). Scholars debate exactly where the book was produced: It could have been made entirely at Iona or at Kells, or started in Iona and finished at Kells.

For eight centuries, the glorious gospel sat regally atop the high altar of the church at Kells, where the priest would read from it during special Masses. In 1654, as Cromwell's puritanical rule settled in, the book was smuggled to Dublin for safety. Here at Trinity College, it was first displayed to the public in the mid-1800s. In 1953, the book got its current covers and was bound into four separate volumes.

The Exhibit: The Turning Darkness into Light exhibit, with a one-way route, puts the illuminated manuscript in its historical and cultural context. This is important as it prepares you to see the original book and other precious manuscripts in the treasury. Make a point to

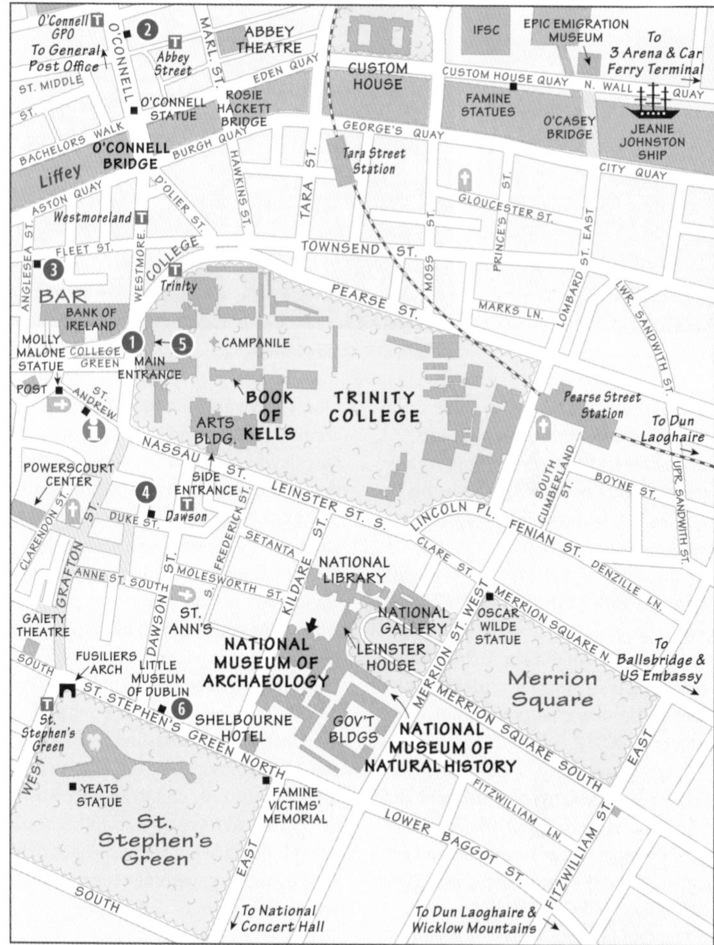

spend some time in this exhibit before reaching the actual Book of Kells.

Especially interesting are the two continuously running video clips that show the ancient art of bookbinding and the exacting care that went into transcribing the monk-uscripts. They vividly depict the skill and patience needed for the monks' work.

The Book: The Book of Kells contains the four gospels of the Bible (two are on display at any given time). Altogether, the manuscript is 680 pages long (or 340 "folios," the equivalent of one sheet, front and back). The Latin calligraphy—all in capital letters—follows ruled lines, forming neat horizontal bars across the page. Sentences end with a "period" of three dots.

The text is elaborately decorated—of the hundreds of pages, only two are without illustration. Each gospel begins with a full-page depiction of an Evangelist and his symbol: Matthew (angel), Mark (lion), Luke (ox), and John (eagle). The apostles pose stiffly, like Byzantine-style icons, with almond-shaped eyes and symmetrically creased robes. Squint at the amazing detail. The true beauty lies in the intricate designs that surround the figures.

Book of Kells

Old Library, Trinity College

The colorful book employs blue, purple, red, pink, green, and yellow pigments—but no gold leaf. Letters and borders are braided together. On most pages, the initial letters are big and flowery, like in a children's fairy-tale book.

Notice how the playful monks might cross a "t" with a fish, form an "h" from a spindly-legged man, or make an "e" out of a coiled snake. Animals crouch between sentences. It's a jungle of intricate designs, inhabited by tiny creatures both real and fanciful.

Scholars think three main artists created the book: the "goldsmith" (who did the filigree-style designs), the "illustrator" (who specialized in animals and grotesques), and the "portrait painter" (who did the Evangelists and Mary).

The Old Library: The Long Room, the 200-foot-long main chamber of the Old Library (from 1732), is stacked to its towering ceiling with 200,000 books. Among the displays here, you'll find a rare first folio of Shakespeare plays and one of a dozen surviving original copies of the **1916 Proclamation of the Irish Republic.** Patrick Pearse read out its words at Dublin's General Post Office on April 24, 1916, starting the Easter Rising that led to Irish independence. Notice the inclusive opening phrase ("Irishmen and Irishwomen") and the seven signatories (each of whom was later executed).

Another national icon is nearby: the oldest surviving **Irish harp,** from the 15th century (while often called the Brian Boru harp, it was crafted 400 years after the death of this Irish king). The brass pins on its oak and willow frame once held 29 strings. In Celtic days, poets—highly influential with kings and druid priests—wandered the land, uniting the people with songs and stories. The harp's inspirational effect on Gaelic culture was so strong that Queen Elizabeth I (1558-1603) ordered Irish harpists to be hung and their instruments smashed. Even today, the love of music here is so intense that Ireland is the only country with a musical instrument as its national symbol. You'll see this harp's likeness on the back of Irish euro coins, on government documents, and on every pint of Guinness.

National Museums

▲▲▲NATIONAL MUSEUM OF ARCHAEOLOGY

Showing off the treasures of Ireland from the Stone Age to modern times, this branch of the National Museum is itself a national treasure. The soggy marshes and peat bogs of Ireland have proven perfect for preserving old objects. You'll see 4,000-year-old gold jewelry, 2,000-year-old bog mummies, 1,000-year-old Viking swords, and the collection's superstar—the exquisitely wrought Tara Brooch. Visit here to get an introduction to the rest of Ireland's historic attractions: You'll find

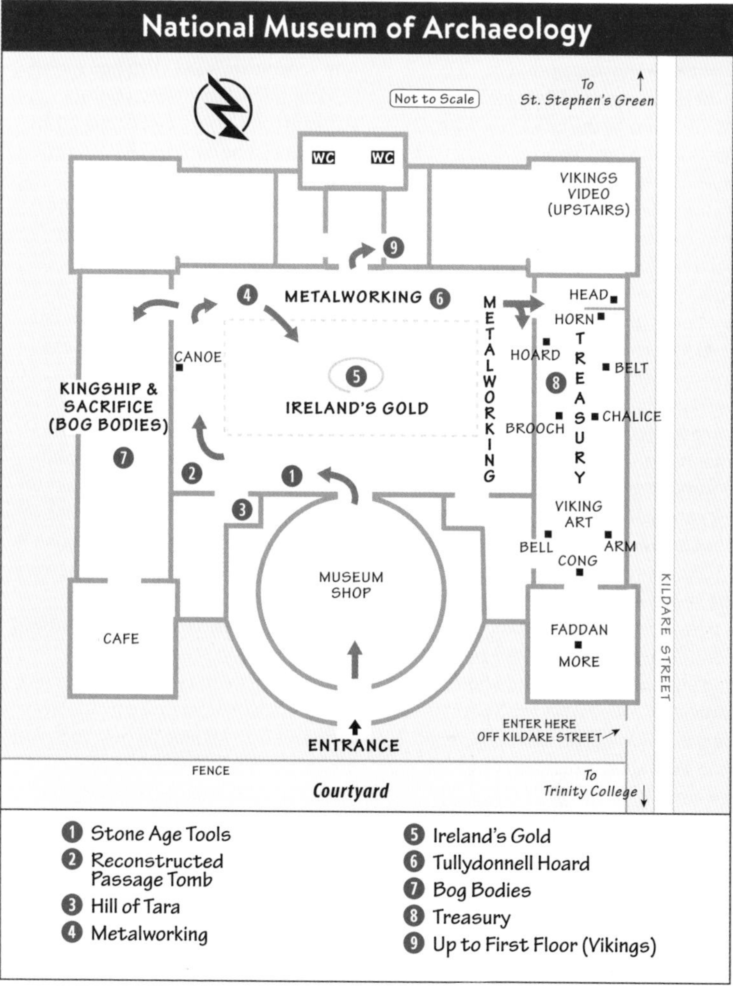

a reconstructed passage tomb like Newgrange, Celtic art like the Book of Kells, Viking objects from Dublin, a model of the Hill of Tara, and a sacred cross from the Cong Abbey. Hit the highlights of my tour, then browse the exhibits at will, all well described throughout.

Cost and Hours: Free, Sun-Mon 13:00-17:00, Tue-Sat 10:00-17:00, free audioguide download covers the Treasury room, good café, between Trinity College and St. Stephen's Green on Kildare Street, tel. 01/677-7444, www.museum.ie.

➲ SELF-GUIDED TOUR

• *Follow this tour with the help of this book's map. On the ground floor, enter the main hall and get oriented: In the center (down four steps, in the little square room) are displays of prehistoric gold jewelry. To the left are the bog bodies, to the right is the Treasury room, and upstairs is the Viking world. Let's start here, at the very beginning.*

❶ **Stone Age Tools:** Glass cases hold flint and stone ax-heads and arrowheads (7,000 BC). Ireland's first inhabitants—hunters and fishers who came from

Scotland—used these tools. These early people also left behind standing stones (dolmens) and passage tombs.

❷ **Reconstructed Passage Tomb:** At the corner of the room, you'll see a typical tomb circa 3,000 BC—a mound-shaped, heavy stone structure, covered with smaller rocks, with a passage leading into a central burial chamber where the deceased's ashes were interred. The vast passage tombs at Newgrange and Knowth are similar but many times bigger.

❸ **The Hill of Tara:** The famous passage-tomb burial site at Tara, known as the Mound of the Hostages, was used for more than 1,500 years as a place to inter human remains. The cases in this side gallery display some of the many exceptional Neolithic and Bronze Age finds uncovered at the site.

Over the millennia, the mound became the very symbol of Irish heritage. This is where Ireland's kings claimed their power, where St. Patrick preached his deal-clinching sermon, and where, in 1843, Daniel O'Connell rallied Irish patriots to demand their independence from Britain (see illustration in the small poster on the left wall).

❹ **The Evolution of Metalworking:** Around 2500 BC, Ireland discovered how to make metal—mining ore, smelting it in furnaces, and casting or hammering it into shapes. The rest is prehistory. You'll travel through the Bronze Age (ax-heads from 2000 BC) and Iron Age (500 BC) as you examine assorted spears, shields, swords, and war horns. The cauldrons made for everyday cooking were also used ceremonially to prepare elaborate ritual feasts for friends and symbolic offerings for the gods.

❺ **Ireland's Gold:** Ireland had only modest gold deposits, mainly gathered by prehistoric people panning for small nuggets and dust in the rivers. But the jewelry they left, some of it more than 4,000 years old, is exquisite. The earliest fashion choice was a broad necklace hammered flat (a *lunula,* so called for its crescent-moon shape). This might be worn with accompanying earrings and sun-disc brooches. The Gleninsheen Collar (c. 700 BC) was found in 1932 by a farmer in one of the limestone crevices characteristic of the Burren region of County Clare. It's thought that this valuable status symbol was hidden there during a time of conflict, then forgotten (or its owner killed)—if it had been meant as an offering to a pagan god it more likely would have been left in a body of water (the portal to the underworld).

A small glass case shows off the ❻ **Tullydonnell Hoard,** discovered in Donegal in 2018. The four heavy gold rings, from about 1000 BC, weigh about two pounds each and are very plain. They likely were just a way to store one's wealth in the days before someone thought of coins and banks.

❼ **Bog Bodies:** When the Celts arrived in Ireland (c. 500 BC-AD 500), they brought with them a mysterious practice: They brutally murdered sacrificial slaves or prisoners and buried them in bogs. Four bodies (each in its own tiny theater with a description outside)—shriveled and leathery, but remarkably preserved—have been dug up from around the Celtic world.

Clonycavan Man is from Ireland. One summer day around 200 BC, this twenty-something man was hacked to death with an ax and disemboweled. In his time, he stood 5'9" and had a Mohawk-style haircut, poofed up with pine-resin hair product imported from France. Today you can still see traces of his hair. Only his upper body survived; the lower part may have been lost in the threshing machine that unearthed him in 2003.

Why were these people killed? It appears to have been a form of ritual human sacrifice of high-status people. Some may have been enemy chiefs or political rivals. The sacrifices could have been offerings to the gods to ensure rich harvests and good luck. Other items

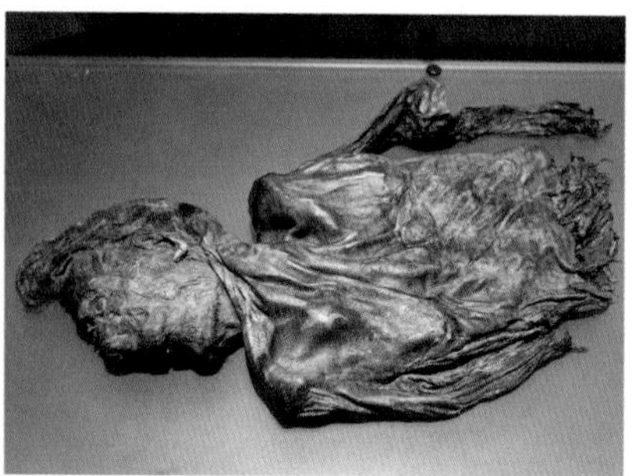

Clonycavan Man

(now on display) were buried along with them—gold bracelets, royal cloaks, finely wrought cauldrons, and leather garments.

❽ **Treasury:** Irish metalworking is legendary, and this room holds 1,500 years of exquisite treasures. Working from one end of the long room to the other, you'll journey from the world of the pagan Celts to the coming of Christianity, explore the stylistic impact of the Viking invasions (9th-12th century), and consider the resurgence of ecclesiastical metalworking (11th-12th century).

Pagan Era Art: The carved stone head of a mysterious pagan god greets you (#19, circa AD 100). The god's three faces express the different aspects of his stony personality. This abstract style—typical of Celtic art—would be at home in a modern art museum. A bronze horn (#17, first century BC) is the kind of curved war trumpet that Celts blasted to freak out the Roman legions on the Continent (the Romans never invaded Ireland). The fine objects of the Broighter Hoard (#15, first century BC) include a king's golden collar decorated in textbook Celtic style, with interlaced vines inhabited by stylized faces. The tiny boat was an offering to the sea god. The coconut-shell-shaped bowl symbolized a cauldron. By custom, the cauldron held food as a constant offering to Danu, the Celtic mother goddess, whose mythical palace was at Brú na Bóinne.

Early Christian Objects: Christianity officially entered Ireland in the fifth century (when St. Patrick converted the pagan king), but Celtic legends and art continued well into the Christian era. You'll see various crosses, shrines (portable reliquaries containing holy relics), and chalices decorated with Celtic motifs. The Belt Shrine (#32)—a circular metal casing that held a saint's leather belt—was thought to have magical properties. When placed around someone's waist, it could heal the wearer or force him or her to tell the truth.

The Ardagh Chalice (#30) and the nearby Silver Paten (#31) were used during Communion to hold blessed wine and bread. Get close to admire the elaborate workmanship. The main bowl of the chalice is gilded bronze, with a contrasting band of intricately patterned gold filigree. It's studded with colorful glass, amber, and enamels. Mirrors below the display case show that even the underside of the chalice was decorated. When the priest grabbed the chalice by its two handles and tipped it to his lips, the base could be admired by God.

Tara Brooch: A wealthy eighth-century Celtic man fastened his cloak at the shoulder with this elaborate ring-shaped brooch (#29), its seven-inch stickpin tilted rakishly upward. Made of cast and gilded silver, it's ornamented with fine, exquisitely filigreed gold panels and studded with amber, enamel, and colored glass. The motifs include Celtic spirals, snakes, and stylized faces, but the symbolism is neither overtly pagan nor Christian—it's art for art's sake. Despite its name, the brooch probably has no connection to the Hill of Tara. In the designs of this elaborate metalwork you can see the Celtic aesthetics that inspired the illuminations of the Book of Kells.

Viking Art Styles: Vikings invaded Dublin around AD 800. As Viking did, they raped and pillaged. But they also opened Ireland to a vast and cosmopolitan trading empire, from which they imported hordes of silver (see the display case of ingots).

Viking influence shows up in the decorative style of reliquaries like the Lismore Crozier (#43, in the shape of a bishop's ceremonial shepherd's crook) and the Shrine of St. Lachtin's Arm (raised in an Irish-power salute). The impressive Bell of St. Patrick (#24) was supposedly owned by Ireland's patron saint. After his death, it was encased within a beautifully worked shrine (displayed above) and kept safe by a single family, who passed it down from generation to generation for 800 years.

Cross of Cong: "By this cross is covered the cross on which the Creator of the world suffered." Running along the sides of the cross (#44), a Latin inscription tells us that it once held a sacred relic, a tiny splinter of the True Cross on which Jesus was crucified. That piece of wood (now lost) had been given in 1123 to the Irish high king, who commissioned this reliquary to preserve the splinter (it would have been placed right in the center, visible through the large piece of rock crystal). Every Christmas and Easter, the cross was fitted onto a staff and paraded through the abbey at Cong, then placed on the altar for High Mass. The extraordinarily detailed decoration features gold filigree interspersed with colored glass, enamel, and (now missing) precious stones. Though fully Christian, the cross has Celtic-style filigree patterning and Viking-style animal heads (notice how they grip the cross in their jaws).

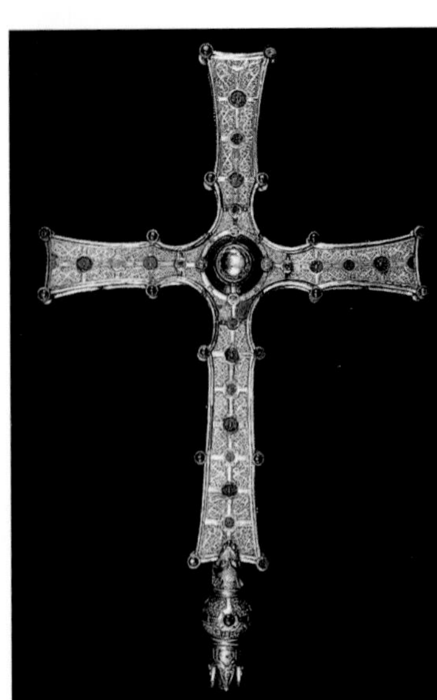

Cross of Cong

• *Now head up to the first floor to the Viking world. Start in the long hall directly above the Treasury, with the informative 25-minute video on the Viking influence on Irish culture.*

❾ **Viking Ireland** (c. 800-1150): Dublin was born as a Viking town. Sometime after 795, Scandinavian warriors rowed their longships up the River Liffey and made camp on the south bank, around the location of today's Dublin Castle and Christ Church Cathedral. Over the next two centuries, they built their encampment into an important trading post, slave market, metalworking center, and the first true city in Ireland. (See a model of Dublin showing a recently excavated area near Kilmainham Gaol.)

The state-of-the-art Viking boats worked equally well in the open ocean and shallow rivers, and were perfect for stealth invasions and far-ranging trading. Soon, provincial Dublin was connected with the wider world—Scotland, England, northern Europe, even Asia. The museum's displays of swords and spears make it clear that, yes, the Vikings were fierce warriors. But you'll also see that they were respected merchants (standardized weights and coins), herders and craftsmen (leather shoes and bags), fashion-conscious (bone combs and jewelry), fun-loving (board games), and literate (runic alphabet). What you won't see are horned helmets, which, despite the stereotype, were not Viking. By 1050, the pagan Vikings had intermarried with the locals, become Christian, and were melting into Irish society.

▲NATIONAL GALLERY OF IRELAND

While not as extensive as the national gallery in London, the collections here

Caravaggio, The Taking of Christ

Dublin Castle

are well worth your time. The beautifully renovated museum boasts an impressive range of works by European masters and displays the works of top Irish painters, including Jack B. Yeats (brother of the famous poet).

Cost and Hours: Free, Sun-Mon 11:00-17:30, Tue-Sat 9:15-17:30, Thu until 20:30, Merrion Square West, tel. 01/661-5133, www.nationalgallery.ie.

Tours: Take advantage of the free audioguide as well as free 45-minute guided tours (usually Sat-Sun—check online or at main information desk for times).

Visiting the Museum: Walk through the series of rooms on the ground floor devoted to Irish painting and get to know artists you may not have heard of before. Visit the National Portrait Gallery on the mezzanine level for an insight into the great personalities of Ireland. European masterworks are on the top floor, including a rare Vermeer (one of only 30-some known works by the Dutch artist), a classic Caravaggio (master of chiaroscuro and dramatic lighting), a Monet riverscape, and an early Cubist Picasso still life.

Perhaps the most iconic of all the Irish art in this museum is the melodramatic (and huge) c. 1854 depiction of the *Marriage of Strongbow and Aiofe* by Daniel Maclise. It captures the chaotic union of Norman and Irish interests that signaled the start of English domination of Ireland 850 years ago. Notice how the defeated Irish writhe and lament in the bright light of the foreground, while the scheming Norman warlords skulk in the dimly lit middle ground. The ruins of conquered Waterford smolder at the back.

Nearby: Just east of the National Gallery, **Merrion Square** was laid out in 1762 and is ringed by elegant Georgian houses decorated with fine doors—a Dublin trademark. The park, once the exclusive domain of the residents (among them, Daniel O'Connell at #58 and W. B. Yeats at #82), is now a delightful public escape.

Dublin Castle and Nearby

▲DUBLIN CASTLE

Built on the spot of the first Viking fortress, this castle was the seat of English rule in Ireland for 700 years. Located where the Poddle and Liffey rivers flowed together, making a black pool (*dubh linn* in Irish), Dublin Castle was the official residence of the viceroy who implemented the will of British royalty. What you see today is the stately Georgian version, built during the late 17th and early 18th centuries on top of the old medieval castle (little of which can still be recognized beyond one remaining round turret). In this stirring setting, the Brits handed power over to Michael Collins and the Irish in 1922, as stipulated by the Anglo-Irish Treaty. Today, the castle is used for fancy state and charity functions, and for presidential inaugurations.

Standing in the courtyard, you can imagine the ugliness of the British-Irish situation. Notice the statue of justice

Modern Ireland's Turbulent Birth

Imagine if our American patriot ancestors had fought both our Revolutionary War and our Civil War back to back—over a span of seven chaotic years—and then appreciate the remarkable resilience of the Irish people. Here's a summary of what happened when.

Easter Rising, 1916: A nationalist militia called the Volunteers (led by **Patrick Pearse**) and the socialist Irish Citizen Army (led by **James Connolly**) join forces in the Easter Rising, a week-long rebellion against British rule that is quickly defeated. The uprising is unpopular with most Irish, who are unhappy with the destruction in Dublin and preoccupied with the "Great War" on the Continent. But when 16 rebel leaders (including Pearse and Connolly) are executed, Irish public opinion reverses as sympathy grows for the martyrs and the cause of Irish independence.

Two important rebel leaders escape execution. Brooklyn-born Éamon de Valera is spared because of his American passport (the British don't want to anger a potential WWI ally). **Michael Collins,** a low-ranking rebel officer who fought in the Rising at the General Post Office, refines urban guerrilla-warfare strategies in prison, and then blossoms after his release as the rebels' military and intelligence leader in the power vacuum that followed the executions.

General Election, 1918: World War I ends and a general election is held in Ireland (the first in which women can vote). Promising to withdraw from the British Parliament and declare an Irish republic, the nationalist **Sinn Féin** party wins 73 out of 79 seats. Only 4 of 32 counties vote to maintain the Union with Britain (all 4 lie in today's Northern Ireland). Rather than take their seats in London, Sinn Féin representatives abstain from participating in a government they see as foreign occupiers.

War of Independence, 1919: On January 19, the abstaining Sinn Féin members set up a rebel government in Dublin called Dáil Éireann. On the same day, the first shots of the Irish War of Independence are fired as rebels begin ambushing police barracks, which are seen as an extension of British rule. De Valera is elected by the Dáil to lead the rebels, with Collins as his deputy. Collins' web of

above the gate—pointedly without her blindfold and admiring her sword. As Dubliners say, "There she stands, above her station, with her face to the palace and her arse to the nation."

The fancy interior offers a sedate room-by-room walk through the lavish state apartments of this most English of Irish palaces. The tour also includes a look at the foundations of the old English tower (from 1204) as well as original Viking defenses, and the best remaining chunk of the 13th-century town wall.

Cost and Hours: Visiting the courtyard is free, €12 for one-hour guided tour, €8 to visit on your own (state apartments only); daily 9:45-16:45, tours depart every 30 minutes, sporadically closed for private events, tickets sold in courtyard under portico opposite clock tower, tel. 01/645-8813, www.dublincastle.ie.

▲▲CHESTER BEATTY LIBRARY

This library—located in the gardens of Dublin Castle (follow the signs)—is an exquisite, delightfully displayed collection of rare ancient manuscripts and beautifully spies infiltrates British intelligence at Dublin Castle. The Volunteers rename themselves the **Irish Republican Army;** meanwhile the British beef up their military presence in Ireland by sending in tough WWI vets, the Black and Tans. A bloody and very personal war ensues.

Anglo-Irish Treaty, 1921: Having endured the slaughter of World War I, the British tire of the extended bloodshed in Ireland and begin negotiations with the rebels. De Valera leads rebel negotiations, but then entrusts them to Collins (a clever politician, De Valera sees that whoever signs a treaty will be blamed for its compromises). Understanding the tricky position he's in, Collins signs the Anglo-Irish Treaty in December 1921, lamenting that in doing so he has signed his "own death warrant."

The Dáil narrowly ratifies the treaty, which ends the war and allows for the establishment of an independent dominion, the Irish Free State. But Collins' followers are unable to convince De Valera's supporters that the treaty's compromises are a stepping-stone to later full independence. De Valera and his anti-treaty disciples resign in protest. **Arthur Griffith,** founder of Sinn Féin, assumes the presidential post.

Irish Civil War, 1922-1923: In June 1922, the anti-treaty forces, holed up in the Four Courts building in Dublin, are fired upon by Collins and his pro-treaty forces—thus igniting the Irish Civil War. The British want the treaty to stand and even supply Collins with cannons, meanwhile threatening to reenter Ireland if the anti-treaty forces aren't put down.

In August 1922, Griffith dies of stress-induced illness, and Collins is assassinated 10 days later. Nevertheless, the pro-treaty forces prevail, as they are backed by popular opinion and better (British-supplied) military equipment. By April 1923, the remaining IRA forces dump (or stash) their arms, ending the civil war...but many bitter IRA vets vow to carry on the fight. De Valera distances himself from the IRA and becomes the dominant Irish political leader for the next 40 years.

illustrated books from around the world, plus a few odd curios. These treasures were bequeathed by Alfred Chester Beatty (1875-1968), a rich American mining magnate who traveled widely, collected 66,000 objects assiduously, and retired in Ireland.

Cost and Hours: Free; Mon-Fri 10:00-17:00, Sat from 11:00, Sun from 13:00; tel. 01/407-0750, www.cbl.ie.

Visiting the Museum: Start on the ground floor, with a 10-minute film about Beatty. Then head upstairs to the second floor to see the treasures he left to his adopted country. Note that exhibits often rotate, so may not be on display in the order outlined here.

Sacred Traditions Gallery: This space is dedicated to sacred texts, illuminated manuscripts, and miniature paintings from around the world. The doors swing open, and you're greeted by a video highlighting a diverse array of religious rites—a Christian wedding, Muslims kneeling for prayer, whirling dervishes, and so on.

Ancient Bible Fragments: Start with Christian texts on the left side of the room. In the 1930s, Beatty acquired these 1,800-year-old manuscripts, which had recently been unearthed in Egypt. The Indiana Jones-like discovery instantly bumped scholars' knowledge of the early Bible up a notch. There were Old Testament books, New Testament books, and—rarest of all—the Letters of Paul. Written in Greek on papyrus more than a century before previously known documents, these are some of the oldest versions of these texts in existence. Unlike most early Christian texts, the manuscripts were not rolled up in a scroll but bound in a book form called a "codex." Jesus died around AD 33, and his words weren't recorded until decades later. Most early manuscripts date from the fourth century, so these pages are about as close to the source as you can get.

Letters (Epistles) of Paul: The Beatty has 112 pages of Saint Paul's collected letters (AD 180-200). Paul, a Roman citizen (c. AD 5-67; see Albrecht Dürer's engraving of the saint), was the apostle most responsible for spreading Christianity beyond Palestine. Originally, Paul reviled Christians. But after a mystical experience, he went on to travel the known world, preaching the Good News in Athens and Rome, where he died a martyr to the cause. Along the way, he kept in touch with Christian congregations in cities like Corinth, Ephesus, and Rome with these letters.

Continuing up the left side of the room, you'll find gloriously illustrated medieval Bibles and prayer books, including an intricate, colorful, gold-speckled Book of Hours (1408).

Islam: In the center of the room you'll find sacred Islamic texts. Muslims believe that the angel Gabriel visited Muhammad (c. 570-632), instructing him to write down his heavenly visions in a book—the Quran. You'll see Qurans with elaborate calligraphy, such as one made in Baghdad in 1001. Nearby are other sacred Islamic texts, some beautifully illustrated, where you may find the rare illuminated manuscript

Islamic manuscript painting, Chester Beatty Library

of the "Life of the Prophet" (c. 1595), produced in Istanbul for an Ottoman sultan.

East Asian Religions: On the right side of the room, statues of Gautama Buddha (c. 563-483 BC) and Chinese Buddhist scrolls attest to the pervasive influence of this wise man. Buddha was born in India, but his philosophy spread to China, Japan, and Tibet (see the mandalas). Continuing clockwise, you'll reach the writings from India, the land of a million gods—and the cradle of Buddhism, Hinduism, Sikhism, and Jainism.

Arts of the Book: Continue your visit in this gallery downstairs on the first floor. The focus here is on the many forms a "book" can take—from the earliest clay tablets and papyrus scrolls, to parchment scrolls and bound codexes, to medieval monks' wondrous illustrations, to the advent of printing and bookbinding, to the dawn of the 21st century and the digital age.

Touring the floor clockwise starting immediately to the left, you'll find displays on **Egyptian and other ancient writings,** including a hieroglyph-covered papyrus

Christ Church Cathedral

scroll from the Book of the Dead (c. 300 BC); displays on **printing, illustrating, and bookbinding;** secular books from the **Islamic World** (science textbooks and poetry, many from the rich Persian culture—modern-day Iran); and albums, scrolls, and other **Far East** treasures.

Dublin's Cathedrals Area

Because of Dublin's English past (particularly Henry VIII's Reformation, and the dissolution of the Catholic monasteries in both Ireland and England in 1539), the city's top two churches are no longer Catholic. Christ Church Cathedral and nearby St. Patrick's Cathedral are both Church of Ireland (Anglican). In the late 19th century, the cathedrals underwent extensive restoration. The rich Guinness brewery family paid to try to make St. Patrick's Cathedral outshine Christ Church—which had patrons who were a rival family of wealthy whiskey barons.

▲CHRIST CHURCH CATHEDRAL

Occupying the same site as the first wooden church built on this spot by the Christianized Viking chieftan Sitric Silkenbeard (c. 1030), the present structure is a mix of periods: Norman and Gothic, but mostly Victorian Neo-Gothic from the late 19th century.

Cost and Hours: €7 includes crypt exhibition, €11 adds a guided tour, €15 combo-ticket includes Dublinia (described next); Mon-Sat 9:30-17:00, Sun 12:00-14:30; guided tours Mon-Fri at 11:00, 12:00, 14:00, 15:00 and 16:00, Sat at 14:00, 15:00 and 16:00; tel. 01/677-8099, www.christchurchcathedral.ie.

Church Services and Evensong: There's a full Anglican service Sun at 11:00, and the public is welcome to a 45-minute evensong service, sung by the esteemed Christ Church choir (Wed-Thu at 18:00, Sun at 15:30).

▲DUBLINIA

This exhibit, which highlights Dublin's Viking and medieval past, is a hit with youngsters. It's cheesy but meaty enough for adults as well.

Cost and Hours: €10, €15 combo-ticket includes Christ Church Cathedral; daily 10:00-18:30, Oct-Feb until 17:30, last entry one hour before closing; top-floor coffee shop, across from Christ Church Cathedral, tel. 01/679-4611, www.dublinia.ie.

Visiting the Exhibits: The displays are laid out on three floors. The ground floor focuses on Viking Dublin, explaining life aboard a Viking ship and inside a Viking house. Viking traders introduced urban life and commerce to Ireland—but kids will be most interested in their gory weaponry.

The next floor up reveals Dublin's day-to-day life in medieval times, from chivalrous knights and damsels in town fairs to the brutal ravages of the plague. Like so much of Europe at that time (1347-1349), Ireland lost one-third of its population to the Black Death. The huge scale model of medieval Dublin is well done. The top floor's "History Hunters" section is devoted to how the puzzles of modern archaeology and science shed light on Dublin's history. From this floor, you can climb a couple of flights of stairs into the tower for so-so views of Dublin, or exit across an enclosed stone bridge to adjacent Christ Church Cathedral.

▲ST. PATRICK'S CATHEDRAL

This Anglican cathedral is a thoughtful learning experience as well as a living church. The first church here was Catholic, supposedly built on the site where St. Patrick baptized local pagan converts. While the core of the Gothic structure you see today was built in the 13th century, most of today's stonework is 19th century. The building passed into the hands of the Anglican Church in the 16th century, after the Reformation. A century later, Oliver Cromwell's puritanical Calvinist troops—who considered the Anglicans to be little more than Catholics without a pope—stabled their horses here as a sign of disrespect.

Cost and Hours: €8 donation; Mon-Fri 9:30-17:00, Sat-Sun 9:00-18:00 except closed during Sun worship 10:30-12:30 & 14:30-16:30, last entry one hour before closing; at the intersection of Patrick Street and Upper Kevin Street, www.stpatrickscathedral.ie.

Tours: Free guided tours run several times a day in summer; check at the front desk for times.

Evensong: You'll get chills listening to the local "choir of angels" (typically Mon-Fri at 17:30 and Sun at 15:30—but schedule can vary, especially in summer, when guest choirs perform; confirm on the church website, under "Music Lists").

▲▲*Temple Bar*

This much-promoted area—with shops, cafés, theaters, galleries, pubs with live music, and restaurants—feels like the heart of the old city. It's Dublin's touristy "Left Bank," on the south shore of the river, filling the cobbled streets between Dame Street and the River Liffey.

Three hundred years ago, this was the city waterfront, where tall sailing ships off-

St. Patrick's Cathedral interior

loaded their goods (a "bar" was a loading dock along the river, and the Temples were a dominant merchant family). Eventually, the city grew eastward, filling in tidal mudflats, to create the docklands of modern Dublin. Once a thriving Georgian center of craftsmen and merchants, this neighborhood fell on hard times in the 20th century. Ensuing low rents attracted students and artists, giving the area a bohemian flair.

With government tax incentives and lots of development money, the Temple Bar district has now become a thriving entertainment (and beer-drinking) hot spot. It can be an absolute spectacle in the evening, when it bursts with revelers. But even if you're just gawking, don't miss the opportunity to wander through this human circus.

Temple Bar Square, just off Temple Bar Street (near Ha' Penny Bridge), hosts street musicians and a Saturday book market. On busy weekends, people-watching here is a contact sport (and pickpocketing is not). Farther west and somewhat hidden, Meeting House Square, with a lively organic-produce market (Sat 10:00-16:30), has become the

Temple Bar

Busy O'Connell Street

neighborhood's living room.

For more on sights in Temple Bar, see the "Dublin City Walk," earlier; for pubs and music, see "Experiences," later.

North of the River Liffey

The River Liffey historically divided the wealthy, cultivated south side of town from the working-class north side. Today there's plenty of culture on the north bank.

▲▲O'CONNELL STREET

Leading from the O'Connell Bridge through the heart of north Dublin, this 45-yard-wide promenade has been Dublin's main drag since 1794. It's named after Daniel O'Connell (1775-1847), Dublin's first Catholic mayor, who earlier had founded the Catholic Association, a political group that demanded Irish Catholic rights in the British Parliament by peaceful, legal means.

These days, the city has made the street more pedestrian-friendly, and a tram line runs alongside the median. Though filled with touristy fast-food joints and souvenir shops, O'Connell Street echoes with history. The median is dotted with statues remembering great figures from Ireland's past (including O'Connell)—particularly the century (1830-1930) when Ireland rediscovered its roots and won its independence. Along this street you'll also see the General Post Office (where nationalist activist Patrick Pearse read the Proclamation of Irish Independence in 1916, kicking off the Easter Rising) with its GPO Witness History exhibit (see later), and the Garden of Remembrance, honoring the victims of the 1916 Easter Rising (pictured on the next page).

🎧 Part 2 of my free Dublin City Walk audio tour covers a stroll up O'Connell Street.

▲▲EPIC: THE IRISH EMIGRATION MUSEUM

Telling the story of the Irish diaspora, this museum celebrates how this little island has had an oversized impact on the world. While the museum has few actual artifacts, this is an entertaining and educational experience. "EPIC" stands for "Every Person Is Connected."

Cost and Hours: €15, daily 10:00-18:45, last entry at 17:00, audioguide-€2 (or download it for free), in the CHQ building on Custom House Quay (at the modern pedestrian bridge a few steps from the famine statues along the riverfront), tel. 01/906-0861, www.epicchq.com.

Visiting the Museum: The museum fills the wine vaults in the basement of an iron-framed warehouse from the 1820s. Its 20 themed galleries take an interactive, high-tech approach to explain the forces that propelled so many Irish around the globe. Featured illustrious emigrants include labor agitator Mother Jones, Caribbean pirate Anne Bonny, Australian bush bandit Ned Kelly, and musical Chicago police chief Francis O'Neill. Historic photos of filthy tenements and early films

Garden of Remembrance

of bustling urban scenes document the plight of the common Irish emigrant. And all along you celebrate Irish heritage in music, literature, sports, and more.

Genealogy Help: The Irish Family History Centre on the ground floor can help you research your Celtic roots (€12.50 to access research stations; consultations—€45/30 minutes, €85/hour; Mon-Fri 10:00-17:00, Sat-Sun 12:00-17:00, tel. 01/905-9216, www.irishfamilyhistorycentre.com).

Nearby: Looking downstream, notice the modern **Samuel Beckett Bridge**—shaped like an old Irish harp and designed by Santiago Calatrava. The areas north and south of this bridge have been rejuvenated over the last 30 years with strikingly modern buildings: on the north bank, with Dublin's contemporary convention center, and just inland from the south bank, with developments such as Google's European headquarters.

Before leaving the area, wander 50 yards up the River Liffey toward the city to contemplate the skeletal sculptures of the city's evocative **Famine Memorial.** Nearby you'll spot the masts of the *Jeanie Johnston* Tall Ship and Famine Museum. A visit here ties in well with the area's emigration theme.

▲*JEANIE JOHNSTON* TALL SHIP AND FAMINE MUSEUM

Docked on the River Liffey, this seagoing sailing ship is a replica of a legendary Irish "famine ship." The original *Jeanie Johnston* embarked on 16 eight-week transatlantic crossings, carrying more than 2,500 Irish emigrants (about 200 per voyage) to their new lives in America and Canada in the decade after the Great Potato Famine of the 1840s. While many barely seaworthy hulks were known as "coffin ships," the people who boarded the *Jeanie Johnston* were lucky: The ship was Irish owned and crewed, with a humanitarian captain and even a doctor on board, and not one life was lost. Your tour guide will introduce you to the ship's main characters and help illuminate day-to-day life aboard a cramped tall ship 160 years ago. Because this ship makes goodwill voyages to Atlantic ports, it may be away during your visit—check ahead.

Cost and Hours: €10.50, visits by 50-minute tour only, easy to book in advance online; daily 10:00-16:00, Oct-March 11:00-15:00, tours depart on the hour (except 13:00); on the north bank of the Liffey just east of Sean O'Casey Bridge, tel. 01/473-0111, jeaniejohnston.ie.

▲DUBLIN WRITERS MUSEUM

No other country so small has produced such a wealth of literature. As interesting

Oscar Wilde

Jeanie Johnston *tall ship*

General Post Office

to those who are fans of Irish literature as it is boring to those who aren't, this three-room museum features the lives and works of Dublin's great writers. It's a low-tech museum, where you read informative plaques while perusing display cases with minor memorabilia—a document signed by Jonathan Swift, a photo of Oscar Wilde reclining thoughtfully, an early edition of Bram Stoker's *Dracula,* a George Bernard Shaw playbill, a not-so-famous author's tuxedo, and a newspaper from Easter 1916 announcing "Two More Executions Today." If unassuming attractions like that stir your blood—or if you simply want a manageable introduction to Irish lit—it's worth a visit.

Cost and Hours: €7.50, includes helpful 45-minute audioguide; Mon-Sat 9:45-17:00, Sun from 11:00, closed Mon Dec-March, 18 Parnell Square North, tel. 01/872-2077, www.writersmuseum.com.

JAMES JOYCE CENTRE

Only aficionados of James Joyce's work will want to visit this micro-museum with videos and displays about the author. Born and raised in Dublin, James Joyce (1882-1941) wrote in great detail about his hometown and mined the local dialect for his pitch-perfect dialogue. His best-known work, *Ulysses,* chronicles one day (June 16, 1904) in the life of the fictional Leopold Bloom as he wanders through the underside of Dublin.

Cost and Hours: €5, Mon-Sat 10:00-17:00, Sun from 12:00, closed Mon Dec-March, two blocks east of the Dublin Writers Museum at 35 North Great George's Street, tel. 01/878-8547, www.jamesjoyce.ie. The center offers walking tours of Joyce sights several times a week.

▲GPO WITNESS HISTORY EXHIBIT

During the 1916 Easter Rising, Irish nationalists took over buildings in Dublin, including the General Post Office (GPO), which became the rebel headquarters. Initial euphoria led to chaotic street battles and ended with the grim realization among the insurgents that surrender was the best option—trusting that their martyrdom would inspire the country to rise more effectively. This engaging exhibit—in the working post office—is primarily focused on that pivotal Easter week. Additional exhibitions cover the related Irish War of Independence and the Irish Civil War.

Cost and Hours: €14, includes audioguide, Mon-Sat 10:00-17:30, Sun from 12:00, last entry one hour before closing, tel. 01/872-1916, www.gpowitnesshistory.ie.

Background: For European nations preoccupied with World War I, the Easter Rising was a sideshow—but it was critical to Irish nationalists. Almost every Irish generation for the preceding 125 years had launched doomed insurrections against the British. But this one had a lasting effect, although it may not have seemed so in its immediate wake—a couple of weeks later, the patriot leaders who held their

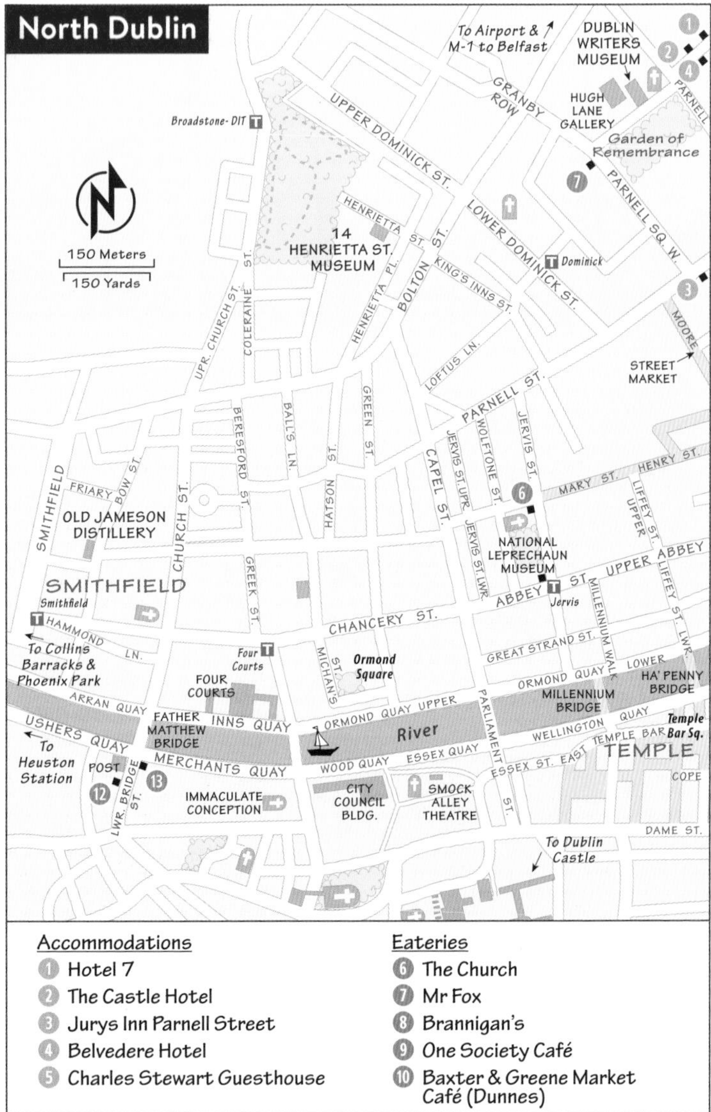

ground at the post office were executed in Kilmainham Gaol. Public sympathies shifted seismically. After seven centuries of dominance, the British were on a slippery slope leading to eventual independence for its nearest and oldest colony.

Visiting the Exhibit: The hardworking exhibit has a few interesting artifacts and lots of videos, photos, and earnest ways to tell the story. It features a fairly balanced view of the rebellion, including the less popular realities (like the lack of widespread support at the beginning of the movement and the civilians who died in the crossfire). Don't miss the 15-minute widescreen depiction of events (called

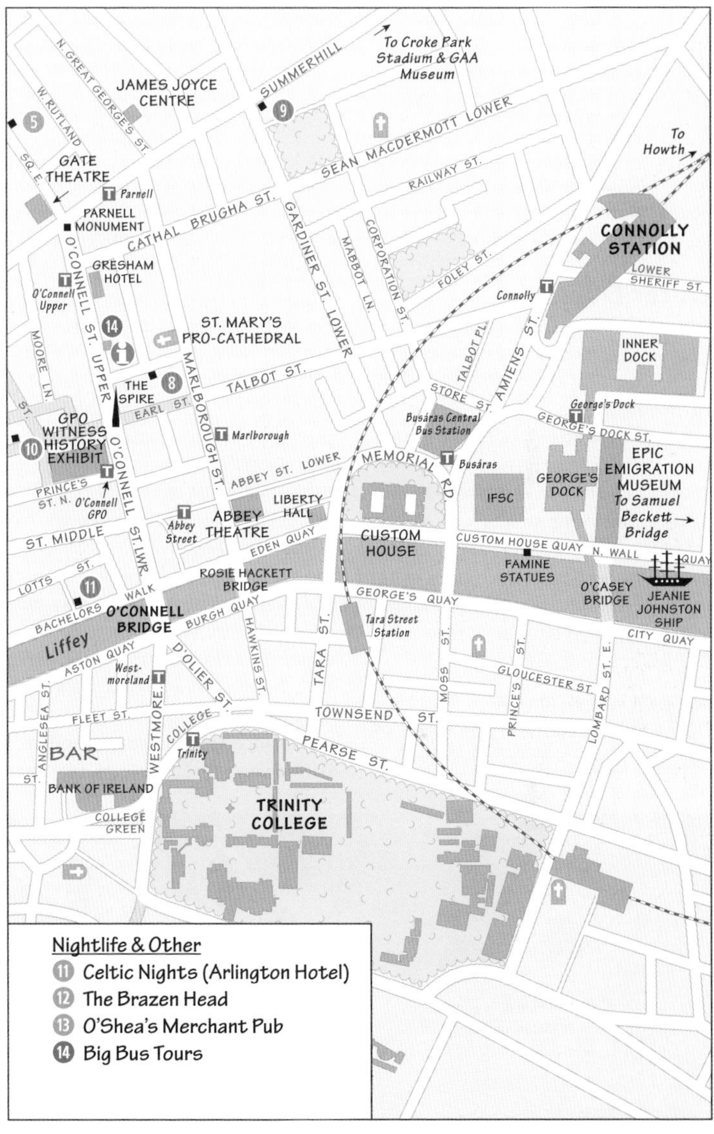

"The Rising") in the tiny theater. An interactive map of Dublin zooms in and out of various neighborhoods, tracking that Easter week's confrontations, with actors dramatizing the events and conversations that shaped the conflict. In video presentations, historians give their take on how the rebellion affected Irish history.

▲▲14 HENRIETTA STREET

This four-story, 18th-century Georgian house, once an affluent mansion, had morphed into a cramped, impoverished, multifamily hovel by the 20th century. Now a museum, it explains tenement life and urban poverty in Dublin. Photos and videos telling the story of the house and its times augment the period architecture and furnishings.

Cost and Hours: €9, visit by 75-minute guided tour only, tours depart on the hour, book online in advance or take your chances; open Wed-Sat 10:00-17:00, Sun from 12:00, closed Mon-Tue; last tour one hour before closing, 14 Henrietta Street, tel. 01/524-0383, www.14henriettastreet.ie.

Outer Dublin

Kilmainham Gaol (JAY-ol) and the Guinness Storehouse are located west of the old center and can be linked by a 20-minute walk, a five-minute taxi ride, or public bus #40 or #13. (To ride the bus from the jail to the Guinness Storehouse, leave the prison and take three rights—crossing no streets—to reach the bus stop.) Another option is to take a hop-on, hop-off bus, which stops at both sights (see "Tours" near the beginning of this chapter). For locations see the "Dublin" map on page 42.

▲▲▲KILMAINHAM GAOL

Opened in 1796 as Dublin's county jail and a debtors' prison, Kilmainham was considered a model in its day. In reality, the British frequently used this jail as a political prison. Many of those who fought for Irish independence were held or executed here, including leaders of the rebellions of 1798, 1803, 1848, 1867, and 1916. James Connolly, unable to stand in front of the firing squad because of a gangrenous ankle, was tied to a chair and shot sitting down. National heroes Robert Emmett and Charles Stewart Parnell each did time here. The last prisoner to be held in the jail was Éamon de Valera, who later became president of Ireland. He was released on July 16, 1924, the day Kilmainham was finally shut down. The buildings, virtually in ruins, were restored in the 1960s. Today, it's a shrine to the Nathan Hales of Ireland.

Cost and Hours: €8, visit by one-hour guided tour only, advance booking highly recommended; daily June-Aug 9:00-19:00, last tour at 17:45; April-May and Sept until 18:00, last tour at 16:45; Oct-March 9:30-17:30, last tour at 16:15; tours run 2/hour, tel. 01/453-5984, www.kilmainhamgaolmuseum.ie.

Advance Tickets Recommended: Book online at least a few days (or up to

Kilmainham Gaol

From Famine to Revolution

After the Great Potato Famine (1845-1849), destitute rural Irish moved to the city in droves, seeking work and causing a housing shortage. Unscrupulous landlords came up with a solution: Subdivide the city's once-grand mansions, vacated by gentry after the 1801 Act of Union transferred all power to London. The mansions' tiny rooms could then be crammed with poor renters. Dublin became one of the most densely populated cities in Europe—one of every three Dubliners lived in a slum. On Henrietta Street, once a wealthy Dublin address, these new tenements bulged with humanity. According to the 1911 census, one district counted 835 people living in 15 houses (many with a single outhouse in back or even sharing a communal chamber pot). In these cramped, neglected quarters, tuberculosis was rampant, and infant mortality skyrocketed.

Those who could get work tenaciously clung to their precious jobs. The terrible working conditions prompted many to join trade unions, but when laborers went on strike in 1913, employers locked them out (the Dublin Lockout lasted for seven months). The picket lines were brutally put down by police in the pocket of rich businessmen, led by newspaper and hotel magnate William Murphy. In response, James Larkin and James Connolly formed the Irish Citizen Army, a militia, to protect the poor trade unionists.

Murphy eventually broke the unions. Larkin headed for the US to organize workers there. Meanwhile, Connolly stayed in Ireland and brought the Irish Citizen Army into the 1916 Easter Rising as an integral part of the rebel forces. During that uprising, he slyly had a rebel flag flown over Murphy's prized hotel on O'Connell Street. The uninformed British artillery battalions took the bait—and pulverized it.

60 days) in advance to guarantee a spot on a tour. While you can try to buy a ticket in person, you'll likely wait in a long line, and walk-up spots go quickly.

Getting There: Hop-on, hop-off buses stop here, or take bus #69 or #79 from Aston Quay or #13 or #40 from O'Connell Street or College Green—confirm with driver. The closest LUAS tram stop is Suir Road (red line, zone 2 ticket from city center). From there, it's a 10-minute, level walk north, crossing over the Grand Canal, to the jail.

Visiting the Jail: Start your visit with a one-hour guided tour (includes 15-minute prison history slideshow in the prison chapel). It's sobering to tour the cells and places of execution—hearing tales of oppressive colonialism and heroic patriotism—alongside Irish schoolkids who know these names well. The museum has an excellent exhibit on Victorian prison life and Ireland's fight for independence.

Don't miss the dimly lit "Last Words 1916" hall upstairs, which displays the stirring final letters that patriots sent to loved ones hours before facing the firing squad. Regrettably, transcriptions of the letters are not posted, denying visitors a better understanding of the passion and patriotism of Ireland's greatest in their own last words—a lost opportunity for Americans not realizing that there are other Nathan Hales in this world who wish they had more than one life to give for their country. (Fortunately, the little bookshop for budding patriots carries the inspirational *Last Words* book.)

▲GUINNESS STOREHOUSE

A visit to the Guinness Storehouse is, for many, a pilgrimage. Arthur Guinness began brewing the renowned stout here in 1759, and by 1868 it was the biggest brewery in the world. Today, the sprawling complex fills several city blocks (64 acres busy brewing 1.5 million pints a day).

Visitors (1.5 million annually) are welcomed to the towering storehouse, where the vibe is glitzy entertainment. Don't look for conveyor belts of beer bottles being stamped with bottle caps. Rather than a brewery tour, this is a Disneyland for beer lovers—huge crowds, high decibel music, and dreamy TV beer ads on big screens.

Cost and Hours: €18.50-25, price depends on entry time—book ahead, admission includes a complimentary pint; daily 9:30-19:00, July-Aug 9:00-20:00, last entry two hours before closing, last beer served 45 minutes before closing; tel. 01/408-4800, www.guinness-storehouse.com.

Advance Tickets Recommended: The brewery is popular with cruise-ship excursions, making an advance ticket the only smart way to visit. Book your timed-entry slot for early or late in the day—it's cheaper, you'll avoid lines, and you'll have a better experience (a midday ticket just assures you'll be part of the mobs).

Getting There: Ride the hop-on, hop-off bus (it stops right at the site), or take bus #13, #40, or #123 from Dame Street and O'Connell Street. The James LUAS stop on the red line is a 15-minute walk west of the Storehouse.

Visiting the Brewery: Enter the brewery on Bellevue Street. The exhibit fills the old fermentation plant, used from 1902 through 1988, and reopened in 2000 as a huge shrine to the Guinness tradition. Step into the middle of the ground floor and look up. A tall, beer-glass-shaped glass atrium—14 million pints big (that's about 10 days' worth of production) soars upward past four floors of exhibitions and cafés to the skylight. Then look down

at Arthur's original 9,000-year lease, enshrined under Plexiglas in the floor. At £45 per year, it was quite a bargain.

As you escalate ever higher, you'll notice that each floor has a theme. The first floor is dedicated to cooperage—the making of wooden barrels (with 1954 film clips showing master kegmakers working at their now virtually extinct trade); the second floor has the tasting rooms; the third floor features advertising and a theater with classic TV ads; the fourth floor is where you can pull your own beer (at the Academy); and the fifth floor has Arthur's Bar. The top floor is the Gravity Bar, providing visitors with a commanding 360-degree view of Dublin—with vistas all the way to the sea—and an included pint of the beloved stout.

▲NATIONAL MUSEUM OF DECORATIVE ARTS AND HISTORY

This branch of the National Museum, which occupies the huge, 18th-century stone Collins Barracks in west Dublin, displays Irish dress, furniture, weapons, silver, and other domestic baubles from the past 700 years. History buffs will linger longest in the Soldiers & Chiefs exhibit, which

Ireland's Gaelic Athletic Association

Ireland's national pastimes of Gaelic football and hurling pack stadiums all over the country, generating revenue that's used to promote Gaelic culture in a grassroots way. So, while Gaelic Athletic Association players participate only for the glory, the money generated funds children's leagues, school coaches, small-town athletic facilities, and traditional arts, music, and dance—as well as the building and maintenance of giant stadiums such as Dublin's Croke Park.

Sports here are a heartfelt expression of Irish identity. There was a time when membership in the GAA was denied to anyone who also attended "foreign games," defined as rugby, soccer, or cricket. If the Brits played it, it was viewed as cultural poison. (The rule was finally abolished in 1971 with the advent of TV sports.)

In 1921, during the War of Independence, a dozen British intelligence agents were assassinated in on a single morning Dublin. The same day, grizzled British WWI veterans—known as the Black and Tan for their black coats and tan army pants—retaliated against the Irish nationalists by firing into the stands during a Gaelic football match at Croke Park, killing 13 spectators as well as a Tipperary player.

Today Croke Park's "Hill 16" grandstands are built on rubble dumped here after the 1916 Easter Rising; it's literally sacred ground. Queen Elizabeth II visited the stadium in 2011. Her warm interest in the stadium and in the institution of the GAA did much to heal old wounds.

covers the Irish at war both at home and abroad since 1500 (including the American Civil War). The sober finale is the Proclaiming a Republic room, offering Ireland's best coverage of the painful birth of this nation. Guns, flags, and personal letters help illustrate the 1916 Easter Rising, the War of Independence against Britain, and Ireland's Civil War. Also on the museum grounds is the historic *Asgard,* a 51-foot yacht used by its owner, Erskine Childers, to smuggle guns to arm Irish rebels in the 1916 Easter Rising. You'll find the boat 50 yards across a small parking lot in a well-marked separate building (free, same hours as museum).

Cost and Hours: Free, Sun-Mon 13:00-17:00, Tue-Sat from 10:00, good café; on north side of the River Liffey in Collins Barracks on Benburb Street, roughly across the river from Guinness Storehouse, LUAS red line: Museum stop; tel. 01/677-7444, www.museum.ie.

▲GAELIC ATHLETIC ASSOCIATION MUSEUM

This museum, at Croke Park Stadium in northeast Dublin, offers a high-tech, interactive introduction to Ireland's favorite games. The GAA, founded in 1884, was created to foster the development of Gaelic sports, specifically Gaelic football and hurling, and to exclude English sports such as cricket and rugby. An expression of the Irish cultural awakening, the GAA played an important part in the fight for independence. Here you can relive the greatest moments in hurling and Irish-football history. Then get involved: Pick up a stick and try hurling, kick a football, and test your speed and balance. A 15-minute film (played on request) gives you a "Sunday at the stadium" experience.

Cost and Hours: €7, Mon-Sat 9:30-17:00, June-Aug until 18:00, Sun 10:30-17:00 year-round—except on game Sundays, when the museum is open

Enjoying Dublin's shopping streets

Dublin lights up at night.

to ticket holders only; café, museum is located under the stands at Croke Park Stadium, enter from St. Joseph's Avenue off Clonliffe Road, tel. 01/819-2323, www.crokepark.ie/gaa-museum.

Tours: The €14, one-hour museum-plus-stadium-tour option is worth it for rabid fans who want a glimpse of the huge stadium and locker rooms. The €20 rooftop Skyline tour offers views 17 stories above the field from lofty catwalks. Both generally run daily—see the website for times.

EXPERIENCES

Shopping

Shops are open roughly Monday-Saturday 9:00-18:00 and until 20:00 on Thursday. Hours are shorter on Sunday (if shops are open at all). The dominant department store in Dublin (and Ireland) is Dunnes (branches throughout town, including on Grafton Street, http://www.dunnesstores.com).

To get a good look at contemporary Irish crafts, visit the mod showrooms of the Irish Design Shop (41 Drury Lane, www.irishdesignshop.com) or Industry & Co (41 a/b Drury Street, www.industryandco.com). The Gutter Bookshop is a fine independent seller that champions Irish writers (Cow's Lane in Temple Bar, www.gutterbookshop.com). Avoca is a mini department store loaded with quality Irish crafts and food (11 Suffolk Street, www.avoca.com).

Good shopping areas include:

Grafton Street, with its neighboring streets and arcades (such as the fun Great George's Arcade between Great George's and Drury Streets), and nearby shopping centers (Powerscourt Townhouse and St. Stephen's Green). Francis Street creaks with antiques.

Henry Street, home to Dublin's top department stores (pedestrian-only, off O'Connell Street).

Nassau Street, lining Trinity College, with the popular Kilkenny Shop (Irish design, with a good cafeteria upstairs, www.kilkennyshop.com) and lots of touristy stores.

Temple Bar, worth a browse for art, jewelry, New Age paraphernalia, books, music (try Claddagh Records), and gift shops. On Saturdays, a couple of markets—one for food and another for books—set up shop.

Millennium Walk, a trendy lane stretching two blocks north from the River Liffey to Abbey Street. It's filled with hip restaurants, shops, and coffee bars. It's easy to miss—look for the south entry at the pedestrian Millennium Bridge, or the north entry at Jervis Street LUAS stop.

Theater

Abbey Theatre is Ireland's national theater, founded by W. B. Yeats in 1904 to preserve Irish culture during British rule (performances generally nightly at 20:00,

Most trad sessions include a fiddle.

Dublin nightlife

Sat matinees at 14:30, 26 Lower Abbey Street, tel. 01/878-7222, www.abbeytheatre.ie). **Gate Theatre** does foreign plays as well as Irish classics (Cavendish Row, tel. 01/874-4045, www.gatetheatre.ie). The **Gaiety Theatre** offers a wide range of quality productions (King Street South, tel. 01/679-5622, www.gaietytheatre.ie). The **Bord Gáis Energy Theatre** (pronounced "Board-GOSH") is Dublin's newest and spiffiest venue (Grand Canal Square, tel. 01/677-7999, www.bordgaisenergytheatre.ie). Less-commercial plays can be seen at the intimate little **Smock Alley Theatre,** with seating surrounding a tiny stage, in a space on the site of the city's first theater—from 1662 (6 Lower Exchange Street—on the western fringe of Temple Bar, tel. 01/677-0014, www.smockalley.com). Browse the listings and fliers at the TI to see what's on.

Music and Dance

The 3 Arena, sited on what was once a dock railway terminus (easy LUAS red line access), is now sponsored by a hip phone company. Residents call it by its geographic nickname: The Point. It's considered one of the country's top live-music venues (East Link Bridge, tel. 01/819-8888, http://3arena.ie).

The **National Concert Hall** supports a varied performance schedule, including the National Symphony Orchestra on most Friday evenings (off St. Stephen's Green at Earlsfort Terrace, tel. 01/417-0077, www.nch.ie).

Celtic Nights combines traditional music and dancing into a big-stage, high-energy, family-friendly, Irish variety show. This touristy dinner act hits all the clichés, from *Riverdance*-style choreography to fun fiddling and comedic *craic.* It comes with a traditional three-course dinner and lots of audience participation (€38, €20 for kids 11 and under, nightly show at 20:30, on the north side of the river by the O'Connell Bridge at the Arlington Hotel, 23 Bachelors Walk—see map on page 74, tel. 01/687-5200, www.celticnights.com).

Pubs and Live Traditional Music

For guided pub crawls (focusing on either Irish literature or music), see "Tours," near the beginning of this chapter. Unless otherwise noted, for locations of the venues described below, see the "South Dublin Restaurants" map on page 88.

Temple Bar and Nearby

This area thrives with music—traditional, jazz, and rock. Pricier than the rest of Dublin and extremely touristy, it's a wild scene and—for party animals—a good place to mix beer and music. The noise, pushy crowds, and inflated prices have driven most local Dubliners away. It's craziest on

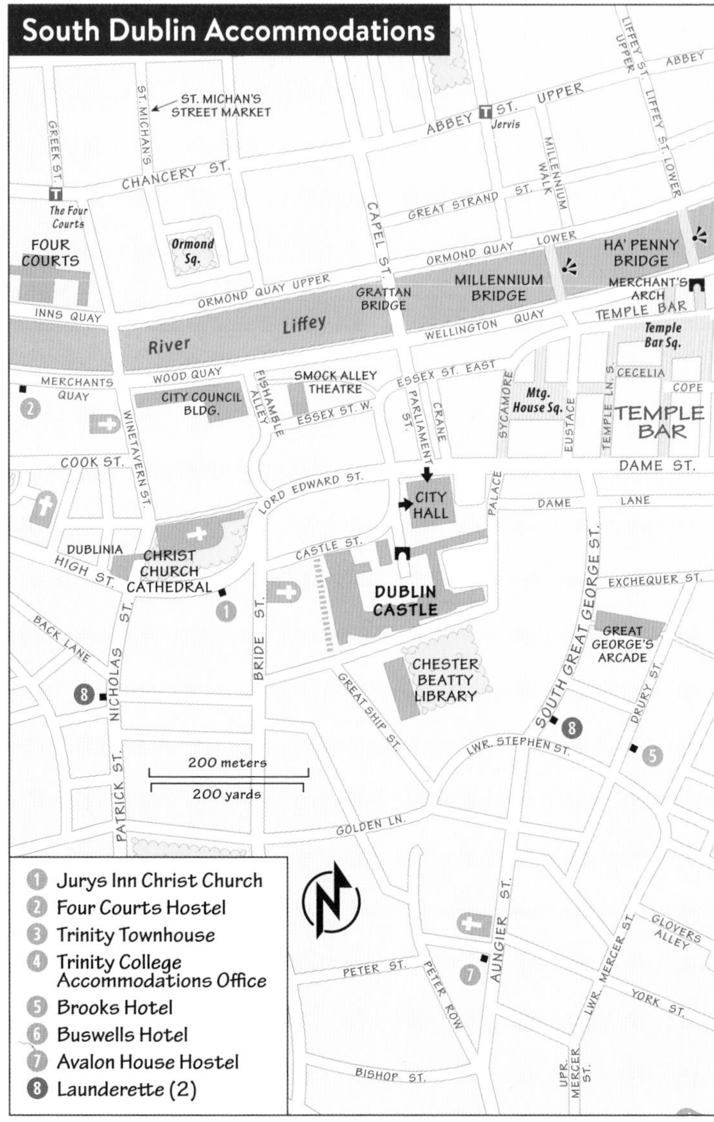

summer weekend nights, holidays, and nights after big sporting events let out.

But several good pubs for traditional music are nearby—a 10-minute hike up the river west of Temple Bar takes you to a more local and less touristy scene. The pubs there have longer histories, tangled floor plans, a fun-loving energy, and a passion for trad.

Gogarty's Pub has long been the leading Temple Bar pub for trad. They have foot-tapping sessions downstairs daily at 13:00 and upstairs nightly from 21:00 (at corner of Fleet and Anglesea, tel. 01/671-1822). This is also where the **Traditional Irish Musical Pub Crawl** starts (see page 44).

Darkey Kelly's Bar is a big, fun-lov-

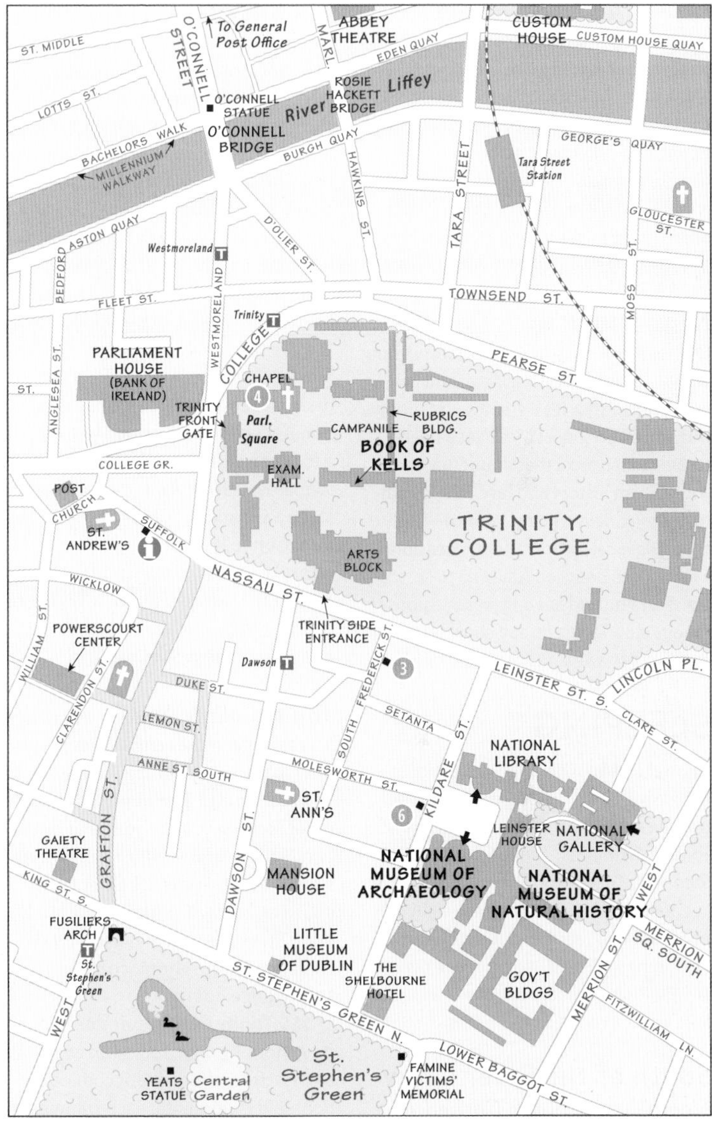

ing place with live music nightly. The traditional folk-music vibe here is more sing-along than hard drinking, and the pub grub is good. See their website for what's on when (daily until 23:30, west end of Temple Bar, near Christ Church Cathedral at 19 Fishamble Street, mobile 083-346-4682, www.darkykellys.ie).

The Brazen Head, which claims to be the oldest pub in Dublin, is a hit for an early dinner and late live music (good food, music nightly from 21:30), with atmospheric rooms and a courtyard perfect for balmy evenings (by south end of Father Mathew Bridge, 2 blocks west of Christ Church Cathedral at 20 Lower Bridge Street—see map on page 74; tel. 01/677-9549).

O'Shea's Merchant Pub, across the street, is encrusted with memories of County Kerry football heroes. It's popular with locals who come for the live traditional music nightly at 22:00 (the front half is a restaurant, the toe-tapping magic is in the back—enter at 12 Lower Bridge Street—see map on page 74, tel. 01/679-3797, www.themerchanttemplebar.com).

North of the River

O'Sheas Pub hosts wonderful storytelling dinners called "Food, Folklore, and Fairies." Even at €52, it's a great value: Along with about 50 tourists, you get a hearty three-course meal that's punctuated by soulful Irish history and fascinating Irish mythology, delivered by Johnny—the engaging local folklorist, with occasional live tunes in between (daily 18:30-21:30, Jan-Feb Thu and Sat only; reservations required; 19 Talbot Street, show tel. 01/218-8555, www.irishfolktours.com).

SLEEPING

Central Dublin is popular, loud, and expensive. You'll find big, practical, central places south of the river, near Christ Church Cathedral, Trinity College, and St. Stephen's Green. For classy, older Dublin accommodations in a quieter neighborhood, stay a bit farther out, southeast of St. Stephen's Green. North of the river are additional reliable options in an urban area well served by LUAS trams.

South of the River Liffey

Near Christ Church Cathedral

These lodging options cluster near Christ Church Cathedral, a 5-minute walk from the rowdy and noisy evening scene (at Temple Bar), and 10 minutes from the sightseeing center (Trinity College and Grafton Street).

$$$$ Jurys Inn Christ Church, part of a no-nonsense, American-style hotel chain, is central and offers business-class comfort in 182 identical rooms. If "ye olde" is getting old—and you don't mind big tour groups—this is a good option. Request a room far from the noisy elevator (breakfast extra, book long in advance for weekends, pay parking, Christ Church Place, tel. 01/454-0000, US tel. 800-423-6953, www.jurysinns.com, jurysinnchristchurch@jurysinns.com).

¢ Four Courts Hostel is a 234-bed hostel well located immediately across the river from the Four Courts. It's within a five-minute walk of Christ Church Cathedral and Temple Bar. Bare and institutional, it's also spacious and well run, with a focus on security and efficiency (private rooms available, elevator, game room, some pay parking, 15 Merchant's Quay, from Connolly Station or Busáras Bus Station take LUAS to Four Courts stop and cross river via Father Mathew Bridge, tel. 01/672-5839, www.fourcourtshostel.com, info@fourcourtshostel.com).

Trinity College Area

You can't get more central; these listings offer a good value for the money.

$$$$ Trinity Townhouse offers fine, quiet lodging in 26 rooms split between two Georgian townhouses on either side of South Frederick Street, just south of Trinity College (12 South Frederick Street, tel. 01/617-0900, www.trinitytownhousehotel.com, info@trinitylodge.com).

$$$ Trinity College turns its 800 student-housing dorm rooms on campus into no-frills, affordable accommodations in the city center each summer. Look for the Accommodations Office (open Mon-Fri 8:00-18:00) on the left after going through the main front gate (rooms available late May-mid-Sept, make sure to book Trinity city center rooms, not suburban Dartry location, specify shared bath or en suite, breakfast extra, tel. 01/896-1177, www.tcd.ie/summeraccommodation, residences@tcd.ie).

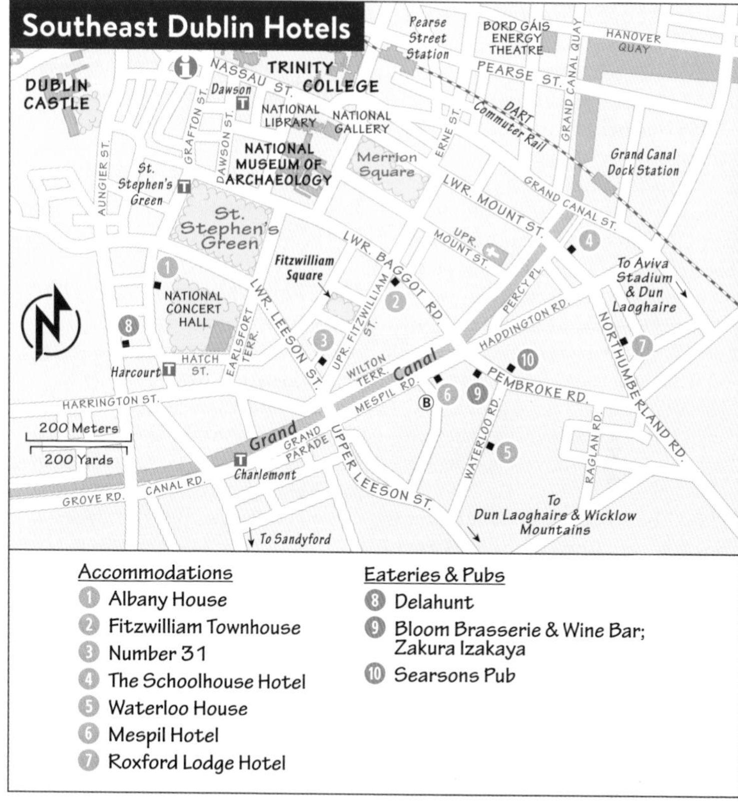

Near St. Stephen's Green

$$$$ Brooks Hotel is a fine choice for great service, tending 98 plush rooms in an ideal central location. This splurge rarely disappoints (Drury Street, tel. 01/670-4000, www.brookshotel.ie, reservations@brookshotel.ie).

$$$$ Buswells Hotel, one of the city's oldest, is a pleasant Georgian-style haven with 67 rooms in the heart of the city (breakfast extra, between Trinity College and St. Stephen's Green at 23 Molesworth Street, tel. 01/614-6500, www.buswells.ie, info@buswells.ie).

$$$ Albany House's 50 good-value rooms come with high ceilings, Georgian ambience, and some stairs. Ask for a quieter room in back, away from streetcar noise (just one block south of St. Stephen's Green at 84 Harcourt Street, tel. 01/475-1092, www.albanyhousedublin.com, info@albanyhousedublin.com).

$$$ Fitzwilliam Townhouse rents 14 renovated rooms in a Georgian townhouse near St. Stephen's Green (family rooms, breakfast extra, 41 Upper Fitzwilliam Street, tel. 01/662-5155, www.fitzwilliamtownhouse.com, info@fitzwilliamtownhouse.com).

¢ Avalon House Hostel, near Grafton Street, rents simple, clean backpacker beds (private rooms available, includes continental breakfast, elevator, a few minutes off Grafton Street at 55 Aungier Street, tel. 01/475-0001, www.avalon-house.ie, info@avalon-house.ie).

Southeast of St. Stephen's Green

This neighborhood is a perfect compromise between busy central lodging options and more sedate choices farther out.

$$$$ Number 31 is a hidden gem reached via gritty little Leeson Close (a lane off Lower Leeson Street). Its understated elegance is top-notch, with six rooms in a former coach house and 15 rooms in an adjacent Georgian house; the two buildings are connected by a quiet little garden. Guests appreciate the special touches (such as a sunken living room with occasional peat fires) and outstanding breakfasts served in a classy glass atrium (family rooms, limited parking, 31 Leeson Close, tel. 01/676-5011, www.number31.ie, stay@number31.ie).

$$$$ The Schoolhouse Hotel taught as many as 300 students in its heyday (1861-1969) and was in the middle of the street fight that was the 1916 Easter Rising. Now it's a serene hideout with 31 pristine rooms and a fine restaurant (breakfast extra, book early, 2 Northumberland Road, tel. 01/667-5014, www.schoolhousehotel.com, reservations@schoolhousehotel.com).

$$$$ Waterloo House stands proudly Georgian on a quiet residential street with 19 comfortable and relaxing rooms and a pleasant back garden (family rooms, parking, 8 Waterloo Road, tel. 01/660-1888, www.waterloohouse.ie, waterloohouse@eircom.net).

$$$ Mespil Hotel is a huge, modern, business-class hotel renting 254 identical three-star rooms at a good price with all the comforts. This place is a cut above Jurys Inn (breakfast extra, elevator; small first-come, first-served free parking; 10-minute walk southeast of St. Stephen's Green or take bus #37, #38, #39, or #46A; 50 Mespil Road, tel. 01/488-4600, www.mespilhotel.com, mespil@leehotels.com).

$$$ Roxford Lodge Hotel is well managed and a great value. In a quiet, residential neighborhood a 20-minute walk from Trinity College, it has 24 tastefully decorated rooms awash with hot tubs and saunas. The executive suite is honeymoon-worthy (family rooms, breakfast extra, elevator, parking, 46 Northumberland Road, tel. 01/668-8572, www.roxfordlodge.ie, reservations@roxfordlodge.ie).

North of the River Liffey

To locate these hotels, see the "North Dublin" map on page 74.

Near Parnell Square

A swanky neighborhood 250 years ago, this is now workaday Dublin with a steady urban hum, made accessible by LUAS trams.

$$$$ Hotel 7 spruces up an old Georgian property with 51 modern rooms that are refined and stylish. It's worth the comparatively high price for this side of town (7 Gardiner Row, tel. 01/873-7777, www.hotel7dublin.com, info@hotel7dublin.com).

$$$$ The Castle Hotel is a formerly grand but still-comfortable Georgian establishment embedded in the urban canyons of North Dublin. A half-block east of the Garden of Remembrance, it's a good value with pleasant rooms and the friendly Castle Vaults pub with live music in its basement (Great Denmark Street, tel. 01/874-6949, www.castle-hotel.ie, info@castle-hotel.ie).

$$$$ Jurys Inn Parnell Street has 253 predictably soulless but modern rooms. It's a block from the north end of O'Connell Street and the cluster of museums on Parnell Square (breakfast extra, tel. 01/878-4900, www.jurysinns.com, jurysinnparnellst@jurysinns.com).

$$$$ Belvedere Hotel has 92 plain-vanilla rooms that are short on character but long on dependable, modern comforts (Great Denmark Street, tel. 01/873-7700, www.belvederehotel.ie, reservations@belvederehotel.ie).

$$$ Charles Stewart Guesthouse, big and basic, offers 60 acceptable rooms in a good location for a fair price (breakfast extra, ask for a quieter room in the back, just beyond top end of O'Connell Street at 5 Parnell Square East, tel. 01/878-0350, www.charlesstewart.ie, info@charles stewart.ie).

EATING

While you can get decent pub grub on just about any corner, there's just no pressing reason to eat Irish in cosmopolitan Dublin. Eating early (17:30-19:00) saves time and money, as many top-end places offer an early-bird special at the same price as a forgettable eatery. Dublin also offers a number of dining-plus-entertainment options.

South Dublin Eateries

"Bib Gourmand" Restaurants

If you want to dine well yet reasonably in Dublin without dressing up, these three restaurants are my favorites. Small, fresh, and untouristy, they've each earned the Michelin "Bib Gourmand" rating for their casual gourmet quality. Reservations are required in the evening. Pig's Ear and Etto offer early-bird dinners (three courses for around €30 weeknights before 18:30).

$$$ Delahunt is a bright star in a newly vibrant neighborhood. In a long and narrow circa-1906 grocery store, it surrounds its diners with original brass and varnished trappings. The waitstaff is friendly and the cuisine—Irish with French/Italian/Japanese flavors—is a delight. At dinner, you'll choose from a two- or three-course menu, with a selection of dishes for each course (casual lunch served Tue-Fri 12:00-14:00, dinner Tue-Sat 17:00-21:30, closed Sun-Mon, 39 Camden Street Lower, tel. 01/598-4880, www.delahunt.ie). For location, see the "Southeast Dublin Hotels" map, earlier.

$$$ The Pig's Ear fills a small and simple, dark-wood-and-candles dining hall. A steep stairway climb above Nassau Street, it overlooks the Trinity College green, and wows diners with its modern Irish menu (Mon-Sat 12:00-14:45 & 17:30-22:00, closed Sun, 4 Nassau Street, tel. 01/670-3865, www.thepigsear.ie).

$$$ Etto is a small restaurant with tight seating, high volume, and a fun energy. The enticing menu is a fusion of Italian and Irish. I enjoy the view from the bar and would consider reserving a spot there (Mon-Sat 12:00-14:30 & 17:30-22:30, closed Sun, 2 blocks off St. Stephen's Green, 18 Merrion Row, tel. 01/678-8872, www.etto.ie).

Other Restaurants in the Center

$$$ Fallon & Byrne Wine Cellar is a fun surprise. From the big, high-end grocery store on the ground floor, you hike down the stairs to a spacious and welcoming wine cellar with a casual mix of regular and barrel-top tables. The wine-friendly menu is international and modern, with €20 main dishes, meat-and-cheese boards, and a fine selection of wine by the glass. Your server can give you good wine advice (daily 12:00-22:00, tel. 01/472-1012). For a more conventional (and pricier) **restaurant** with modern Irish dishes and good pre-theater menus, climb upstairs (daily 17:30-22:00, tel. 01/472-1000, reservations smart, 11 Exchequer Street, www.fallonandbyrne.com).

$$$$ Trocadero is an old-school fixture serving beefy European and modern Irish cuisine to Dubliners interested in a slow, romantic meal. The dressy, red-velvet interior is draped with photos of local actors (daily 17:00-23:30, 4 St. Andrew Street, tel. 01/677-5545, www.trocadero.ie, Robert). Popular with theatergoers, the three-course early-bird special is a fine value at €30 (17:00-19:00, leave by 19:45).

Fast, Easy, and Cheap

$$ Bewley's Oriental Café is a grand, traditional eatery, centrally located on Grafton Street. Good-value breakfast, lunch, and early-evening meals are offered in a wonderful human bustle that epitomizes urban Dublin. The fine Harry Clarke stained-glass windows (against the back wall), fun lunch theater (upstairs), and snack-worthy baked treats (inside the front door) are all great excuses to linger

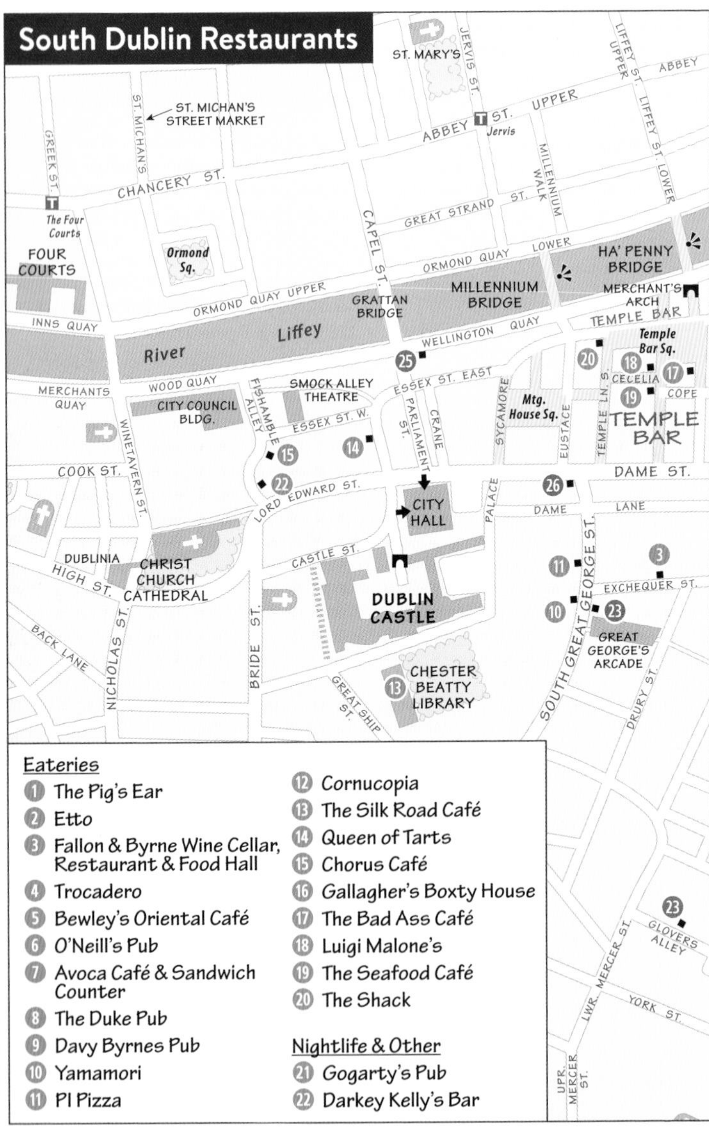

(Mon-Wed 7:30-19:00, Thu until 21:00, Fri until 20:00, Sat-Sun 9:00-20:00, 78 Grafton Street, tel. 01/564-0900). For the lunch theater schedule, see www.bewleyscafetheatre.com (€12, performances at 13:00, arrive at 12:45 to settle in and order before the performance begins).

$$ O'Neill's Pub is a venerable, touristy, dark, and tangled retreat offering sling-'em-out pub grub, including breakfasts and carvery lunches. While you can order from the menu, most diners grab a tray and go through their self-service cafeteria line (daily 12:00-22:30, across from the Molly Malone statue on Suffolk Street, tel. 01/679-3656).

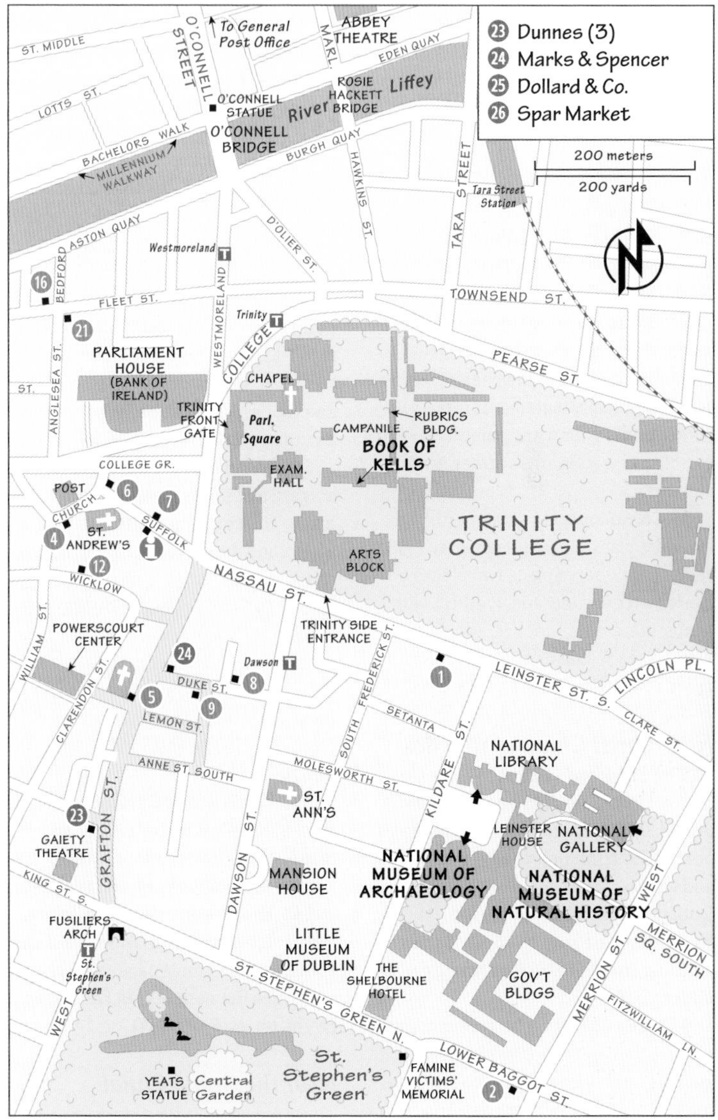

$$ Avoca Café, on the second floor above the Avoca department store, is a cheery eatery thriving with smart local shoppers. They serve healthy foodie plates and great salads (daily 9:30-17:30, 11 Suffolk Street, tel. 01/672-6019).

$ Avoca Sandwich Counter, in the Avoca store basement, has simple seating and a cheap buffet and salad bar counter that sells food priced by weight. They also offer deli sandwiches and enticing baked goodies (good for takeaway, daily generally 10:00-18:00, 11 Suffolk Street).

$$ The Duke and **Davy Byrnes,** neighbors on Duke Street, serve reliable pub lunches. Davy Byrnes feels like pub-meets-diner (at #21, also serves dinner, tel. 01/677-5217). The Duke has a buffet lunch counter in the back from 12:00 to 16:00 (at #8, tel. 01/679-9553). Both are favorites for Irish lit fans whose heroes (James Joyce, Brendan Behan, and Patrick Kavanagh) frequented them.

$$$ Yamamori is a plain, mellow, and modern Japanese place serving seas of sushi and noodles (daily 12:00-22:30, 73 South Great George's Street, tel. 01/475-5001).

$ PI Pizza is a hit for its short list of wood-fired, thin-crust Naples-style pizza. It's mod and fun, and the chef is passionate about quality ingredients (you're welcome to split your pizza, daily 12:00-22:00, 83 South Great George's Street, www.pipizzas.it).

$$ Cornucopia is a small, earth-mama-with-class, proudly vegetarian ("98% vegan"), self-serve place two blocks off Grafton. It's friendly and youthful, with hearty breakfasts, lunches, and dinner specials (Mon-Sat 8:30-22:00, Sun 12:00-21:00, 19 Wicklow Street, tel. 01/677-7583).

Near Christ Church Cathedral

$$ The Silk Road Café at the Chester Beatty Library serves an enticing selection of Middle Eastern and Mediterranean cuisine for lunch daily (good salads and vegetarian dishes, on the grounds of Dublin Castle, tel. 01/407-0770). While you're there, be sure to pop into the amazing (free) library (see listing earlier, under "Sights").

$ Queen of Tarts, with nice outdoor seating, does yummy breakfasts, light lunches, sandwiches, and wonderful pastries (Mon-Fri 8:00-19:00, Sat-Sun from 9:00, just off Dame Street, go 100 yards up from City Hall and left on Cow's Lane, tel. 01/670-7499).

$ Chorus Café is a friendly and plain little hole-in-the-wall diner serving breakfast, salads, panini, and pastas (daily 8:30-17:00, 7 Fishamble Street, next door to the site of the first performance of Handel's "Messiah," tel. 01/616-7088, Cyrus).

In Temple Bar

Temple Bar, while overrun with tourists, has a strange magnetism—you'll likely be drawn here to be part of the scene. It's lined with sloppy eateries charging a premium for their location. Everything's open long hours daily. If I were to eat in Temple Bar, I'd consider these places:

$$ Gallagher's Boxty House, with creaky floorboards and old Dublin ambience, serves stews and corned beef, but the specialty is boxty, the generally bland-tasting Irish potato pancake filled and rolled with various meats, veggies, and sauces (reservations wise, 20 Temple Bar, tel. 01/677-2762).

$$ The Bad Ass Café serves pizza, pasta, burgers, and salads. There's even a fun kids' menu. Their big patio fronts the Temple Bar action, and there's live music nightly from about 19:00 in the dark, sprawling, pubby interior (9 Crown Alley, tel. 01/675-3005).

$$ Luigi Malone's, with its fun atmosphere and varied menu of pizza, ribs, pasta, sandwiches, and fajitas, is just the place to take your high-school date (corner of Cecilia and Fownes streets, tel. 01/679-2723).

$$$ The Seafood Café, across from Luigi Malone's, is pricey but serves top-quality Irish oysters, lobster rolls, and more (11 Sprangers Yard, tel. 01/515-3717).

$$$ The Shack, offering traditional Irish, chicken, seafood, and steak dishes, comes with the most sanity of this bunch of Temple Bar eateries (24 East Essex Street, tel. 01/679-0043).

Near the Grand Canal

These are within a long block of one another in the emerging Grand Canal neighborhood. This area, southeast of St. Stephen's Green (just walk straight out Lower Baggot Street until you cross the canal), feels comfortably workaday with fewer tourists (near the intersection of Baggot Street and Mespil Road). For locations, see the "Southeast Dublin Hotels" map, earlier.

$$$ Bloom Brasserie & Wine Bar has a woody, candlelit ambience with beautifully presented dishes based on locally sourced meats (beef, lamb, duck) and seafood (Irish salmon). The menu is modern Irish meets France and changes with the seasons (daily 12:00-14:30 & 17:00-22:30, 11 Upper Baggot Street, tel. 01/668-7170).

$$ Searsons Pub, a sprawling neighborhood favorite, is a gastropub known for its roast beef, lamb, and salmon, with an open kitchen, classy-for-a-sports-bar energy, and friendly service. If there's a horse race or rugby match on, it'll be on the screens here (it's located near the rugby stadium and a betting office). You can escape the clamor out back on the patio (daily 12:00-22:00, 42 Upper Baggot Street, tel. 01/660-0330).

$$ Zakura Izakaya is a classy if noisy Japanese place—small and tight, like a sushi wine bar (daily 12:00-22:00, 7 Upper Baggot Street, tel. 01/563-8000).

Hip and Fun in North Dublin

For locations, see the "North Dublin" map on page 74.

The Church is a trendy café/bar/restaurant/nightclub/beer garden housed in the former St. Mary's Church (which hosted the baptism of Irish rebel Wolfe Tone and the marriage of brewing legend Arthur Guinness). Today the **$$$ Choir Balcony** has a huge pipe organ and a refined menu (daily 17:00-22:30). The less-expensive ground floor **Nave** is dominated by a long bar and pub grub (daily 12:00-21:00). A disco thumps away in the bunker-like basement until the wee hours on Friday and Saturday. On warm summer nights, the outdoor terrace is packed. Eating here is more about the scene than the cuisine (corner of St. Mary's and Jervis Streets, tel. 01/828-0102, www.thechurch.ie).

$$$ Mr Fox is an elegant and serene little basement operation serving locally sourced dishes created by chef Anthony Smith (Tue-Fri 12:00-14:00 & 17:00-21:30, Sat 17:30-22:00, closed Sun-Mon; behind the Garden of Remembrance at 38 Parnell Square West, tel. 01/874-7778, www.mrfox.ie)

$$ Brannigan's is an inviting family-run traditional pub—it's been a "beer emporium since 1909." They offer a lunch buffet (Mon-Fri 12:00-15:00). Its location—roughly halfway between the Gate and Abbey theaters—makes it convenient for theatergoers and those exploring O'Connell Street (daily 10:30-23:30, 9 Cathedral Street, 50 yards from the Spire, tel. 01/874-0137).

$ One Society Café goes for "tasty, healthy, simple" in an unpretentious little space a few blocks east of the Parnell Monument. But it surprises with inventive breakfasts and lunches as well as unique specialty pizza dinners (pizza only at night, dinner reservations required, Tue-Fri 7:30-21:00, Sat-Sun from 9:30, closed Mon, 1 Gardiner Street Lower, tel. 01/537-5261, www.onesociety.ie).

Delis and Markets with Practical Eateries

Department stores with fancy grocery sections also generally have what picnickers need: Try **Dunnes** (daily until 21:00, with several locations) or **Marks & Spencer** (daily until 20:00 or so, at 20 Grafton Street).

$$ Dollard & Co. is a gourmet grocery... and much more. The spacious dining hall has a fun, trendy energy with views of the river (Mon-Fri 8:00-21:00, Sat 9:00-22:00, Sun 10:00-20:00; on the south bank at 2 Wellington Quay, tel. 01/616-9606).

$ Fallon & Byrne Food Hall is like eating at an upscale Trader Joe's. Just point to what you like (a main dish with two sides for €11) and they'll microwave it (Mon-Sat 8:00-21:00, Sun 11:00-19:00, 11 Exchequer Street, tel. 01/472-1010).

$ Spar Market is open 24/7. Shop for your groceries, then sit down right there and eat them (a block above the Temple

Bar commotion at the corner of Dame Street and South Great George's Street, tel. 01/633-9070).

$ Baxter & Greene Market Café, north of the river behind the General Post Office, is a handy cafeteria on the third floor of the Dunnes department store in the Ilac Centre (daily 9:00-18:30, Henry Street; for location, see map on page 74).

TRANSPORTATION

Getting Around Dublin

You'll do most of Dublin on foot, though when you need public transportation, you'll find it readily available and easy to use. And Dublin is a great taxi town, with reasonable, metered cabs easy to hail. With a little planning, sightseers can make excellent use of a two-day hop-on, hop-off bus ticket to link the best sights (see "Tours," earlier). For cross-city travel, the expanding LUAS tram system beats bus service for reliability and ease of transporting bags.

Transit Cards: The **Leap Card** is good for travel on Dublin's bus, DART (speedy commuter trains running along the coast), and LUAS routes, and fares are lower than buying individual tickets. Leap Cards are sold at TIs, newsstands, and markets citywide—look for the leaping-frog logo—and can be topped up (€5 refundable deposit, www.leapcard.ie).

The **Do Dublin Freedom Card** covers the Airlink Express, public buses in Dublin, and the Do Dublin hop-on, hop-off bus, and also offers some sight discounts. You can buy it in advance online, at the Do Dublin airport desk (Terminal 1), or the Dublin Bus office (€35/72 hours, tel. 01/844-4265, www.dodublin.ie).

By Bus

Public buses are cheap and cover the city thoroughly. Most lines start at the four quays (riverfront streets) nearest O'Connell Bridge. If you're away from the center, nearly any bus takes you back downtown. Some bus stops are "request only": Be alert to the numbers of approaching buses, and when you see yours coming, flag it down. Tell the driver where you're going, and he'll ask for €2.15-3.30 depending on the number of stops. Bring coins, as drivers don't make change. The Dublin Bus office has free route maps and sells transit cards (Mon-Fri 9:00-17:30, Sat-Sun 9:30-14:00, 59 Upper O'Connell Street, tel. 01/873-4222, www.dublinbus.ie).

By LUAS Tram

The city's street-tram system has two main lines, red and green. The **red line** is most useful for tourists, with an east-west section connecting the Heuston and Connolly train stations (a 20-minute ride apart) at opposite edges of the central zone. In between, the Busáras, Smithfield, and Museum stops are handy. Useful north-south **green line** stops are at St. Stephen's Green, Trinity College, and both ends of O'Connell Street. The lines don't intersect: The closest transfer point is a 100-yard walk between the red-line Abbey Street stop and the green-line General Post Office (GPO) stop on O'Connell Street. Monitors at boarding platforms display the time and end destination of the next tram; make sure you're on the right platform for the direction you want to go (€2.10, buy at machine, 6/hour, runs until 24:45, tel. 1-800-300-604, www.luas.ie).

By Taxi or Uber

Taxis are everywhere and easy to hail. Cabbies are generally honest, friendly, and good sources of information (drop charge—€3.80 daytime, €4.20 nighttime, €1/each additional adult, figure about €10 for most crosstown rides, €50/hour for guided joyride). Your Uber app will get you two choices in Dublin: "Uber" is actually a taxi (with the standard metered rate, but no tipping and billed to your account); "Uber Black" is a more expensive chauffeur-driven car.

Arriving and Departing

By Train

Dublin has two train stations, both with ATMs but no lockers. **Heuston Station,** on the west end of town, serves west and southwest Ireland (nearest baggage storage is a 5-minute walk across the river at Tipperary House B&B, daily 8:00-20:00, hidden beside huge Ashcroft Hotel at 7 Parkgate Street, tel. 01/679-5317, www.tipperaryhousedublin.com). **Connolly Station** is closer to the center and serves the north, northwest, and Rosslare (nearest baggage storage is directly across from station at the Internet & Call Shop, Mon-Fri 9:00-23:30, Sat-Sun from 10:00, 16 Amiens Street, tel. 01/537-7413).

The frequencies listed below are for Monday-Saturday (departures are less frequent on Sunday).

From Dublin's Heuston Station to: Tralee (every 2 hours, most change in Mallow but one direct evening train, 4 hours), **Ennis** (10/day, 4 hours, change in Limerick, Limerick Junction, or Athenry), **Galway** (8/day, 3 hours), **Westport** (5/day, 3.25 hours). Irish Rail train info: Tel. 01/836-6222, www.irishrail.ie.

From Dublin's Connolly Station to: Rosslare (3-4/day, 3 hours), **Portrush** (7/day, 5 hours, transfer in Belfast or Coleraine). The **Dublin-Belfast train** connects the capitals in two hours at 90 mph (8/day). Northern Ireland train info: Tel. 048/9089-9400, www.translink.co.uk.

By Bus

Bus Éireann, Ireland's national bus company, uses the Busáras Central Bus Station (pronounced bu-SAUR-us), located one block south of Connolly Station. The frequencies listed below are for Monday-Saturday (departures are less frequent on Sunday).

From Dublin by Bus to: Belfast (hourly, most via Dublin Airport, 3 hours), **Trim** (almost hourly, 1 hour), **Ennis** (almost hourly, 5 hours), **Galway** (hourly, 3.5 hours; faster on CityLink—hourly, 2.5 hours, tel. 091/564-164, www.citylink.ie), **Westport** (6/day, 6 hours), **Limerick** (7/day, 3.5 hours), **Tralee** (7/day, 6 hours), **Dingle** (4/day, 8.5 hours, transfer at Limerick and Tralee). Bus info: Tel. 01/836-6111, www.buseireann.ie.

By Plane

Dublin Airport has two terminals located an easily walkable 100 yards apart (code: DUB, tel. 01/814-1111, www.dublinairport.com). Both have ATMs, cafés, Wi-Fi, and luggage storage (www.leftluggage.ie). There is no TI at the airport.

Getting Downtown by Bus: Airlink (double-decker turquoise buses) and Aircoach (single-deck blue buses) pick up on the street directly in front of arrivals, at ground level, at both terminals.

Airlink Express bus #747 generally runs an east-west route that parallels the River Liffey and includes stops at or near the Busáras Central Bus Station, Connolly Station, O'Connell Street, Temple Bar, Christ Church, and Heuston Station. Airlink bus #757 links the airport to the center along a generally north-south axis, including Trinity College, St. Stephen's Green (eastern end), and the National Concert Hall. Ask the driver which stop is closest to your destination (€7, pay driver, 3-5/hour, about 40 minutes; runs Mon-Sat 5:00-late, Sun from 7:25; tel. 01/873-4222, www.dublinbus.ie). This bus is covered by the Do Dublin Freedom transit card, which can be purchased at the airport.

Aircoach generally runs a north-south route that follows the O'Connell and Grafton streets axis. To reach recommended hotels south of the city center, the Aircoach bus #700 works well (€8, pay driver, discount if booked online, discount with Dublin Pass, 4/hour, fewer late at night, runs 24 hours, tel. 01/844-7118, www.aircoach.ie). Aircoach also runs a bus between Dublin Airport and Belfast (see the Belfast chapter).

By Taxi: Taxis from the airport into Dublin cost about €30.

By Car

If you plan to drive in Ireland, save your car rental for the countryside. Consider renting a car at Dublin airport, where you'll find all the standard car-rental agencies with longer hours than those in the city and easier access to the M-50. If you have no option but to rent in Dublin, the Hertz office on the Grand Canal in southeast Dublin is workable if you are headed south out of the city (at 2 Haddington Road, tel. 01/668-7566).

Don't drive in downtown Dublin—traffic's terrible and parking is expensive. If you must park in central Dublin, a good option is Q-Park Christ Church, on Werburgh Street behind Jurys Inn Christ Church (€3/hour, €12/day, tel. 01/634-9805, www.ncps.ie).

M-50 Toll Road: Drivers renting a car at Dublin Airport and heading for the countryside can bypass the worst of the big-city traffic by taking the M-50 ring road south or west. The M-50 uses an automatic tolling system called eFlow. Your rental should come with an eFlow tag installed; confirm this when you pick up your car. The €3.10 per-trip toll is automatically charged to the credit card you used to rent the car (www.eflow.ie).

Other Toll Roads: Your rental car's eFlow tag will work only for the M-50 ring road around Dublin. On any other Irish toll roads, you'll need to pay with cash (about €2/toll). These roads mostly run outward from Dublin toward Waterford, Cork, Limerick, and Galway (roads farther west are free).

By Ferry

Irish Ferries (tel. 0818-300-400, www.irishferries.com) and Stena Line (tel. 01/907-5555, www.stenaline.ie) combine to make eight daily crossings between Dublin Port (two miles east of O'Connell Bridge) and Holyhead, Wales. Most trips take 3.5 hours, but Irish Ferries offers a twice-daily fast boat that makes the trip in 2 hours. Since these boats can fill up on summer weekends, book at least a week ahead during the peak period.

NEAR DUBLIN

Not far from urban Dublin, the stony skeletons of evocative ruins sprout from the lush Irish countryside. The story of Irish history is told by ancient burial mounds, early Christian monastic settlements, huge Norman castles, and pampered estate gardens.

These sights are separated into two regions: north of Dublin (the Boyne Valley, including Brú na Bóinne and the town of Trim) and south of Dublin (Powerscourt Estate Gardens, Glendalough, and the Wicklow Mountains).

BOYNE VALLEY

The peaceful, green Boyne Valley, 30 miles north of Dublin, is worth a visit for the prehistoric and spiritual sights at Brú na Bóinne. The town of Trim makes an easy overnight stop for drivers (on the first or last night of your trip) and boasts a 13th-century castle—Ireland's biggest.

Brú na Bóinne

The famous archaeological site of Brú na Bóinne—"dwelling place of the Boyne"—is also commonly called "Newgrange," after its star attraction. Here you can visit two ▲▲▲ 5,000-year-old passage tombs—**Newgrange** and **Knowth** (rhymes with "south"). These are massive grass-covered burial mounds built atop separate hills, each with a chamber inside reached by a narrow stone passage. Mysterious, thought-provoking, and mind-bogglingly old, these tombs can give you chills.

Access to Newgrange and Knowth is by guided tour only (book ahead for Brú na Bóinne Plus tour). You'll start your visit at the visitors center with its excellent exhibit, then catch a shuttle bus to the tomb sites.

Orientation

Cost: Visitors center only-€5; Brú na Bóinne Tour (outside only)-€12, Brú na Bóinne Plus (includes Newgrange chamber)-€18; visitors center is included in tour prices.

Hours: Daily 9:00-19:00, slightly shorter hours Sept-April, last bus to the tombs leaves 1.75 hours before closing, last entry to visitors center 45 minutes before closing.

Information: Tel. 041/988-0300, www.heritageireland.ie.

Tours: Both tour options visit both Newgrange and Knowth, but the Brú na Bóinne Tour does not go inside Newgrange. There is no access to Knowth's interior on either tour. All tours take about 2.75 hours including the visitors center exhibits.

Advance Tickets Recommended: It's smart to reserve timed-entry tickets online at https://brunaboinne.admit-one.eu (online tickets available only for Brú na Bóinne Plus tour). Without a tour reservation, arrive early—ideally before 9:30.

Getting There

By Car: Drive 45 minutes north from Dublin on N-1 toward Drogheda, where signs direct you to the visitors center. If you're using a GPS, input "Brú na Bóinne" rather than "Newgrange" to get to the visitors center, where you must check in.

By Train and Taxi: First take a train departing Dublin Connolly station at 8:00, which puts you in the town of Drogheda around 9:00 (€12 round-trip; confirm train times at www.irishrail.ie). From here it's a short six-mile taxi ride to the Brú na Bóinne visitors center (approximately €10 one-way).

By Bus: Take bus #100x from Dublin to Drogheda, then bus #163 to the visitors center. Aim to depart the Drogheda bus station at 11:15 (return bus from the visitors center to Drogheda at 15:10, allow about 1.5 hours each way, including the connection in Drogheda).

By Tour from Dublin: Newgrange Tours visits Brú na Bóinne (including

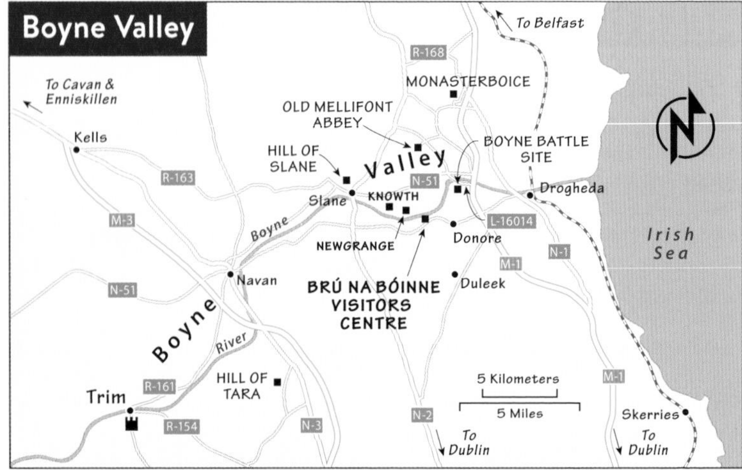

inside the Newgrange tomb), the Hill of Tara, and the Hill of Slane in a seven-hour trip (€40, daily pickup from several Dublin hotels, book direct via website, mobile 086-355-1355, www.newgrangetours.com).

Sights

BRÚ NA BÓINNE VISITORS CENTER EXHIBIT

The exhibit introduces you to the Boyne River Valley and its tombs. No one knows exactly who built the 40 burial mounds found in the surrounding hills. Exhibits re-create what these pre-Celtic people might have been like—simple farmers and hunters living in huts, fishing in the Boyne, equipped with crude tools of stone, bone, or wood.

Then around 3200 BC, someone had a bold idea. They constructed a chamber of large stones, with a long stone-lined passage leading up to it. They covered it with a huge mound of dirt and rocks in successive layers. Sailing down the Boyne to the sea, they beached at Clogherhead (12.5 miles from here), where they found hundreds of five-ton stones, weathered smooth by the tides. Somehow they transported them back up the Boyne, possibly by tying a raft to the top of the stone so it was lifted free by a high tide. They then hauled these stones up the hill by rolling them atop logs and up dirt ramps, and laid them around the perimeter of the burial mound to hold everything in place. It would have taken anywhere from five years to a generation to construct a single large tomb.

Why build these vast structures? Partially, it was to bury VIPs. A dead king might be carried up the hill to be cremated on a pyre. Then they'd bring his ashes into the tomb, parading by torchlight down the passage to the central chamber. The remains were placed in a ceremonial basin, mingling with those of his illustrious ancestors.

The museum displays replicas of tools and objects found at the sites, including the ceremonial basin stone and a head made from flint, which may have been carried atop a pole during the funeral procession. Marvel at the craftsmanship of the perfectly spherical stones (and the phallic one) and wonder at their purpose.

The tombs also served an astronomical function; they're precisely aligned to the movements of the sun, as displays and a video illustrate. You can request a short tour and winter solstice light-show demo at a full-size replica of the Newgrange passage and interior chamber.

The Newgrange burial tomb predates the Egyptian pyramids.

▲▲▲NEWGRANGE

This grassy mound atop a hill is 250 feet across and 40 feet high. Dating from 3200 BC, it's 500 years older than the pyramids at Giza. The base of the mound is ringed by dozens of curbstones, each about nine feet long and weighing five tons.

The entrance facade is a mosaic of white quartz and dark granite. This is a reconstruction done in the 1970s, and not every archaeologist agrees it originally looked like this. Above the doorway is a square window called the roofbox, which played a key role (as we'll see). In front of the doorway lies the most famous of the curbstones, the 10- by 4-foot entrance stone. Its left half is carved with three mysterious spirals, which have become a kind of poster child for prehistoric art.

Most of Newgrange's curbstones have designs carved into them. This was done with super-hard flint tools; the Neolithic ("New Stone Age") people had not mastered metal. The stones feature common Neolithic motifs: not people or animals, but geometric shapes—spirals, cross-hatches, bull's-eyes, and chevrons.

Entering the tomb, you walk down a narrow 60-foot passage lined with big boulders. The passage opens into a central room—a cross-shaped central chamber with three alcoves, topped by a 20-foot-high igloo-type stone dome. Bones and ashes were placed here in a ceremonial stone basin, under 200,000 tons of stone and dirt.

While we know nothing of Newgrange's builders, it most certainly was a sacred spot—for a cult of the dead, a cult of the sun, or both. The tomb is aligned precisely east-west. As the sun rises around the shortest day of the year (winter solstice—usually on Dec 21—and two days before and after), a ray of light enters through the roofbox and creeps slowly down the passageway. For 17 minutes, it lights the center of the sacred chamber (your guide will demonstrate this). Perhaps this was the moment when the souls of the dead were transported to the afterlife, via that ray of light. Then the light passes on, and, for the next 361 days, the tomb sits again in total darkness.

▲▲▲KNOWTH

This site is an impressive necropolis, with one grand hill-topping mound surrounded by several smaller satellite tombs. The central mound is 220 feet wide, 40 feet high, and covers 1.5 acres. You'll see plenty of mysteriously carved curbstones and new-feeling grassy mounds that you can look down on from atop the grand tomb.

Knowth's big tomb has two passages: one entering from the east, and one from the west. Like Newgrange, it's likely aligned so the rising and setting sun shone down the passageways to light the two interior chambers. Neither passage is open to the public, but you can visit a room carved into the mound by archaeologists, where a cutaway lets you see the layers of dirt and rock used to build the mound. You also get a glimpse down one of the passages.

The Knowth site thrived from 3000 to 2000 BC. The central tomb dates from about 2000 BC. It was likely used for burial rituals and sun-tracking ceremonies to please the gods and ensure the regular progression of seasons for crops. The site then evolved into the domain of fairies and myths for the next 2,000 years and became an Iron Age fortress in the early centuries after Christ. Around AD 1000, it was an all-Ireland political center, and later, a Norman fortress was built atop the mound.

Trim

The sleepy, workaday town of Trim, straddling the River Boyne, is marked by the towering ruins of Trim Castle, which seem to say, "This little town was big-time...800 years ago."

Trim makes a great landing pad into—or launching pad out of—Ireland. If you're flying into or out of Dublin Airport and don't want to deal with big-city Dublin, this is a perfect alternative—an easy 45-minute, 30-mile drive away. You can rent a car at the airport and make Trim your first overnight base, or spend your last night here before returning your car at the airport.

Orientation

Trim's main square is a traffic roundabout, and everything's within a block or two. Most of the shops and eateries are on or near Market Street, along with banks and a supermarket.

Tourist Information: The TI is right next to the castle entrance and has a handy coffee shop (open daily, Castle Street, tel. 046/943-7227).

Laundry: The launderette is located close to Market Street (Mon-Sat 9:00-13:00 & 13:30-17:30, closed Sun, Watergate Street, tel. 046/943-7176).

Taxi: For visits to nearby Boyne sites, **Donie Quinn** can give you a lift (tel. 046/943-7777).

Getting There

Buses run from Dublin's Busáras bus station to Trim nearly hourly, dropping off at the bus shelter next to Trim's TI and the castle entrance on Castle Street (1-hour trip, www.buseireann.ie). Trim has no train station.

Day-tripping drivers can park on the street or in a public lot (pay-and-display system, 2-hour maximum, Mon-Sat 9:00-18:00, free Sun).

Sights

▲▲TRIM CASTLE

This is the biggest Norman castle in Ireland. Set in a grassy riverside park at the edge of this sleepy town, its mighty keep towers above a ruined outer wall. It replaced a wooden fortification that was destroyed in 1173 by Irish High King Rory O'Connor, who led a raid against the invading Normans. The current castle was completed in the 1220s and served as a powerful Norman statement to the restless Irish natives.

Today the castle remains an impressive sight. The best-preserved walls ring the castle's southern perimeter and

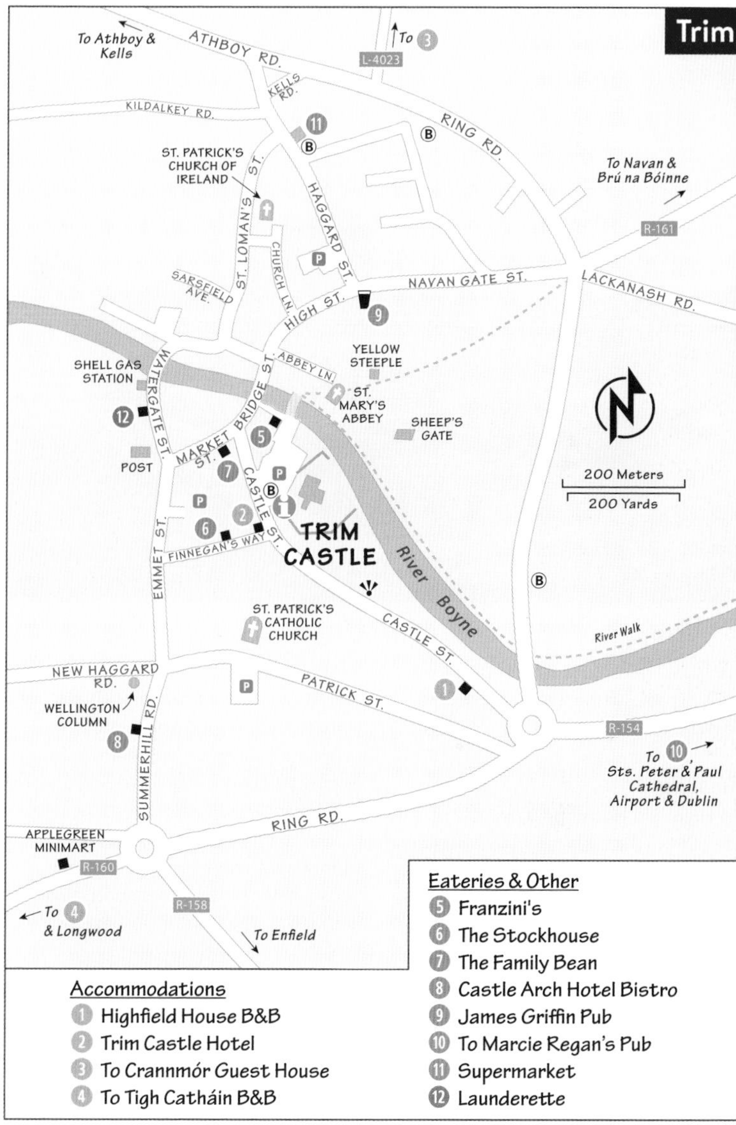

sport a barbican gate that contained two drawbridges.

The massive 70-foot-high central keep, which is mostly a hollow shell, has 20 sides. This experimental design was not implemented elsewhere because it increased the number of defenders needed to cover all the angles. Make time to take a 15-minute walk outside, circling the castle walls and stopping at the informative plaques.

Cost and Hours: Keep and required tour-€5, grounds only-€2, daily 10:00-17:00, Nov-mid-March open Sat-Sun only 9:30-16:00, last entry one hour before closing, 45-minute tours run 2/hour but

Trim's huge Norman castle overlooks the Boyne River.

spots are limited and can fill up—arrive early in peak season, tel. 046/943-8619, www.heritageireland.ie.

Sleeping

$$ Highfield House B&B, across the street from the castle and a five-minute walk from town, is a stately former maternity hospital with hardwood floors and 10 spacious, high-ceilinged rooms (family rooms; above the roundabout where the road from Dublin hits Trim, Castle Street, tel. 046/943-6386, mobile 086-857-7115, www.highfieldguesthouse.com, info@highfieldguesthouse.com, Geraldine and Edward Duignan).

$$ Trim Castle Hotel is the town's modern option with 68 immaculate rooms, some with direct views of the castle, and a friendly downstairs pub (family rooms, parking, Castle Street, tel. 046/948-3000, www.trimcastlehotel.com, info@trimcastlehotel.com).

Countryside B&Bs: These two B&Bs are about a mile outside Trim (phone ahead for driving directions).

$ At ivy-draped **Crannmór Guest House,** Anne O'Regan decorates five rooms with cheery color schemes (family room; north of the Ring Road on Dunderry Road L-4023, then veer right at the first fork; tel. 046/943-1635, mobile 087-288-7390, www.crannmor.com, cranmor@eircom.net). Anne's professional-guide husband Marc knows all the best fishing holes.

$ Marie Keane's **Tigh Catháin B&B,** southwest of town, has four large, bright, lacy rooms with a comfy, rural feel and organically grown produce at breakfast (cash only, on R-160/Longwood Road, 200 yards past the Applegreen minimart, tel. 046/943-1996, mobile 086-257-7313, www.tighcathain-bnb.com, tighcathain.bnb@gmail.com).

Eating

My first two listings are the only full restaurants in town. Otherwise, the spots along Market Street are friendly, wholesome, and unassuming.

$$$ Franzini's has a fun dinner menu and an excellent location next to the castle. They serve pasta, steak, fish, and great salads in a modern, plush space (Mon-Sat 17:00-21:00, Sun 14:00-20:00, on French's Lane across from the castle parking lot, tel. 046/943-1002).

$$$ The Stockhouse serves hearty steaks and poultry, plus creative desserts. Sit upstairs and take in the history of Trim from the walls while you wait (Mon-Thu 17:00-21:00, Fri-Sat until 22:00, Sun 13:00-20:30, Finnegan's Way, tel. 046/943-7388).

$$ The Family Bean is a good local joint along Market Street for omelettes, sandwiches, and meat pies (daily 8:30-17:00, tel. 046/948-1481).

$$ The **Castle Arch Hotel,** popular with locals, serves hearty pub grub at reasonable prices in its bistro on Summerhill Road (daily 12:30-21:00, tel. 046/943-1516).

Pubs: For a fun pub experience, check out Trim's two best watering holes. The **James Griffin** (on High Street) is full of local characters with traditional Irish music sessions on Monday, Wednesday, and Thursday nights. Locals fill the tiny, low-ceilinged **Marcie Regan's,** a creaky, unpretentious pub at the north end of the old Norman bridge over the River Boyne—it's a half-mile stroll outside town, next to the ruins of Newtown.

Supermarket: The large **Super Valu** is your best bet (daily 8:00-22:00, on Haggard Street, a short walk from the town center).

WICKLOW MOUNTAINS

The Wicklow Mountains, while only 15 miles south of Dublin, feel remote—enough so to have provided a handy refuge for opponents to English rule. Rebels who took part in the 1798 Irish Rebellion hid out here. The area became more accessible in 1800, when the frustrated British built a military road to help flush out the rebels. Today, this same road—now R-115—takes you through the Wicklow area, with the Powerscourt Estate Gardens on the north end and the monastic settlement of Glendalough at the south end.

Getting There

By car or tour, it's easy. It's not worth the trouble on public transport.

By Car: Take N-11 south from Dublin toward Bray, then R-117 to Enniskerry, the gateway to the Wicklow Mountains. Signs direct you to the gardens and on to Glendalough. From Glendalough, if you're heading west, you can leave the valley and pick up the highway over the famous but dull mountain pass called the Wicklow Gap.

By Tour from Dublin: Wild Wicklow Tours packs every minute of an all-day excursion covering the windy military road over scenic Sally Gap and the Glendalough monasteries (€33, RS%, runs daily year-round, stop for lunch at a pub—cost not included, several Dublin hotel pickup points, advance booking required, tel. 01/280-1899, www.wildwicklow.ie).

Do Dublin Tours offers a shorter trip focusing on Glendalough and Powerscourt Gardens (€27, daily departures from Dublin Bus head office, 59 Upper O'Connell Street, tel. 01/844-4265, www.dodublin.ie).

Friendly and knowledgeable **Lisa Tully** can pick you up in Dublin for a full-day private driving tour to all the best spots (from €425/up to 3 people, March-Nov, tel. 086/898-6457, www.wicklowguidedtours.ie). If you have your own car, consider meeting her there for a scenic two-hour walking tour of the lush Wicklow countryside (€120/up to 4 people).

Sights

▲▲POWERSCOURT ESTATE GARDENS

A mile above the village of Enniskerry, these gardens from the Victorian era are Ireland's best, covering 47 acres within a

Powerscourt House is surrounded by Italian Renaissance–style gardens.

700-acre estate. The mansion's interior is still only partially restored after a 1974 fire (and only available for special events).

Upon entry to the gardens, you'll get a flier laying out two walks. The "one-hour" walk (actually 30 minutes at a relaxed amble) features the impressive summit of the Great Sugar Loaf Mountain as a backdrop, and a fine Japanese garden, Italian garden, and goofy pet cemetery along the way.

Cost and Hours: €10.50, daily 9:30-17:30, Nov-Feb until dusk, great cafeteria, tel. 01/204-6000, www.powerscourt.com.

▲▲GLENDALOUGH

The steep wooded slopes of Glendalough (GLEN-da-lock, "Valley of the Two Lakes"), at the south end of Wicklow's old military road, hide Ireland's most impressive monastic settlement. Founded by St. Kevin in the sixth century, the monastery flourished (despite repeated Viking raids) throughout the Age of Saints and Scholars until the English destroyed it in 1398. A few hardy holy men continued to live here until it was finally abandoned during the Dissolution of the Monasteries in 1539. But pilgrims kept coming, especially on St. Kevin's Day, June 3. While much restoration was done in the 1870s, most of the buildings date from the 10th to 12th century.

In an Ireland without cities, these monastic communities were mainstays of civilization. At such remote outposts, ascetics gathered to commune with God. Today, Ireland is dotted with the reminders of this age: illuminated manuscripts, simple churches, carved crosses, and about 100 round towers.

The valley sights are split between the two lakes. The smaller, lower lake is just beyond the visitors center and nearer the best remaining ruins. The upper lake has scant ruins and feels like a state

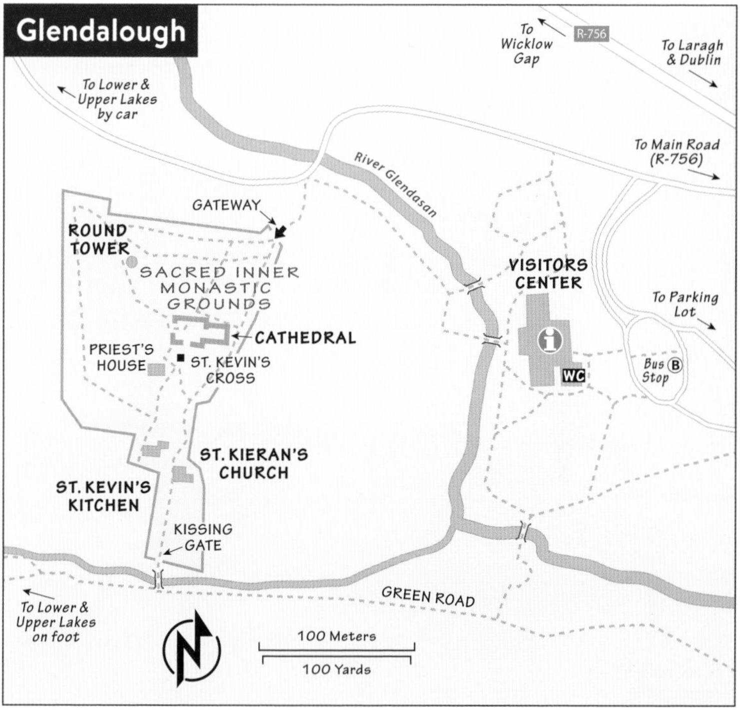

Glendalough

To Wicklow Gap
R-756
To Laragh & Dublin
To Lower & Upper Lakes by car
River Glendasan
To Main Road (R-756)
GATEWAY
ROUND TOWER
SACRED INNER MONASTIC GROUNDS
VISITORS CENTER
To Parking Lot
CATHEDRAL
PRIEST'S HOUSE
ST. KEVIN'S CROSS
WC
Bus Stop
ST. KIERAN'S CHURCH
ST. KEVIN'S KITCHEN
KISSING GATE
GREEN ROAD
To Lower & Upper Lakes on foot
100 Meters
100 Yards

park. Walkers and hikers will enjoy a choice of nine different trails of varying lengths through the lush Wicklow countryside (longest loop takes four hours, hiking-trail maps available at visitors center).

Cost and Hours: Free to enter site, €5 for visitors center, €4 to park at upper lake; open daily 9:30-18:00, mid-Oct-mid-March until 17:00; last entry 45 minutes before closing, tel. 0404/45352.

Visiting Glendalough: Park for free at the visitors center. Visit the center; take the guided tour if possible; wander the ruins surrounding the round tower on your own (free); or walk the traffic-free Green Road a half-mile to the upper lake, and then walk back to the visitors center and your car along the trail that parallels the public road (an easy, roughly one-mile loop). Or you can drive to the upper lake (skippable, if you're rushed).

The monastic ruins of Glendalough in the lush Wicklow Mountains

Kilkenny & the Rock of Cashel

Driving west across Ireland from Dublin to Dingle, the best two stops to break up a journey across the Irish interior are Kilkenny, Ireland's finest medieval town; and the Rock of Cashel, a thought-provoking early Christian site crowning the Plain of Tipperary.

Counties Kilkenny and Tipperary ("Tipp" to locals) are friendly neighbors geographically, yet blood rivals on the hurling field, with the lion's share of the GAA national championships split between them. Watch for kids heading home from school carrying hurlies (ash-wood sticks with broad, flat ends) and dressed in their local colors (black and yellow, like bumblebees, for Kilkenny; blue and gold for Tipperary).

These two counties also boast some of the finest agricultural land on this rocky and boggy island. These days, farm tractors rumble the back roads where it's not a long way to Tipperary.

KILKENNY & THE ROCK OF CASHEL IN 1 DAY

With one day, drivers connecting Dublin with Kinsale can get an early start, stop in Kilkenny for lunch, and then tour the Rock of Cashel before ending up in Kinsale to spend the night. For a longer visit, Kilkenny makes a good overnight for drivers from Dublin who drive slower back roads to visit the Powerscourt Estate Gardens and Glendalough (see previous chapter).

I've listed accommodations for both Kilkenny and the Rock of Cashel: A night in Kilkenny comes with plenty of traditional folk music in its pubs and more to do. With extra time, you could visit sights stretching south to Waterford (monastic ruins, a famine ship replica, and crystal factory). If you're driving between Dublin and Dingle (or Kenmare), the Rock of Cashel is a more direct overnight.

Kilkenny

KILKENNY & THE ROCK OF CASHEL AT A GLANCE

In Kilkenny

▲▲**Kilkenny Castle** Historic castle and gardens, later converted into an opulent château. **Hours:** Daily June-Aug 9:00-17:30, shorter hours off-season. See page 109.

▲**Rothe House and Garden** Sprawling 17th-century merchant's townhouse complex displaying upper-crust Elizabethan life. **Hours:** Mon-Sat 10:30-17:00, Sun from 12:00; Nov-March Mon-Sat until 16:30, closed all day Sun. See page 109.

Between Kilkenny and Waterford

▲▲**Jerpoint Abbey** Informatively presented abbey ruins with carvings, bringing to life a monastic culture from 850 years ago. **Hours:** Daily 9:00-17:30; shorter hours Oct-Nov, Dec-March by appointment only. See page 115.

▲▲**Kells Priory** Deserted, monastic ruins of a vast complex, with tower houses bordering a huge courtyard, and rock walls that once supported a church, a cloister, and more. See page 116.

▲▲***Dunbrody* Famine Ship** Replica of a typical famine ship that brought emigrants to America. **Hours:** Daily 9:00-18:00, Oct-March 10:00-17:00. See page 116.

▲▲**Waterford Crystal Visitor Centre** Popular tour of glass factory with live demos and glittering sales shop. **Hours:** Mon-Sat 9:00-18:00, Sun from 9:30, shorter hours Nov-March. See page 117.

At Cashel

▲▲**Rock of Cashel** Ireland's best tangle of ecclesiastical ruins atop a rocky perch surveying the plains of Tipperary. **Hours:** Daily 9:00-19:00 in summer, closes earlier rest of year. See page 117.

KILKENNY

Lovely Kilkenny gives you a feel for salt-of-the-earth Ireland. The town earned its nickname, the "Marble City," because of the stone from the local quarry (actually black limestone, not marble). You can see white seashells fossilized within the black stone steps around town. While an average-size town today (around 25,000 residents), Kilkenny has a big history. It was even the capital of Ireland for a short spell in the turbulent 1640s.

Orientation

Kilkenny's castle and cathedral stand like historic bookends on a higgledy-piggledy High Street of colorful shops and medieval facades. This stretch of town has been rebranded as "The Medieval Mile."

Tourist Information: The TI is a block off the bridge in the 16th-century Shee (a wealthy medieval donor family) Alms poorhouse (Mon-Sat 9:00-17:30, Sun 11:00-17:00, shorter hours and closed Sun off-season; Rose Inn Street, tel. 056/775-1500).

Helpful Hints

Market: The square in front of Kilkenny Castle hosts a friendly produce, cheese, and crafts market on Thursday (8:00-14:30).

Laundry: At the south end of town, the full-service **Laundry Basket** trumpets its existence in vivid red at 21 Patrick Street (Mon-Fri 9:00-17:00, Sat 10:00-15:00, closed Sun, tel. 056/777-0355).

Bike Rental: Kilkenny Cycling rents bikes and provides safety gear and route maps for exploring the pastoral charms of County Kilkenny (€25/day, €50 refundable deposit, office behind The Wine Centre shop at 15 John Street, mobile 086-895-4961, www.kilkennycyclingtours.com).

Walking Tours: **Pat Tynan** and his staff offer the only regularly scheduled walking tours in town. They last one hour and depart from the TI (€10, daily at 11:00 and 14:00, Nov-mid-March by prior arrangement only, mobile 087-265-1745, www.kilkennywalkingtours.ie).

Local Guides: **Frank Kavanagh** offers custom walks of the town and castle and full- or half-day driving tours (Feb-Nov, book ahead, €75/half-day, €150/full day, gas and

Kilkenny Castle

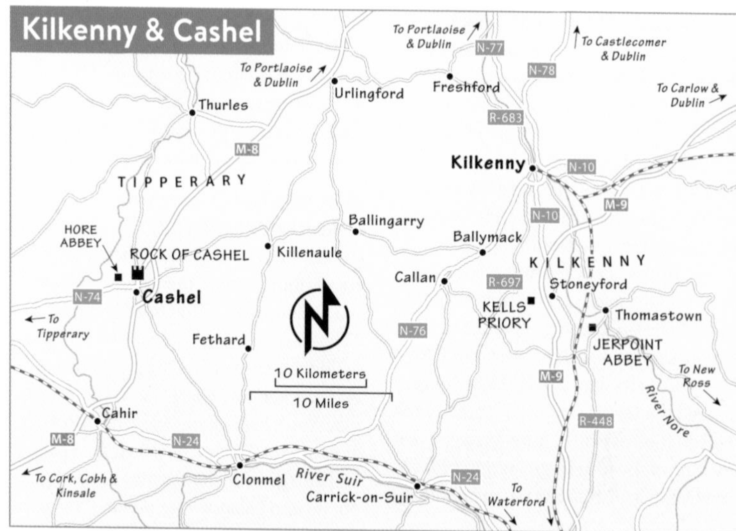

lunch extra, mobile 086-839-2468, http://visitkilkenny.ie/franks_medieval_tours, fkav1948@gmail.com). **Amanda Pitcairn**'s tours focus on medieval Kilkenny and the life of its inhabitants (€15/person, €12/person for groups of 4-6, book ahead, mobile 087-277-6107, www.touchthepastireland.com, pitcaira@tcd.ie).

Sights

▲▲KILKENNY CASTLE

Dominating the town, this castle is a stony reminder that the Anglo-Norman Butler family controlled Kilkenny for 500 years. The castle once had four sides, but Oliver Cromwell's army knocked down one wall when it took the castle, leaving it as the rough "U" shape we see today.

Cost and Hours: €8; daily 9:30-17:30, June-Aug from 9:00, shorter hours in winter; tel. 056/770-4100, www.kilkennycastle.ie.

Visiting the Castle: Enter the castle gate, turn right in the courtyard, and head into the base of the turret. Here you'll find a 12-minute video explaining how the 12th-century wooden fort evolved into a 17th-century château. Then go into the main castle entrance, diagonally across the courtyard from the turret, to buy your entry ticket. You'll be free to walk through the castle. A pamphlet explains the exhibits, and you can also talk to stewards in the important rooms.

Now restored to its Victorian splendor, the castle's highlight is the beautiful family-portrait gallery, which puts you face-to-face with the wealthy Butler family ghosts.

Nearby: The **Kilkenny Design Centre,** across the street from the castle in some grand old stables, is full of local crafts and offers cafeteria-style lunches in its food hall (shops open Mon-Sat 10:00-19:00, Sun until 18:00; food hall open daily 9:00-18:30; tel. 056/772-2118, www.kilkennydesign.com).

▲ROTHE HOUSE AND GARDEN

This is the crown jewel of Kilkenny's medieval architecture: a well-preserved merchant's house that expanded around interior courtyards as the prosperous Rothe family grew in the early 1600s.

Cost and Hours: €7.50; Mon-Sat 10:30-17:00, Sun from 12:00; Nov-March Mon-Sat until 16:30, closed Sun; Parliament Street, tel. 056/772-2893, www.rothehouse.com.

Visiting the House and Garden: Check out the graceful top-floor timberwork supporting the roof, which uses wooden dowels (pegs) instead of nails. The museum, which also serves as the County Kilkenny genealogy center, gives a glimpse of life here in late Elizabethan and early Stuart times. The walled gardens at the far back were a real luxury in their time.

The Rothe family eventually lost the house when Oliver Cromwell banished all Catholic landowners, sending them to live on less desirable land west of the River Shannon. In the late 1800s, the building housed the Gaelic League, devoted to the rejuvenation of Irish culture through preservation of the Irish language and promotion of native Irish sports (such as hurling).

▲MEDIEVAL MILE MUSEUM

This fine museum covers Kilkenny's brutal yet pious Dark Age past and rounds out the story begun at the Rothe House (listed above). Housed in the 13th-century St. Mary's Church (much of which was rebuilt in the 1700s), the museum displays medieval artifacts, including ornately carved tomb lids, ceremonial swords and scepters, and neatly penned 800-year-old civic records.

Cost and Hours: €8, €12 with 45-minute tour; daily 10:00-18:00, Nov-March 11:00-16:30; tours daily at 10:30, 12:30, 14:30, and 16:30; 2 Mary's Lane, tel. 056/781-7022, www.medievalmilemuseum.ie.

▲HURLING MUSEUM AND STADIUM EXPERIENCE

The sport of hurling is historically and culturally important to the Irish, and Kilkenny is a hurling mecca. Run by PJ Lanigan, "The Kilkenny Way" is a walking tour that includes visits to a hurling pub/museum and the stadium where the Kilkenny Cats play. You'll learn about the long history and rules of this lightning-fast field game, and also get a chance to play as you figure out how to balance your *sliotar*—and how to pronounce it.

Cost and Hours: €25 for two-hour tour, includes pub meal; Mon-Sat at 14:00, reserve ahead in summer; leaves from Legends Hurling Bar, 28 Rose Inn Street, tel. 056/772-1718, www.thekilkennyway.com.

ST. CANICE'S CATHEDRAL

This 13th-century cathedral is early English Gothic, rich with stained glass,

St. Canice's Cathedral

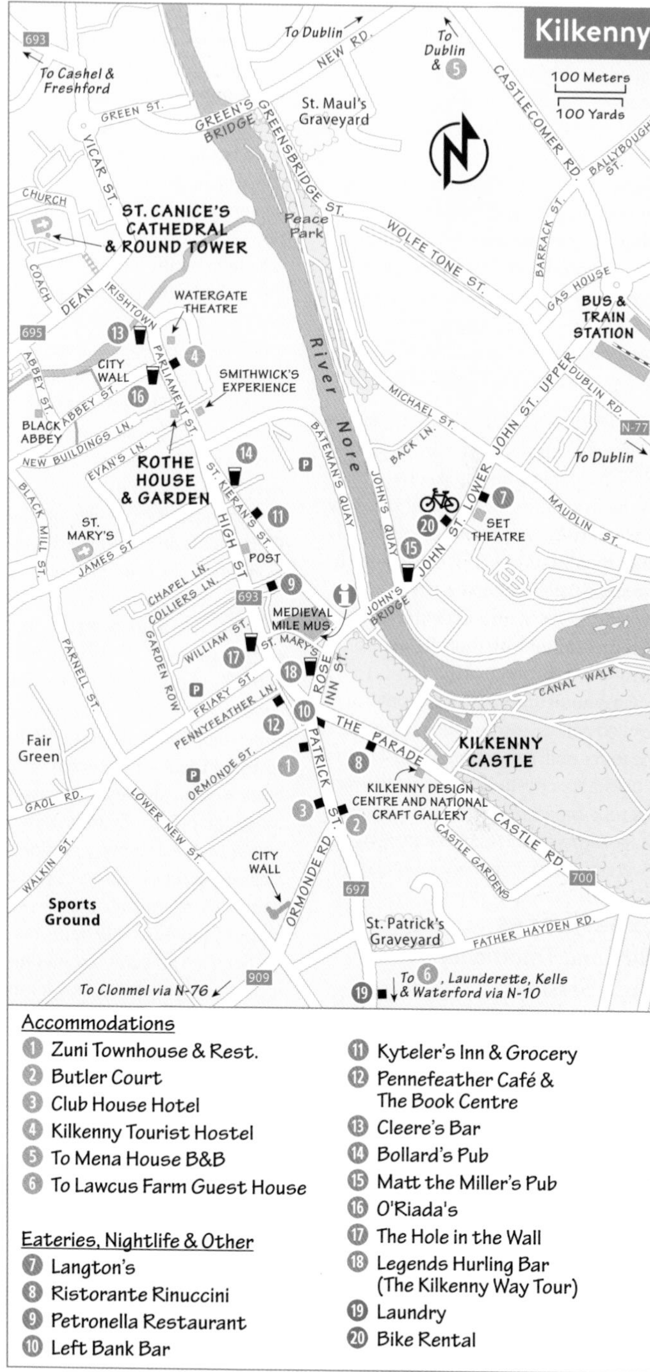
Kilkenny
100 Meters
100 Yards
To Dublin
To Dublin & 5
To Cashel & Freshford
To Dublin
To Clonmel via N-76
To 6, Launderette, Kells & Waterford via N-10
693
695
697
700
909
N-77
NEW RD.
GREEN ST.
GREEN'S BRIDGE
GREENSBRIDGE ST.
St. Maul's Graveyard
CASTLECOMER RD.
BALLYBOUGHT ST.
VICAR ST.
CHURCH
ST. CANICE'S CATHEDRAL & ROUND TOWER
Peace Park
WOLFE TONE ST.
BARRACK ST.
GAS HOUSE
BUS & TRAIN STATION
COACH
DEAN
IRISHTOWN
WATERGATE THEATRE
River Nore
CITY WALL
PARLIAMENT ST.
SMITHWICK'S EXPERIENCE
ABBEY ST.
BLACK ABBEY
NEW BUILDINGS LN.
EVAN'S LN.
ROTHE HOUSE & GARDEN
BATEMAN'S QUAY
MICHAEL ST.
BACK LN.
JOHN ST. UPPER
DUBLIN RD.
ST. KIERAN'S ST.
HIGH ST.
JOHN'S QUAY
JOHN ST. LOWER
SET THEATRE
MAUDLIN ST.
BLACK MILL ST.
ST. MARY'S
JAMES ST.
POST
CHAPEL LN.
COLLIERS LN.
MEDIEVAL MILE MUS.
JOHN'S BRIDGE
WILLIAM ST.
ST. MARY'S
GARDEN ROW
ROSE INN ST.
PARNELL ST.
FRIARY ST.
PENNYFEATHER LN.
CANAL WALK
THE PARADE
KILKENNY CASTLE
Fair Green
ORMONDE ST.
PATRICK ST.
KILKENNY DESIGN CENTRE AND NATIONAL CRAFT GALLERY
GAOL RD.
LOWER NEW ST.
CASTLE RD.
CASTLE GARDENS
WALKIN ST.
CITY WALL
ORMONDE RD.
Sports Ground
St. Patrick's Graveyard
FATHER HAYDEN RD.
Accommodations
1 Zuni Townhouse & Rest.
2 Butler Court
3 Club House Hotel
4 Kilkenny Tourist Hostel
5 To Mena House B&B
6 To Lawcus Farm Guest House
Eateries, Nightlife & Other
7 Langton's
8 Ristorante Rinuccini
9 Petronella Restaurant
10 Left Bank Bar
11 Kyteler's Inn & Grocery
12 Pennefeather Café & The Book Centre
13 Cleere's Bar
14 Bollard's Pub
15 Matt the Miller's Pub
16 O'Riada's
17 The Hole in the Wall
18 Legends Hurling Bar (The Kilkenny Way Tour)
19 Laundry
20 Bike Rental

medieval carvings, and floors paved in history. Check out the model of the old walled town in its 1641 heyday, as well as a couple of modest audiovisuals. The 100-foot-tall round tower, built as part of a long-gone pre-Norman church, recalls the need for a watchtower, treasury, and refuge. The fun ladder-climb to the top affords a grand view of the countryside.

Cost and Hours: Cathedral-€4.50, tower-€4, combo-ticket-€7; Mon-Sat 9:00-18:00, Sun from 13:00; shorter hours and closed for lunch off-season; tel. 056/776-4971, www.stcanicescathedral.com.

SMITHWICK'S EXPERIENCE KILKENNY

Smithwick's (pronounced SMIT-icks) reddish ale was born in Kilkenny...and has been my favorite Irish beer since my first visit to Ireland. Founded in 1710, it is older than Guinness (but now owned by the same parent company). No longer a working brewery, the building now houses a visitors center with tours focused on the historic origins of the tasty ale.

Cost and Hours: €16, discount if booked online, entry includes a pint at the tour's end; daily 10:00-18:00, Nov-Feb 11:00-16:00, one-hour tours run hourly, last tour departs one hour before closing; 44 Parliament Street, tel. 056/778-6377, www.smithwicksexperience.com.

Experiences

Pubs and Traditional Music Sessions

Kilkenny has its fair share of atmospheric pubs. Visitors seeking fun traditional music sessions can try the first four places listed here. Those seeking friendly conversation in utterly unvarnished Irish surroundings should seek out the memorable duo at the end of these listings. A fun pub crawl could link all of these places with 20 minutes of walking (30 minutes crawling). Confirm the nightly pub trad session schedules as you explore town during the day.

Starting at the north end of town and working south, **Cleere's Bar** is a friendly throwback with surprisingly good pub grub served until 20:00 (music Mon and Wed at 21:30, 28 Parliament Street). **Bollard's Pub,** an unpretentious landmark at the north end of St. Kieran's Street, is a good bet for lively traditional music sessions, or sit out front under the awning and enjoy a pint as Kilkenny's humanity flows past you. Just down the same street is **Kyteler's Inn,** with a stony facade and medieval witch-haunted cellar (music nightly in summer at 18:00, 27 St. Kieran's Street). You can saunter over John's Bridge to check out the tunes at **Matt the Miller's Pub,** with its multilevel, dark-wood interior (around 18:30 most nights, next to bridge on John Street across the river from the castle).

Lacking music but high on character, **O'Riada's** is an endangered species—a wonderful, old-fashioned place that your Irish grandfather would recognize and linger in. This is an ideal place to chat with engaging locals (across from the Watergate Theatre at 25 Parliament Street).

At the other end of the conversational spectrum, **The Hole in the Wall** is a tiny, restored Elizabethan tavern (c. 1582) hidden down an alley (capacity 15-20, mostly standing). Charmingly eccentric owner Michael Conway presides over sing-alongs of Irish classics that include helpful lyrics and explanations of Irish idioms (unpredictable hours but typically Fri-Sat from 20:00 and sometimes weeknights, confirm ahead, look for the alley beside Bourkes shop at 17 High Street, tel. 087/807-5650, www.holeinthewall.ie).

Theater

The **Watergate Theatre** houses live plays and other performances in its 300-seat space (€15-25, Parliament Street, tel. 056/776-1674, www.watergatetheatre.ie). The **Set Theatre,** adjacent to sprawling Langton's Restaurant, is a fine, modern, 250-seat music venue attracting top-notch Irish acts in an intimate setting (€15-30, John Street, tel. 056/776-5133, www.set.ie).

Rick's Tip: *Kilkenny is a popular destination for rowdy bachelor and bachelorette parties. For quiet at night,* **avoid hotels with bars nearby,** *and stick with smaller B&Bs, guesthouses, or rural lodging (especially Fri-Sat nights).*

Sleeping

$$$ Zuni Townhouse, above a fashionable restaurant, has 13 boutique-chic rooms sporting colorfully angular furnishings. Ask about two-night weekend breaks and midweek specials that include a four-course dinner (parking in back, 26 Patrick Street, tel. 056/772-3999, www.zuni.ie, info@zuni.ie).

$$ Butler Court is Kilkenny's best lodging value. Ever-helpful Yvonne and John offer 10 modern, spacious rooms (wheelchair-accessible, continental breakfast in room, will validate parking in nearby multistory garage on Ormonde Street for length of your stay, 14 Patrick Street, tel. 056/776-1178, www.butlercourt.com, info@butlercourt.com).

$$ Club House Hotel, originally a gentlemen's sporting club, comes with fading Georgian elegance; a musty, creaking ambience; a palatial, well-antlered breakfast room; and 35 comfy bedrooms (secure parking, 19 Patrick Street, tel. 056/772-1994, www.clubhousehotel.com, info@clubhousehotel.com).

¢ Kilkenny Tourist Hostel fills a fine Georgian townhouse with ramshackle fellowship at the north end of the town center, right in the action (private rooms available, cash only, pay self-serve laundry, 2 blocks from cathedral at 35 Parliament Street, tel. 056/776-3541, www.kilkennyhostel.ie, info@kilkennyhostel.ie).

Near Kilkenny

$$ Lawcus Farm Guest House, hosted by Mark and Ann Marie, offers quirky, rural comfort 10 miles south of Kilkenny between Kells Priory and the village of Stoneyford. Mark, an inventive craftsman, renovated the original house and built the rest. A menagerie of friendly pets and farm animals shares property (family rooms, cash only, parking, mobile 086-603-1667 or 087-291-1056, www.lawcusfarmguesthouse.com, lawcusfarm@hotmail.com). To reach the farm, go south out of Kilkenny on N-10, which becomes R-713 after crossing over the M-9 motorway. Just as you enter the village of Stoneyford, turn right onto L-1023. Go 500 yards down that lane and watch for a brown sign directing you to turn right into a gravel driveway.

$ Mena House B&B is a traditional, good-value option quietly nestled a mile north of town. Behind its Tudor-style facade you'll find seven large, spotless rooms, well kept by hostess Katherine. It's about a 15-minute walk from the center and easy for drivers (family rooms, cash only, parking, located roughly across from the Newpark Hotel and just south of the Kilkenny Golf Club on Castlecomer Road, tel. 056/776-5362, www.menahousebandb.com, menahouse@eircom.net).

Eating

$$$ Langton's is every local's first choice, serving high-quality Irish dishes under a labyrinthine, multichambered, Tiffany-skylight expanse (daily 12:00-22:00, 69 John Street, tel. 056/776-5133).

$$$$ Ristorante Rinuccini serves classy, romantic, candlelit Italian meals (daily 12:00-14:30 & 17:00-22:00, reservations smart, 1 The Parade, tel. 056/776-1575, www.rinuccini.com).

$$ Petronella Restaurant warms its medieval surroundings with dependable traditional entrées and a welcoming vibe dished out by jovial Frank (Mon-Sat 12:00-15:00 & 17:00-21:00, closed Sun, Butterslip Lane off High Street, tel. 056/776-1899).

$$$$ Zuni, in one of my recommended accommodations, is a stylish splurge

Kyteler's Inn

offering international cuisine (daily 12:30-17:00 & 18:00-20:45, weekend reservations a good idea, 26 Patrick Street, tel. 056/772-3999, www.zuni.ie).

$$$ Left Bank Bar is a dimly lit gastropub with better-than-average fare and a fun patio. Come early—its top-floor nightclub zooms with stag/hen party bedlam on weekends (food served Mon-Thu 12:00-21:00, Fri-Sun until 19:00, 1 Parade Gardens, tel. 056/775-0016).

$$$ Kyteler's Inn serves decent pub grub in a timber-and-stone atmosphere with a heated and covered beer garden out back. Visit their fun 14th-century cellar and ask about their witch (Mon-Sat 12:00-21:00, Sun until 20:00, 27 St. Kieran's Street, tel. 056/772-1064).

$ Pennefeather Café, above the Kilkenny Book Centre, is good for a quick, cheap, light lunch (Mon-Sat 9:00-17:30, closed Sun, 10 High Street, tel. 056/776-4063).

Grocery Store: You'll find an ample selection of picnic supplies at **Dunnes Stores** (a few doors down from Kyteler's Inn on St. Kieran's Street, Mon-Sat 8:00-21:00, Sun 10:00-20:00).

Transportation

Arriving and Departing

BY TRAIN OR BUS

The train/bus station is four blocks from John's Bridge, which marks the center of town.

From Kilkenny by Train to: Dublin (6/day, 1.5 hours), **Waterford** (6/day, 35 minutes). Train info: www.irishrail.ie.

By Bus to: Dublin (8/day, 2 hours), **Waterford** (Dublin Coach every 2 hours, 40 minutes, www.dublincoach.ie), **Galway** (2/day, change in Athlone, 5 hours). Bus info: www.buseireann.ie.

BY CAR

Drivers can find parking at the Market Yard Car Park behind Kyteler's Inn (daily 8:00-18:00, entry off Bateman's Quay) or the pay-and-display spots on the street (enforced Mon-Sat 8:00-19:00). The multistory parking garage on Ormonde Street is the best long-term bet (3-day pass for €13.50 allows you to come and go; open 7:00-23:00, Fri-Sat until 24:00).

BETWEEN KILKENNY AND WATERFORD

The fast M-9 motorway links Kilkenny and Waterford on a 45-minute drive. But drivers in no rush can savor the journey by spending a couple of enjoyable back-road hours taking in two pastoral sights: Jerpoint Abbey and Kells Priory. Farther along, in the tiny port of New Ross is the Dunbrody Famine Ship. And in Waterford itself, you can see one of the most famous glassworks in the world. The rural roads come with old stone bridges spanning placid rivers that weave among tiny villages and abandoned mills.

▲▲JERPOINT ABBEY

Evocative abbey ruins dot the Irish landscape, but few are as well presented as Jerpoint (founded in 1180). Its claim to fame is fine stone carvings on the sides of tombs and on the columns of the cloister arcade. If you visit only one abbey in Ireland, make it this one.

Without the excellent guided tours, the site is a cold, rigid ruin. But in the hands of unusually well-versed hosts, the place truly comes alive with insights into the monastic culture that imprinted Ireland 850 years ago.

Cost and Hours: €5; daily 9:00-17:30, shorter hours Oct-Nov, Dec-March by appointment only; tel. 056/772-4623.

Getting There: It's located about 11 miles (17 km) south of Kilkenny or 2 miles (3 km) south of Thomastown, beside R-700.

Visiting the Abbey: The Cistercian monks, who came to Ireland from France in the 12th century, were devoted reformers bent on following the strict rules of St. Benedict. Their holy mission was to bring the wild Irish Christian church (which had evolved, unsupervised, for centuries on the European fringe) back in line with Rome. They steamrolled their belief system across the island and stamped the landscape with a network of identical, sprawling monasteries. The preexisting form of Celtic Christianity that had thrived in the Dark Ages was no match for the organization and determination of the Cistercians. For the next 350 years, these new monasteries were the dominant local religious authority.

The cloister at Jerpoint Abbey

What eventually did them in? King Henry VIII's marriage problems, his subsequent creation of the (Protestant) Church of England, and his eventual dissolution of the (Catholic) monasteries.

▲▲KELLS PRIORY

This place is a wonderful lonely gem. Locals claim that the massive religious complex of Kells Priory (more than 3 acres) is the largest monastic site in Europe. It's an isolated, deserted ruin that begs a curious wander (and alert side-stepping of sheep droppings).

Cost and Hours: Free, no set hours.

Getting There: You'll find Kells Priory about 9 miles (15 km) south of Kilkenny or 6 miles (10 km) west of Jerpoint Abbey, just off the R-697 road. From Jerpoint Abbey, turn left, then take your first right through the village of Stoneyford. At the end of the village, turn left (at the sign for Kells Priory), then continue straight.

The main parking lot lies on a slope above the south side of the ruins (a good place for a quick overview photo stop). But I prefer to park beside the Kings River on the north side of the ruins. To get there, cross the pretty stone bridge over the river, and turn right onto the L-5067 road. Drive about 100 yards past the first mill (with a craft shop in an adjacent building); when you come to the second mill (completely shuttered and abandoned), park in the gravel lot in front.

Visiting the Priory: From the parking lot by the abandoned mill (described above), stroll past the mill's rusty waterwheel and enjoy the wander downstream for the remaining 100 yards along the riverside path. Once inside the complex, watch where you walk and explore at your leisure. Consider bringing a picnic to enjoy—but please respect the site and leave no trash.

Founded in 1193 by Norman soldiers of fortune with Augustinian monks in tow, this priory grew into the intimidating structure that locals call "the seven castles" today. These "castles," however, were actually Norman tower houses connected by a wall that enclosed the religious functions within. Inside the walls, the site is divided into two main areas: One is a huge interior common grazing area (larger than a football field) dominated by the encircling tower houses; the other is a tangled medieval maze of rock walls (remnants of a cloister, a church, cellars, a medieval dormitory, and a graveyard).

▲▲*DUNBRODY* FAMINE SHIP

Permanently moored on a river in the tiny port of New Ross, this ship is a full-scale reconstruction of a 19th-century three-masted bark built in Quebec in 1845. It's typical of the trading vessels that originally sailed, empty, to America to pick up goods; during the famine, ship owners found that they could make a little money on the westward voyage by transporting hungry Irish emigrants. Commonly, boats like this would arrive in America with only 80 percent of their original human cargo. Those who succumbed to "famine fever" (often typhus or cholera) were dumped overboard, and the ships gained their morbid moniker: "coffin ships."

Cost and Hours: €11; daily 9:00-18:00, Oct-March 10:00-17:00, 45-minute tours go 2/hour, last tour starts one hour before closing; upstairs café handy for lunch with nice views of the ship, tel. 051/425-239, www.dunbrody.com.

Getting There: The *Dunbrody* is in New Ross, a 30-minute drive southeast from Jerpoint Abbey via highway R-700.

Visiting the Ship: Your visit starts with an audiovisual presentation on the life Irish emigrants were leaving behind, followed by coverage about the building of the vessel. Then you'll follow an excellent guide on board the ship, encountering a couple of passengers (one traveling first class, the other second) who tell vivid tales about life onboard. At the end, you'll get a glimpse of the new life Irish immigrants would encounter in New York.

Roots seekers are welcome to peruse the computerized file of the names of the

Dunbrody Famine Ship

Crystal cutting at Waterford

million immigrants who sailed on these ships from 1846 through 1865.

▲▲WATERFORD CRYSTAL VISITOR CENTRE

With a tradition dating back to 1783, Waterford was once the largest—and is still the most respected—glassworks in the world. While 70 percent of Waterford Crystal is now manufactured by cheaper labor in Poland, Slovenia, and the Czech Republic, the finest glass craftsmen still reside here, where they create "prestige pieces" for special-order customers. The one-hour tour of this hardworking little factory is a joy. It's more intimate than the old, larger factory, and you're encouraged to interact with the craftsmen. Large tour groups descend midday, so try to visit before 10:00 or after 15:30.

Cost and Hours: Tours cost €14.50 and depart every 30 minutes (cheaper online); Mon-Sat 9:00-18:00, Sun from 9:30, last tour at 16:15; shorter hours Nov-March with last tour at 15:15; shop open longer hours; on The Mall, one block south of Reginald's Tower; tel. 051/317-000, www.waterfordvisitorcentre.com.

Visiting the Factory: The tour begins with a bit of history and a glitzy and pointless five-minute fireworks film montage set to a techno beat. But things pick up again as your guide takes you into the factory to meet the craftsmen in their element. Glassblowers magically spin glowing blobs of molten crystal into exquisite and recognizable shapes in minutes.

The crystal vases and bowls may look light and delicate, but hold an unfinished piece (with its lead-enhanced heft) and you'll gain a new appreciation for the strength, touch, and hand-eye coordination of the glasscutters.

Afterward, visit the glittering salesroom. If you make a significant purchase, be sure to ask about a VAT refund (see page 340).

ROCK OF CASHEL

Rising high above the fertile Plain of Tipperary, the Rock of Cashel, worth ▲▲, is one of Ireland's most historic and evocative sights. Seat of the ancient kings of Munster (c. AD 300-1100), this is where St. Patrick baptized King Aengus in about AD 450. Strategically located and perfect for fortification, the Rock was fought over by local clans for hundreds of years. Finally, in 1101, clever Murtagh O'Brien gave the Rock to the Church.

Nowhere else in Ireland can you better see the evolution of Irish devotion expressed in stone. This large lump of rock is a pedestal supporting a compact tangle of three dramatic architectural styles: early Christian (round tower and St. Patrick's high cross), Romanesque (Cormac's Chapel), and Gothic (the main cathedral).

The Rock of Cashel looms above the Tipperary countryside.

Orientation

Cost and Hours: €8, families-€20, ticket includes guided tour—see below; daily 9:00-17:30, summer until 19:00, winter until 16:30, last entry 45 minutes before closing; tel. 062/61437, www.heritageireland.ie.

Crowd-Beating Tips: Summer crowds flock to the Rock (worst June-Aug 11:00-15:00). Try to plan your visit for early or late in the day.

Tours: Guided walks are included with your entrance (2/hour, about 45 minutes). Otherwise, set your own pace with my self-guided tour.

Parking: Pay the €6 fee at the machine (under the Plexiglas shelter to the left of the exit) before returning to your car.

Services: You'll find basic WCs at the base of the Rock next to the parking lot (there are none up on the Rock).

Rick's Tip: **Dress warmly**—*the Rock is exposed and often cold and windy.*

➲ Self-Guided Tour

From the parking lot, it's a steep 100-yard walk up to the Rock itself. On this 200-foot-high outcrop of limestone, the first building you'll enter is the 15th-century Hall of the Vicars Choral, housing the ticket desk, a tiny museum (with a stunted original 12th-century high cross dedicated to St. Patrick and a few replica artifacts), and a 20-minute video (2/hour, shown in the hall's former dormitory). From there you'll explore the following: a round tower, an early Christian cross, a delightful Romanesque chapel, and a ruined Gothic cathedral, all surrounded by my favorite Celtic-cross graveyard with views for miles.

• *Follow this tour counterclockwise around the Rock. Start by descending the indoor stairs opposite the ticket desk into the one-room, vaulted cellar museum.*

❶ **Hall of the Vicars Choral:** You are in the cellar of the youngest building on the Rock (early 1400s). This would have been the storage room for the vicars (minor clerics) appointed to sing during cathedral services. Today it contains a sparse collection of artifacts (some copies) associated with the religious site. Two glass cases display brooches and primitive axes, while the walls are hung with stone slab carvings. The impressively ornate shrine bell of St. Patrick is a reproduction (the bell would not have been used by him, but rather, dedicated to him, centuries later). But the star of the vault is the **original Cross of St. Patrick** at the far end. The

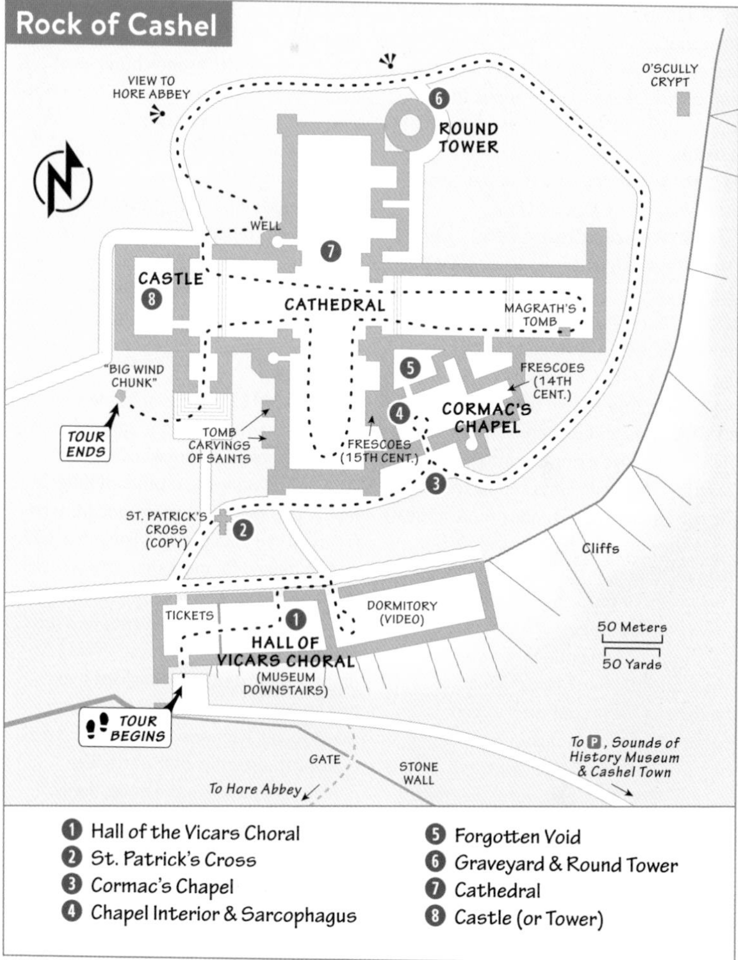

massive stone base is hollow (see the mirror underneath it). Was it a hiding place for valuable religious objects during raids? Or just too heavy to move otherwise? The cross stood outside for centuries, but hundreds of years of wind and rain slowly buffeted away important detail, scouring it into a stub of its former glory. We'll soon see a copy outside.

• *Climb back up to the ticket desk level and continue up the indoor stairs into the living space of the vicars.*

Walk to the **great hall** with the big brown tapestry. Vicars were granted nearby lands by the archbishop and lived comfortably here, with a large fireplace and white, lime-washed walls (to reflect light and act as a natural disinfectant that discouraged bugs). Window seats gave the blessedly literate vicars the best light to read by. The furniture is original, but the colorfully ornamented oak timber roof is a reconstruction, built to medieval specifications using wooden dowels instead of nails. The large wall tapestry shows King Solomon with the Queen of Sheba.

The vicars, who formed a sort of corporate body to assist the bishop with local administration, used a special seal to authorize documents such as land leases. You can see an enlarged wooden copy of the seal (hanging above the fireplace), depicting eight vicars surrounding a seated organist.

• *Go outside the hall into the grassy space, veer left about 30 feet, and find...*

❷ **St. Patrick's Cross:** St. Patrick baptized King Aengus on the Rock of Cashel in about AD 450. This is a copy of the 12th-century cross carved to celebrate the handing over of the Rock to the Church 650 years after St. Patrick's visit (the original is in the museum in the Hall of the Vicars Choral, described earlier). Typical Irish high crosses use a ring around the cross' head to support its arms and to symbolize the sun (making Christianity more appealing to the sun-worshipping Celts). But instead, this cross uses the Latin design: The weight of the arms was supported by two vertical beams on each side of the main shaft, representing the two criminals who were crucified beside Christ (today only one of these supports remains).

• *Walk about 100 feet slightly uphill along the gravel path beside the cathedral. Roughly opposite the far end of the Hall of the Vicars Choral is the entry (a glass door) to the chapel.*

❸ **Cormac's Chapel** (Exterior): As the wild Celtic Christian church was reined in and reorganized by Rome 850 years ago, new architectural influences from continental Europe began to emerge on the remote Irish landscape. This small chapel—Ireland's first and finest Romanesque church, constructed in 1134 by King Cormac MacCarthy—reflects this evolution. Imagine being here in the 12th century, when this chapel and the tall round tower were the only stone structures sprouting from the Rock (among a few long-gone, humble wooden structures).

The "new" Romanesque style reflected the ancient Roman basilica floor plan. Its columns and rounded arches created an overall effect of massiveness and strength. Romanesque churches were like dark fortresses, with thick walls, squat towers, and few windows. Irish stone churches of this period (like the one at Glendalough in the Wicklow Mountains) were simple rectangular buildings emphasizing function.

Before stepping inside, notice the weathered tympanum above the door. The carved "hippo" is actually an ox, representing Gospel author St. Luke.

• *The modern, dark-glass chapel door is a recent addition to keep out nesting birds. Enter the chapel and let your eyes adjust to the low light.*

❹ **Chapel Interior:** Just inside, on your left, is an empty stone **sarcophagus.** Nobody knows for sure whose body once lay here (possibly the brother of King Cormac MacCarthy). The damaged front relief is carved in a Viking style. Vikings had been raiding Ireland for more than 200 years by the time this was carved; they had already intermarried with the Irish and were seeping into Irish society. Some scholars interpret the relief design (a tangle of snakes and beasts) as a figure-eight lying on its side, looping back and forth forever, symbolizing the eternity of the afterlife.

You're standing in the **nave,** dimly lit by three small windows. Overhead is an arched vaulted ceiling with support ribs. The strong round arches support not only the heavy stone roof, but also the unseen second-story scriptorium chamber, where monks once carefully copied manuscripts by candlelight (their work was amazingly skillful and ornate, considering the poor light).

The big main arch overhead, studded with fist-size heads, framed the altar (now gone). Walk into the chancel and look up at the ceiling, examining the faint **frescoes,** a labor of love from 850 years ago. Frescoes are rare in Ireland because of the perpetually moist climate. Once vividly colorful, then fading over time, these frescoes were further damaged during and after the Reformation, when Protestants piously whitewashed them. These surviving frescoes were discovered under multiple layers of whitewash during painstaking modern restoration.

• *Walk through the other modern, dark-glass doorway, opposite the door you used to enter the chapel. You'll find yourself in a...*

❺ **Forgotten Void:** This enclosed little space was created when the newer cathedral was wedged between the older chapel and the round tower. Once the main entrance into the chapel, this forgotten doorway is crowned by a finely carved tympanum that decorates the arch above it. It's perfectly preserved because the huge cathedral shielded it from the wind and rain. The large lion (symbol of St. Mark's gospel) is being hunted by a centaur (half-man, half-horse) archer wearing a Norman helmet.

• *Exit the chapel, turning left, and tiptoe through the tombstones around the east end of the cathedral to the base of the round tower.*

❻ **Graveyard and Round Tower:** This graveyard is full. The 20-foot-tall stone shaft at the edge of the graveyard, marking the O'Scully family crypt, was once crowned by an elaborately carved Irish high cross—destroyed during a lightning storm in 1976. The fortified wall dates from the 15th century, when the riches of this outpost merited a little extra protection.

Look out over the **Plain of Tipperary.** Called the "Golden Vale," its rich soil makes it Ireland's most fertile farmland. In St. Patrick's time, it was covered with oak forests. From the corner of the church, beyond the fortified wall on the left, you can see the ruined 13th-century **Hore Abbey** dominating the fields below (free, always open and peaceful).

Gaze up at the **round tower,** the first stone structure built on the Rock after the Church took over in 1101. The shape of these towers is unique to Ireland. Though you might think towers like this were chiefly intended as a place to hide in case of invasion, they were instead used primarily as bell towers and lookout posts. The tower stands 92 feet tall, with walls more than three feet thick. The doorway, which once had a rope ladder, was built high up not only for security, but also because having it at ground level would have weakened the foundation of the top-heavy structure. The interior once contained wooden floors connected by ladders and served as safe storage for the monks' precious sacramental treasures.

Continue walking around the cathedral's north transept, noticing the square "put-log" holes in the exterior walls. During construction, wooden scaffolding was anchored into these holes. After the structure was completed, the builders simply sawed off the scaffolding, leaving small blocks of wood embedded in the walls. With time, the blocks rotted away, and the holes became favorite spots for birds to build their nests.

On your way to the cathedral entrance find the small **well** (in the corner on the left, built into the wall). Its stone lip is groovy from ropes after centuries of use. Without this essential water source, the Rock could never have withstood a siege and would not have been as valuable to clans and clergy. In 1848, a chalice was dredged from the well, likely thrown there by fleeing medieval monks intending to survive a raid. They didn't make it. (If they had, they would have retrieved the chalice.)

• *Now enter the...*

❼ **Cathedral:** Traditionally, churches face east toward Jerusalem and the rising sun. Because this cathedral was squeezed between the preexisting chapel, round tower, and drinking well, to make it face east the builders were forced to improvise by giving it a cramped nave and an extra-long choir (where the clergy gathered to celebrate Mass).

Built between 1230 and 1290, the church's pointed arches and high, narrow windows proclaim the Gothic style of the period (and let in more light than earlier Romanesque churches). Walk under the central bell tower and look up at the rib-vaulted **ceiling.** The hole in the middle

Ornate tomb at cathedral

Graveyard and round tower

was for a rope used to ring the church bells. The wooden roof is long gone. When the Protestant Lord Inchiquin (who became one of Oliver Cromwell's generals) attacked the Catholic town of Cashel in 1647, hundreds of townsfolk fled to the sanctuary of this cathedral. Inchiquin packed turf around the exterior and burned the cathedral down, massacring those inside.

Ascend the terraces at the choir end of the cathedral, where the main altar once stood. Stand on the gravestones (of the 16th-century rich and famous) with your back to the east wall (where the narrow windows have crumbled away) and look back down toward the nave. The right wall of the choir is filled with graceful Gothic windows, while the solid left wall hides Cormac's Chapel (which would have blocked most sunlight). The line of stone supports on the left wall once held the long, wooden balcony where the vicars sang. Closer to the altar, high on the same wall (directly above the pointed doorway), is a small, rectangular window called the "leper's squint"—which allowed unsightly lepers to view the altar during Mass without offending the congregation.

The grand **wall tomb** on the left contains the remains of archbishop Miler Magrath, the "scoundrel of Cashel," who lived to be 100. From 1570 to 1622, Magrath was the Protestant archbishop of Cashel who simultaneously profited from his previous position as Catholic bishop of Down. He married twice, had lots of kids, confiscated the ornate tomb lid here from another bishop's grave, and converted back to Catholicism on his deathbed.

• *Walk back down the nave and turn left into the south transept.*

Peek into the modern-roofed wooden structure against the wall on your left. It's protecting 15th-century **frescoes** of the Crucifixion of Christ that were rediscovered during renovations in 2005. They're as patchy and hard to make out (and just as rare, for Ireland) as the century-older frescoes in the ceiling of Cormac's Chapel.

On the opposite side of this transept, in alcoves built into the wall, enjoy the wonderful **carvings** of early Christian saints lining the outside walls of tombs (look down at shin level).

• *Exit the cathedral opposite where you entered.*

❽ **Castle** (or Tower): Back outside, stand beside the huge chunk of wall debris. (This is not "the rock" of Cashel.) Try to picture where it might have perched in the ragged puzzle of ruins above. This end of the cathedral was converted into an archbishop's castle in the 1400s (shortening the nave even more). Looking high into the castle's damaged top floors, you can see the bishop's residence chamber and the secret passageways that were once hidden inside the thick walls. Lord Inchiquin's cannons weakened the structure during the 1647 massacre, and in 1848, a massive storm (known as "Night of the Big Wind" in Irish lore) flung the huge chunk next to you from the ruins above.

In the mid-1700s, the Anglican Church transferred cathedral status to St. John's in town, and the archbishop abandoned the drafty Rock for a more comfortable residence, leaving the ruins that you see today.

Rick's Tip: *Fans of Irish music will enjoy the small* **Sounds of History Museum** *in the Brú Ború Cultural Centre next to the Rock of Cashel (€5, tel. 062/61122, www.bruboru.ie).*

Cashel Town

The huggable town at the base of the Rock affords a good break on the long drive from Dublin to Dingle (**TI** open daily 9:30-17:30 in season, tel. 062/61333). The Heritage Centre, next door to the TI, presents a modest six-minute audio explanation of Cashel's history around a walled town model. Parking is pay-and-display (enforced Mon-Sat 9:00-18:00).

Sleeping

If you spend the night in Cashel, you'll be treated to beautifully illuminated views of the ruins. The first listing is in the center of town (a 15-minute walk from the Rock). The rest are cozy, old-fashioned, and closer to the Rock.

$$$ Bailey's Hotel is Cashel's best boutique hotel, housed in a fine Georgian townhouse (1709). Its 19 refurbished rooms are large, inviting, and well appointed, perched above a great cellar-pub restaurant (parking, 42 Main Street, tel. 062/61937, www.baileyshotelcashel.com, info@baileyshotelcashel.com).

$ Cashel Lodge is a well-kept rural oasis housed in an old stone grain warehouse, a 10-minute walk from the Rock near the Hore Abbey ruins. Its seven comfortable rooms combine unpretentious practicality with Irish country charm. Guests have a ringside seat for beautiful views of the Rock lit up at night (camping spots, parking, Dundrum Road R-505, tel. 062/61003, www.cashel-lodge.com, info@cashel-lodge.com, Tom and Brid O'Brien).

$ Rockville House, 100 yards from the Rock, is a traditional place run by gentleman owner Patrick Hayes. The house itself has six fine rooms, and its old stablehouse, lovingly converted by Patrick, has five more (family room, cash only, 10 Dominic Street, tel. 062/61760, www.rockvillehousebb.com, rockvillehse@eircom.net).

$ Wattie's B&B has three rooms that feel lived-in and comfy (cash only, parking, 14 Dominic Street, tel. 062/61923, www.wattiesbandb.ie, wattiesbandbcashel@gmail.com, Maria Dunne).

Eating

Near the Rock, **$ Granny's Kitchen** is a tiny, violet-colored place with basic soup-and-sandwich lunches (daily 11:00-16:00, just past parking lot at the base of the Rock). **$$ Café Hans** has the best lunch selection and biggest crowds (Tue-Sat 12:00-17:30, closed Sun-Mon, 75 yards down the road from the parking lot). **$$$$ Chez Hans,** filling an old stone church, is good for a splurge dinner (Tue-Sat 18:00-21:30, closed Sun-Mon, a block below the Rock, tel. 062/61177, www.chezhans.net).

In town, you'll find several options. Next door to the TI, **$ Feehan's Bar** is a convenient stop for a pub grub lunch (daily 12:00-16:00, tel. 062/61929). A couple of blocks farther into town, the **$$ Cellar Pub** hides beneath Bailey's Hotel and serves satisfying dishes (daily 12:00-21:30, tel. 062/61937). **Super Valu** is the town's supermarket (Mon-Sat 7:00-22:00, Sun 8:00-21:00, 30 Main Street).

Transportation

Cashel has no train station; the closest one is 10 miles away in the town of Cahir. Buses run from Cashel to **Dublin** (6/day, 2.5 hours) and **Waterford** (6/day, 2 hours; bus-train combination also possible via Cahir). Bus info: www.buseireann.ie.

STONE MAD
22
STONE MAD
STONE MAD GALLERY

Kinsale

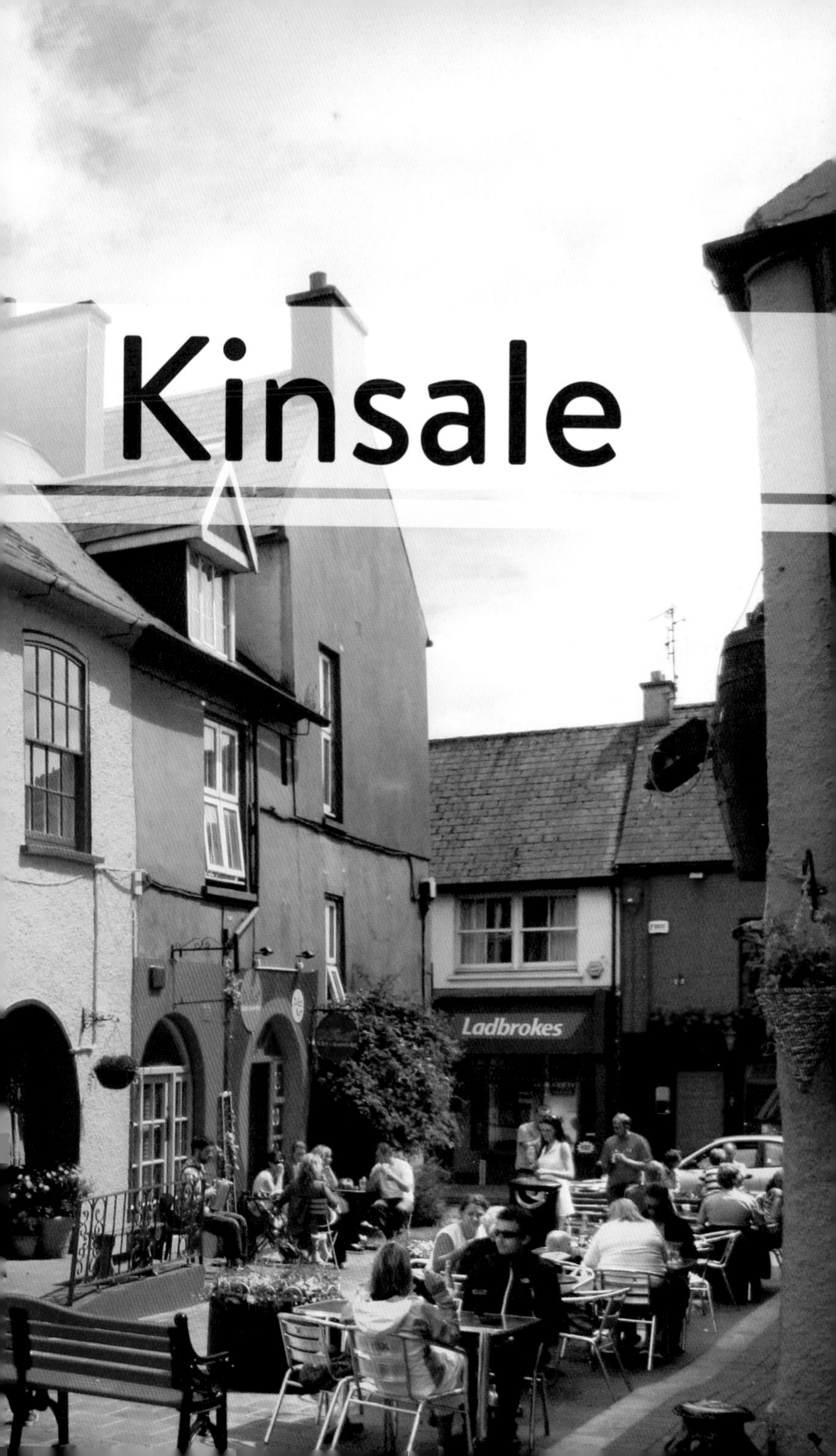

County Cork, on Ireland's south coast, is fringed with historic port towns and scenic peninsulas. Spend your time in County Cork enjoying the bustling, historic maritime town of Kinsale. Pint-sized and friendly, Kinsale is delightful to visit. Thanks to the naturally sheltered bay barbed by a massive 17th-century star fort, you can submerge yourself in history, from the Spanish Armada to the sailor who inspired Daniel Defoe's *Robinson Crusoe* to the *Lusitania* (torpedoed by the Germans just off the point in 1915). Kinsale also makes a great home base (the easy-to-visit port of Cobh is nearby).

And if you just can't go home without kissing the Blarney Stone, it's a convenient stop when connecting to the Ring of Kerry or Dingle.

KINSALE IN 1 DAY

Kinsale is worth two nights and a day. Spend the morning checking out one or two of the town's sights, and make sure to take Don and Barry's excellent Kinsale walking tour (9:15 or 11:15 most days). After lunch, head out to Charles Fort for great bay views and insights into British military life in colonial Ireland. (You can drive, or take a taxi out and walk back.) On the way back, stop for a pint at the Bulman Bar. Finish the day with a good dinner and live music in a pub.

With extra time, fit in a visit to Cobh. If you have Irish roots, your ancestors likely sailed from here. Coming from Kilkenny or the Rock of Cashel, you could visit Cobh on your way to Kinsale.

ORIENTATION

Kinsale has a great natural harbor, and while the town is prettier than the actual harbor, the harbor was its reason for being. Today, Kinsale is a vibrant bustle of about 5,000 residents. Its population swells to 9,000 with the many "blow-ins" who live here each summer. The town's long and skinny old center is part modern marina (attracting wealthy yachters) and part pedestrian-friendly medieval town (attracting scalawags like us). It's an easy 20-minute stroll from end to end.

Tourist Information: The TI is at the head of the harbor (Mon-Sat 9:00-17:00, closed Sun, shorter hours in winter; tel. 021/477-2234, www.kinsale.ie).

Helpful Hints

Market: An open-air market enlivens the town square (on Market Quay) on Wednesdays in summer (9:00-14:00).

Laundry: Full-service laundry is available at **Elite Laundry** (Mon-Fri 9:00-17:30, Sat 10:00-17:00, closed Sun, The Glen, tel. 021/477-7345).

Bike Rental: Mylie Murphy's rents bikes from a handy spot near the Centra Market (€15/day, includes lock and helmet; Mon-Sat 9:30-18:00, Sun 11:00-17:00

KINSALE AT A GLANCE

In Kinsale

▲▲**Don & Barry's Kinsale Historic Stroll** Duo of fascinating guides weave through town revealing the pivotal role Kinsale played in the history of the British Empire. **Hours:** Daily tours mid-March-mid-Oct. See page 128.

▲▲**Charles Fort** Stout 17th-century fortress guarding harbor with great tour explaining British military life and featuring fine views; also the starting point of Scilly Walk—a fine harborside walk back into town. **Hours:** Daily 10:00-18:00, Nov-mid-March until 17:00. See page 132.

▲**Kinsale Regional Museum** Grab-bag of domestic and maritime knickknacks, starring *Lusitania* debris beachcombed after the famous sinking. **Hours:** Tue-Sat 10:30-13:30, closed Sun-Mon. See page 134.

Nearby

▲**Cobh** Historic port with two worthwhile sights (both open daily): Titanic Experience (simulation of the last day the ill-fated ship picked up passengers here) and Queenstown Story (Cobh's history as Ireland's busiest emigration port). See page 138.

Blarney Castle Commercial, touristy castle featuring the stone that visitors kiss to gain the gift of gab, surrounded by beautifully lush parkland. **Hours:** Mon-Sat 9:00-18:30, Sun until 18:00, later in peak season, shorter hours in winter. See page 141.

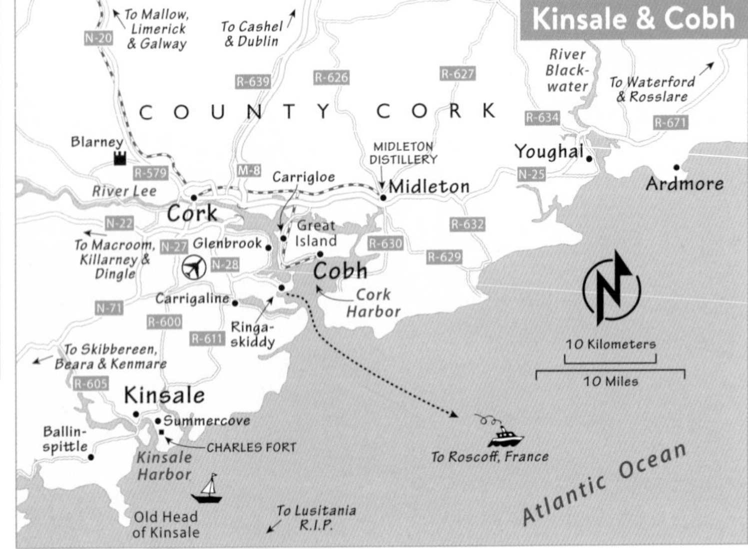

May-Aug only, shorter hours in winter; arrangements can be made for pickup or drop-off, 8 Pearse Street, tel. 021/477-2703, MylieMurphyShop@hotmail.com). They can recommend paths good for biking or walking.

Taxi: Contact **Tom Canty,** whose destinations include Cork Airport for €25 or Cork city for €30 (mobile 087-237-1022).

Rick's Tip: *On the first weekend in May, the* **Kinsale Rugby Sevens Tournament** *draws dozens of teams and hundreds of loud-and-proud, rowdy rugby fans. If you're not up for the scrum, then scram.*

Tours

▲▲DON & BARRY'S KINSALE HISTORIC STROLL

To understand the important role Kinsale played in Irish, English, and Spanish history, join gentlemen Don Herlihy or Barry Moloney on a fascinating 1.5-hour walking tour (€8, daily mid-March-mid-Oct at 11:15, also Mon-Sat at 9:15 in May-Sept, no reservation necessary, by appointment only off-season, meet outside the TI, private tours possible, tel. 021/477-2873 or 087-250-0731, www.historicstrollkinsale.com). Both guides are a joy, creatively bringing to life Kinsale's past, placing its story in the wider sweep of history, and making the stony sights more than just buildings. This walk is Kinsale's single best attraction.

GHOST WALK TOUR

This is not just any ghost tour; it's more Monty Python-style slapstick comedy than horror. Two high-energy actors

Barry and Don lead outstanding walking tours.

(Brian and David) weave funny stunts and stories into a 75-minute loose history on Kinsale's after-dark streets (€12, April-Oct Sun-Fri at 21:00, no tours Sat, leaves from The Tap Tavern, call ahead to confirm, mobile 087-948-0910). You'll spend the first 15 minutes in the back of the tavern—time to finish your drink and get to know some of the group. This tour doesn't overlap with Don and Barry's more serious historic town walk described above.

KINSALE HARBOUR CRUISE

Enjoy a 45-minute voyage around the historic harbor aboard the nimble little 50-passenger *Spirit of Kinsale*, with informative commentary from captain/historian/naturalist Jerome (€13, June-Sept daily at 14:00 and 15:00, July-Aug also at 11:00 and 12:00, one sailing per day April-May and Oct, check schedule online; departs from Pier Road in front of Acton's Hotel roughly 200 yards south of the TI; not necessary to book ahead; mobile 086-250-5456, www.kinsaleharbourcruises.com).

KINSALE TOWN WANDER

To trace our route, see the "Kinsale" map. Start on the harbor (just below the TI and across from Dinos Fish & Chips).

➲ *Self-Guided Walk*

Harborfront: The medieval walled town's economy was fueled by its harbor, where ships came to be stocked. The old walls defined the original town and created a fortified zone that facilitated the taxation of goods. In the 17th and 18th centuries, this small and easily defended harbor was busy with rich and hungry tall ships getting provisions and assembling into convoys for the trip to America.

Look for the **memorial** shaped like the mast of a tall ship, farther out toward the marina. It's a reminder that this was also a port of military consequence. Dozens of ships from the Spanish Armada could moor here, threatening England.

Clear-cutting of the once-plentiful oak forest upriver (for shipbuilding and barrel-making) hastened erosion and silted up

Wandering through colorful Kinsale

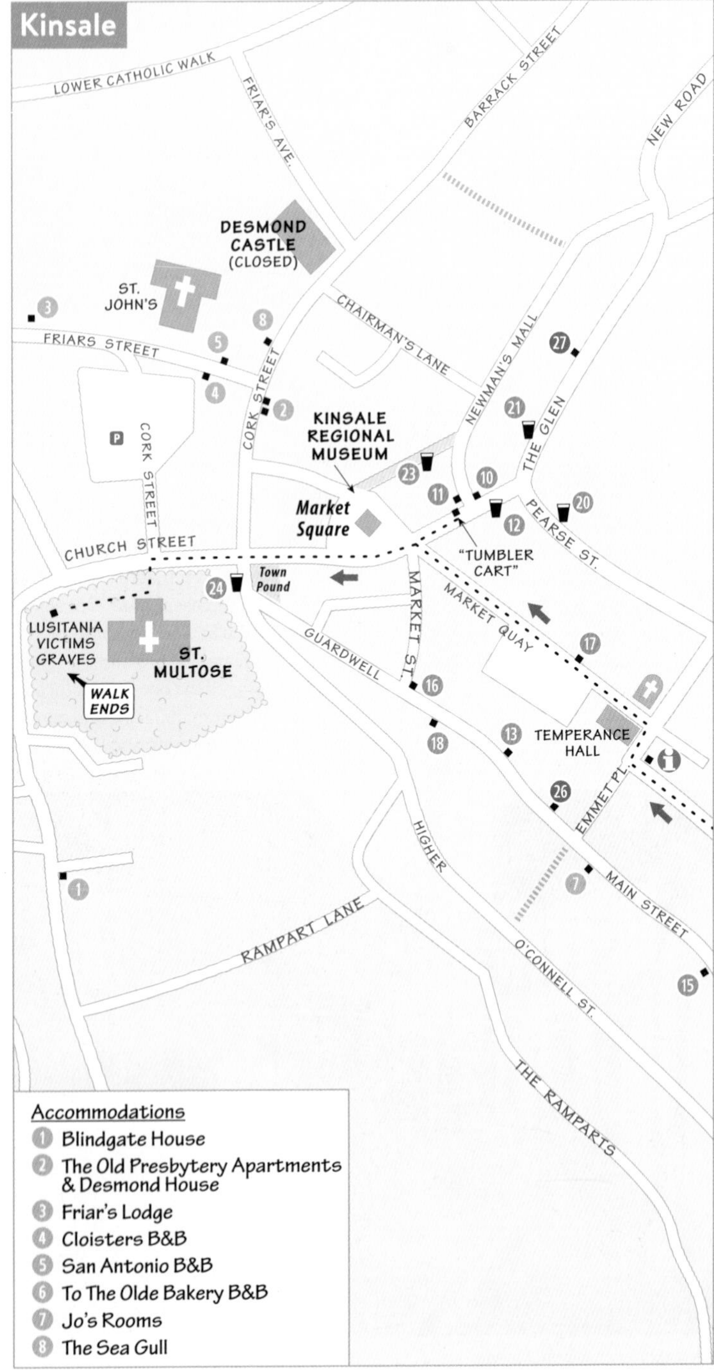
Kinsale
LOWER CATHOLIC WALK
FRIAR'S AVE.
BARRACK STREET
NEW ROAD
DESMOND CASTLE (CLOSED)
ST. JOHN'S
FRIARS STREET
CORK STREET
CHAIRMAN'S LANE
NEWMAN'S MALL
THE GLEN
KINSALE REGIONAL MUSEUM
Market Square
PEARSE ST.
"TUMBLER CART"
CHURCH STREET
Town Pound
MARKET ST.
MARKET QUAY
GUARDWELL
LUSITANIA VICTIMS GRAVES
ST. MULTOSE
WALK ENDS
TEMPERANCE HALL
EMMET PL.
HIGHER
MAIN STREET
RAMPART LANE
O'CONNELL ST.
THE RAMPARTS
Accommodations
1 Blindgate House
2 The Old Presbytery Apartments & Desmond House
3 Friar's Lodge
4 Cloisters B&B
5 San Antonio B&B
6 To The Olde Bakery B&B
7 Jo's Rooms
8 The Sea Gull

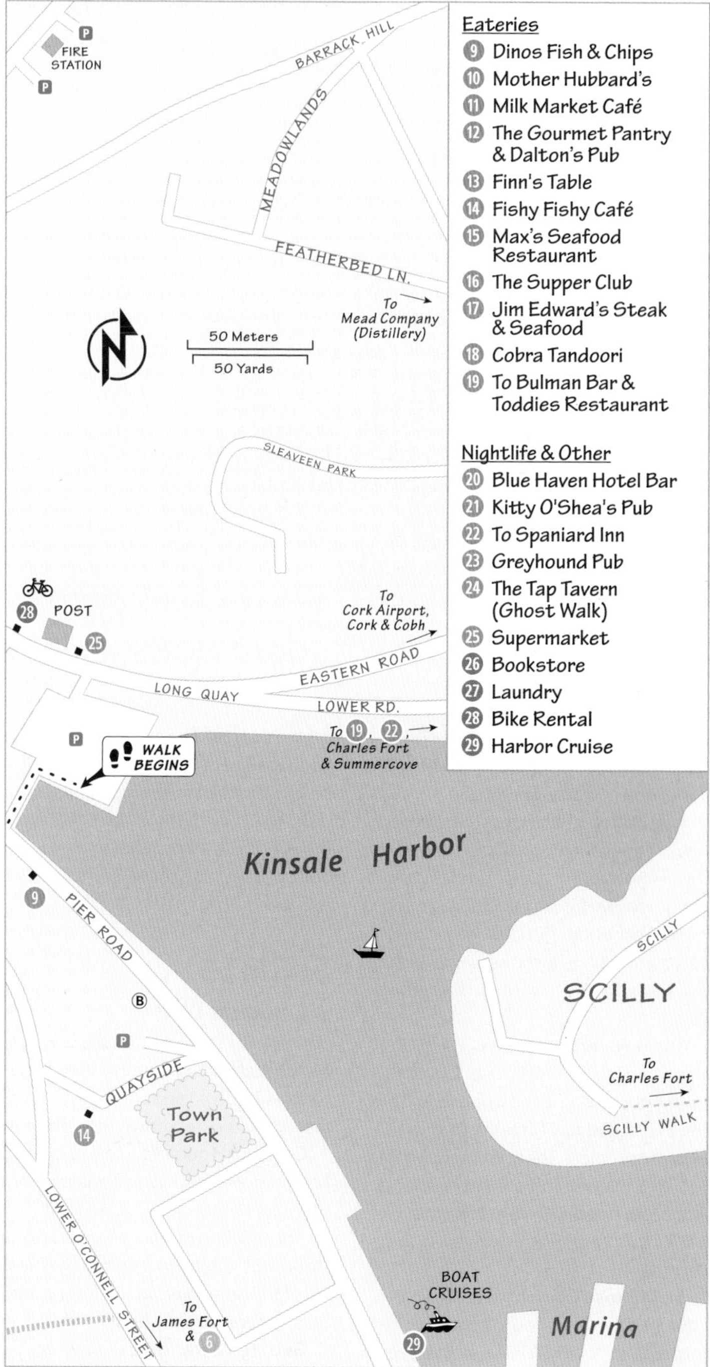

Eateries
9 Dinos Fish & Chips
10 Mother Hubbard's
11 Milk Market Café
12 The Gourmet Pantry & Dalton's Pub
13 Finn's Table
14 Fishy Fishy Café
15 Max's Seafood Restaurant
16 The Supper Club
17 Jim Edward's Steak & Seafood
18 Cobra Tandoori
19 To Bulman Bar & Toddies Restaurant
Nightlife & Other
20 Blue Haven Hotel Bar
21 Kitty O'Shea's Pub
22 To Spaniard Inn
23 Greyhound Pub
24 The Tap Tavern (Ghost Walk)
25 Supermarket
26 Bookstore
27 Laundry
28 Bike Rental
29 Harbor Cruise
FIRE STATION
BARRACK HILL
MEADOWLANDS
FEATHERBED LN.
To Mead Company (Distillery)
50 Meters
50 Yards
SLEAVEEN PARK
POST
To Cork Airport, Cork & Cobh
EASTERN ROAD
LONG QUAY
LOWER RD.
To 19, 22, Charles Fort & Summercove
WALK BEGINS
Kinsale Harbor
PIER ROAD
SCILLY
To Charles Fort
SCILLY WALK
QUAYSIDE
Town Park
LOWER O'CONNELL STREET
To James Fort & 6
BOAT CRUISES
Marina

the harbor. By the early 1800s, nearby Cobh's deep-water port took over the lion's share of shipping. Kinsale settled into a quieter existence as a fishing port.

• *From the TI, walk inland (between the Temperance Hall and the old Methodist church) up Market Quay. Take your first right on Market Street and find an old vehicle on big wheels at the Milk Market Café, across from Dalton's Pub.*

Town Center: Parked like a big flower-box is a 19th-century **"tumbler cart."** This rolled through town like a garbage service, collecting sewage from the townsfolk, then spread the human waste as fertilizer on the fields outside of town.

Study the green metal medieval **Kinsale model** (c. 1381) and the information panel on the wall with another map. It shows the narrow confines of the town, hiding behind its once-proud walls, before much of the bay was reclaimed. You can see how the wall lined the main street along the tidal flats. The subtle curves of Main Street trace the original coastline. (Walking this street, you'll see tiny lanes leading to today's harbor. These originated as piers—just wide enough to roll a barrel down to an awaiting ship.)

Find **Dalton's Pub** across the street—one of 25 pubs in this small but never-thirsty town. This is one of many inviting local pubs famous for live folk and traditional music.

• *Backtrack to cross Market Square, pass the old courthouse (now the Regional Museum), and take Church Street to a vacant little lot across from The Tap Tavern.*

Town Pound: This small enclosure was where goods and livestock used to be impounded until the owner could pay the associated tax. After the town wall became obsolete, the townspeople disassembled the wall and used its ready-cut stones for building projects like this.

• *Walk uphill past The Tap Tavern to the church.*

St. Multose Church: This Anglican church (open after noon) comes with a fortress-like tower. While rebuilt in recent centuries, it goes back to the Middle Ages. In its very proper Anglican interior, you'll see a list of vicars going back to 1377. The humble base of the baptismal font dates from the 6th century.

• *Leave the church and turn left, walking around the outside of it to the west end (facing most of the graves).*

Check out the **old doorway** into the church. These days, this door is always locked, but it was once the main entrance. Notice the worn lines scratched into the stone around eye level. Oliver Cromwell's soldiers garrisoned in the church in the mid-1600s and sharpened their swords on the doorway. Facing this door you can tell there were (not surprisingly) more right-handed swordsmen.

• *Walk back to the current main entrance (north side of church), then walk 20 paces, veering left and uphill to two gray, concrete-bordered, grass-covered graves (near the gate to the street).*

***Lusitania* Victim Graves:** This remembers "Victims of the *Lusitania* Outrage 1915." Nine months into World War I, just off the coast of Kinsale, the Germans torpedoed the *Lusitania* with 128 Americans on board. It sank within 20 minutes, and more than half of the 2,000 passengers drowned. This tragedy led to the United States going "over there" and joining what was called "The Great War."

SIGHTS

▲▲CHARLES FORT

Strategically set to be the gatekeeper for this critical harbor, Kinsale's star-shaped Charles Fort is a testimony to the importance of this little town in the 17th century.

Cost and Hours: €5, daily 10:00-18:00, Nov-mid-March until 17:00, last entry one hour before closing, café a half-mile southeast of town, tel. 021/477-2263.

Good, free guided tours cover the harsh life of British soldiers at the fort (45 minutes, generally on the hour).

Getting There: You can drive, taxi, walk

Kinsale Is Key

Kinsale's remarkable harbor has made this an important port since prehistoric times. Its importance peaked during the 16th, 17th, and 18th centuries, when it was the gateway to both Spain and France—potentially providing a base for either of these two powers in cutting off English shipping.

In about 1500, the pope divided newly discovered lands outside Europe between Spain and Portugal. With the Reformation breaking Rome's lock on Europe, maritime powers such as England were ignoring the pope's grant. England threatened Spain's New World piñata, and Ireland was Catholic. Spain had an economic and a religious reason to defend the pope and Catholicism. The showdown between Spain and England for mastery of the seas was in Ireland. The excuse: to rescue the dear Catholics of Ireland from the terrible treachery of Protestant England.

So the Irish disaster unfolded. The powerful Ulster chieftains Hugh O'Neill and Red Hugh O'Donnell and their clans had been on a roll in their guerilla battles against the English. With Spanish aid, they figured they could drive the English out of Ireland. In 1601, a Spanish fleet dropped off 3,000 soldiers, who established a beachhead in Kinsale. After the ships left, the Spaniards were pinned down in Kinsale by the English commander. In harsh winter conditions, virtually the entire Irish-clan fighting force left the north and marched to the south coast, thinking they could liberate their Spanish allies and win freedom from England.

The numbers seemed reasonable (8,000 Englishmen versus 3,000 Spaniards with 7,000 Irish clansmen approaching). The Irish attacked on Christmas Eve in 1601. But, holding the high ground around fortified and Spanish-occupied Kinsale, the relatively small English force kept the Spaniards hemmed in, leaving the bulk of the English troops to rout the fighting Irish, who were adept at ambushes but not at open-field warfare.

The Irish resistance was broken, and its leaders fled to Europe (the "flight of the Earls"). England made peace with Spain and began the "plantation" of mostly Scottish Protestants in Ireland (the seeds of the long-running Troubles in Ulster). England ruled the waves, and it ruled Ireland. The lesson: Kinsale is key. England eventually built two huge, star-shaped fortresses to ensure control of the narrow waterway.

(see the "Scilly Walk," next), or take bus #253, which runs a few times daily from the bus stop on Pier Road.

Visiting the Fort: When built, Charles Fort was Britain's biggest star-shaped fort—a state-of-the-art defense when artillery made the traditional castle obsolete (low, thick walls were tougher for cannons to breach than the tall, thinner walls of older castles). The star design made defending any attack on its walls safer and more effective. Notice how the strongest walls face the sea and how the oldest buildings are crouched down below the potential cannon fire of attacking ships.

The British occupied this fort until Irish independence in 1922. Its interior buildings were torched in 1923 by anti-treaty IRA forces to keep it from being used by Free

Charles Fort guards Kinsale harbor.

State troops during the Irish Civil War. While most of the fort is just ruined buildings with nice views, there is an important exhibit filling two floors of the Barracks Stores building (the tall intact building, just below and to the right of the entry).

Nearby: For a beer or meal nearby, try the recommended **Bulman Bar** in Summercove, 100 yards downhill where the road runs low near the water on the way back to town (with small parking lot).

SCILLY WALK (KINSALE TO CHARLES FORT)

The 45-minute walk between Kinsale and Charles Fort offers a delightful chance to connect the town with its top historic attraction. Along the way you'll pass great harbor views, quaint cottages, dry-stone walls, and the recommended Bulman Bar. While the couple of hundred yards at the beginning and end are along roads without sidewalks, the middle 80 percent of the walk is along a peaceful, pedestrian-only trail through lush vegetation. From Kinsale, follow the Lower Road east until you wind around onto Scilly peninsula. From the fort, look for *Scilly Walk* signs on the left when walking toward town (near top of hill, 100 yards beyond Bulman Bar).

DESMOND CASTLE

This 15th-century fortified customs house (at the top of Cork Street) has had a long and varied history (but is currently closed to visitors). It was the Spanish armory during Spain's 1601 occupation of Kinsale, a British prison during the Napoleonic Wars, and a famine-relief center in the late 1840s. In its days as the customs house, this evocative little tower was an important cog in the international wine trade. In the late Middle Ages, local merchants traded their top-quality wooden casks for casks full of wine. Later, Kinsale became a "designated wine port" for tax-collection purposes.

▲KINSALE REGIONAL MUSEUM

In the center of the Old Town, this modest museum is worth a quick visit for its fun mishmash of domestic and maritime bygones. Its Dutch architecture reflects the influence of Dutch-born King William of Orange at the end of the 1600s. Among its exhibits, the museum gives a good perspective on the controversial *Lusitania*

Desmond Castle

tragedy. Drop by at least to read the fun 1788 tax code for all Kinsale commercial transactions (outside the front door).

Cost and Hours: Free, Tue-Sat 10:30-13:30, closed Sun-Mon, staffed by volunteers—hours can be erratic, Market Square, tel. 021/477-7930.

KINSALE MEAD COMPANY

A tour of this working distillery in a modern warehouse on the outskirts of Kinsale offers a rare opportunity to learn about (and taste) mead, a wine made with honey that's one of the world's oldest alcoholic drinks.

Cost and Hours: €12, best to book in advance; hour-long tours Tue-Sun at 13:00, 15:00, and 17:00, closed Mon; Nov-March Fri-Sun only at 13:00 and 15:00; 15-minute walk east of town center, located at Unit 5, Barracks Lane, Troopers-Close, tel. 021/477-3538, www.kinsalemeadco.ie.

EXPERIENCES

Live Folk and Traditional Music

In the Town Center: Kinsale's pubs are packed with atmosphere and live music (more likely folk, but plenty of traditional Irish, too). Rather than target a certain place, simply walk the area between Guardwell, Pearse Street, and the Market Square. Music starts up after 21:00—you'll hear it as you wander. **Dalton's Pub** hosts informal amateur sessions with locals after 21:00 (grab a seat by 20:30). The **Blue Haven Hotel Bar** and **Kitty O'Shea's** are also good bets.

Outside of Town: Irish music purists can get their trad fix at the charmingly claustrophobic **Spaniard Inn,** a 10-minute walk out to the Scilly peninsula across the harbor from town. The darkly atmospheric interior is about the size of a rail car, so only about 10 seats get an actual view of the musicians (weekend nights at 21:30, arrive before 20:30 to avoid standing all night, tel. 021/477-2436).

Pubs for Craic Rather than Music

For conversation or an introspective pint, I like the **Greyhound** (off Newman's Mall, behind the Milk Market Café)—no live music, just a scruffy, multichambered throwback with no pretense. Another joint filled with characters who haven't changed in decades is **The Tap Tavern** (corner of Church Street and Guardwell). It's presided over by Mary O'Neill, the unofficial godmother of Kinsale, and her slyly humorous son Brian, who runs the town's recommended ghost tours.

SLEEPING

Kinsale is a popular place in summer for yachters and golfers. It's wise to book your room in advance. These places are all within a 15-minute walk of the town center.

$$$ Blindgate House, high up on the fringe of town behind St. Multose Church, offers 11 pristine rooms in fine modern comfort (tel. 021/477-7858, mobile 087-237-6676, www.blindgatehouse.com, info@blindgatehouse.com, Maeve Coakley).

$$$ The Old Presbytery Apartments, occupy a fine, quiet house that's been converted into four lovely apartments. Daily light breakfast is included. The rooms are stocking-feet cozy, and Noreen McEvoy runs the place with a passion for excellence (2-night minimum, RS%, family rooms, private parking, 43 Cork Street, tel. 021/477-2027, www.oldpres.com, info@oldpres.com).

$$$ Desmond House, next door to the Old Presbytery, has four spotless, tastefully furnished rooms and tons of space to stretch out. Grainne Barnett takes pride in her homemade bread served with their fine breakfast (private parking, 42 Cork Street, tel. 021/477-3575, mobile 087-205-5566, www.desmondhousekinsale.com, desmondhouse@gmail.com).

$$$ Friar's Lodge is a slate-shingled hotel perched on the hill past St. John's Catholic Church (and frequently booked up by Rick Steves tours). What its 17 spacious rooms lack in Old World character, they make up for in dependable quality (family rooms, private parking, 5 Friar Street, tel. 021/477-7384, www.friars-lodge.com, mtierney@indigo.ie).

$$ Cloisters B&B has four snug but bright and inviting rooms with a friendly atmosphere fostered by Orla Kenneally and Aileen Healy (2 Friars Street, tel. 021/470-0680, www.cloisterskinsale.com, info@cloisterskinsale.com).

$$ San Antonio B&B is a 200-year-old house with five rooms and a funky feel, lovingly looked after by gentleman Jimmie Conron (cash only, 1 Friar Street, tel. 021/477-2341, mobile 086-878-9800, jimmiesan@yahoo.ie).

$ The Olde Bakery B&B makes you feel at home with three quilt-bedded rooms and charmingly chatty hostess Chrissie Quigley. This friendly tech-free gem can only be booked by phone (cash only, 56 Lower O'Connell Street, tel. 021/477-3012).

$ Jo's Rooms is a good value, offering five fresh, practical rooms in the center of town (breakfast extra in downstairs café, cash only, small rooms with smaller double beds, 55 Main Street, mobile 087-948-1026, www.joskinsale.com, joskinsale@gmail.com).

$ The Sea Gull, perched up the hill right next to Desmond Castle, offers four retro-homey rooms. It's run by Mary O'Neill, who also runs The Tap Tavern down the hill (RS%, cash only, Cork Street, tel. 021/477-2240, mobile 087-241-6592, marytap@iol.ie).

EATING

Back in the 1990s, when Ireland was just getting its cuisine act together, Kinsale was the island's self-proclaimed gourmet capital. While good restaurants are commonplace in Irish towns today, Kinsale still has an edge at mealtime. Reservations are smart, especially if eating late or on a weekend. Restaurant connoisseurs can check the menu details of Kinsale's top restaurants at www.kinsalerestaurants.com.

Picnickers seek out the **SuperValu** supermarket (daily until 21:00, New Road).

Cheap and Cheery

$ Dinos Fish & Chips, with big windows overlooking the harbor, is a fun and family-friendly chain for budget fish-and-chips (daily 9:00-21:30, across from the TI, tel. 021/477-4561). **$ Mother Hubbard's,** tiny with six tables near Market Square, serves all-day breakfast, toasties, sandwiches, and salads (daily 8:30-15:00,

1 Market Street, tel. 021/477-2440).
$ Milk Market Café—right next door—is a hit with kids, offering burgers, pizza, and fish-and-chips (daily 10:00-18:00, 3 Market Street). **$ The Gourmet Pantry** is an above-average takeout option (Mon-Sat 9:00-18:00, Sun 10:30-17:30, 4 Market Street, tel. 021/470-9215).

Good Dinners in the Old Center

$$$$ Finn's Table is dressy, refined, and romantic. John Finn cooks and Julie Finn serves enticing dinner plates ranging from lamb to lobster. Meat is their passion—John comes from a long line of butchers and still gets the best cuts from his dad's butcher shop. Their three-course early-bird menu, served until 18:30, makes this pricey place more affordable (Thu-Tue 18:00-22:00, closed Wed; Nov-April Thu-Sat only, if open at all; 6 Main Street, tel. 021/470-9636, www.finnstable.com).

$$$ Fishy Fishy Café, a high-energy destination seafood restaurant with spacious seating (indoor, balcony, and terrace) and a wonderful menu, is run by Martin and Maria Shanahan. It's a good lunch or early dinner option. Martin's culinary prowess has led him to host a weekly cooking show on Irish TV (daily 12:00-21:00, reservations recommended, Pier Road, tel. 021/470-0415, www.fishyfishy.ie).

$$$ Max's Seafood Restaurant is spacious and stylish, but not overly romantic. There's no pretense—the focus is simply on great seafood. Chef Olivier Queva from France offers a fresh and classic selection and a French flair (nice wines by the glass), while wife Anne Marie serves. While this place gets pricey, there's a good early-bird special until 19:15 (daily 18:00-21:30, 48 Main Street, tel. 021/477-2443).

$$$ The Supper Club is a linen-and-leather upmarket joint with a meat smoker, strong cocktails, and creative desserts (Tue-Sat 17:30-22:30, closed Sun-Mon, 2 Main Street, tel. 021/470-9233).

$$$ Jim Edward's Steak & Seafood Restaurant and Bar is an energetic place that's a favorite for its steaks, seafood, and vegetables. Choose between the restaurant's maritime setting or the more intimate, pub-like bar (same menu, bar open daily 12:00-22:00, restaurant from 18:00, Market Quay, tel. 021/477-2541).

$$ Cobra Tandoori is good for tasty Punjabi/Indian cuisine (daily 16:00-23:00, 69 Main Street, tel. 021/477-7911).

Near Charles Fort

$$$ Bulman Bar and Toddies Restaurant serves seafood with seasonal produce. The mussels are especially tasty; on a balmy day or evening, diners take a bucket and a beer out to the seawall. This is the only way to eat on the water in Kinsale. The **$$ pub,** sporting a big fireplace, is also good for a coffee or beer after your visit to Charles Fort (pub open daily 12:30-21:00, restaurant open Tue-Sat from 18:30, 200 yards toward Kinsale from Charles Fort in hamlet of Summercove, tel. 021/477-2131).

TRANSPORTATION

Arriving and Departing

By Bus

The closest train station is in Cork, 15 miles north. Buses run frequently between Kinsale (stop is on Pier Road, 100 yards behind TI) and Cork's bus station (14/day Mon-Sat, fewer on Sun, 50 minutes).

In **Cork,** the bus station and train station are a 10-minute walk apart. The bus station (corner of Merchant's Quay and Parnell Place) is on the south bank of the River Lee, just over the nearest bridge from the train station (north of the river on Lower Glanmire Road).

From Cork by Train to: Dublin (hourly, 2.5 hours, www.irishrail.ie).

From Cork by Bus to: Dublin (every 2 hours, 3.5 hours), **Galway** (hourly, 4.5 hours), **Tralee** (hourly, 2.5 hours), **Kilkenny** (7/day, 2.5 hours, www.dublincoach.ie). Bus info: Tel. 021/450-8188 or www.buseireann.ie.

By Car

Drivers should park and walk. The most central lot is at the head of the harbor behind the TI (pay-and-display, exact change required, 2-hour maximum, enforced Mon-Sat 10:30-18:00, free on Sun). A big, safe, free parking lot is across the street from St. Multose Church at the top of town, a 5-minute walk from most recommended hotels and restaurants. An even larger free lot is east of town by the fire station (10-minute walk). Street parking is pay-and-display. Outlying streets, a 10-minute stroll from the action, have wide-open parking.

By Plane

Cork Airport is handy for travelers starting or ending their trip in southern Ireland (located four miles south of Cork city, on N-27/R-600 to Kinsale, a 30-minute drive away, code: ORK, tel. 021/431-3131, www.corkairport.com). Airport buses run to Kinsale (2/hour, 30 minutes, www.buseireann.ie).

NEAR KINSALE

Cobh

If your ancestry is Irish, there's a good chance that Cobh, rated ▲, was the last Irish soil your ancestors had under their feet. Cobh (pronounced "cove") was the major port of Irish emigration in the 19th century. Of the six million Irish who have emigrated to America, Canada, and Australia since 1815, nearly half left from Cobh.

The first steam-powered ship to make a transatlantic crossing departed from Cobh in 1838—cutting the journey time from 50 days to 18. When Queen Victoria came to Ireland for the first time in 1849, Cobh was the first Irish ground she set foot on. Giddy, the town renamed itself "Queenstown" in her honor. It was still going by that name in 1912, when the *Titanic* made its final fateful stop here before heading out on its maiden (and only) voyage. To celebrate their new independence from British royalty in 1922, locals changed the town's name back to its original Irish moniker. Today the town's deep harbor attracts dozens of cruise ships per year (with their large packs of eager visitors).

Orientation

Cobh sits on a large island in Cork Harbor, connected to the mainland via a short bridge (on the north shore) and a drive-on ferry (on the west shore). The town's inviting waterfront is colorful yet salty, with a playful promenade. The butcher's

St. Colman's Cathedral is a Cobh landmark.

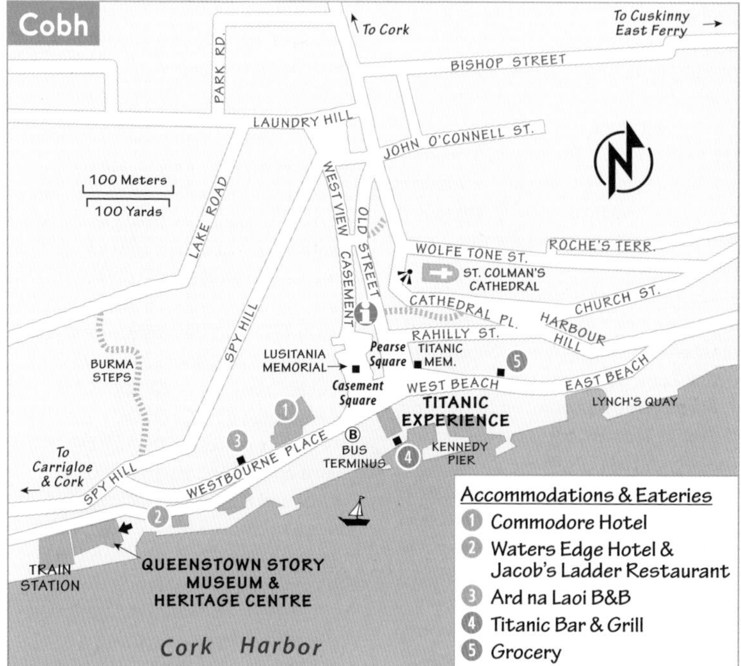

advertisement reads, "Always pleased to meet you and always with meat to please you." Stroll past the shops along the water. Ponder the large and dramatic *Lusitania* memorial on Casement Square and the modest *Titanic* memorial nearby on Pearse Square.

A hike up the hill to the towering Neo-Gothic St. Colman's Cathedral rewards you with a fine view of the port. To get to the cathedral, walk behind the *Lusitania* memorial, go under the stone arch, and strut up steep Westview Street, passing the photogenic row of colorful houses on your right (nicknamed the "deck of cards" by locals). After panting your way to the top, turn right—you can't miss the cathedral steeple.

Tourist Information: The TI is in the old courthouse at the base of Westview Street, inside of the arch on the left wall as you head uphill (Mon-Fri 9:00-17:30, Sat-Sun 10:30-16:30, tel. 021/481-3301, www.cobhharbourchamber.ie).

Walking Tours: Michael Martin and his staff lead one-hour **Titanic Trail** walking tours that give you unexpected insights into the tragic *Titanic* and *Lusitania* voyages, Spike Island, and Cobh's maritime history (€13, RS%—show this book when you pay, daily at 11:00, also 14:00 in summer with required advance booking, call ahead to confirm tour times in winter, private tours available, meet in lobby of Commodore Hotel, tel. 021/481-5211, mobile 087-276-7218, www.titanic.ie, info@titanic.ie).

Getting There

If you're **driving** to Cobh from either Cork or Waterford, exit N-25 about 8 miles (13 km) east of Cork, following little R-624 over a bridge, onto the Great Island, and directly into Cobh.

Cork's Kent Station has frequent **train** service to Cobh (hourly, usually departs on the hour and returns on the half-hour, 25 minutes, www.irishrail.ie).

Sights

▲THE TITANIC EXPERIENCE

It's stirring to think that this modest little port town was the ship's final anchorage—and the last chance to get off. Occupying the former White Star Line building where the *Titanic*'s final passengers boarded, this compact museum packs a decent punch as it recounts the story of the ship and its final moments.

Cost and Hours: €10; daily 9:00-18:00, Oct-April until 17:30, last entry 45 minutes before closing; Casement Square, tel. 021/481-4412, www.titanicexperiencecobh.ie.

Visiting the Museum: As you look off the back balcony into the harbor, note the decayed pilings in front of you. These once supported the old pier and represent the passengers' last chance to turn back. One lucky surviving crewman with a premonition did.

Inside the museum, you travel room to room with your host, the ship's fourth mate, in audiovisual form. He meets you at the boarding dock, full of pride in the new vessel. He joins you in replicas of a posh first-class cabin and a no-frills third-class cabin before his commentary is interrupted by the sound of ice tearing at the hull. You then enter an exhibition room featuring an animation that silently depicts the ship sinking in its steel-twisting, slow-motion ballet to the bottom (settling as two crunched hulls 600 yards apart and 12,000 feet deep).

The last stop is a room highlighting the luxurious ship's innovative firsts. It was one of the first equipped with a wireless "Marconi room" to send messages from sea to shore—or to other ships. *Titanic* was the first ever to issue an SOS message by Morse code. Another wall explains in grim detail the effects of hypothermia on the human body.

Before you leave, check out the list of 123 passengers who boarded the *Titanic* in Cobh. Your entry ticket has one of these passenger's names on it. See if you survived (you've got a 30 percent chance). A passenger with the same name as one of this book's co-authors is listed among the third-class passengers lost.

▲THE QUEENSTOWN STORY

Filling a harborside Victorian train station, this museum is an earnest attempt to make the city's history come to life. The topics—the Famine, Irish emigration, Australia-bound prison ships, the sinking of the *Lusitania,* and the ill-fated voyage of the *Titanic*—are interesting enough to make it a worthwhile stop. Before departing, walk over to the Annie Moore statue next to the water, 25 yards from the front door. She emigrated from Cobh and was the first person to be processed through Ellis Island when it opened on January 1, 1892.

Cost and Hours: €10, includes audioguide; Mon-Sat 9:30-18:00, Sun from 11:00, Nov-April until 17:00, last entry one hour before closing; Cobh Heritage Centre, handy café, tel. 021/481-3591, www.cobhheritage.com.

Nearby: Those with Irish roots to trace can use the Heritage Centre's **genealogy search service,** located right across from the Queenstown Story ticket booth. Since Cobh was the primary Irish emigration port, this can be a great place to start your search (€50/hour consultation and research assistance by appointment only, email ahead to book—genealogy@cobhheritage.com). For more on tracing your Irish roots, see the sidebar in Practicalities.

Sleeping

These hotels are all centrally located near the harbor.

$$$ Commodore Hotel is a grand 170-year-old historic landmark with 40 rooms (Westbourne Place, www.commodorehotel.ie). **$$$ Waters Edge Hotel** has 19 bright, modern rooms and a pleasant harbor-view restaurant (Yacht Club Quay, www.watersedgehotel.ie). **$ Ard na Laoi B&B** is a friendly place with five fresh rooms in a great central location (cash only, 15 Westbourne Place, www.ardnalaoi.ie, Michael O'Shea).

Eating

The nicest place in town is the **$$$ Titanic Bar & Grill,** sunken under the Titanic Experience, with fun outdoor seating on fine days. I also like **$$$ Jacob's Ladder** restaurant in the Waters Edge Hotel, with another great outdoor deck option. For picnic fixings, there's the **Centra Market,** facing the water on West Beach Street.

Blarney Castle

If you're driving between Kinsale and the Ring of Kerry, it's easy to stop here, though many find it a tourist trap. The town of Blarney is of no importance, and the 15th-century Blarney Castle is an empty hulk. It's only famous as the place of tourist pilgrimage, where busloads line up to kiss a stone on its top rampart and get "the gift of gab." After a day of tour groups mindlessly climbing up here to perform this ritual, the stone can be literally slathered with spit and lipstick.

The tradition goes back to the late 16th century, when Queen Elizabeth I was trying to plant loyal English settlers in Ireland to tighten her grip on the rebellious island. She demanded that the Irish clan chiefs recognize the Crown, rather than the clan chiefs, as the legitimate title-holder of all lands. One of those chiefs was Cormac MacCarthy, Lord of Blarney Castle (who was supposedly loyal to the queen). He was smart enough never to disagree with the queen—instead, he would cleverly avoid acquiescing to her demands by sending a never-ending stream of lengthy and deceptive excuses, disguised with liberal doses of flattery (while subtly maintaining his native Gaelic loyalties). In her frustration, the queen declared his endless words nothing but "blarney."

While the castle is a shell, the surrounding grounds are beautiful and well kept, and the fine gardens and lush forested Rock Close are photogenic.

Cost and Hours: €18, cheaper online; Mon-Sat 9:00-18:30, Sun until 18:00, later in peak season, shorter hours in winter; free parking lot, helpful TI, tel. 021/438-5252, www.blarneycastle.ie.

Getting There: It's 5 miles (8 km) northwest of Cork, 20 miles northwest of Cobh, and 24 miles north of Kinsale.

Kissing the Blarney Stone

Kenmare & the Ring of Kerry

It's no wonder that, since Victorian times, visitors have been attracted to this dramatic chunk of Ireland. Mysterious ancient ring forts stand sentinel on mossy hillsides. Early Christian hermit-monks left a lonely imprint of their devotion, in the form of simple stone dwellings atop an isolated rock crag far from shore...a holy retreat on the edge of the then-known world. And beloved Irish statesman Daniel O'Connell maintained his ancestral estate here, far from 19th-century politics.

Today, it seems like every tour bus in Ireland makes the ritual loop around the scenic Ring of Kerry, using the bustling and famous tourist town of Killarney as a springboard. Killarney National Park is gorgeous and well worth driving through. But I prefer to skip Killarney town (useful only for its transportation connections). Instead, make the tidy town of Kenmare your home base, and use my suggestions to cleverly circle the much-loved peninsula—entirely missing the convoy of tour buses.

If you have time for only one peninsula tour, I recommend Dingle's Slea Head Loop. But with more time, you could do both. For a comparison of the two peninsulas, see the sidebar on page 155.

KENMARE & THE RING OF KERRY IN 1 DAY

All you need in compact Kenmare is one night and an early start the next day to drive the Ring of Kerry. Without a car, you can take a private tour from Kenmare, though it's not as enjoyable as driving the loop yourself.

Coming to Kenmare from Kinsale, you'll likely drive through the town of Killarney. After Killarney, you can see any of these sights on your way to Kenmare: Muckross House, Killarney National Park, and the Kissane Sheep Farm.

Ideally, arrive in Kenmare by late afternoon and see the town's sights, then get an early start on the Ring of Kerry in the morning. After driving the Ring, head to Dingle for the night. (Don't attempt to depart Kinsale, drive the entire Ring, and reach Dingle all in one day.)

Hardy hikers might consider adding another day to visit the rugged island of Skellig Michael, which requires an overnight in Portmagee or St. Finian's Bay. Be aware that boats can book up months in advance, and bad weather can cancel boat crossings.

KENMARE

Cradled in a lush valley, this charming little town (known as Neidín, "little nest" in Irish) hooks you right away with its rows of vividly colored shop fronts and go-for-a-stroll atmosphere. The nearby finger of the gentle sea feels more like a large lake (called the Kenmare River, just to confuse things). Far from the assembly-line tourism of Killarney town, Kenmare (rhymes with "been there") also makes a great launchpad for enjoying the sights along the road around the Iveragh (eev-er-AH) Peninsula—known to shamrock lovers everywhere as the Ring of Kerry.

Orientation

Carefully planned Kenmare is shaped like an "X," forming two triangles. The upper (northern) triangle contains the town square—where fairs and markets have been held for centuries (colorful market Wed in summer), the adjacent TI and Heritage Centre, and a cozy park. The lower (southern) triangle contains three one-way streets busy with shops, lodgings, and restaurants. Use the tall Holy Cross Church spire to get your bearings (next to the northeast parking lot, handy public WC across the street).

Tourist Information: The helpful TI on the town square offers "The Trail," a brochure with a short self-guided tour; they occasionally have €10 1.5-hour guided town walks (TI open Mon-Sat 9:30-17:30; closed Thu in spring and fall, Sun year-round, and all of Nov-March; tel. 064/664-1233, www.kenmare.ie).

Helpful Hints

Laundry: O'Shea's Cleaners and Launderette offers daily self-service and Monday-Friday drop-off service (Mon-Sat 9:00-20:00, Sun 12:00-18:00; across from Lansdowne Arms Hotel on Main Street, hidden in back of O'Shea's photography shop, tel. 064/664-0808).

Bike Rental: Finnegan's Corner rents bikes and has route maps and advice on maximizing scenery and minimizing traffic (standard bike-€15/day, €20/24 hours, beefed-up road bike-€30/day; Mon-Sat 9:30-18:30, July-Aug until 19:00; Sun 12:00-18:00; leave ID for deposit, office in gift shop at 37 Henry Street, tel. 064/664-1083, www.finneganscycles.com).

Taxi: Try **Murnane Cabs** (mobile 087-236-4353) or **Kenmare Coach and Cab** (mobile 087-248-0800).

Tours: Finnegan's Tours runs day tours with guides who provide casual, anecdotal

Welcome to Kenmare.

KENMARE & THE RING OF KERRY AT A GLANCE

In Kenmare

Kenmare Lace and Design Centre Modest cubbyhole with lovingly displayed examples of the lacemaking craftsmanship that put Kenmare on the map. **Hours:** Mon-Sat 10:15-17:00, closed off-season and Sun year-round. See page 147.

Ancient Stone Circle One of Ireland's most intact and easily accessible stone circles—more than 3,000 years old. See page 148.

The Ring of Kerry

▲▲▲Ring of Kerry Loop Drive Famous, scenic 135-mile loop road, featuring Iron Age ring forts, Daniel O'Connell's Derrynane estate, and grand views of the rugged coast and islands. See page 155.

▲▲Kissane Sheep Farm Working sheep farm on scenic hillside, with demonstrations of sheep shearing and dog herding. **Hours:** Most afternoons April-Oct by appointment only (minimum 20 people), closed Sun and Nov-March. See page 154.

▲Muckross House and ▲Muckross Traditional Farms Fine lakeside manor house surrounded by lush gardens, adjacent to folk park devoted to rural farm life over the past 200 years. **Hours:** House—daily 9:00-18:00, July-Aug until 19:00. Farms—daily June-Aug 10:00-18:00, May and Sept from 13:00, March-April and Oct Sat-Sun only 13:00-18:00, closed Nov-Feb. See page 152.

▲Killarney National Park Ireland's best national park, laced with hiking trails, waterfalls, and drives through old-growth forests dotted with postcard views of the lakes of Killarney. See page 153.

Side Trip

▲▲▲Skellig Michael A craggy pinnacle of an island, topped with monks' huts, reachable by a boat from Portmagee, then a steep hike—an excursion for hardy hikers with extra time. See page 164.

Nuns' Lace

Sister Margaret Cusack, a.k.a. Sister Mary Francis Clare, lived in the town from 1862 to 1881, becoming the famous Nun of Kenmare. Her controversial religious life began when she decided to become an Anglican nun after her fiancé's sudden death. Failing to be accepted as one of Florence Nightingale's nurses during the Crimean War, she converted to Catholicism, joined the Poor Clare order as Sister Mary Francis Clare, and moved with the order to Kenmare.

Sister Clare became an outspoken writer who favored women's rights and lambasted the tyranny of the landlords during the Great Potato Famine (1845-1849). She eventually took church funds and attempted to set herself up as abbess of a convent in Knock. Her renegade behavior led to her leaving the Catholic faith, converting back to Protestantism, writing an autobiography, and lecturing about the "sinister influence of the Roman Church."

After the devastation of the famine, an industrial school was founded in Kenmare to teach trades to destitute youngsters. The school, run by the Poor Clare sisters, excelled in teaching young girls the art of lacemaking. Inspired by lace created earlier in Italy, Kenmare lace caught the eye of Queen Victoria and became much coveted by Victorian society. Examples of it are now on display in the Victoria and Albert Museum (London), the Irish National Museum (Dublin), and the US National Gallery (Washington, DC).

narration. The route depends on the day: Ring of Kerry (Mon, Wed, and Fri); Beara Peninsula (Tue); and Glengarriff and Garnish Island (Thu, all tours €40/person, reserve a day in advance by phone or 3 days in advance by email; for Sept-June, call to arrange; tel. 064/664-1491, mobile 087-248-0800, www.kenmarecoachandcab.com, info@kenmarecoachandcab.com).

Sights

HERITAGE CENTRE

This humble museum, in the back rooms of the TI, explains the nearby ancient stone circle, the history of Kenmare's lacemaking fame, and the story of a feisty, troublemaking nun (free, same hours as TI).

KENMARE LACE AND DESIGN CENTRE

A single large room above the TI displays the delicate lacework that put Kenmare on the map. From the 1860s until World War I, the Poor Clare convent at Kenmare was the center of excellence for Irish lacemaking. Inspired by antique Venetian lace, nuns created their own designs and taught needlepoint lacemaking as a trade to girls in a region struggling to get back on its feet in the wake of the catastrophic famine. Queen Victoria commissioned five pieces of lace in 1885, and by the end of the century tourists began visiting Kenmare on their way to Killarney just for a peek at the lace. Nora Finnegan, who runs the center, usually has a work in progress to demonstrate the complexity of fine lacemaking.

Cost and Hours: Free; Mon-Sat 10:15-17:00, closed off-season and Sun year-round; mobile 087-234-6998, www.kenmarelace.ie.

ANCIENT STONE CIRCLE

Of the approximately 100 stone circles that dot southwest Ireland (Counties Cork and Kerry), Kenmare's is one of the most accessible. More than 3,000 years old, the circle has a diameter of 50 feet and consists of 15 stones ringing a large center boulder (possibly a burial monument). Experts think this stone circle (like most) functioned as a celestial calendar—it tracked the position of the setting sun to determine the two solstices (in June and December).

Cost and Hours: €2, drop coins into honor box in hut by entry when attendant is away, always open.

Getting There: It's a 10-minute walk from the TI. From the city center, face the TI, turn left, and walk 200 yards down Market Street, passing a row of cute 18th-century houses on your right. Beyond the row of houses, veer right through an unmarked modern gate mounted in stone columns, and continue 50 yards down the paved road. You'll pass the entry hut on your right. The stone circle is behind the adjacent hedge.

Experiences

Horseback Riding

River Valley Riding Stables offers day treks through beautiful hill scenery (at Sheen Falls Lodge, 1.5 miles southeast of Kenmare, mobile 087-958-5895, www.kenmare.com/rivervalleystables, rivervalleystables@hotmail.com).

Boating and Hiking

Star Sailing rents boats, gives sailing lessons, and organizes hill walks. Phone ahead to reserve (daily 10:00-17:00, 5 miles southwest of Kenmare on R-571, courtesy shuttle, tel. 064/664-1222, www.staroutdoors.ie).

Golfing

Kenmare Golf Club is on the edge of town (€50, on R-569 toward Cork, tel. 064/664-1291, www.kenmaregolfclub.com). Or try the **Ring of Kerry Golf and Country Club** (€80, 4 miles west on N-70, tel. 064/664-2000, www.ringofkerrygolf.com).

Kenmare's ancient stone circle

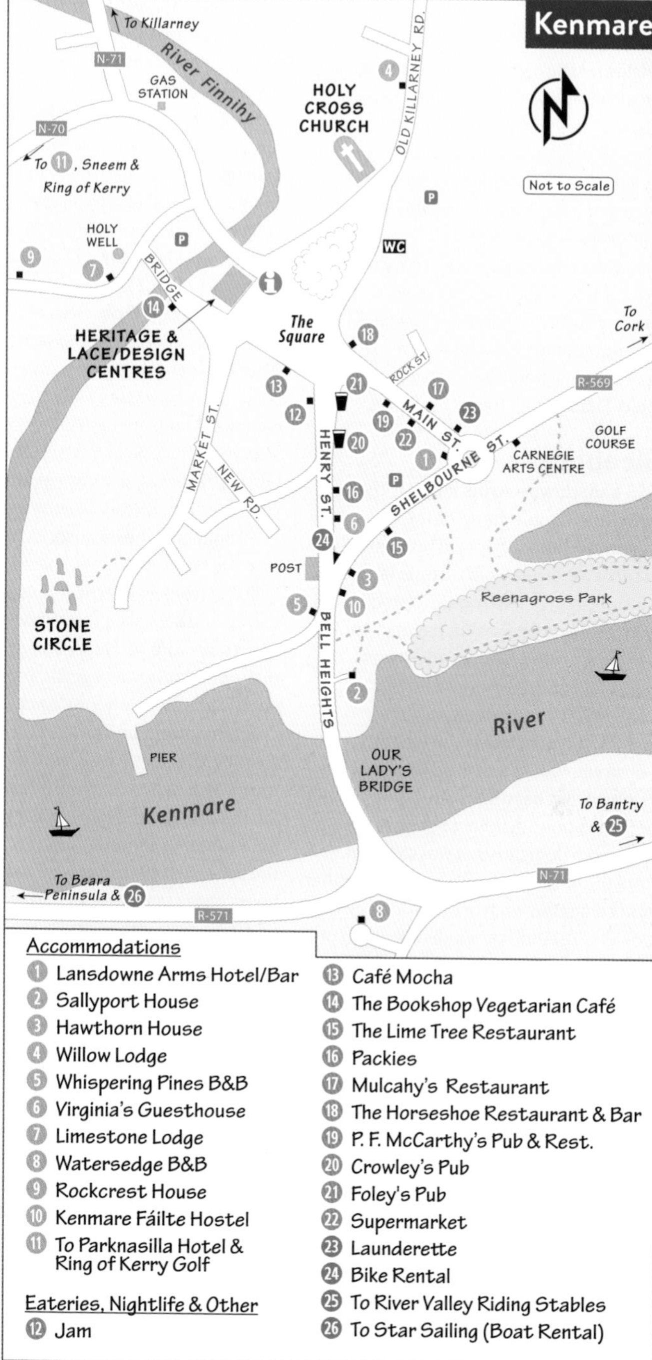
Kenmare
Not to Scale
To Killarney
N-71
River Finnihy
GAS STATION
HOLY CROSS CHURCH
OLD KILLARNEY RD.
N-70
To 11, Sneem & Ring of Kerry
HOLY WELL
BRIDGE
WC
The Square
HERITAGE & LACE/DESIGN CENTRES
To Cork
ROCK ST.
R-569
MAIN ST.
GOLF COURSE
CARNEGIE ARTS CENTRE
SHELBOURNE ST.
MARKET ST.
NEW RD.
HENRY ST.
POST
Reenagross Park
STONE CIRCLE
BELL HEIGHTS
River
PIER
OUR LADY'S BRIDGE
Kenmare
To Bantry & 25
To Beara Peninsula & 26
N-71
R-571
Accommodations
1 Lansdowne Arms Hotel/Bar
2 Sallyport House
3 Hawthorn House
4 Willow Lodge
5 Whispering Pines B&B
6 Virginia's Guesthouse
7 Limestone Lodge
8 Watersedge B&B
9 Rockcrest House
10 Kenmare Fáilte Hostel
11 To Parknasilla Hotel & Ring of Kerry Golf
Eateries, Nightlife & Other
12 Jam
13 Café Mocha
14 The Bookshop Vegetarian Café
15 The Lime Tree Restaurant
16 Packies
17 Mulcahy's Restaurant
18 The Horseshoe Restaurant & Bar
19 P. F. McCarthy's Pub & Rest.
20 Crowley's Pub
21 Foley's Pub
22 Supermarket
23 Launderette
24 Bike Rental
25 To River Valley Riding Stables
26 To Star Sailing (Boat Rental)

Nightlife

Wander the compact Kenmare town triangle and stick your head in wherever you hear something you like. Music usually starts at 21:30 (although some pubs have early 18:30 sessions—ask at the TI) and ranges from Irish traditional sessions to sing-along strummers. **Crowley's** is an atmospheric little shoebox of a pub with an unpretentious clientele. **Foley's** whiskey tube collection adorns its window, inviting you in for a folksy songfest. The recommended Lansdowne Arms Hotel sponsors live traditional sessions in their **Bold Thady Quill Bar.**

Sleeping

$$$ Lansdowne Arms Hotel is the town's venerable grand hotel, with generous public spaces. This centrally located, 200-year-old historic landmark rents 25 large, crisp rooms (music in pub until late on Fri-Sat, parking, corner of Main and Shelbourne streets, tel. 064/664-1368, www.lansdownearms.com, info@lansdownearms.com).

$$$ Sallyport House, an elegant, quiet house with five rooms filled with antique furniture, has been in Helen Arthur's family for generations. Ask her to point out the foot-worn doorstep that was salvaged from the local workhouse and built into her stone chimney (cash only, no kids, parking, closed Oct-April, 5-minute walk south of town before crossing Our Lady's Bridge, tel. 064/664-2066, www.sallyporthouse.com, port@iol.ie).

$$ Hawthorn House, a fine, modern, freestanding house with a lounge and 10 comfy rooms, is in a quiet residential location just a block from all the pub and restaurant action. Warm and friendly hostess Mary O'Brien's front parlor is an homage to her son Stephen's success on the dominant County Kerry Irish football team (family rooms, parking, Shelbourne Street, tel. 064/664-1035, www.hawthornhousekenmare.com, hawthorn@eircom.net). Mary's modern, self-catering apartment next door works well for those wanting to linger (weekly rentals).

$$ Willow Lodge, on the main road at the edge of town, feels American-suburban, with friendly hosts and seven comfortable rooms (cash only, family rooms, parking, 100 yards beyond Holy Cross Church, tel. 064/664-2301, www.willowlodgekenmare.com, willowlodgekenmare@yahoo.com, jovial Paul and talkative Gretta Gleeson-O'Byrne).

$ Whispering Pines B&B offers five rooms with sincere, traditional Irish hospitality in a spacious house warmed by the presence of hostesses Mary Fitzgerald and daughter Kathleen (cash only, closed Oct-March, at the edge of town on Bell Heights, tel. 064/664-1194, www.whisperingpineskenmare.com, wpines@eircom.net).

$ Virginia's Guesthouse, ideally located near the best restaurants, is well kept by Neil and Noreen. Its nine rooms are fresh, roomy, and appealing (breakfast extra in downstairs café, 36 Henry Street, mobile 086-306-5291, www.virginias-kenmare.com, virginias.guesthouse@gmail.com).

$ Limestone Lodge stands rock-solid beside a holy well, with five comfy rooms in a quiet location. Friendly hosts Sinead and Siobhan Thoma are experts on Kenmare's famous lace, and Casey the Jack Russell terrier is an expert at being cute (family rooms, parking, tel. 064/664-2231, mobile 087-757-4411, www.limestonelodgekenmare.com, info@limestonelodgekenmare.com).

$ Watersedge B&B is a mile south of town, serenely isolated on a forested hillside and overlooking the estuary. The modern house has four clean, colorful rooms and a kid-pleasing backyard (cash only, parking, tel. 064/664-1707, mobile 087-413-4235, www.watersedgekenmare.com, watersedgekenmare@gmail.com, Noreen and Vincent O'Shea). To get here, drive south over Our Lady's Bridge, bear left, immediately look for the B&B sign, and take the first right onto the road heading uphill. Go 100 yards up the paved road, then—at the end of the white cinder-block wall (on left)—turn right onto the private lane and drive 100 yards to the dead-end. It's worth it.

$ Rockcrest House is secluded down a quiet, leafy lane, with five large rooms and a fine front-porch view (cash only; as you pass the TI heading north out of town, take the first left after crossing the bridge; tel. 064/664-1248, mobile 087-904-3788, www.visit-kenmare.com, info@visit-kenmare.com, Marian and David O'Dwyer). Ask about their two self-catering cottage rentals.

¢ Kenmare Fáilte Hostel (FAWL-chuh) maintains 34 budget beds in a well-kept, centrally located building with more charm than most hostels (private rooms available, closed mid-Oct-April, Shelbourne Street, tel. 064/664-2333, mobile 087-711-6092, run by Finnegan's Corner bike-rental folks directly across street, www.kenmarehostel.com, info@kenmarehostel.com).

Sleeping in Luxury on the Ring of Kerry

$$$$ Parknasilla Hotel is a 19th-century hotel with 82 rooms, lost in 500 plush acres of a subtropical park overlooking the wild Atlantic Ocean. With old-fashioned service and Victorian elegance, this luxe spot is a ritual splurge for Irish families and wedding groups. Activities include boating, archery, tennis, cycling, and walks (highest rates July-Aug, tel. 064/667-5600, www.parknasillahotel.ie, reservationsinfo@parknasillahotel.ie).

Eating

Make a reservation or have dinner early, as many finer places book up on summer evenings. Pub dinners are a good value, but pub kitchens close earlier than restaurants.

Lunch

$ Jam, with soups, salads, and sandwiches, is an inviting place with delightful seating inside and out. They also make sandwiches or wraps to go for picnics (daily 8:00-17:00, 6 Henry Street, tel. 064/664-1591).

$ Café Mocha is a basic sandwich shop (daily 9:00-17:30, on the town square, tel. 064/664-2133).

$ The Bookshop Vegetarian Café is delightful for a healthy, peaceful lunch or some coffee, cakes, and pastries (daily 10:30-16:30, on Bridge Street just around the corner from the TI, tel. 064/667-9911).

Supermarket: Stock up for a Ring of Kerry picnic at **Murphy's Daybreak** (Mon-Sat 8:00-22:00, Sun 9:00-21:00, Main Street).

Dinner

$$$ The Lime Tree Restaurant occupies the former Lansdowne Estate office, which gave more than 4,000 people free passage to America in the 1840s. These days, it serves delicious, locally caught seafood in a modern yet cozy dining hall (daily 18:30-21:30, closed Nov-March, Shelbourne Street, tel. 064/664-1225, www.limetreerestaurant.com).

$$$$ Packies, a popular bistro with a leafy, low-light interior and cottage ambience, serves traditional cuisine with French influence. Their seafood gets rave reviews (Mon-Sat 17:30-22:00, closed Sun, Henry Street, tel. 064/664-1508, www.packiesrestaurant.ie).

$$$$ Mulcahy's Restaurant has a jazz-mellowed, elegant vibe and creatively presented gourmet dishes with Indian, Japanese, and American influences. There's always a good vegetarian entrée available (Thu-Tue 17:00-22:00, closed Wed, Main Street, tel. 064/664-2383, www.mulcahyskenmare.ie).

$$$ The Horseshoe Restaurant and Bar, specializing in steak and spareribs, somehow turns rustic farm-tool decor into a romantic candlelit sanctuary (daily 17:00-22:00, 3 Main Street, tel. 064/664-1553, www.thehorseshoekenmare.com).

$$ P. F. McCarthy's Pub and Restaurant feels like a sloppy saloon, serving reasonable salad or sandwich lunches and filling dinner fare (daily 12:00-21:00, 14 Main Street, tel. 064/664-1516).

Transportation

Arriving and Departing

BY CAR

Parking: Two large public parking lots (behind the TI and across from the church, free overnight) cling to the two main roads departing town to the north. Street parking is free (2 hours).

BY BUS

Kenmare has no train station (the nearest is in Killarney, 20 miles away) and only a few bus connections. Most buses transfer in Killarney. Bus info: www.buseireann.ie.

From Kenmare by Bus to: Killarney (3/day, 45 minutes), **Tralee** (3/day, 2 hours), **Dingle** (3/day, 3-4 hours, change in Killarney and Tralee), **Kinsale** (3/day, 4 hours, 2 changes). To reach **Dublin,** take a bus to Killarney and then transfer to a train.

KILLARNEY

Killarney's value is its location. And for most tour organizers, it's the logical jumping-off point for excursions around the famous Ring of Kerry peninsula. If you're approaching the region from Kinsale and Cobh, drive through Killarney and hop on the Ring to visit Muckross House, Killarney National Park, and Kissane Sheep Farm (in the mountains) en route to Kenmare. By taking a bite out of the Ring the day before you sleep in Kenmare, you'll be better situated to drive most of the remainder of the Ring of Kerry loop the next day.

If you're traveling in the region without a car, you'll have to stop here. The Killarney bus and train stations flank the big, modern Killarney Outlet Centre mall. Springing from the bus and train station are a few colorful streets lined with tourist-friendly shops and restaurants. If you have a layover between connections, walk five minutes straight out from the front of the mall and check out Killarney's shop-lined High Street and New Street. The **TI** is a 15-minute walk from the train station, on Beech Street.

Sights near Killarney

▲MUCKROSS HOUSE AND FARMS

Perhaps the best stately Victorian home you'll see in the Republic of Ireland, Muckross House (built in 1843) is magnificently set at the edge of Killarney National Park. It's adjacent to Muckross Farms, a fascinating open-air farm museum that shows rural life in the 1930s. Besides the mansion and farms, this regular stop on the tour-bus circuit also includes a fine garden idyllically set on a lake and an information center for the national park. The juxtaposition of the magnificent mansion and the humble farmhouses illustrates in a thought-provoking way the vast gap that once separated rich and poor in Ireland.

Cost and Hours: House or farms-€9.25 each, €15.50 combo-ticket includes both (Heritage Cards not accepted for farms); **house** open daily 9:00-18:00, July-Aug until 19:00, last entry one hour before closing; **farms** open daily June-Aug 10:00-18:00, May and Sept from 13:00, March-April and Oct Sat-Sun only 13:00-18:00, closed Nov-Feb; good cafeteria; house tel. 064/667-0144, farms tel. 064/663-0804, www.muckross-house.ie.

Tours: The only way to see the interior of the house is with the 45-minute guided tour (included with admission, offered frequently throughout the day). Book your tour as soon as you arrive (they can fill up). Then enjoy a walk in the gardens or have lunch before your tour begins.

Getting There: Muckross House is conveniently located on the long ride from Kinsale or Cashel to Dingle or Kenmare. From Killarney, follow signs to Kenmare, where you'll find Muckross House three miles (5 km) south of town. As you approach from Killarney, you'll see a small parking lot two miles before the actual parking lot. This is used by horse-and-

Muckross House

buggy bandits to hoodwink tourists into thinking they have to pay to clip-clop to the house. Pass by to find a big, safe, and free parking lot right at the mansion.

Visiting the House and Farms: A visit to **Muckross House** takes you back to the Victorian period—the 19th-century boom time when the sun never set on the British Empire and the Industrial Revolution (born in England) was chugging the world into the modern age. Of course, Ireland was a colony back then, with big-shot English landlords. During the Great Potato Famine of 1845-1849, most English gentry lived very well—profiting off the export of their handsome crops to lands with greater buying power—while a third of Ireland's population starved.

Muckross House feels lived-in (and it was, until 1933). Its fine Victorian furniture is arranged around the fireplace under Waterford crystal chandeliers and lots of antlers. The bedroom prepared for Queen Victoria was on the ground floor, since she was afraid of house fires. The owners spent a couple of years preparing for the royal visit in 1861, eager to gain coveted titles and nearly bankrupting themselves in the process. The queen stayed only three nights and her beloved Prince Albert died soon after the visit. The depressed queen never granted the titles that the grand house's owners had so hoped for.

The house exit takes you through an **information center** for Killarney National Park, with a relaxing 15-minute video explaining the park's geology, flora, and fauna (free, shown on request).

Muckross Traditional Farms features six vintage farmhouses strung along a mile-long road, with an old bus shuttling those who don't want to hike (free, 4/hour). The farm visits are a great experience—but only if you engage the attendants in conversation. Each farm is staffed by a Kerry local who enjoys talking about farm life in the old days—from the 1920s until electricity arrived in 1955.

▲KILLARNEY NATIONAL PARK

This 25,000-acre park (Ireland's oldest) was established when Muckross Estate was donated to the nation in 1932. Walking trails attract hikers of all levels for views of flora and fauna. Glacially sculpted rock ridges cradle three large lakes teeming with trout and salmon, which lure sport fishermen.

Getting There: It's just south of Killarney town on N-71 toward Kenmare, on the most mountainous stretch of the Ring of Kerry.

Visiting the Park: The park information center is at Muckross House (see earlier). Take a moment to contemplate your lush surroundings. This is what the majority of Ireland looked like 8,000 years ago, before Neolithic man settled and began rudimentary slash-and-burn farming. Later English colonial harvesting of timber exacerbated the deforestation process. Today, Ireland has the smallest proportion of forested land—10.5 percent—of any EU nation. The park's old-growth oak, yew, and alder groves are the best preserved in Ireland, and rhododendrons explode beside the road in late May and June. If you visit early or late in the day, keep an eye out for Ireland's only native herd of red deer.

Torc Waterfall in Killarney National Park

Enjoy an easy 10-minute stroll along a trail bordered by mossy rocks from the roadside up to **Torc Waterfall** (look for small parking lot beside N-71, 2 miles—3 km—south of Muckross House). Hikers will find more strenuous trails beyond.

Leaving the Park: Enjoy expansive lake views from **Ladies View,** right beside the N-71 road, a half-mile (1 km) from the park's southern exit. Just south of the park exit, you'll pass long, thin Looscaunagh Lough (beside the road on the left). A few hundred yards farther, the Black Valley opens up beneath you on the right. This remote valley was the last chunk of Ireland to get electricity—in 1978. The highest bump on the distant ridge across the Black Valley to the west is Carrantuohill, Ireland's tallest mountain at 3,400 feet.

▲▲KISSANE SHEEP FARM

Call ahead to arrange an hour's visit to this hardworking 2,500-acre Irish farm, perched on a scenic slope above the Black Valley. The Kissane family has raised sheep here for five generations. John (or his brother Noel) explains the sheep-shearing process and invites you to touch the pile of fresh wool afterward. You can feel the lanolin, which acts as natural waterproofing for the sheep and is extracted from the wool to sell to pharmaceutical firms (synthetic manufacturing has driven the price of wool so low, it's not worth selling otherwise). But the highlight of any visit is the demonstration of sheepherding by the highly alert border collies who have trained here since puppyhood. John (or Evan) commands the dogs from afar using an array of verbal calls, whistles, and hand signals. Sheep shearing takes place from mid-May to early October; spring visitors will also see newborn lambs.

Cost and Hours: €8; by appointment only most afternoons April-Oct, closed Sun and Nov-March, check website for times, minimum 20 people—call ahead to coordinate your visit with a big bus group, gates open 15 minutes prior to demo; on N-71 between Ladies View and Moll's Gap, tel. 064/663-4791, mobile 087-260-0410, www.kissanesheepfarm.com, noel@kissanesheepfarm.com.

From Kissane Sheep Farm to Kenmare: Drive south on N-71. Going over Moll's Gap (WCs and Avoca Café beside parking lot), you'll descend into Kenmare. The rugged, bare rock on either side of the road was rounded and smoothed by the grinding action of glaciers over thousands of years. In the distance to the north (on your right) look for the Gap of Dunloe, a perfect example of a U-shaped glacial valley notch.

Kissane Sheep Farm

The Ring of Kerry vs. the Dingle Peninsula

If I had to choose one spot to enjoy the small-town charm of traditional Ireland, it would be Dingle and its history-laden scenic peninsula. But the Ring of Kerry—a much bigger, more famous, and more touristed peninsula just to its south—is also great to visit. If you go to Ireland and don't see the famous Ring of Kerry, your uncle Pat will never forgive you. Here's a comparison to help with your itinerary planning.

Both peninsulas come with a scenic loop drive. Dingle's Slea Head Loop Drive is 30 miles. The Ring of Kerry is 135 miles. Both loops come with lots of megalithic wonder. Dingle's prehistory is more intimate, with numerous little evocative stony structures. The Ring of Kerry's prehistory shows itself in three massive ring forts—far bigger than anything on Dingle.

Dingle town is the perfect little Irish burg—alive with traditional music pubs, an active fishing harbor, and the sturdy cultural atmosphere of an Irish-speaking Gaeltacht region. You can easily spend three fun nights here. In comparison, Kenmare (the best base for the Ring of Kerry loop) is pleasant but forgettable. Those spending a night on the west end of the Ring of Kerry find a rustic atmosphere in Portmagee (the base for a cruise to magical Skellig Michael).

Both regions are beyond the reach of the Irish train system and require a car or spotty bus service to access. Both offer memorable scenery, great restaurants, warm B&B hospitality, and similar prices. The bottom line: With limited time, choose Dingle. If you have a day or two to spare, the Ring of Kerry is also a delight.

RING OF KERRY

More than twice the size of the Dingle Peninsula, the Ring of Kerry (Iveragh Peninsula) can seem overwhelming. Lassoed by a winding coastal road (the Ring), this mountainous, lake-splattered region comes with breathtaking scenery and the highest peak in Ireland. While a veritable fleet of big, tourist-laden buses circles it each day, they generally depart Killarney around the same time, head the same direction, and stop at the same handful of attractions. But if you avoid those places at rush hour, the Ring feels remarkably unspoiled and dramatically isolated, allowing you to enjoy one of the most rewarding days in Ireland.

You can explore the Ring by car in one satisfying day with the following plan. To see the Ring of Kerry without a car, it's easiest to take a private tour from Kenmare; see page 145.

Rick's Tip: *The flat, inland, northeastern section of the Ring—from Killorglin to Killarney on N-72—is* **skippable.**

Ring of Kerry Loop Drive

The entire Ring of Kerry loop, worth ▲▲▲, is 135 miles and takes 4.5 hours without stops. Factoring in time for lunch and sightseeing, the Ring is easily an all-day experience. Get an early start (by 8:30 at the latest) and drive clockwise around the Ring to minimize afternoon encounters with the oncoming chain of tour buses on the narrowest stretches (buses are required to drive it counterclockwise). Tank up before leaving, as gas in Kenmare is cheaper than out on the Ring.

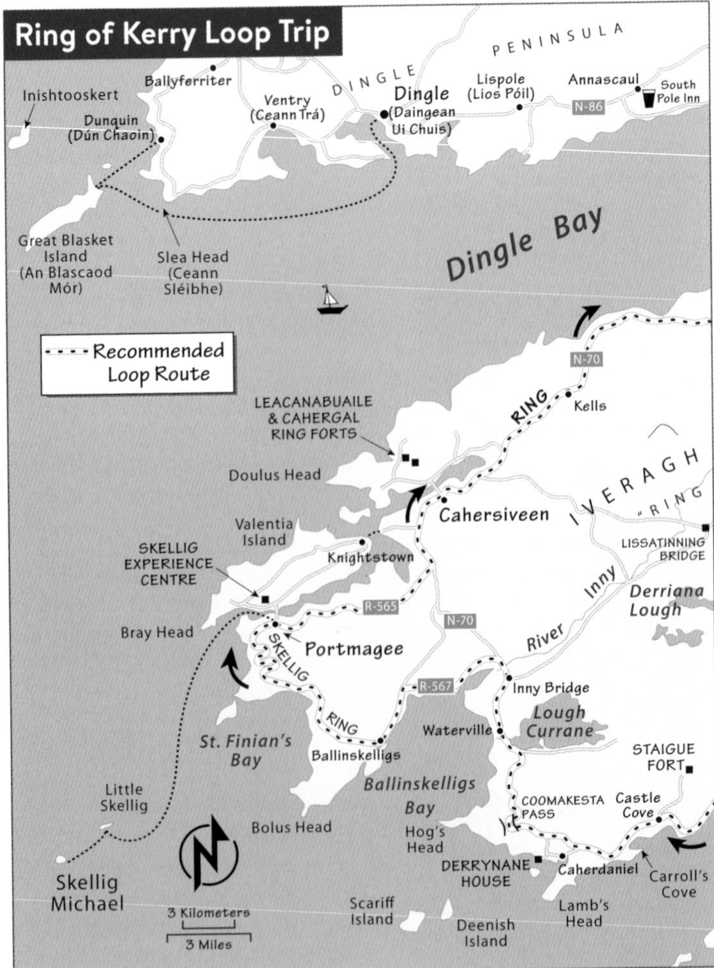

Leaving Kenmare, head clockwise on N-70. Allow time for stops at Staigue Ring Fort (45 minutes) and Derrynane House (1 hour), and get to Waterville before noon. Shortly after Waterville, leave the main N-70 Ring for the Skellig Ring (consisting of the R-567, R-566, and R-565—roads that are too narrow for big buses). Have lunch out on the Skellig Ring, either as a picnic on the lovely beach at St. Finian's Bay, or in Portmagee. By the time you rejoin the main N-70 route, the big buses will have slunk by. On the last half of the route, there are two more hour-long stops: the Skellig Experience Centre (near Portmagee) and two additional big ring forts (near Cahersiveen).

For me, the two most photogenic coastal stretches are out near the tip of the peninsula: between Caherdaniel and Waterville (on the Ring of Kerry) and from Ballinskelligs to Portmagee (on the Skellig Ring).

The only downside of going against the bus traffic is that, on the narrow parts of the Ring road, buses always have the right-of-way. If there's a bottleneck, you'll need to back up to the nearest wide spot in the road to let the bus through. The main sticking point is the 30-foot-long, one-lane tunnel in Killarney National Park between Muckross House and the Kissane Sheep Farm. With an early start, you can generally avoid these hassles.

Equip yourself with a good map before driving the Ring of Kerry loop, such as the *Complete Road Atlas of Ireland* by Ordnance Survey (sold in most TIs and bookstores in Ireland) or the *Fir Tree Aerial* series, with a

Lakes of Killarney

The Ring Forts of Kerry

The Ring of Kerry comes with three awe-inspiring prehistoric ring forts—among the largest and best preserved in all of Ireland. Staigue Fort (near the beginning of my recommended Ring route) is most impressive but in a desolate setting. The two others—Cahergal and Leacanabuaile, 200 yards apart just north of Cahersiveen (closer to the end of the Ring, after Valentia Island)—are easier to visit and plenty evocative. Each ring fort is about a 2.5-mile (4-km) side trip off the main drag. If you're trying to beat the tour-bus convoy, Staigue Fort is problematic because it eats up morning time before the buses have passed you. The Cahersiveen ring forts are your last stop in the Ring of Kerry, once bus traffic is of no concern.

Staigue Fort

All of these ring forts are roughly the same age and have the similar basic features. The circular dry-stone walls were built sometime between 500 BC and AD 300 without the aid of mortar or cement. About 80 feet across, with walls 12 feet thick at the base and up to 25 feet high, these brutish structures would have taken 100 men six months to complete.

Expert opinion is divided on the reason they were built. Civilization was morphing from nomadic hunter-gatherers to settled farmers, so herders used these forts to gather their valuable cattle inside and protect them from ancient rustlers. Other experts see the round design as a kind of amphitheater, where local clan chieftains would have gathered for important meetings or rituals. However, the ditch surrounding the outer walls of Staigue Fort suggests a defensive, rather than ceremonial, function. Without written records, we can only imagine the part these magnificent piles of finely stacked stones played in ancient dramas.

map that covers both the Iveragh (Ring of Kerry) and Dingle peninsulas, giving you a bird's-eye feel for the terrain (sold in most bookstores in County Kerry).

➲ *Self-Guided Drive*

Here's a kilometer by kilometer guide to my recommended clockwise route. Several of these stops are listed later in this chapter.

0 km: Leave Kenmare.

17.6 km: On the right is Glacier Lake, with a long, smooth limestone "banister" carved by a glacier 10,000 years ago.

22.8 km: The recommended Parknasilla Hotel—a posh 19th-century hotel—is a great stop for tea and scones.

26 km: Visit the town of Sneem.

40.4 km: Turn off for the Staigue Ring Fort.

41.5 km: Enjoy great views across the bay of the Beara Peninsula beyond a ruined hospital with IRA ties. No one wants to touch these ruins today, out of fear of "kicking up a beehive."

43.5 km: Carroll's Cove has a fine beach with some of the warmest water in Ireland, grand views of Kenmare Bay, a trailer park, and "Ireland's only beachside bar."

46.4 km: Take the turnoff for Derrynane House (home of Daniel O'Connell).

50.4 km: Enjoy brilliant views for the next two kilometers to Coomakesta Pass.

52.4 km: The Coomakesta Pass lookout point (700-foot altitude) offers grand vistas in both directions.

54.5 km: On a clear day, look for the distant Skellig Islands with their pointy summits.

59.6 km: In the town of Waterville, you'll see a sculpture of Charlie Chaplin standing on the waterfront. Waterville is also home to the Butler Arms Hotel—a fine stop for tea and scones in its Charlie Chaplin room (with lots of photos of the silent-film icon and his young wife frolicking as they lived well in Ireland).

65 km: After rejoining the main road, cross the small bridge that's locally famous for salmon fly-fishing. Take the first left (R-567) for the Skellig Ring loop (follow brown *Skellig Ring* signs through Ballinskelligs, and then scenically to Portmagee). At this point, you've left the big-bus route.

75 km: St. Finian's Bay lies about halfway around, with a pleasant little picnic-friendly beach that's recently been discovered by surfers (no WCs). Just before the bay is the small, modern Skelligs Chocolate Factory, with free, tasty samples as well as a café for coffee and muffins (Mon-Fri 10:00-17:00—but longer hours in summer, Sat-Sun from 11:00, especially fun for kids, tel. 066/947-9119, www.skelligschocolate.com).

St. Finian's Bay

80 km: Signs for the *Kerry Cliffs* lure photographers and walkers to turn left into the driveway that advertises "Best View in County Kerry." Park and pay the €4 fee at the hut. Then walk 10 minutes straight up the gravel road to a dramatic coastal cliff that opens up onto expansive coastal views. The beehive huts nearby are replicas but true to the originals.

83 km: You reach Portmagee, a small port town and jumping-off point for boats to the Skellig Islands.

83.2 km: Cross the bridge to the Skellig Experience Centre. You're now on Valentia Island, its name hinting at medieval trading connections with nearby Spain—which lies due south. Dinosaur hunters may want to detour and follow the signs to the modest but ancient tetrapod tracks, frozen in stone, on the north side of the island (ask for directions at the visitors center).

91.2 km: At the church in Knightstown, turn left for the Knightstown Heritage Museum.

93 km: Return to the main road and go through Knightstown to the tiny ferry (€7/car, runs constantly 8:00-21:00, 1-km trip).

95 km: Leaving the ferry, rejoin N-70 (the main Ring of Kerry route), turning left for the town of Cahersiveen. From here, you can detour a few kilometers to two impressive stone ring forts, Cahergal and Leacanabuaile.

100 km: Return to N-70 at Cahersiveen and follow signs for *Glenbeigh* and *Killorglin.* Enjoy views of the Dingle Peninsula across Dingle Bay. Eagle eyes can spot stumpy Eask Tower and Inch Beach.

The rest of the loop is less scenic. At Killorglin, you've seen the best of it. From here, go either to Dingle (left) or to Kenmare/Killarney/Kinsale (right).

From Kenmare to Portmagee

SNEEM

Inundated by tour buses daily from 14:00 to 16:00, the town of Sneem is peaceful and laid-back the rest of the day. This humble place has two entertaining squares. The Irish joke, "Since we're in Kerry, the square on the east side is called South Square and the one on the west is called North Square." On the first (South) square, you'll see a statue of Steve "Crusher" Casey, the local boy who reigned as world-champion heavyweight wrestler (1938-1947). A sweet little peat-toned rapid gurgles under the one-lane bridge connecting the two Sneem squares. The North Square features a memorial to former French president Charles de Gaulle's visit (Irish on his mother's side, de Gaulle came here for two weeks of R&R after his final retirement from office in 1969). Locals call it "da gallstone."

Statue of Steve "Crusher" Casey

▲STAIGUE FORT

This impressive ring fort is worth a stop on your way around the Ring (always open, drop €1 in the gray donation box beside the gate). While viewing the imposing pile of stone, read "The Ring Forts of Kerry" sidebar.

Getting There: The fort is 2.5 miles (4 km) off the main N-70 road up a narrow rural access lane (look for signs just after the hamlet of Castle Cove). Honk on blind corners to warn oncoming traffic as you drive up the hedge-lined lane.

▲DERRYNANE HOUSE

This is the home of Daniel O'Connell, Ireland's most influential 19th-century politician, whose tireless nonviolent agitation gained equality for Catholics 185 years ago. The coastal lands of the O'Connell estate that surround Derrynane (rhymes with Maryann) House are now a national historic park. A visit here is a window into the life of a man who not only liberated Ireland from the last oppressive anti-Catholic penal laws, but also first developed the idea of a grassroots movement—organizing on a massive scale to achieve political ends without bloodshed (see the "Daniel O'Connell" sidebar).

Cost and Hours: €5; daily 10:30-18:00; mid-March-April and Oct Wed-Sun 10:30-17:00, closed Mon-Tue; weekends only in Nov, closed Dec-mid-March; last entry 45 minutes before closing, tel. 066/947-5113.

Getting There: Just outside the town of Derrynane, pick up a handy free map of the area from the little private TI inside the brown Wave Crest market (TI open daily 9:00-18:00, closed in off-season, tel. 066/947-5188; market is a great place to buy picnic food). One mile after the market, take a left and follow the signs into Derrynane National Historic Park.

Visiting the House: The house has a quirky floor plan. Ask about the next scheduled 20-minute audiovisual show, which fleshes out the highlights of O'Connell's turbulent life and makes the contents of the house more interesting. Self-guided info sheets are available in the main rooms.

Downstairs in the study, look for the

Daniel O'Connell (1775-1847)

Born in Cahersiveen and elected from Ennis as the first Catholic member of the British Parliament, O'Connell was the hero of Catholic emancipation in Ireland. Educated in France at a time when punitive anti-Catholic laws limited schooling for Irish Catholics at home, he witnessed the carnage of the French Revolution. Upon his return to Ireland, he saw more bloodshed during the futile Rebellion of 1798.

Abhorring all this violence, O'Connell dedicated himself to peacefully gaining equal rights for Catholics in an Ireland dominated by a wealthy Protestant minority. He formed the Catholic Association with a one-penny-per-month membership fee and quickly gained a huge following (especially among the poor) with his persuasive speaking skills. Although Catholics weren't allowed to hold office, he ran for election to Parliament anyway and won a seat in 1828. His unwillingness to take the anti-Catholic Oath of Supremacy initially kept him out of Westminster, but the moral force of his victory caused the government to concede Catholic emancipation the following year.

Known as "The Liberator," O'Connell began working toward his next goal—repealing the Act of Union with Britain. When his massive "monster meeting" rallies attracted thousands, his popularity spooked the British authorities, who threw him in jail on trumped-up charges of seditious conspiracy in 1844. When the Great Potato Famine hit in 1845, some Irish protesters advocated for more violent action against the British, which O'Connell had long opposed. He died two years later in Genoa on his way to Rome, but his ideals lived on: His Catholic Association was the model of grassroots organization for the Irish, both in their homeland and in America.

glass case containing the pistols used in O'Connell's famous duel. Beside them are his black gloves, one of which he always wore on his right hand when he went to Mass (out of remorse for the part it played in taking a man's life). The dining room is lined with family portraits. Upstairs in the drawing room, you'll find his ornately carved chair with tiny harp strings and wolfhound collars made of gold. And in another upstairs room is his deathbed, brought back from Genoa.

The coach house (out back) shows off the enormous grand chariot that carried O'Connell through throngs of joyous Dubliners after his release from prison in 1844. In a glass case opposite the chariot is a copy of O'Connell's celebrated speech imploring the Irish not to riot when he was arrested. He added the small chapel wing to the house in gratitude to God for his prison release.

PORTMAGEE

Just a short row of snoozy buildings lining the bay, Portmagee is the best harbor for boat excursions out to the Skellig Islands (see "Getting There" on page 165). It's a quiet village with a handful of B&Bs, two pubs, a bakery, a market, and no ATMs—the closest ATM is 6 miles (10 km) east in Cahersiveen. On the rough harborfront, a slate memorial to sailors from here who were lost at sea reads, "In the nets of God may we be gathered."

A 100-yard-long bridge connects Portmagee to gentle Valentia Island, where you'll find the Skellig Experience Centre (on the left at the Valentia end of the bridge). A public parking lot is at the Portmagee end of the bridge, with WCs. The first permanent transatlantic cable (for telegraph communication) was laid from Valentia Island in 1866.

Sleeping in Portmagee: $$$ Moorings Guesthouse feels like a small hotel, with 17 rooms, a pub and a good restaurant downstairs, and the most convenient location in town, 50 yards from the end of the pier (family rooms, tel. 066/947-7108, www.moorings.ie, moorings@iol.ie, Gerard and Patricia Kennedy). **$$ Portmagee Heights B&B** is a modern, solid slate home up above town, renting eight fine rooms (cash only, family rooms, on the road into town, tel. 066/947-7251, www.portmageeheights.com, portmageeheights@gmail.com, Monica Hussey). **$ Beach Cove Lodge** offers three comfortable, fresh, and lovingly decorated rooms (but no breakfast) in splendid isolation four miles south of Portmagee. Bridie O'Connor's adjacent cottage out back has two double rooms (tel. 066/947-9301, mobile 087-139-0224, www.stayatbeachcove.com, beachcove@eircom.net).

Eating in Portmagee: These options all line the waterfront (between the pier and the bridge to Valentia Island). **$$$ The Moorings** is a nice restaurant with great seafood caught literally just outside its front door (Tue-Sun 18:00-22:00, closed Mon and in winter, reservations smart, tel.

Portmagee's harbor

066/947-7108, www.moorings.ie). The **$$ Bridge Bar,** next door, does traditional pub grub. Call ahead to check on their traditional music and dance schedule (daily 12:00-22:00, live music Fri and Sun nights, tel. 066/947-7108). The **$$ Fisherman's Bar** is less flashy, with more locals and cheaper prices (daily 10:00-21:00, tel. 066/947-7103).

O'Connell's Market is the only grocery (Mon-Sat 9:00-19:00, Sun 9:30-12:30). **Smugglers Cafe** offers lunch options of fresh seafood dishes and salads. They can also make great sandwiches to take on Skellig boat excursions (daily 9:30-17:00, tel. 066/947-7250).

Valentia Island

These two sights are on Valentia Island, across the bridge from Portmagee.

SKELLIG EXPERIENCE CENTRE

Whether or not you're actually sailing to Skellig Michael (described later), this little center (with basic exhibits and a fine 15-minute film) explains it well—both the story of the monks and the natural environment.

Cost and Hours: €5; daily 10:00-18:00, July-Aug until 19:00, off-season until 17:00, closed Dec-Feb; last entry one hour before closing, call ahead outside of peak season as hours may vary, on Valentia Island beside bridge linking it to Portmagee, tel. 066/947-6306, www.skelligexperience.com.

Boat Trips: The Skellig Experience Centre arranges two-hour boat trips, circling both Skellig Michael and Little Skellig (without actually bringing people ashore)—ideal for those who want a close look without the stair climb and vertigo that go with a visit to the island (€40, sailings daily at 10:30, 13:30, and 15:00—weather permitting, depart from Valentia Island pier 50 yards below the Skellig Experience Centre).

Rick's Tip: *If you're interested in* **tetrapods,** *the actual* **"first footprints"** *are a 15-minute drive from the Valentia Heritage Museum, on a rugged bit of rocky shoreline, a 10-minute hike below a parking lot. Get details locally.*

VALENTIA HERITAGE MUSEUM

The humble Knightstown schoolhouse, built in 1861, houses an equally humble but interesting museum. You'll see a 19th-century schoolroom and learn about tetrapods (those first fish to climb onto land—which locals claim happened here). You'll also follow the long story of the expensive, frustrating, and heroic battle to lay telegraph cable across the Atlantic, which finally succeeded in 1866

Leacanabuaile ring fort

when the largest ship in the world connected the tiny island of Valentia with Newfoundland.

Cost and Hours: €3.50, daily 10:30-17:30, closed Oct-April, tel. 066/947-6985, www.valentiaisland.ie.

Rest of the Ring

CAHERGAL AND LEACANABUAILE RING FORTS

Crowning bluffs in farm country, 2.5 miles (4 km) off the main road at Cahersiveen, these two windy and desolate forts are each different and worth a look. Just beyond the Cahersiveen town church at the tourist office, turn left, cross the narrow bridge, turn left again, and follow signs to the ancient forts—you'll see the huge stone structures in the distance. You'll hike 10 minutes from the tiny parking lot (free, always open, no museum). Both forts are roughly 100 yards off the road (uphill on the right) and are 200 yards from each other. For details, see "The Ring Forts of Kerry" sidebar, earlier.

SKELLIG MICHAEL

A trip to this jagged, isolated pyramid—the Holy Grail of Irish monastic island settlements—rates as a truly memorable ▲▲▲ experience. After visiting Skellig Michael a hundred years ago, Nobel Prize-winning Irish playwright George Bernard Shaw called it "the most fantastic and impossible rock in the world."

Rising seven miles offshore, the Skelligs (Irish for "splinter") are two gigantic slate-and-sandstone rocks crouched aggressively on the ocean horizon. The larger of the two, Skellig Michael, is more than 700 feet tall and a mile around, with a tiny cluster of abandoned beehive huts clinging near its summit like stubborn barnacles. The smaller island, Little Skellig, is home to a huge colony of gannet birds (like large, graceful seagulls with six-foot wingspans), protected by law from visitors setting foot onshore.

Skellig Michael (dedicated to the archangel) was first inhabited by sixth-century Christian monks. Inspired by earlier hermit-monks in the Egyptian desert,

Jagged, isolated Skellig Michael

they sought the purity of isolation to get closer to God. Neither Viking raids nor winter storms could dislodge them, as they patiently built a half-dozen small, stone, igloo-like dwellings and a couple of tiny oratories. Their remote cliff-terrace perch is still connected to the sea 600 feet below by an amazing series of rock stairs. Viking Olav Tryggvason, who later became king of Norway and introduced Christianity to his country, was baptized here in 993.

Chiseling the most rudimentary life from solid rock, the monks lived a harsh, lonely, disciplined existence here, their colony surviving for more than 500 years. They collected rainwater in cisterns and lived off fish and birds. To supplement their meager existence, they traded bird eggs and feathers with passing boats for cereals, candles, and animal hides (used for clothing and for copying scripture). They finally moved their holy community ashore to Ballinskelligs in the early 1100s. But Christian pilgrims continued to visit Skellig Michael for centuries as penance...edging out onto a ledge to kiss a stone cross that has since toppled into the ocean.

In 2014, the ruggedly exotic Skellig Michael was used as a filming location for *Star Wars: The Force Awakens.* To keep the filming top-secret, the Irish Navy was called in to enforce a two-mile exclusionary zone around the island. Environmental concerns about the impact on the island's fragile ecosystem, especially native seabirds, led Disney to scrap plans for filming the next installment on the island. Instead it built its own version of the location at Sybil Head on the Dingle Peninsula. Expect a constant stream of *Star Wars* tourists at both locations. *Go mbeidh an Fórsa leat!* (May the Force be with you!)

Getting There

Boats sail to Skellig Michael daily from mid-May through September, but are heavily dependent on weather conditions. If the seas are too choppy, boats cannot safely drop people at the concrete island pier.

The number of daily visitors is limited due to the island's fragile ecosystem as a puffin breeding ground. Just 15 boats carrying 12 passengers each are licensed to land on the island once a day. Additional boats circle the island without landing, with multiple departure times each day.

Booking a Trip: Boats that land on the island cost €125, and generally depart Portmagee between 9:30 and 10:30 (depending on tides), sail for an hour, leave you on the island, and get you back into Portmagee between 14:30 and 16:30. Boat trips that just circle the island cost €40.

Tickets sell out months in advance. The best first step is to ask the host at your accommodations as soon as you know your travel dates; many know of a limited number of sailing slots through their local connections. You can also email skelligadventure@gmail.com. Or, contact the boat captains: **Paul Devane** (mobile 087-617-8114, www.skelligmichaelcruises.com), **Patrick Murphy** (mobile 087-234-2168), or **Brendan Casey** (tel. 066/947-2437, mobile 087-450-1211). For a list of everyone who runs trips to the island, see www.skelligexperience.com/other-sea-tours.

Planning Tips: Your best bet is to reserve a room near Portmagee or St. Finian's Bay. Contact the boat operator on the morning of departure to get the final word about whether the sailing is on or off.

Bring your camera, lunch (easy to buy at the recommended Smugglers Cafe in Portmagee), water, sunscreen, rain gear, hiking shoes, and your sense of wonder.

Visiting Skellig Michael

Since you'll have only about 2.5 hours to explore the island, begin by climbing the seemingly unending series of stone stairs to the monastic ruins (600 vertical feet of uneven steps with no handrails). Save most of your photographing for the way down. Those who linger too long below

The stone stairs on Skellig Michael

risk missing the enlightening 20-minute free talk among the beehive huts, given by guides who camp on the island from May through September. Afterward, poke your head into some of the huts and try to imagine the dark, damp, and devoted life of a monk here more than 1,000 years ago. After rambling through the ruins, you can give in to the puffin-spotting photo frenzy as you wander back down the stairs.

The two lighthouses on the far side of the island are now automated, and access to them has been blocked off. There are no WCs or modern shelters of any kind on Skellig Michael.

If you visit between May and early August, you'll be surrounded by fearless rainbow-beaked puffins, which nest here in underground burrows. Their bizarre swallowed cooing sounds like a distant chainsaw. These portly little birds live off fish, and divers have reported seeing them 20 feet underwater in pursuit of their prey.

Your return boat journey usually includes a pass near Little Skellig, which looms like an iceberg with a white coat of guano—courtesy of the 20,000 gannets that circle overhead like feathered confetti. These large birds suddenly morph into sleek darts when pursuing a fish, piercing the water from more than 100 feet above. You're also likely to get a glimpse of gray seals lazing on rocks near the water's edge.

Evolution in Ireland: Tetrapods to Marconi

Evolution, literacy, communication—Ireland has played a starring role in all three.

Many Irish paleontologists believe that the fossilized tetrapod tracks preserved on Valentia Island are the oldest in Europe. It was here that some of the first fish slithered out of the water on four stubby legs 385 million years ago, onto what would become the Isle of Saints and Scholars. Over time, those tetrapods evolved into the ancestors of today's amphibians, reptiles, birds, mammals...and humans, with the desire to record their thoughts and history, and communicate with others across the miles.

Irish scribes—living in remote outposts like the Skellig Islands, just off this coast—kept literate life alive in Europe through the darkest depths of the so-called Dark Ages. In fact, in about the year 800, Charlemagne imported monks from this part of Ireland to be his scribes.

Just more than a thousand years later, in the mid-19th century, Paul Julius Reuter—who provided a financial news service in Europe—knew his pigeons couldn't fly across the Atlantic. So, he relied on ships coming from America to drop a news capsule overboard as they rounded this southwest corner of Ireland. His boys would wait in their little boats with nets to "get the scoop." They say Europe learned of Lincoln's assassination (1865) from a capsule tossed out of a boat here.

The first permanent telegraph cables were laid across the Atlantic from here to Newfoundland, giving the two hemispheres instantaneous electronic communication. Queen Victoria was the first to send a message—greeting American president James Buchanan in 1858. The cable broke more than once, but it was finally permanently secured in 1866. Radio inventor Guglielmo Marconi, who was half-Irish, achieved the first wireless transatlantic communication from this corner of Ireland to America in 1901.

Today, driving under the 21st-century mobile-phone and satellite tower that crowns a hilltop above Valentia Island, while gazing out at the Skellig Islands, a traveler has to marvel at humanity's progress—and the part this remote corner of Ireland played in it.

Dingle Town & Peninsula

The Dingle Peninsula, the westernmost tip of Ireland, offers just the right mix of far-and-away beauty, isolated wanders, and ancient wonders—all within convenient reach of its main town. Dingle town is just large enough to have all the necessary tourist services and the steady nocturnal beat of Ireland's best traditional music scene.

Dingle feels so traditionally Irish because it's part of the Gaeltacht, a region where the government subsidizes the survival of the Irish language and culture. While English is always there, the signs, chitchat, and songs come in Irish Gaelic. Children carry Gaelic footballs to class, and the local preschool brags "ALL Gaelic."

Despite growing more touristy, Dingle's charms are resilient. As the older generation slows down and fades away, a new generation of entrepreneurs is giving Dingle fresh vitality.

West of Dingle town, the Dingle Peninsula is home to thousands of sheep and the scenic Slea Head Loop. You can do the loop by car (or bike it, if you're hardy), stopping to enjoy sights along the way. Off the tip of the peninsula is Great Blasket Island, reachable by ferry.

DINGLE TOWN & PENINSULA IN 2 DAYS

Take one day to sightsee and relax in Dingle town. Follow my self-guided walks (through town and to the harbor), marvel at the chapel's stained-glass windows, have an excellent dinner, and enjoy trad music in the pubs.

On your second day, explore the 30-mile loop around the peninsula by car or bike (see route specifics on page 190). By spending at least two nights, you'll feel more like a local on your second evening in the pubs. With more time (and in good weather), Great Blasket Island (off the western tip of the Dingle Peninsula, with the best ferry options from Dingle town) is a rewarding and easy-to-navigate hiking option.

DINGLE TOWN

Of the peninsula's 10,000 residents, about 2,000 live in Dingle town (Daingean Ui Chuis). Its few streets, lined with ramshackle but gaily painted shops and pubs, run up from a rain-stung harbor always sheltering fishing boats and leisure sailboats. Traditionally, the buildings were drab gray or whitewashed, but Ireland's "Tidy Town" competition a few decades back prompted everyone to paint their buildings in playful pastels.

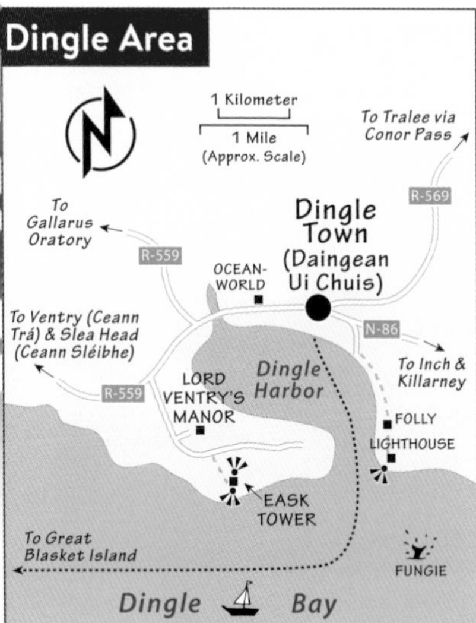

The courthouse (1832) is open one day per month. The judge does his best to wrap up business within a few hours. During the day, you'll see teenagers—already working on ruddy, beer-glow cheeks—roll kegs up the streets and into the pubs in preparation for another night of music and *craic* (fun conversation and atmosphere). It's a friendly town.

Rick's Tip: *Expect to* **use cash** *rather than credit cards to pay for most peninsula activities. You'll find ATMs on Dingle's Main Street.*

Orientation

Dingle—extremely comfortable on foot—hangs on a medieval grid of streets between the harbor (where the bus to Tralee, with the nearest train station, stops) and Main Street (three blocks inland). Nothing in town is more than a 10-minute walk away. Street numbers are rarely used. Everyone knows each other, and people on the street are fine sources of information.

Tourist Information: The TI has a great town map (free) and staff who know the town, but less about the rest of the peninsula (Mon-Sat 9:00-13:00 & 13:30-17:00, generally closed Sun, shorter hours off-season, on Strand Street by the water, tel. 066/915-1188). For advice on outdoor activities, drop by the Mountain Man shop on Strand Street, or talk to your B&B host.

Helpful Hints

Farmers Market: From mid-April to mid-October on Fridays from 9:00 to 15:00, farmers sell fresh produce, homemade marmalade, and homespun crafts in a small parking lot across the street from SuperValu grocery store.

Laundry: Dingle Cleaners is convenient (Mon-Sat 9:00-18:00, closed Sun, up Spa Road—see map on page 187, tel. 066/915-0680, mobile 087-793-5621). There's no self-service laundry in Dingle.

Bike Rental: Try **Paddy's Bike Hire,** with reliably maintained 21-speed hybrids (€15/day, includes helmet and lock, daily 9:00-19:00, must leave driver's license, directly across Dykegate from An Café Liteartha—see map on page 187, tel. 066/915-2311). **Dingle Electric Bike Experience** rents electric bikes as well as 24-speed hybrid bikes, and can deliver them to your hotel and pick them up later (electric–€45/day, hybrid–€20/day, mobile 086-084-8378, www.dinglebikes.com, info@dinglebikes.com). Be aware that Dingle and the Dingle Peninsula have no bike lanes and increasing traffic volume.

Falconry Experience: At the **Dingle Falconry Experience,** master falconer Eric leads encounters with hawks, falcons, owls, and eagles (€15, reserve in advance, most days at 17:00 at Milltown House,

DINGLE TOWN & PENINSULA AT A GLANCE

In Dingle Town

▲▲▲**Dingle Town Walk** This short stroll introduces you to the town, its finest craft shops, and its characteristic pubs. See page 174.

▲▲▲**Traditional Music** Best enjoyed at one of Dingle's many pubs; early birds can take in early-evening folk concerts at St. James' Church or the Siopa Ceoil music shop. See page 182.

▲▲**Harry Clarke Windows** Imaginative stained-glass Bible scenes inside a lovely Neo-Gothic chapel in the middle of Dingle town. **Hours:** Mon-Fri 9:00-17:00, Sat-Sun 10:00-15:00. See page 179.

▲**Fungie** Dingle Harbor's resident dolphin (and town mascot), who makes regular appearances in the bay. See page 181.

▲**Oceanworld** Aquarium with penguin exhibit, touch pools, and Fungie lore. **Hours:** Daily 10:00-18:00, shorter hours off-season. See page 181.

The Dingle Peninsula

▲▲▲**Slea Head Loop Drive** Scenic 30-mile loop from Dingle, featuring the Gallarus Oratory (impressive early Christian church), Iron Age stone huts and "fairy forts," Norman ruins, and spectacular coastal views. See page 190.

▲▲▲**Sciúird Archaeology Tours** Fascinating three-hour minibus tours offer an up-close look into the peninsula's ancient history. **Hours:** Tours generally depart at 10:00 in peak season. See page 173.

▲▲**Great Blasket Island** Until quite recently home to one of Ireland's most traditional communities; best appreciated after a visit to the excellent Great Blasket Centre on the mainland. **Hours:** Great Blasket Centre open daily 10:00-18:00, closed Nov-Easter; boat tours and ferry to the island run regularly in good weather. See page 200.

What's in a Name?

Linguistic politics have stirred up a controversy over the name of this town and peninsula. As a Gaeltacht, the entire region gets subsidies from the government (which supports the survival of the traditional Irish culture and language). A precondition of this financial support is that towns use their Irish Gaelic name. In 2005, government officials in Dublin dictated that Dingle convert its name to the Irish Gaelic "An Daingean" (on DANG-un). But, in fact, four separate Irish towns are named Daingean ("fortress"), so in 2012 Dingle's name was changed again—to Daingean Ui Chuis ("Fortress of the Husseys," a medieval Norman founding family).

The town has resisted these dictates. Dingle has become so wealthy from the tourist trade that it sees its famous name as a trademark, and doesn't want to become "the cute tourist town with the unpronounceable name, formerly known as Dingle." Official road signs that identified the town only as *Daingean Ui Chuis* were modified by stubborn locals, who stenciled in a crude *DINGLE*. The government eventually gave up and changed the signs back to *Dingle*. In town, nearly everyone—locals and tourists alike—refers to it as Dingle.

In this book, I follow the predominant convention: Dingle instead of An Daingean or Daingean Ui Chuis, Great Blasket Island instead of An Blascaod Mór, and so on. But for ease of navigation, I've also generally included the place's Irish name in parentheses. For a list of these bilingual place names, see the sidebar on page 190.

just over the bridge west of town; private falconry experience-€150/5 people, "hawk walk" (hawks only) at nearby beach or forest-€100/2 people; mobile 087-055-2313, www.dinglefalconry.com).

Tours

Sciúird Archaeology Tours, worth ▲▲▲, are offered by a father-son team with a passion for sharing the long history of the Dingle Peninsula. Stops include beehive huts, the Reasc Monastery, the Gallarus Oratory, and Kilmalkedar Church with its ancient ogham stone—but not the Great Blasket Centre (€30, departs daily at 10:00 from the Fungie statue at the TI or at your B&B by request, book by email as soon as you know your dates, mobile 087-419-8617, www.ancientdingle.com, info@ancientdingle.com).

Dingle Slea Head Tours does single- and multiday private driving tours of the region from Dingle. They also run Slea Head tours daily at 9:30 and 13:30 (4 hours, €30, minimum 4 people, www.dinglesleaheadtours.com).

Dingle Dolphin Boat Tours offers a one-hour bay cruise with a guarantee to see Fungie the dolphin (€16, at least 4 times daily in summer) and a day trip to Great Blasket Island (€55, six-hour round-trip, must book ahead, schedules vary with weather and tides, office in back corner of TI beside Fungie sculpture, tel. 066/915-2626, www.dingledolphin.com). **Dingle Boat Tours** covers a similar lineup at competitive prices. Their office is at the base of the large Dingle Marina jetty—not to be confused with the shorter commercial fishing pier (tel. 066/915-1344, www.dingleboattours.com).

Blasket Island Ferry shuttles visitors from Dunquin Pier at the far west end of the peninsula to Great Blasket Island (€30, kids-€15, hourly starting at 10:00, weather permitting, advanced booking recommended, tel. 066/915-6422, www.blasketisland.com).

➲ Dingle Town Walk

• *Start this walk, worth ▲▲▲, just beyond the "old roundabout" and beside the playground at the...*

❶ **Tiny Bridge:** This pedestrian bridge, with its black-and-gold wrought-iron railing, was part of the original train line coming into Dingle (the westernmost train station in all of Europe from 1891 to 1953). The train once picked up fish in Dingle; its operators boasted that the cargo would be in London markets within 24 hours. The narrow-gauge tracks ran right along the harborfront.

All the land beyond the old buildings you see today has been reclaimed from the sea. Look inland and find the building on the left with the slate siding (the back wall of O'Flaherty's pub), facing the worst storms coming in from the sea. This was the typical design for 19th-century weatherproofing.

• *From here, cross the roundabout and walk up the big street called...*

❷ **The Mall:** After about 20 yards, two stubby red-brick pillars mark the entry to the police station. These pillars are all that remain of the 19th-century British Constabulary, which afforded a kind of Green Zone for British troops when they tried to subdue the local insurgents here. It was burned down in 1922, during the Civil War; the present building dates from 1938.

The big white **crucifix** across the street and 50 yards up The Mall is a memorial to heroes who died in the 1916 Rising. Note that it says in the people's language, "For honor and glory of Ireland, 1916 to 19__." The date is unfinished until Ireland is united and free.

• *Just past the Russel's B&B sign, take 15 paces up the B&B's driveway to see an old stone etched with a cross sitting atop the wall (on the right).*

This marks the site of a former **Celtic holy well,** a sacred spot for people here 2,000 years ago. Now, cross over the street, and continue walking uphill along the delightful gurgling stream.

Fifty yards farther up is another much-honored spot: the distribution center for **Guinness.** From this warehouse, pubs throughout the peninsula are stocked with beer. The wooden kegs have been replaced by what locals fondly call "iron lungs."

Across the street is the blocky, riot-resistant 19th-century **courthouse.** Once a symbol of British oppression, today it's a laid-back place where the roving County Kerry judge drops by to adjudicate cases on the last Friday of each month (mostly domestic disputes and drunken disorderliness). Next door, the blue building is the popular (and recommended for trad music) **Courthouse Pub.**

• *Continue to the big intersection and pause at the small bridge over a little stream.*

Notice the colors. A century ago, all these buildings were just shades of black and white. Their exteriors were originally exposed stonework (like the houses upstream). Then in the 1920s came the plaster (notice the bumps on the yellow Small Bridge Pub), and in the 1970s, cheery pastels (along with modern tourism).

• *Now head left into the commercial heart of the town on...*

❸ **Main Street:** First, find the little **Fiadh Handwoven Design Shop,** on the left just past the first little corner, across from Ashes Bar. Fiadh (pronounced Fia) Durham creates locally inspired contemporary designs with local wool at her loom and welcomes curious visitors.

A few steps farther up on the left is **Benner's Hotel.** This was Dingle's first hotel, where the old Tralee stagecoach route ended. Note the surviving Georgian facade and door.

Across the street, up a short gravel alley, is **St. James' Church.** Since the 13th century, a church has stood here (just inside the medieval wall, closed to public during the day). Today, it's Anglican on Sundays and filled with great traditional music several nights a week. In 2003, a midwinter concert series sprang up at the church, featuring internationally known artists seeking an intimate venue. It became known as the "Other Voices" series and

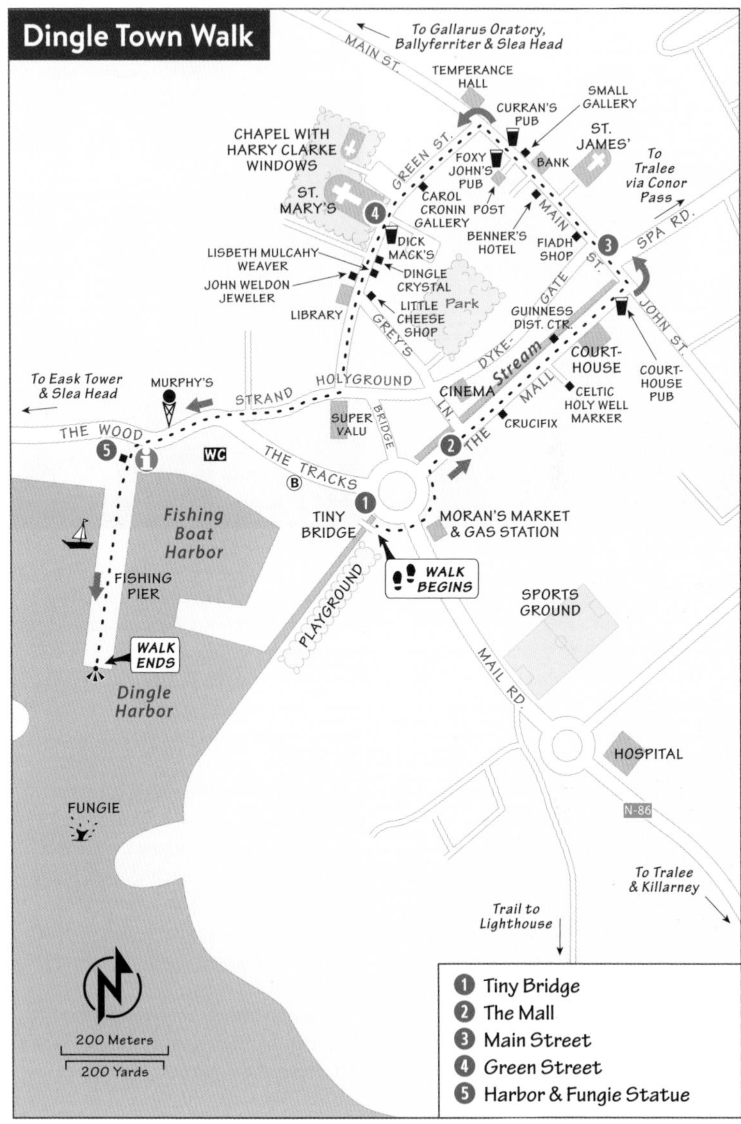

grew to become an annual event.

• *Farther uphill on the same side is a co-op gallery.*

The Small Gallery (An Gailearai Beagg) is the cute little showroom of the West Kerry Craft Guild, a collective of 14 local artists and artisans who each man the shop two days a month to show off their work. Drop in and learn about their work.

Facing each other just uphill are two of Dingle's most unapologetically **traditional drinking holes,** Curran's and Foxy John's. You're welcome to pop in and look around, though you'll feel a little more welcome if you order a drink. The publicans are happy to reminisce about old

Courthouse Pub

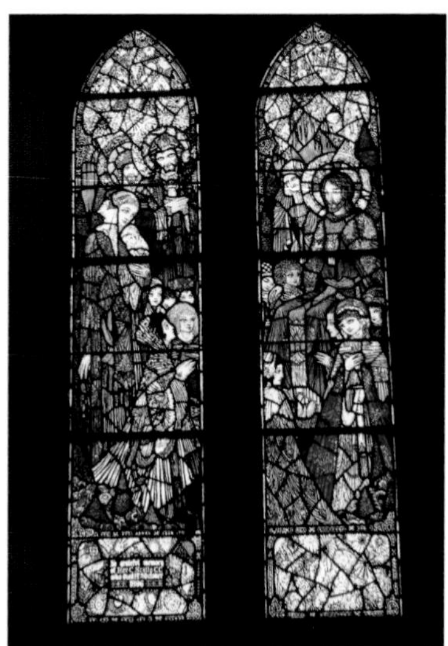

Harry Clarke windows

Dingle. These pubs are throwbacks to the humble day when a single hole-in-the-wall address would do double duty: commercial shop by day, pub by night.

James Curran runs **Curran's Pub** out of what was once his grandma's general store. On the last Saturday of every month—when farm families were in town for the market—the wives would pick up their basics here, ordering butter, tea, sugar, jams, and salted meat through the little window. Notice the "snug" in front. Until the 1950s, women weren't really welcome to drink in Irish pubs, but they could discreetly nurse a sherry in the "snug" while their men enjoyed the main room.

Foxy John's Pub, across the street, is still a working hardware store. Any time of day, you can order a bag of nails with your pint. Notice the back room; while pubs historically have had a legal "last call" at 11:30, the action would often migrate to the back room after the front door was locked.

• *Walk uphill to the Green Street intersection.*

On your right, notice the big **Temperance Hall,** which dates back to a 19th-century church-promoted movement that attempted to cut down the consumption of alcohol. To this day Ireland has a serious alcohol problem behind the happy veneer of all this pub fun. Today the Temperance Hall is a meeting place for AA groups, youth clubs, scouts, and other various social and support groups.

Directly across the street, you'll find a small **plaque** on the wall. This marked a safe house prepared during the French Revolution for the French Queen, Marie Antoinette. But the queen refused to leave France and was beheaded in 1789.

• *Now head downhill opposite the Temperance Hall to discover...*

❹ **Green Street:** Green Street is a reminder that 16th-century Dingle traded with Spain and was a port of embarkation for pilgrims on their way to Santiago de Compostela. A few steps down Green Street on the left, look above Kanon's Korner Fish shop to find a stone carved with the year "1586"—perhaps a remnant of that Spanish influence.

Down the street on the right, pop into the beautiful, modern **St. Mary's Church.** The former convent behind it shows off its delightful **Harry Clarke stained-glass**

Medieval Dingle

In the dimmest depths of the Dark Ages, peace-loving, bookish monks fled the chaos of the Continent and its barbarian raids. They sailed to the drizzly fringe of the known world—to places like Dingle. These monks kept literacy alive in Europe, and later provided scribes to Charlemagne, who ruled much of central Europe in the year 800.

It was from this peninsula that the semi-mythical explorer-monk St. Brendan is said to have set sail in the sixth century in search of a legendary western paradise. Some think he beat Columbus to North America by almost a thousand years.

Dingle was a busy seaport in the late Middle Ages. Dingle and Tralee were the only walled towns in Kerry. Castles stood at the low and high ends of Dingle's Main Street, protecting the Normans from the angry and dispossessed Irish outside. Dingle was a gateway to northern Spain—a three-day sail due south. Many 14th- and 15th-century pilgrims left from Dingle for the revered Spanish church in Santiago de Compostela, thought to house the bones of St. James.

windows—the single most important cultural sight in Dingle (described later, under "Sights"). Then, wander in the backyard to check out the tranquil nuns' cemetery, with its white-painted iron crosses huddling peacefully together under a big copper beech tree.

Across from St. Mary's (hence the nickname "the last pew") is **Dick Mack's Pub,** another traditional pub well worth a peek, even for nondrinkers. This was once a tiny leather shop that expanded into a pub at night. The pub was established in 1899 by great-grandpa Mack, whose mission was to provide "liquid replenishment" to travelers. Today, Dick Mack retains its old leather-shop ambience. In fact it's popular for handcrafted belts. (Their motto: "Step up and get waisted.")

Green Street continues downhill past inviting boutiques, cafés, and estate agents. Many fine Dingle shops show off work by local artisans.

Dingle Crystal features Sean Daly and his Waterford-trained crystal-cutting skills. Sean prides himself on the deep, sharp cuts in his designs—see the video of him at work.

A few steps farther on is the shop of **Lisbeth Mulcahy Weaver,** filled with traditional but stylish woven woolen wear. It's also the Dingle sales outlet of her husband, a well-known potter from Slea Head. Across the street is **John Weldon Jewellers**—ideal for those interested in handcrafted gold and silver with Celtic designs.

• *At the corner, take a left on Grey's Lane and follow your nose.*

The **little cheese shop** is a foodie shrine playfully governed by Maja Binder, a German who trained in Switzerland. Poke your head inside, even if only for a whiff of her handmade cheeses.

Back on Green Street you'll see **Dingle's library,** a gift from the Carnegie Foundation, with a small exhibit about local patriot Thomas Ashe and the Blasket Island writers. The best historic photos you'll find in town decorate the library's walls with images of 19th-century Dingle.

• *At the bottom of Green Street, take a right and head (past recommended Murphy's ice cream) to...*

❺ The Harbor and the Fungie Statue: The harbor was built in 1992 on reclaimed land. The string of old stone shops facing the harbor was the loading station for the railway that hauled fish from Dingle until 1953. Dingle's fishing industry survives, but it's an international endeavor. Most fishing boats that now ply these waters are Spanish, French, and Basque. Rather than going home with their catch, they offload their fish (mackerel, tuna, cod, herring, and prawns) onto trucks that lumber directly to their homelands. (European

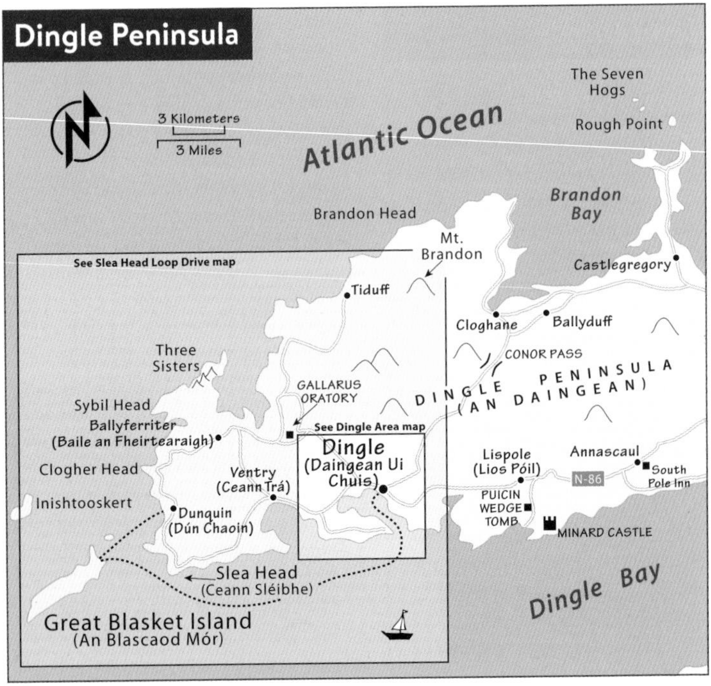

Dingle Peninsula

Atlantic Ocean
3 Kilometers
3 Miles
The Seven Hogs
Rough Point
Brandon Bay
Brandon Head
Mt. Brandon
Castlegregory
See Slea Head Loop Drive map
Tiduff
Cloghane
Ballyduff
CONOR PASS
Three Sisters
DINGLE PENINSULA (AN DAINGEAN)
GALLARUS ORATORY
Sybil Head
Ballyferriter (Baile an Fheirtearaigh)
See Dingle Area map
Dingle (Daingean Ui Chuis)
Lispole (Lios Póil)
Annascaul
South Pole Inn
N-86
Clogher Head
Ventry (Ceann Trá)
Inishtooskert
Dunquin (Dún Chaoin)
PUICIN WEDGE TOMB
MINARD CASTLE
Slea Head (Ceann Sléibhe)
Dingle Bay
Great Blasket Island (An Blascaod Mór)

Union member countries can fish in other countries' waters, which can leave a little country like Ireland at the mercy of other nations that have many times the people, appetite, and purchasing power.) The trucks that haul their catch home return to Ireland loaded with provisions for their fishermen, a situation that does very little to bolster Dingle's economy. But don't be too sad for Dingle. The parking lot to the right is often filled with tour buses, as Dingle is on the big-bus route from Killarney to Slea Head (in season, thousands stop here daily for a few hours).

Dingle's harbor

Enjoy the kid-friendly scene around the **bronze statue** of Dingle's beloved dolphin, Fungie (described later). From the Fungie statue, look straight out. Dead ahead on the distant hill is the Eask Tower. While it serves the useful purpose of marking this hidden harbor for those far out at sea, it was built primarily as a famine-era make-work project. A bit to the right, the big, yellow 18th-century manor house across the harbor was owned by Lord Ventry, the dominant English landlord of the time, and is now a school. The pyramid in the distance is Mount Eagle, marking Slea Head at the end of Dingle Peninsula. The building to the left with two big basement doors is a boathouse. At high tide, boats would float in, and be dry-docked at low tide for repairs. Beyond the boathouse and the harbor wall is the mouth of Dingle Harbor, playful Fungie, and the open sea.

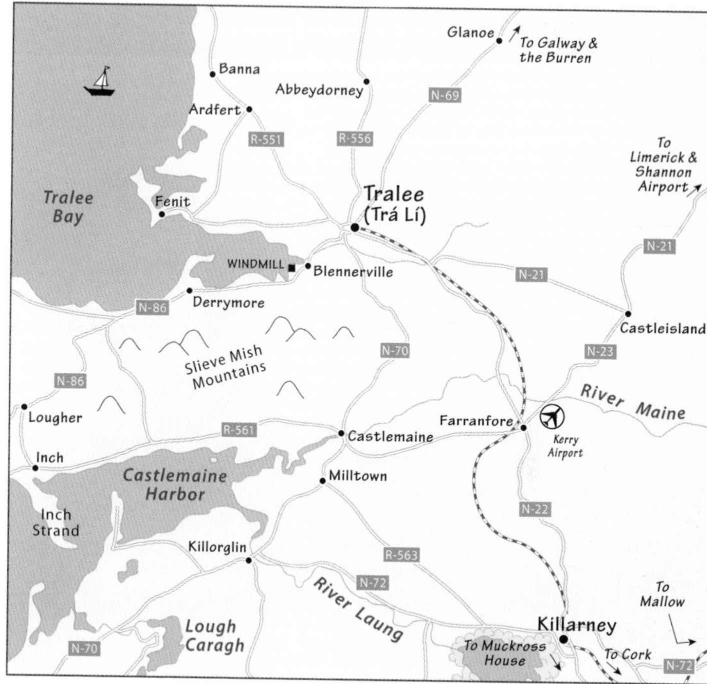

Sights

▲▲HARRY CLARKE WINDOWS

Just behind Dingle's St. Mary's Church stands the former Presentation Sisters' convent, now home to the Díseart (dee-SHIRT) Institute of Education and Celtic Culture. The sisters of this order, who came to Dingle in 1829 to educate local girls, worked heroically during the famine. The convent contains the beautiful Neo-Gothic Chapel of the Sacred Heart, built in 1884. During Mass in the chapel, the Mother Superior would sit in the covered stall in the rear, while the sisters—filling the carved stalls—chanted in response.

The chapel was graced in 1922 with 12 windows—the work of Ireland's top stained-glass man, Harry Clarke. Long appreciated only by the sisters, these special windows—showing scenes from the life of Christ—are now open to the public. The convent has become a center for sharing Christian Celtic culture and spirituality.

Cost and Hours: €3, Mon-Fri 9:00-17:00, Sat-Sun 10:00-15:00, tel. 066/915-2476, www.diseart.ie.

Visiting the Chapel: Stop at the reception room to pick up a loaner description with a self-guided walk. While Harry Clarke's neo-medieval windows are the big draw, it's also worth noting the recently painted, charming art of Coloradan Eleanor Yates, especially her *Last Supper* that pictures Dingle Harbor out the window. Upstairs is the chapel with the beloved stained glass of Harry Clarke. While the windows behind the altar are Victorian, Clarke's early-20th-century windows ring the chapel with six easy-to-read scenes. Clockwise from the back entrance, they are the visit of the Magi, the Baptism of Jesus, "Let the little children come to me," the Sermon on the Mount, the Agony in the Garden, and Jesus appearing to Mary Magdalene.

Tom Crean, Unsung Antarctic Explorer

Kerrymen are a hardy lot, and probably none more so than Antarctic explorer Thomas Crean. In 1901, Crean volunteered to join the crew of the RSS *Discovery.* Onboard were Captain Robert Falcon Scott and other soon-to-be famous explorers, including Ernest Shackleton. Their mission: to be the first men to reach the South Pole.

The effort required pulling sleds laden with tons of supplies across miles and miles of ice in extreme conditions. Crean quickly gained his mates' respect for his hard work, calm presence, and cheerful (if tuneless) singing. The *Discovery* Expedition pushed the boundaries of Antarctic exploration, but didn't reach the pole (Britain's second attempt, in 1909 under Shackleton, got much closer before also turning back).

Determined to try again, Scott chose Crean among the first of his handpicked crew for the *Terra Nova* Expedition (1910-1913). Early on, Crean saved some expedition members stranded on a drifting ice floe—encircled by orcas—by leaping between floating chunks of ice, then scaling an ice wall to get help. Later, Crean and two others were the last support team ordered to turn back as Scott made the final push to the pole (having come so close, the unshakable Crean wept at the news). Near the end of the 730-mile return trip, Crean's two mates, sick and freezing, could go no farther. Exhausted and provisioned with only three cookies and two sticks of chocolate, Crean made a nonstop, solo, 35-mile march through a blizzard to reach help, saving his mates' lives. (Though Scott's party did reach the pole, a Norwegian team led by Roald Amundsen beat them to it—by a month; Scott and his men didn't survive the trip back.)

Crean's most famous act of heroism took place on his third and final polar expedition (1914-1917), led by Shackleton. Their ship, the *Endurance,* was crushed by ice, marooning the crew on Elephant Island. Hoping to find help at a whaling station, Shackleton, Crean, and four others sailed a modified open lifeboat 800 miles in 17 days to South Georgia Island. There they were forced to hike across the rugged, unexplored interior to reach the station on the other side. A ship was sent to rescue the exhausted and malnourished crew, all of whom had miraculously survived the 18-month ordeal.

Crean never did reach the South Pole himself, turning down Shackleton's request to join him on his next (and last) trek. But Crean distinguished himself as a hero among explorers—who named both a mountain and a glacier after him in Antarctica—and was honored by King George V. In 1920, he retired from the navy, returned to County Kerry, and stashed his medals away, never again speaking of his experiences.

Fungie, Dingle's resident dolphin

▲FUNGIE

In 1983, a bottlenose dolphin moved into Dingle Harbor and became a local celebrity. Fungie (FOON-ghee) is now the darling of the town's tourist trade and one reason you'll find so many tour buses parked along the harbor. A recent study theorizes that he may be one of a half-dozen dolphins released from "Dolphinariums" (under pressure from animal-rights activists) on the southern coast of Britain. This would account for Fungie's loner ways and comfort around humans.

Hardy little tour boats thrive by baiting passengers with the chance of an up-close Fungie encounter, then motoring out to the mouth of the harbor, where they troll around looking for him (see "Tours," earlier). You don't pay unless you see the dolphin.

▲OCEANWORLD

This aquarium offers a little peninsula history, 300 different species of fish in thoughtfully described tanks, a penguin exhibit, and the easiest way to see Fungie the dolphin: on video. Newer additions include young otters, tiny crocodiles, and a steamy "butterfly oasis" chamber.

Cost and Hours: €15.50, from €47 for families with children (4-6 people), daily 10:00-18:00, shorter hours off-season, cafeteria, just past harbor on west edge of town, tel. 066/915-2111, www.dingle-oceanworld.ie.

DINGLE DISTILLERY TOUR

Whiskey is as trendy as Dingle, and the hometown distillery would love to give you a sample. The one-hour tour includes earnest explanations and two hard drinks—a whiskey and a gin or vodka. The distillery is a 20-minute walk from town, just over the bridge on Slea Head Drive (€15, tours run daily in season at 12:00, 14:00, and 16:00, tel. 066/402-9011, www.dingledistillery.ie).

Experiences

▲*Bike and Hike to Eask Tower*

This bike-and-hike trek to Eask Tower totals about 10 miles round-trip.Rent a bike in town and pedal west past the aquarium, going left at the roundabout that takes you over the bridge onto R-559

Biking outside Dingle Town

Eask Tower

toward Slea Head. After almost two miles, turn left at the brown sign to *Holden's Leather Workshop*. A narrow leafy lane leads another two miles or so to a hut on the right marked *Eask Tower* (the tower looms on the bare hill above). Pay the €2 trail fee at the hut (if unattended, feed the honor box) and hike about a mile straight up the steep trail. You'll need to navigate through (possibly climb) a couple of waist-high, metal-rung gates. After 45 minutes, you'll reach the stone signal tower on the crown of the hill. Enjoy fantastic views of Dingle town (to the north) and Dingle Bay with the Iveragh Peninsula (home of the Ring of Kerry to the south). Spot the two jagged Skellig Islands off the distant tip of the Iveragh Peninsula.

▲▲▲*Music in Dingle Pubs*

Traditional pub music is Dingle town's best experience. Even if you're not into pubs, take an afternoon nap and then give these an evening whirl. Dingle is renowned among traditional musicians as an ideal place to perform. The town has piles of pubs that feature music most nights, and there's never a cover charge—just buy a beer. The scene is a decent mix of locals, Americans, Brits, and Germans. Music normally starts at 21:30ish, and the last call for drinks is at "half eleven" (23:30), sometimes later on weekends. For a seat near the music, arrive early. By midnight, the door is usually closed and the chairs are stacked. Note that from October through April the music hibernates.

Make a point to wander the town and follow your ear. Irish culture is very accessible in the pubs; they're like highly interactive museums waiting to be explored. If you sit at a table, you'll be left alone. But stand or sit at the bar and you'll be engulfed in conversation with new friends.

Dingle Pub Crawl: The best place to start a pub crawl is at **O'Flaherty's,** the first music pub in Dingle, located on Holyground street. Quietly intense owner Fergus O'Flaherty sings and plays a half-dozen different instruments during almost nightly traditional-music sessions. His domain has a high ceiling and is dripping in old-time photos and town memorabilia—it's unpretentious, cluttered fun.

Moving up Strand Street, find **John Benny's.** Its dependably good traditional-

Enjoying the pub experience

Dick Mack's Pub

music sessions come with John himself joining in on accordion when he's not pouring pints. **Paddy Bawn Brosnan's Pub** (also on the Strand) brags no music and no food—just beer and sports. If a game is on TV—especially Gaelic football or hurling—you can watch it here with the locals. Then head up Green Street. **Dick Mack's,** across from the church, is nicknamed "the last pew." Once a leather shop, today the pub sells only drinks, with a fine snug and a fascinating ambience.

Green Street climbs to Main Street, where two more Dick Mack-type places are filled with locals deep in conversation (but no music): **Foxy John's** (a hardware shop by day) and **Curran's** (across the street, a small clothing shop by day). For more on each of these (and Dick Mack), see the town walk, earlier.

Wander down Main Street. The **Dingle Pub** seems designed for John Denver and Irish Rovers fans. It's well established as *the* place for folk-ballad singing rather than the churning traditional beat of an Irish folk session. Just downhill, **Neligan's** is another lively traditional music session option with fun dance lessons for beginners on summer Thursday nights. At the bottom of Main Street, **Small Bridge Bar** offers live music nightly.

I'd finish my night at the **Courthouse Pub** (on The Mall, next to the old gray courthouse). This is a steamy little hideaway with low ceilings and high-caliber musicians who perform nightly at 21:00, and my favorite men's room in Ireland—with kegs for urinals.

▲▲*Folk Concerts*

If you're not a night owl, these are your best opportunities to hear Irish traditional music in a more controlled, early evening environment.

St. James' Church: Top local musicians offer a quality evening acoustic, traditional Irish music in the fine little St. James' Church (100 seats), just off Main Street. They are organized by local piper Eoin Duignan, whose command of the melodic *uileann* bagpipes is a highlight most nights. Surprisingly, this humble church is the home venue of the acclaimed "Other Voices" winter concert TV series that has drawn the likes of Amy Winehouse, Sinéad O'Connor, and Donovan, among others (€13 in advance, €15 at the door; Mon, Wed, and Fri at 19:30, May-Oct only; see sign on church gate or, for more details or to book a ticket, drop by Paul Geaneys Pub, Leac a Ré craft shop, or Siopa Ceoil music shop).

The Siopa Ceoil Trad Concert: The Siopa Ceoil music shop hosts intimate traditional Irish music sessions in its cozily cramped, 45-seat space (€20, includes a

Music performance at St. James' Church

tasty Irish decaf between sets; May-Sept Tue, Thu, and Sat at 19:00, plus Sun July-Sept; 2 The Colony, mobile 086-080-8448, www.siopaceoil.ie).

Sleeping

In or near the Town Center

$$$$ Benners Hotel was the only hotel in town a hundred years ago. It stands bewildered by the modern world on Main Street, with sprawling public spaces and 52 abundant, overpriced rooms (tel. 066/915-1638, www.dinglebenners.com, info@dinglebenners.com).

$$$ Greenmount House sits among chilly palm trees a five-minute hike up from the town center. This guesthouse commands a fine view of the bay and mountains, with two fine rooms, three superb rooms, and nine sprawling suites in a modern building with lavish public areas and wonderful breakfasts (parking, top of John Street, tel. 066/915-1414, www.greenmounthouse.ie, info@greenmounthouse.ie). Seek out the hot tub in their back-garden cabin.

$$$ Barr Na Sráide Inn, central and hotel-like, has 29 nicely refurbished rooms (huge family room sleeps 5, self-service laundry, bar, parking, past McCarthy's pub on Upper Main Street, tel. 066/915-1331, www.barrnasraide.ie, barrnasraide@eircom.net).

$$ Bambury's Guesthouse is big and modern with views of grazing sheep and the harbor. The 12 rooms are airy and comfy (coming in from Tralee it's on your left on Mail Road, 2 blocks before the Texaco station; tel. 066/915-1244, mobile 086-324-4281, www.bamburysguesthouse.com, bamburysguesthouse@gmail.com).

$$ Alpine Guesthouse looks like a Monopoly hotel, and is fittingly comfortable and efficient. Its 14 bright and fresh rooms come with pastoral views, a cozy lounge, and friendly owner Paul O'Shea (RS%, family rooms, easy parking, Mail Road, tel. 066/915-1250, www.alpineguesthouse.com, alpinedingle@gmail.com). Driving into town from Tralee, it's the first lodging on your right, next to the sports field and a block uphill from the Texaco station.

$$ Sraíd Eoin House offers five pleasant, top-floor rooms above Galvin's Travel Agency (RS%, family rooms, John Street, tel. 066/915-1409, www.sraideoinbnb.com, sraideoinhouse@hotmail.com, friendly Kathleen and Maurice O'Connor).

$$ O'Neill's B&B is homey and friendly, with six nifty rooms on a quiet street at the top of town (cash only, parking, John Street, tel. 066/915-1639, www.oneillsbedandbreakfast.com, info@oneillsbedandbreakfast.com, Mary and Stephen O'Neill).

$ Eileen Collins Kirrary B&B is run by the same Collins family that does archaeological tours of the peninsula (see "Tours," earlier). They offer five pleasant rooms, great prices, a large garden, and a homey friendliness (cash only, Kirrary House, just off The Mall on Avondale at Dykegate and Grey's Lane, tel. 066/915-1606 or mobile 087-150-0017, www.collinskirrary.com, collinskirrary@eircom.net).

Beyond the Pier

A 10- to 15-minute walk from Dingle's town center, these places tend to be quieter, since they are farther from the late-night pub scene.

$$$ Heaton's Guesthouse, big, peaceful, and comfortable, is on the water just west of town at the end of Dingle Bay—a five-minute walk past Oceanworld on The Wood. The 16 thoughtfully appointed rooms come with all the amenities (creative breakfasts, parking, The Wood, tel. 066/915-2288, www.heatonsdingle.com, info@heatonsdingle.com, David Heaton).

$$$ Castlewood House is a palatial refuge with 12 tasteful rooms, classy furnishings, and delicious breakfasts. The breakfast room and patio have a wonderful view of Dingle Harbor (parking, The Wood, tel. 066/915-2788, www.castlewooddingle.com, info@castlewooddingle.com, Brian and Helen Heaton).

$$ Harbour Nights B&B weaves together a line of old row houses to create a 17-room guesthouse facing the harbor (parking, just past the aquarium on The Wood, tel. 066/915-2499, mobile 087-686-8190, www.dinglebandb.com, info@dinglebandb.com, Seán and Kathleen Lynch).

Above Town

$$ Tower View B&B is a big, modern home just outside of town on a lovely quiet lot. This kid-friendly mini farm rents eight fine rooms (family rooms, High Road, tel. 066/915-2990, www.towerviewdingle.com, info@towerviewdingle.com, Aidan and Helen Murphy).

$$ The Lighthouse B&B is a cozy place with six prim rooms, wonderful views near the crest of the hill, and Lucky the fluff-ball mutt (family rooms, High Road, tel. 066/915-1829, www.lighthousedingle.com, info@lighthousedingle.com, Denis and Mary Murphy).

$$ Bolands B&B is family-run with a traditional, welcoming atmosphere and eight comfortable rooms (family rooms, Goat Street, tel. 066/915-1426, mobile 085-714-2297, www.bolandsdingle.ie, info@bolandsdingle.ie, Breda and Michael Boland).

$ Devane's B&B caters to the active bike-and-hike crowd, with six clean and practical rooms that are a good value given their close proximity to town (cash only, Goat Street, tel. 066/915-1193, www.devanesdingle.com, devanesdingle@eircom.net, Kevin and Geraldine Devane).

Over the Bridge, West of Town

These options are a 25- to 30-minute level walk along the Dingle Bay shore from town, on the far side of an unlit stone bridge with no sidewalks (making a walk back at night a bit dodgy). A taxi from town should only cost about €6. All three have parking.

$$$ Milltown House has 10 nicely refurbished rooms—some with bay views. The casual vibe comes with a cozy in-house bar and three gentle-giant Irish wolfhounds dozing nearby. In warmer months, Dingle Falconry shows off birds of prey in the huge front yard. With room to run, unusual animals, and its proximity to Dingle Pitch & Putt, kids love this place (family rooms, The Wood, first left after crossing the bridge, tel. 066-915-1372, www.milltownhouse.com, info@milltownhouse.com, Stephen McPhilemy).

$$$ Milestone House is farthest out, but an ideal option for longer stays, with two separate self-catering apartments. The front yard sports a 3,500-year-old standing stone as an ancient territorial marker (3-night minimum, on road R-559, tel. 066/915-1831, www.milestonedingle.com, milestonehousedingle@gmail.com).

$$ Clonmara B&B's host Blandina O'Connor grew up next door to Milltown House and knows the area well. You'll find five homey rooms in a peaceful setting with grand views across Dingle Bay (cash only, tel. 066/915-1656, mobile 087-204-2243, www.clonmara.com, clonmara@hotmail.com).

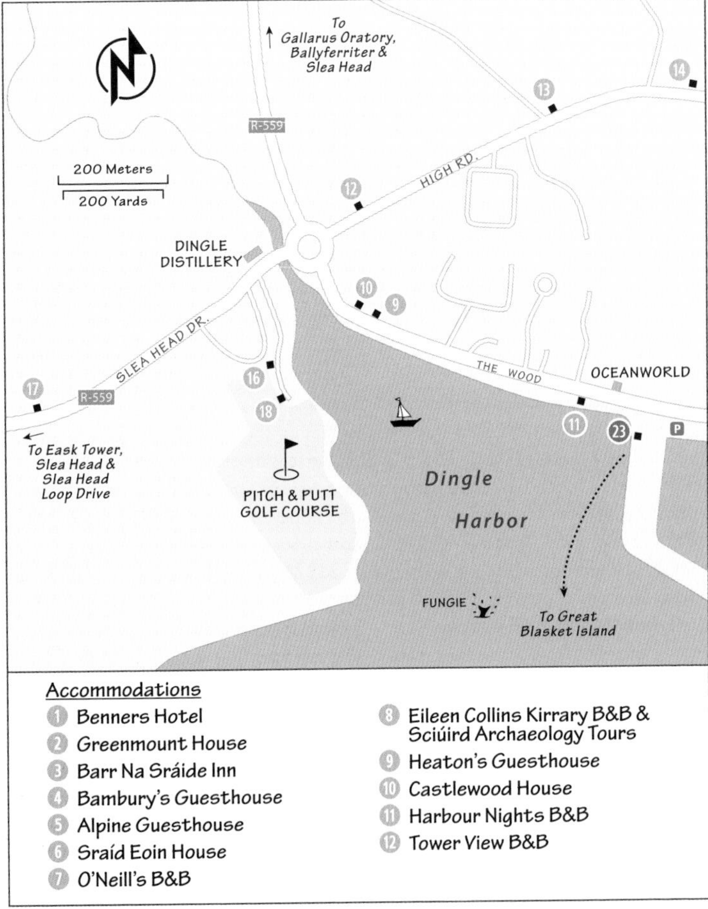

Eating

Dining in Dingle

The top-end places generally offer good-value, multicourse, early-bird specials from about 17:30 to 19:00. Remember that while seafood is a treat here, so is the lamb.

$$$$ Out of the Blue Seafood-Only Restaurant is the locals' choice for great fresh fish. The interior is bright and elegantly simple. The chalkboard menu is dictated by what the fishermen caught that morning. If they're closed, there's been a storm and the fishermen couldn't go out (Mon-Sat 17:00-21:30, Sun 12:30-15:00, reservations smart, some outdoor picnic-table seating, just past the TI, facing the harbor on The Waterside, tel. 066/915-0811, www.outoftheblue.ie).

$$$ James G. Ashe Pub and Restaurant, an old-fashioned joint, is popular with locals for its nicely presented, top-quality, traditional Irish food and seafood at good prices. I like their beef-and-Guinness stew (daily 12:00-15:00 & 17:30-21:30, Main Street, tel. 066/915-0989).

$$$$ Global Village Restaurant is where Martin Bealin gives dishes a creative twist with inspiration gleaned

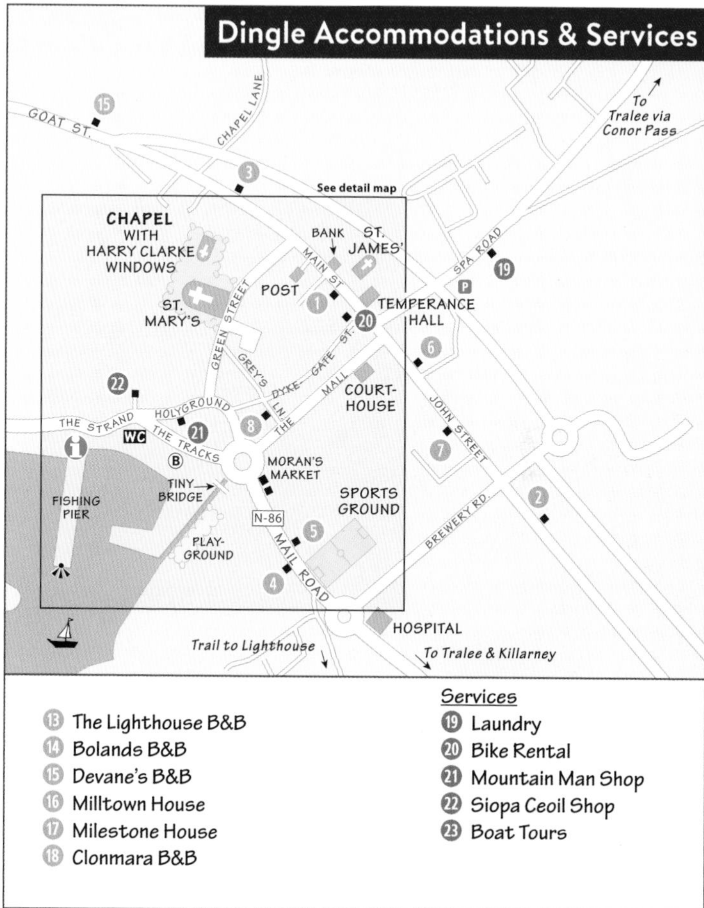

from his world travels. It's an eclectic, healthy, fresh seafood-eaters' place (daily 17:30-22:00, Nov-Feb Fri-Sun only, good salads, top of Main Street, tel. 066/915-2325, mobile 087-917-5920).

$$$$ Chart House Restaurant serves contemporary cuisine in a sleek, well-varnished dining room. Settle back into the shipshape, lantern-lit space. The menu is shaped by what's fresh and seasonal (daily 18:00-22:00 except closed Mon Oct-May, reservations wise, at roundabout at base of town, tel. 066/915-2255, www.thecharthousedingle.com, Jim McCarthy).

$$$$ Lord Baker's is the venerable elder among fine Dingle dining options. John Moriarty and his family concoct quality dishes served in a friendly yet refined atmosphere. The seafood soup is a memorable specialty (Fri-Wed 18:00-21:30, closed Thu, reservations smart, Main Street, tel. 066/915-1277 or 066/915-1141, www.lordbakers.ie).

$$$$ Fenton's is good for seafood meals with a memorable apple-and-berry-crumble dessert (Tue-Sun 18:00-21:30, closed Mon, reservations smart, on Green Street down the hill below the church, tel. 066/915-2172, mobile 087-248-2487).

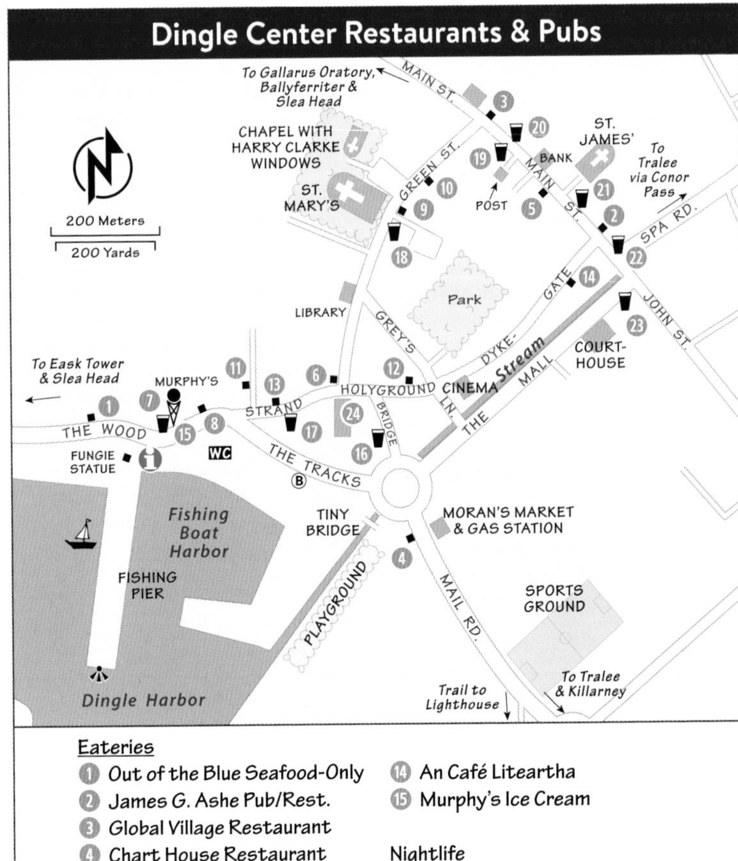

Less Expensive Dingle Meals

$$ John Benny's Pub dishes up traditional Irish fare on the waterfront. John, the proprietor and a Dingle fixture since my first visits, takes his outstanding selection of whiskeys as seriously as his choice of quality local musicians. Come here for dinner, and stay for a drink and great nightly live music (food daily 12:30-21:30, music after 21:30, The Pier, tel. 066/915-1215).

$$ Danno's Restaurant and Bar is a sprawling and fun-loving eatery popular with tourists and locals for inexpensive burgers, fish-and-chips, and pub grub. Danno's interior is a mix of railroad and rugby memorabilia. He offers some of the best outdoor seating in town with a heated and leafy patio out back (closed Mon, Strand Street, mobile 086-236-4404).

$$ The Blue Zone is a hip jazz wine bar offering pizza, salad, and an international cosmopolitan vibe. Tight, busy, and family-friendly, it's a tasty alternative to Dingle's pub grub and fish-dominated fare. Or just kick back and enjoy a late-night conversation over a glass of wine set to eclectic background music (Thu-Tue 17:30-11:30, closed Wed, Green Street across from St. Mary's Church, tel. 066/915-0303).

$$ Fish Box connects generations of Flannery family fishing to this pleasant little brightly white-tiled fish restaurant (daily 12:00-21:00, takeout available, Green Street just up from St. Mary's Church, mobile 087-052-6896).

$$ Anchor Down is a fresh fish option that's easy on the wallet. The Sheehy family, who are local fishermen, supply their simple little cottage with a variety of fresh fish—and chips if you want them (daily 11:30-21:30, closed Dec-Feb, up a lane off Strand Street, 3 The Colony, tel. 066/915-1545).

$ Reel Dingle Fish & Chips is the best chippy in town, serving mostly takeout, but with a few stools. It's not fast, because they cook the fish fresh to order. They serve generous portions—consider splitting—and are also good for burgers (daily 13:00-22:00, near SuperValu grocery store on Holyground, tel. 066/915-1713).

$ Strand House Café is a cozy spot where their fresh-made pastry tempts you to hang out with an extra cup of coffee (daily 10:00-17:00, Sun from 11:00, perched above the centrally located Strand House on Strand Street, tel. 066/915-2703).

$ An Café Liteartha, a simple refuge hidden behind a wonderfully cluttered bookstore, serves soup and sandwiches to a good-natured crowd of Irish speakers (daily 10:00-18:00, Oct-April until 17:00 and closed Sun, Dykegate Street, tel. 066/915-2204).

Ice Cream: For two decades **Murphy's** ice cream has been a Dingle favorite. Their famously adventurous "handmade" flavors include lavender, candied chili pepper, rosewater, clove, and even gin (daily 11:00-22:00, shorter hours off-season, on Strand Street).

Picnics

The **SuperValu** supermarket/department store, at the base of town, has everything and stays open late (Mon-Sat 8:00-21:00, Sun until 19:00, daily until 22:00 July-Aug). Smaller groceries, such as **Centra** on Main Street (daily 8:00-21:00), are scattered throughout the town. Consider a grand-view picnic out on the end of the newer pier (as you face the harbor, it's the pleasure-boat pier on your right). You'll find picnic tables on the harbor side of the roundabout and benches along the busy harborfront.

Transportation

Arriving and Departing

Tralee (Trá Lí), 30 miles from Dingle, is the region's transportation hub (with the nearest train station). Most bus trips make connections in Tralee.

BY BUS

Dingle has no bus station and only one bus stop, on the waterfront behind the SuperValu supermarket: Look for the bus shelter with the roof made from an overturned traditional black-tarred boat (bus info tel. 01/836-6111, www.buseireann.ie, or Tralee station at 066/712-3566; Tralee train info tel. 066/712-3522).

From Dingle by Bus to: Galway (5/day, 6 hours, transfer in Tralee and Limerick), **Dublin** (3/day, 7 hours, transfer in Tralee and Limerick), **Tralee** (5/day, fewer off-season and Sun, 1.5 hours). Most bus trips out of Dingle require at least one or two (easy) transfers.

All Roads Lead to Daingean Ui Chuis

The western half of the Dingle Peninsula is part of the Gaeltacht, where locals speak the Irish Gaelic language. In an effort to ward off English-language encroachment, all place names on road signs were controversially changed to Irish-only, though some are now back in English. As you travel along Slea Head Drive (known as Ceann Sléibhe in Irish), refer to this cheat sheet of the most useful destination names.

English Name	Irish Gaelic Name
Dingle	*Daingean Ui Chuis* (DANG-un e koosh)
Ventry	*Ceann Trá* (k'yown—rhymes with "crown" traw)
Slea Head	*Ceann Sléibhe* (k'yown SHLAY-veh)
Dunquin	*Dún Chaoin* (doon qween)
Blasket Islands	*Na Blascaodaí* (nuh BLAS-kud-ee)
Great Blasket Island	*An Blascoad Mór* (on BLAS-kade moor)
Ballyferriter	*Baile an Fheirtearaigh* (BALL-yuh on ERR-ter-ee)
Reasc Monastery	*Mainistir Riaisc* (MON-ish-ter REE-isk)
Gallarus	*Gallaras* (GAHL-russ)
Kilmalkedar	*Cill Mhaoil-cheadair* (kill moyle-KAY-dir)
Annascaul	*Abhainn an Scáil* (ow'en on skahl)
Lispole	*Lios Póil* (leesh pohl)
Tralee	*Trá Lí* (tra-LEE)

BY CAR

Drivers choose from two routes into Dingle: the easy southern route on N-86 or the much more dramatic, scenic, and treacherous Conor Pass on the R-560 leading into the R-569. It's 30 miles (48 km) from Tralee either way. If you're not staying overnight, use the waterfront parking lot extending west from the TI, or the lot four blocks inland on Spa Road (€1/hour, pay-and-display, daily 8:00-18:00).

SLEA HEAD LOOP DRIVE

The gloriously green Dingle Peninsula is 10 miles wide and runs 40 miles from Tralee to Slea Head. The top of its mountainous spine is Mount Brandon—at 3,130 feet, it's the second-tallest mountain in Ireland. The Slea Head Loop, worth ▲▲▲, is a scenic road that lassoes the peninsula in about 30 miles (45 km). It must be driven (or biked) in a clockwise direction. It's easy by car, or a demanding five hours by bike. Remember that minibus tours are offered, too (see page 173).

As you navigate the loop, you'll see lots of grass-fed Friesian (or Holstein) cows, the belted Galloway cow from Scotland (looking like they have a white blanket tossed over them), and some of the peninsula's 50,000 sheep. In spring or summer, you'll likely enjoy a festival of flowers as you follow the blue signs with white squiggles—a stylized "WAW"—reminding you that this is "The Wild Atlantic Way" (part of a marketing campaign by the Irish Tourist Board).

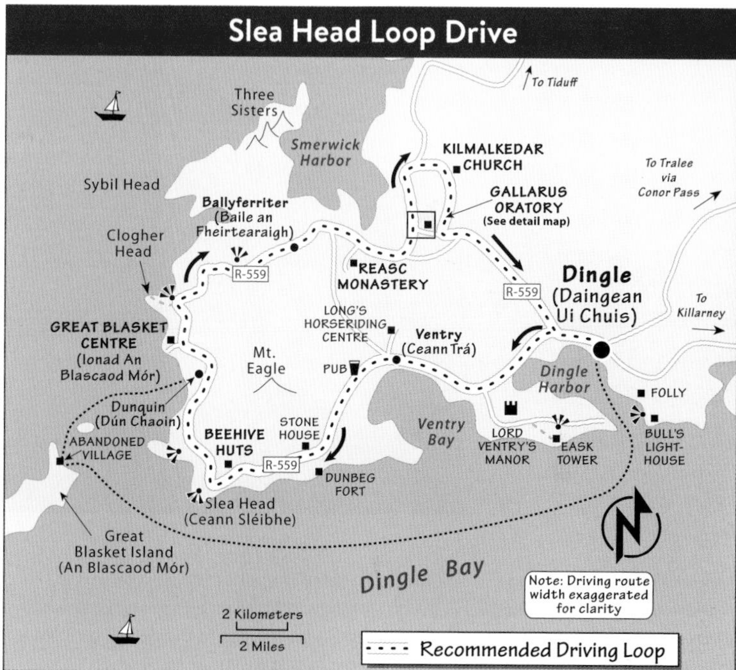

To help locate points of interest, I've given distances in kilometers so you can follow along with your odometer. To match my listed distances, set your odometer to zero at Oceanworld as you leave Dingle. You'll stay on R-559 the entire way, following brown *Slea Head Drive* signs for most of the route (through kilometer 37). The road is narrow and can be congested from mid-July to late August.

If you'll be visiting Great Blasket Island later, allow time for a stop at the Great Blasket Centre, with interesting exhibits and views across to the island (about halfway around the loop).

Self-Guided Drive

FROM DINGLE TOWN TO VENTRY

Leave Dingle town west along the waterfront (0.0 km at Oceanworld). Driving out of town, on the left you'll see a row of humble "two up and two down" cottages from a 1908 affordable-housing government initiative.

0.5 km: Dingle Harbor has an eight-foot tide. The seaweed was used to make formerly worthless land arable. (Seaweed is a natural source of potash—organic farming, before it was trendy.) Across the River Milltown estuary, the recommended **Milltown House** was Robert Mitchum's home during the 1969 filming of the Academy Award-winning movie *Ryan's Daughter.* (Behind that is Dingle's pitch-and-putt golf course.) Look for the narrow mouth of this blind harbor (behind you, in the distance at the opposite end of the harbor) and the Ring of Kerry beyond that. Dingle Harbor is so hidden that ships needed the hilltop Eask Tower to find its mouth. If a group of small boats are gathered at the mouth of the harbor, Fungie has come out to play.

0.7 km: At the roundabout, turn left over the bridge. On the far side, the blue building on the right was the site of a corn-grinding mill in the 18th century (with a ghostly black waterwheel hiding

Slea Head Loop drive

behind it). Today it's a modern warehouse that shelters the **Dingle Distillery** (tours daily—see "Sights," earlier). Just beyond that on the right, you'll pass the junction where you'll complete this loop 30 miles from now. The gas station on your left is the westernmost on the peninsula (you won't see another on this drive, so consider topping up the tank).

1.3 km: The recommended Milestone House is named for the stone **pillar** (*gallaun* in Irish) in its front yard. This pillar may have been a prehistoric grave or a boundary marker between two tribes. This peninsula, literally an open-air archaeological museum, is dotted with more than 2,000 such monuments dating from the Neolithic Age (roughly 3000 BC) through early Christian times. Another stone pillar stands in the field across the road (100 yards away, on the left).

The land ahead on the left holds the estate and mansion of Lord Ventry, whose family came to Dingle as post-Cromwellian War landlords in 1666. Today his mansion (built in 1750, out of view) houses an all-Irish-language girls boarding school.

As you drive past the **Ventry estate** (at 2.8 km, on the right, is Ventry's slate-roofed blacksmith shop), you'll pass palms, magnolias, and exotic flora, which were introduced to Dingle by Lord Ventry. Fuchsias—imported from Chile and spreading like weeds—line the roads all over the peninsula and redden the countryside from June through September. About 75 inches of rain a year gives this area its "40 shades of green."

4.6 km: Stay off the "soft margin" as you enjoy views of Ventry Harbor, its long beach (to your right as you face the water), and distant **Skellig Michael**—the pyramid-shaped island in the distance that holds the rocky remains of a sixth-century monastic settlement. Mount Eagle (1,660 feet), rising across the bay, marks the end of Ireland—and that's where you're heading.

FROM VENTRY TO SLEA HEAD

6.6 km: In the town of **Ventry**—a.k.a. Ceann Trá (translated roughly as "beach head")—Irish is the first language. Urban Irish families love to come here in the summer to immerse their kids in the traditional culture and wild nature.

Just past town, a lane leads left to a fine beach and mobile-home vacation community. An information board explains the history, geology, and bird life of the harbor. The humble trailer park has no running water or electricity. Locals like it for its economy and proximity to the beach. From here, a lane leads inland to **Long's Horseriding Centre.**

7.3 km: The bamboo-like **rushes** on either side of the road are the kind used to make the local thatched roofs. Thatching, which nearly died out because of fire danger, is more popular now that anti-flame treatments are available. It's expensive, as few qualified thatchers remain in Ireland.

8.5 km: This intersection has the "Three Gs"—God (a church), groceries, and Guinness. The pub just past the church is **Paddy O'Shea's.** The Irish football star Páidí Ó Sé (Paddy O'Shea) was a household name in Ireland. He won eight all-Ireland football titles for Kerry as a player from 1970 to 1988. He then trained the Kerry team for many years before further endearing himself to his fans by running this pub. A **statue** remembers Paddy, who died in 2012.

10.7 km: *Taisteal go Mall* means "go slowly"; the building on the right, surrounded by a tall net to keep the balls in, is the **village schoolhouse.** In summer it's used for Irish Gaelic courses for kids from the big cities. On the left is the small Celtic and Prehistoric Museum, a quirky private collection of prehistoric artifacts, including arrowheads and ancient jewelry, collected by a retired busker (musician) named Harris (€5, daily 10:00-17:00).

11.1 km: The circular mound on the right is a late Stone Age **ring fort.** It was a petty Celtic chieftain's headquarters—a stone-and-earth stockade filled with little thatched dwellings. Such mysterious sites survived untouched through the centuries because of superstitious beliefs that they were "fairy forts." While this site is unexcavated, archaeologists have found evidence that people have lived on this peninsula since about 4000 BC.

11.7 km: Look ahead up Mount Eagle at the patchwork of stone-fenced fields. In the distance on the left is another view of Skellig Michael.

12.5 km: Dunbeg Fort (50 yards downhill on the left) is made up of a series of defensive ramparts and ditches around a central *clochan* (€3, May-Sept 9:00-18:00, July-Aug until 19:00). A third of the fort fell into the sea during a violent storm in 2014. Forts like this are the most important relics left from Ireland's Iron Age (500 BC-AD 500).

The modern stone-roofed dwelling across the street was built to blend in with the landscape and the region's ancient rock-slab architecture (AD 2000). It's the welcoming and recommended **Stone House Restaurant,** with an adjacent visitors center, where you can check out a 10-minute video (€2.50) that gives a bigger picture of the prehistory of the peninsula (included with Dunberg Fort ticket). A traditional *currach* boat is permanently dry-docked in the parking lot.

Roughly 50 yards up the road and 100 yards off the road to the right is a thatched **cottage** abandoned by a family named Kavanaugh during the famine (around 1848). With a few rusty and chipped old artifacts and good descriptions, it offers an evocative peek into the simple lifestyles of the area in the 19th century (€3, daily 10:00-18:00, closed Nov-April). The owner, Gabriel, also runs working sheepdog demonstrations (in Irish for the dogs, English for tourists; €5, €7 combo-ticket covers cottage and dog demo, must book ahead by phone, mobile 087-762-2617, www.dinglesheepdogs.com).

13.2 km: A group of **beehive huts** (*clochans*) is a short walk uphill (€3, daily 9:00-19:00, WC). While reconstructed, these mysterious stone igloos, which cluster together within a circular wall, are a better sight than the similar group of beehive huts down the road.

Farther on (at 14.0 km), you'll ford a stream. There's never been a bridge here; this bit of road—nicknamed the "upside-down bridge"—was designed as a ford.

14.7 km: Pull off to the left at this second group of beehive huts. (Aedan runs this family enterprise where you can see more *clochans*, hold a baby lamb, and use the WC for €3.) Look across the bay at the Ring of Kerry in the distance and ahead at the Blasket Islands.

FROM SLEA HEAD TO BALLYFERRITER

16.0 km: At **Slea Head** (Ceann Sléibhe)—marked by a crucifix, a pullout, and great views of the Blasket Islands—you turn the corner on this tour. On stormy days, the waves are "racing in like white horses."

16.7 km: Pull into the little parking lot (at *Dún Chaoin* sign) for views of **Great Blasket Island** and **Dunmore Head** (the westernmost point in Europe) and to review the roadside map (which traces your route) posted in the parking lot.

Great Blasket Island is an icon of traditional Irish culture. Because the islanders subsisted off the sea, rather than on potatoes, they survived the famine. The most traditional of Irish communities, about 100 people lived there until 1953, when the government evacuated the island. While the island is uninhabited today, small tour boats shuttle visitors from Dingle and from Dunquin Harbor (just ahead). To read more about this fascinating island, see the next section of this chapter. And to learn more, visit the Great Blasket Centre (a few miles farther down the road).

As you drive on, notice the ruined stone houses. The scattered village just down the road was abandoned during the famine. Some homes are now fixed up, as this is a popular place these days for summer vacationers. You can see more good examples of land reclamation, patch by patch, climbing up the hillside. Mount Eagle was the first bit of land that Charles Lindbergh saw after crossing the Atlantic on his way to Paris in 1927. Villagers here were as excited as he was—they had never seen anything so big in the air.

Look above, at the patches of land slowly made into farmland by the inhabitants of this westernmost piece of Europe. Rocks were cleared and piled into fences. Sand and seaweed were laid on the clay, and in time it was good for grass. The created land, if at all tillable, was generally used for growing potatoes; otherwise, it was only good for grazing. Much of this farmland has now fallen out of use.

19.0 km: The Blasket Islands' residents had no church or cemetery on the island. On the left stretches their **cemetery.** The famous Blascaod storyteller Peig Sayers (1873-1958) is buried at its center. Just off this coast is the 1588 shipwreck of the *Santa María de la Rosa* of the Spanish Armada. And ahead is the often-tempestuous Dunquin Harbor. Blasket Island farmers—who on a calm day could row

Building a Rock Fence

The Emerald Isle is as rocky as it is green. When the English took the best land, they told the Irish to "go to hell or go to Connaught" (the rugged western part of Ireland where the soil was particularly poor and rocky). Every spring, farmers "harvest" rocks driven up by the winter frost in order to plant more edible fare. Over generations, Irish farmers stacked these rocks into fences, which still divide so much of the land.

The fences generally have no visible gates. But upon closer look, you'll see a "V" built into the wall by larger rocks, which are then filled in with smaller rocks. When a farmer needs to move some cattle, he slowly unstacks the smaller rocks, moves the cattle through, and then restacks them. Flying low over western Ireland, the fields—alligatored by these rock fences—seem to stretch forever. And nearly all have these labor-intensive V-shaped gates built in.

View from Slea Head

Great Blasket Centre

across in 30 minutes—would dock here and hike over the saddle and 12 miles into Dingle to sell their produce.

Hey! There's a dead man floating out at sea. Oh, it's just an island. (While its official name is The Sleeping Giant, that island has always been known to Blasket Islanders as "The Dead Man.")

21.3 km: From here a lane leads a kilometer to the **Great Blasket Centre,** worth ▲▲. This excellent modern cultural museum is an essential stop if you plan to visit the islands—or a good place to learn about them if you won't be making the crossing (€5, daily 10:00-18:00, closed Nov-Easter, fine cafeteria run by friendly Christy, tel. 066/915-6444, www.blasket.ie).

The state-of-the-art Blascaod and Gaelic heritage center gives visitors the best look possible at the language, literature, and way of life of Blasket Islanders. The building's spine, built to resemble a sloping village lane, leads to an almost sacred view of the actual island. Don't miss the exceptional 20-minute video, a virtual visit to the island back when it was inhabited (shows on the half-hour), then hear the sounds, read the poems, browse through old photos, and gaze out the big windows at those rugged islands.

23.1 km: Grab the scenic **Clogher Head pullout.** Ahead is Mount Brandon, Ireland's second highest peak (at 3,130 feet). Working to the left you'll see Butter Harbor (the name believed to originate from times when Vikings stopped here to grease up their hulls). Then spot the three swoopy peaks—the Three Sisters. Left of that is Sybil Head (where scenes from *Star Wars: The Force Awakens* were shot). On the summit of Sybil Head, the tiny black square is a watchtower from the days when Britain feared an invasion from Napoleon. The entire coast was lined with these, all within sight of each other to relay a warning signal if under attack by the bloody French. And under the Three Sisters is the popular Dingle Links golf course.

Ahead, on the right, study the top fields, untouched since the planting of 1845, when the potatoes didn't grow, but rotted in the ground. The faint vertical ridges of the potato beds can still be seen—a reminder of the famine. Before the famine, 40,000 people inhabited this peninsula. After the famine, the population was so small that there was never again a need to farm so high up. Today, only 10,000 people live on the peninsula.

From this pullout, a breezy 15-minute walk leads out to **Clogher Head.** The dirt road stretches off to the left and peters out after 200 yards. But it's all open ground and easy to navigate. Just step carefully over bog puddles and head uphill through the rocky heather to the lumpy summit. There you'll be rewarded with postcard-worthy panoramic views.

FROM BALLYFERRITER TO DINGLE

28.0 km: The town of **Ballyferriter,** established by a Norman family in the 12th century, is the largest on this side of Dingle Peninsula. The pubs serve grub, the fine old church dates to the 1860s, and the old schoolhouse (on the left) is a museum with modest exhibits that provide the best coverage of this very historic peninsula (€3, generally daily 10:00-17:00, closed Oct-May, tel. 066/915-6333, www.westkerrymuseum.com).

Keep on Slea Head Drive (R-559), following signs to *Dingle.*

30.0 km: The road bends over a tiny yellow bridge, past a pub and microbrewery (on the right); 50 yards after that watch for a tiny unmarked paved road going uphill on the right. Detour right up this lane, where you'll find the scant remains of **Reasc Monastery** about 300 yards up (no sign).

This is the stony footprint of a monastic settlement dating from the 6th to 12th century (free, always open). The inner wall divided the community into sections for prayer and business (cottage industries helped support the monastery). In 1975, only the stone pillar was visible, as the entire site was buried. The layer of black tar paper (near the base of the walls) marks where the original rocks stop and the excavators' reconstruction begins. The stone pillar is Celtic (c. 500 BC).

Reasc standing stone

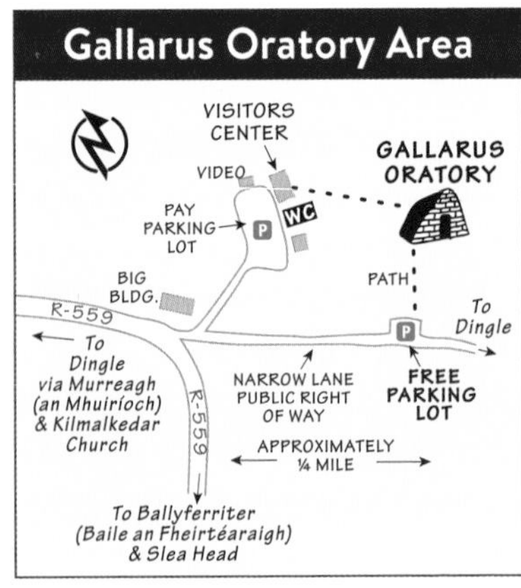

When Christians arrived in the fifth century, they didn't throw out the Celtic society. Instead, they carved a Maltese-type cross over the Celtic scrollwork.

One of the cottage industries operated by the monastery was a double-duty kiln. Just outside the wall (opposite the oratory, past the duplex *clochan,* at the bottom end), find a stone hole with a passage facing the southwest wind. This was the kiln—fanned by the wind, it was used for cooking and drying grain. Locals would bring their grain to be dried and ground, and the monks would keep a tithe (their 10 percent cut). With the arrival of the Normans in the 12th century, these small religious communities were pushed aside by a militaristic feudal system.

Return to the main road and continue on.

32.0 km: Go left at the big Dingle Peninsula Hotel, following *Gallarus* signs and staying on Slea Head Drive.

33.0 km: Turn right up the narrow lane. The "free" car park is a private enterprise on private land (with a short video, WC,

Gallarus Oratory

and shop), where you'll be charged €3 to see the site. To park for free, go farther up the lane (at 33.4 km) to a tiny five-car pullout on the left, where a path leads through a gate 200 yards to the amazing **Gallarus Oratory** (free, always open).

Built about 1,300 years ago, the Gallarus Oratory is one of Ireland's best-preserved early Christian churches. Shaped like an upturned boat, its finely fitted dry-stone walls are still waterproof. As you step in, notice how thick the walls are. A simple, small arched window offers scant daylight over where the altar would have stood. Picture the interior lit by candles during medieval monastic services. It would have been tough to fit more than about a dozen monks inside. Notice the holes once used to secure covering at the door, and the fine alternating stonework on the corners.

From the oratory, return to the main road and continue, following the brown *Slea Head Drive* signs. (To skip the Kilmalkedar Church—last stop on this tour—and go directly back to Dingle, continue up the narrow lane and turn right when you hit the bigger road.)

35.5 km: At the junction in the center of the next village, leave Slea Head Drive by taking a right on R-559 (signed with *Dingle, 10 km*). For an optional stop (your own private mini Gallarus Oratory), pull off at 37.1 km at the cemetery, cross the road, and hike 200 yards to St. Brandon's Oratory, which dates to the sixth century (even older than Gallarus).

37.3 km: The **ruined church of Kilmalkedar** (Cill Mhaoil-cheadair, on the left at the yellow hiker sign) was the Norman center of worship for this end of the peninsula. It was built when England replaced the old monastic settlements in an attempt to centralize their rule. The 12th-century church has a classic Romanesque arch and a well-worn cross atop its roof. It's surrounded by a densely populated graveyard (which has risen noticeably above the surrounding fields over the centuries). In front of the church, you'll find the oldest (late medieval) tombs, a stately early Christian cross (substantially buried by the rising graveyard and therefore oddly proportioned), and a much older ogham stone. This stone, which had

Ruined church of Kilmalkedar

already stood here 900 years when the church was built, is notched with the mysterious Morse code-type ogham script used from the third to seventh century. It may have marked a grave or a clan border, indicating that this was an important pre-Christian gathering place. The church fell into ruin during the Reformation.

38.0 km: Continue uphill, overlooking the water. You'll pass another ancient **"fairy fort"** on the right. The bay stretched out below you is Smerwick Harbor. In 1580 a force of 600 Italian and Spanish troops (sent by the pope to aid a rebellion against the Protestant English) surrendered at this bay to the English. All 600 were beheaded by the English forces, which included Sir Walter Raleigh.

41.7 km: At the crest of the hill you may see the belted Galloway beef cattle with their white blankets. The spruce forest on the right was planted with government supplements (to minimize Ireland's carbon footprint). From here, enjoy a long coast back into Dingle town (sighting, as old-time mariners did, the Eask Tower).

44.0 km: Take a left past the Dingle Distillery, go over the bridge, and head back into Dingle. At 45 km, you're back at the Oceanarium where you started. Well done!

BLASKET ISLANDS

This rugged group of six islands off the tip of Dingle Peninsula seems particularly close to the soul of Ireland. The only one you can visit, Great Blasket Island (worth ▲▲), was once home to as many as 160 people. Life here was hard, but the sea provided for all, and no one went hungry. Each family had a cow, a few sheep, and a plot of potatoes. They cut their peat from the high ridge and harvested fish from the sea. There was no priest, pub, or doctor. Because they were not entirely dependent upon the potato, island inhabitants survived the famine relatively unscathed. To these folk, World War I provided a bonus, as occasionally valuable cargo washed ashore from merchant ships sunk by U-boats. These people formed the most traditional Irish community of the 20th century—the symbol of ancient Gaelic culture.

Blasket Islands

From this simple but proud fishing/farming community came three writers of international repute whose Gaelic works—basically tales of life on Great Blasket Island—have been translated into many languages. You'll find *Peig* (by Peig Sayers) and *The Islandman* (Thomas O'Crohan) in shops everywhere. But the most readable and upbeat is *Twenty Years A-Growing* (Maurice O'Sullivan), a somewhat-true, Huck Finn-esque account of the author's childhood and adolescence and of island life as it was a hundred years ago.

The population dwindled until the government moved the last handful of elderly residents to the mainland in 1953. Today Great Blasket is little more than a ghost town overrun with rabbits on a peaceful, grassy, three-mile-long poem.

Getting To the Blasket Islands

In summer, various boats run between **Dingle town** and the Blasket Islands, with anywhere from a 3.5- to 6-hour stop to explore Great Blasket. The ride (which may include a quick look at Fungie the dolphin) traces the spectacular coastline all the way to Slea Head. Competing boats offer similar services from Dingle town and operate when there's enough demand. The tricky landing at Great Blasket Island's primitive and slippery little boat ramp makes getting off a challenge and landing virtually impossible in wet weather. Boats generally depart from the marina pier in Dingle at 9:00 or 11:00 and return from Great Blasket at 15:00 or 17:30. For details, see the boat tour listings under "Tours," earlier.

Schedules are soft—reconfirm the day before. Hikers (bringing their own picnic) should take the early boat out and a late boat back. With a bit of planning, you can spend a half-day and really do the island justice. Nonhikers can put ashore for an hour or two just to explore the ghost-town ruins.

Boats also go from **Dunquin Harbor** to the Blasket Islands (book ahead; see Blasket Island Ferry listing under "Tours," earlier).

Visiting Great Blasket Island

Boats bring visitors ashore at the abandoned village, next to the beach, at the east end of the island (the only landing on the island). Be sure to reconfirm the return boat schedule with the crew before you disembark.

Upon dropping anchor, you'll be ferried from the boat to the boat ramp in a six-person RIB/zodiac. Ask the Office of Public Works guide on shore when the next guided walk of the abandoned village starts; or, start your trek immediately if it's a long wait. There are no eateries, so bring a picnic. Note that there are also no modern WCs or dependable shelters.

Tourist Information: Before you go, visit the **Great Blasket Centre** on the mainland near Dunquin (see page 195) and spend some time on the excellent **website** of the Office of Public Works, devoted to both the island and the visitors center (www.blasket.ie).

Great Blasket Hike: Wear good shoes rain or shine. The long (roughly 3.5 miles), thin island is flanked by easy-to-follow hiking trails.

Think of the island as a giant hog's back running generally northeast to southwest, with parallel trails running along the south-facing and north-facing slopes. An easy loop circles the lowest and closest ridge, linking the south- and north-flank trails (do this if you're short on time). Beyond that junction, the trail becomes a single heather-clumped path that heads right up the ridge to two taller summits.

The only steep section of the hike is the first hundred-yard slope behind the abandoned village that you'll take to reach the flanks of the ridge, which the rest of the trail follows. I like to take the south-facing trail outbound with the morning light and save the north side for the return, when parts of the trail are brought out of the shade by the afternoon sun.

You could simply hike out for an hour and then hike back. You'll know you've reached the third summit when you encounter a stubby hip-high concrete pylon marker (there's no need to go farther as the views are best from here).

TRALEE

While Killarney is the tour-bus capital of County Kerry, Tralee (Trá Lí in Irish, both pronounced Tra-LEE) is its workaday market and transit hub. For drivers zipping between Dingle and Galway, this amiable town near the base of the Dingle Peninsula is worth an hour's stop.

The town comes alive for the famous Rose of Tralee International Festival, usually held in mid-August. It's a celebration of arts and music, culminating in the election of the Rose of Tralee—the most beautiful woman at the festival (no matter which country she was born in, as long as she has Irish heritage).

Sights

▲KERRY COUNTY MUSEUM

Easily the best place to learn about life in Kerry, this museum (located in Ashe Memorial Hall in the center of town) has three parts: Kerry slide show, museum, and medieval-town walk.

Tralee

Cost and Hours: €5; daily 9:30-17:30, Oct-May until 17:00 and closed Sun-Mon; tel. 066/712-7777, www.kerrymuseum.ie.

Visiting the Museum: Get in the mood by relaxing for 10 minutes through the continuous slide show of Kerry's spectacular scenery. Then wander through 7,000 years of Kerry history in the museum. It starts with good background info on the archaeological sites of Dingle, progresses through Viking artifacts found in the area, and goes right up to a video showing highlights of the Kerry football team (a fun look at Irish football, which is more like rugby than soccer). Good coverage is given to adventurous Kerryman Tom Crean, who survived three Antarctic expeditions with Scott and Shackleton (see sidebar on page 180).

BLENNERVILLE WINDMILL

On the western edge of Tralee, just off the N-86 Dingle road, spins a restored mill originally built in 1780. Its eight-minute video tells the story of the windmill, which ground grain to feed Britain as that country steamed into the Industrial Age. In the 19th century, Blennerville was a major port for America-bound emigrants.

Blennerville Windmill

Cost and Hours: €7 gets you a one-room emigration exhibit, the video, and a peek at the spartan interior of the working windmill; daily 9:00-18:00, April-May and Sept-Oct 9:30-17:30, closed Nov-March, last entry 45 minutes before closing, tel. 066/712-1064, www.blennerville-windmill.ie.

Transportation

Arriving and Departing

BY TRAIN AND BUS

Travelers headed for Dingle using public transportation will likely go through Tralee.

From Tralee by Train to: Dublin (every 2 hours, 6/day on Sun, 1 direct in morning, otherwise change in mellow Mallow, 4 hours, arrives at Heuston Station), **Killarney** (8/day, 35 minutes). Train info: Tel. 066/712-3522, www.irishrail.ie.

By Bus to: Dingle (6/day, fewer off-season and on Sun, 1 hour), **Galway** (8/day, 4 hours), **Limerick** (7/day, 2 hours), **Doolin/Cliffs of Moher** (5/day, 5 hours), **Ennis** (6/day, 3.5 hours, change in Limerick), **Dublin** (5/day, 6 hours). Tralee's bus station is across the parking lot from the train station. Bus info: Tel. 066/716-4700, www.buseireann.ie.

BY PLANE

Kerry Airport is a 20-minute drive from Tralee and a one-hour drive from Dingle (code: KIR, tel. 066/976-4644, www.kerryairport.ie). It's just off the main N-22 road, halfway between Killarney and Tralee. Dingle Shuttle Bus is your best connection to Dingle town, but you must reserve in advance (about €30-40/person one-way, minimum 3 passengers, mobile 087-250-4767, www.dingleshuttlebus.com). You can also connect to the airport via taxi (€35 from Tralee, €90 from Dingle) or bus (3/day to Dingle via Tralee).

County Clare

Those connecting Dingle in the south with Galway up the coast to the north can joyride through the fascinating landscape and tidy villages of County Clare. Ennis, the county's major city, is a workaday Irish place with a medieval history, a great traditional Irish music scene, and a market bustle. Near Ennis are the open-air folk park of Craggaunowen and the sobering Irish Workhouse Centre in Portuma. Overlooking the Atlantic, the dramatic Cliffs of Moher offer tenderfeet a thrilling hike. The Burren is a unique, windblown limestone moonscape that hides an abundance of flora, fauna, caves, and history. If you stick around for the evening, join a tour-bus group for a medieval banquet in a castle in Kinvarra or meet up with trad-music enthusiasts in Doolin.

COUNTY CLARE IN 1 DAY

A car is the best way to experience County Clare and the Burren. The region can be an enjoyable daylong drive-through or a destination itself. None of the sights take much time. But do get out and walk a bit.

With more time, you could take a walking tour (of the Cliffs of Moher or the Burren) or a cruise from Doolin (to see the Cliffs of Moher and the Aran Island of Inisheer). For an overnight stay, good choices are Doolin and Ennis.

Driving from Dingle to Galway, I'd recommend the following day plan: Rather than taking the main N-21 road via Limerick, drive north from Tralee on N-69 via Listowel to catch the Tarbert-Killimer car ferry (avoiding Limerick traffic with a direct route to the Burren; for ferry specifics, see page 217).

From Killimer, drive north on N-67 via Kilkee and Milltown Malbay. The little surf-and-golf village of Lahinch makes a good lunch stop. Then drive the coastal route to the Cliffs of Moher for an hour-long break. The scenic drive from the cliffs through the Burren, with a couple of stops, takes about two hours. For dinner, consider the 17:30 medieval banquet at Dunguaire Castle (reservations required), near Kinvarra, one hour south of Galway.

By Train or Bus: Using public transportation, your gateways to this region are Ennis from the south and Galway from the north. Linking the smaller sights within County Clare and the Burren by bus is difficult: Book a tour instead (see page 216).

ENNIS

This bustling market town (pop. 25,000), the main town of County Clare, rated ▲, is a handy transportation hub, with good rail connections to Limerick, Dublin, and Galway. Ennis is 15 miles from Shannon Airport and makes a good first- or last-night base in Ireland for travelers not locked into Dublin flights. It also offers a chance to wander around an Irish town that is not reliant upon the tourist dollar (though not shunning it either).

COUNTY CLARE AT A GLANCE

▲▲▲**Cliffs of Moher** Steep cliffs bordered by a bluff-top trail—offering breathtaking coastal views—perched precariously 600 feet above the churning Atlantic. **Hours:** Visitors center open daily 8:00-19:00, gradually later closing times toward midsummer—as late as 21:00 May-Aug, Nov-Feb 9:00-17:00. See page 212.

▲▲**The Burren** Desolate but botanically diverse, a limestone wonderland for hikers, sheltering evocative 4,000-year-old burial structures that witnessed humans' transition from hunter-gatherers to farmer-herders. See page 215.

▲**Doolin** A friendly crossroads town drawing great musicians to its pubs and serving as an easy base for cruising along the Cliffs of Moher and day-tripping to the Aran Island of Inisheer. See page 214.

▲**Ennis** County's main market town (a great overnight base for nearby Shannon Airport) sporting fun trad music pubs, and historic abbey ruins. Craggaunowen open-air folk park is nearby; the Irish Workhouse Centre is an hour away. See page 204.

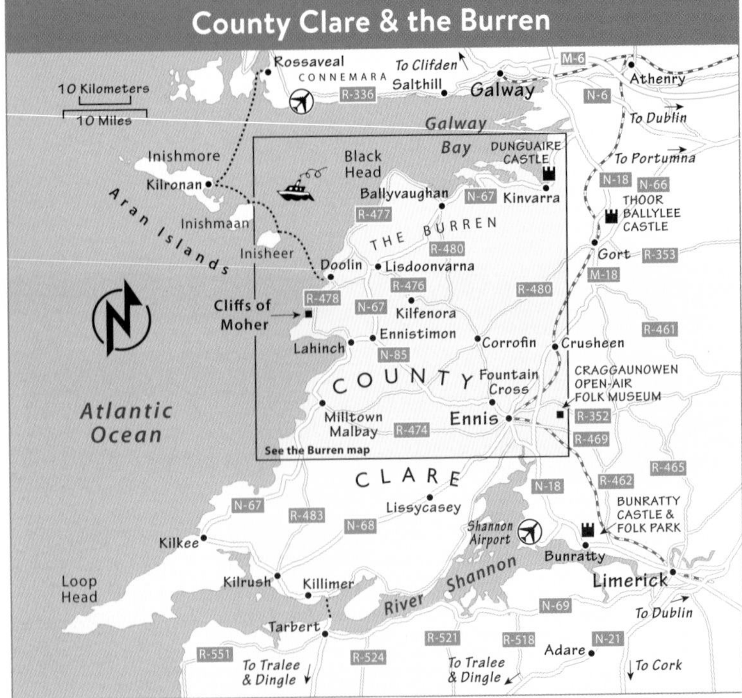

Orientation

The center of Ennis is a tangle of contorted streets (often one-way). Use the steeple of Saints Peter and Paul Cathedral and the Daniel O'Connell monument column (at either end of the main shopping drag, O'Connell Street) as landmarks.

Tourist Information: The TI is just off O'Connell Square (closed Sun year-round and Mon Oct-May, some lunchtime closures, tel. 065/682-8366).

Helpful Hints

Laundry: Fergus launderette is opposite the Harvey's Quay parking lot (Mon-Sat 8:30-18:00, closed Sun, tel. 065/682-3122).

Taxi: A good local bet is **Burren Taxis** (tel. 065/682-3456).

Walking Tours: Jane O'Brien leads 1.5-hour walking tours of Ennis departing from the TI (€10, mid-May-mid-Sept Mon-Tue and Thu-Sat at 11:00, available for private tours, mobile 087-648-3714, www.enniswalkingtours.com). **Ollie's Tours** operates 1.5-hour walking tours, departing from the O'Connell Monument (€10, May-Sept daily at 10:45, mobile 086-202-3534, www.olliestours.com).

Sights

CLARE MUSEUM

This small but worthwhile museum, housed in the large TI building, has eclectic displays about ancient ax heads, submarine development, and local boys who made good—from 10th-century High King Brian Ború to 20th-century statesman Éamon de Valera. Coverage includes the Battle of Dysert O'Dea in 1318. One of the few Irish victories over the invading Normans, it delayed English domination of most of County Clare for another 200 years.

Cost and Hours: Free, Mon-Sat 9:30-13:00 & 14:00-17:30, closed Sun year-round and Mon Oct-May, tel. 065/682-3382, www.clarelibrary.ie.

ENNIS FRIARY

The Franciscan monks arrived here in the 13th century, and the town grew up around their friary (which is like a monastery). Today, it's still worth a look for its 15th-century limestone carvings (now protected by a modern roof to keep their details from further deterioration).

Cost and Hours: €5, may include a tour—depends on staffing, daily 10:00-18:00, closed Nov-March, tel. 065/682-9100.

Visiting the Friary: If more than one guide is on duty, ask for a brief introduction to the five carvings taken from the McMahon family tomb. The last one, of Christ rising on the third day, has a banner with a tiny swastika. But look closely: It's reversed so that it rotates as the rising sun would. Despite the swastika's later Nazi association, it's actually a centuries-old symbol of good luck (the word "swastika" comes from Sanskrit and means "well-being"). Postwar visitors, unaware of the symbol's older meaning, misunderstood it and tried to rub it out of the carving, thus its very faint presence today.

Craggaunowen tower house

▲CRAGGAUNOWEN

This open-air folk museum nestles in a pretty forest, an easy 20-minute drive east of Ennis. The structures are replicas, except for the small 16th-century castle (tower house), which the park was built around. A friendly weaver, spinning her wool on the castle's ground floor, is glad to tell you the tricks of her trade. A highlight is the Crannog, a fortified Iron Age thatch-roofed dwelling built on a small man-made island, which gives you a grubby idea of how clans lived 2,000 years ago. A modern surprise hides in a corner of the park under a large glass teepee: the *Brendan,* the original humble boat that scholar Tim Severin sailed from Ireland to North America in 1976 (via frosty stepping-stones like Iceland and Greenland). He built this boat out of tanned hides, sewn together using primitive methods, to prove that Ireland's St. Brendan may indeed have been the first European to visit America on his legendary voyage, 900 years before Columbus and 500 years before the Vikings.

Cost and Hours: €11, daily 10:00-17:00, shorter hours off-season, last entry one hour before closing, tel. 061/711-222, www.shannonheritage.com.

Getting There: The park is well signposted nine miles (15 km) east of Ennis off R-469, which leads out of town past the train station.

IRISH WORKHOUSE CENTRE

To see the Victorian "cure" for poverty, the Irish Workhouse Centre in Portumna is a memorable side trip from Ennis. One of the few remaining intact workhouses in Ireland, it has been restored but not renovated; it stands, grim and foreboding, in much the same condition as when it was closed.

Workhouses were set up by the British government in the 1830s to provide the destitute with an alternative to starvation and death. But they were a poor alternative. To enter, you had to give up any assets you still had. Men and women were

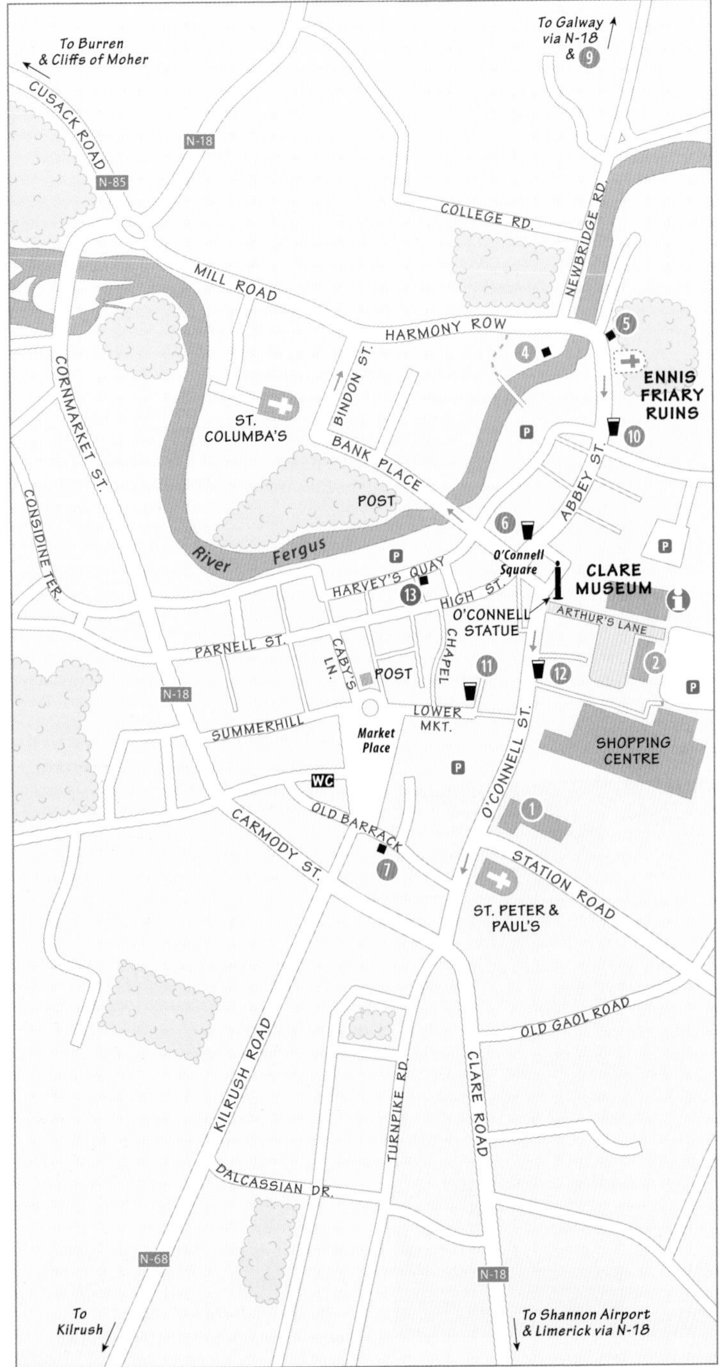
To Burren & Cliffs of Moher
To Galway via N-18 & 9
CUSACK ROAD
N-18
N-85
COLLEGE RD.
NEWBRIDGE RD.
MILL ROAD
HARMONY ROW
BINDON ST.
ST. COLUMBA'S
ENNIS FRIARY RUINS
CORNMARKET ST.
BANK PLACE
POST
ABBEY ST.
CONSIDINE TER.
River Fergus
O'Connell Square
CLARE MUSEUM
HARVEY'S QUAY
HIGH ST.
O'CONNELL STATUE
ARTHUR'S LANE
PARNELL ST.
CABY'S LN.
CHAPEL
POST
N-18
LOWER MKT.
SUMMERHILL
Market Place
O'CONNELL ST.
SHOPPING CENTRE
WC
OLD BARRACK
CARMODY ST.
STATION ROAD
ST. PETER & PAUL'S
OLD GAOL ROAD
KILRUSH ROAD
TURNPIKE RD.
CLARE ROAD
DALCASSIAN DR.
N-68
N-18
To Kilrush
To Shannon Airport & Limerick via N-18

Ennis
Accommodations
1 Old Ground Hotel & Poet's Corner Pub
2 Temple Gate Hotel
3 Grey Gables B&B
4 Rowan Tree Hostel
Eateries
5 The Cloisters Restaurant & Pub
6 Knox's Pub
7 Numero Uno Pizzeria
Nightlife & Other
8 Glór Irish Music Centre
9 To Cois na hAbhna Show
10 Cruise's Pub
11 Quinn's Pub
12 Brogan's Pub
13 Launderette
NEW ROAD
River Fergus
CUSACK PARK STADIUM
FRANCIS STREET
ENNIS SHOPPING CENTRE
CLON ROAD
GLÓR IRISH MUSIC CENTRE
PARKING GARAGE
P
To Galway
One-way streets
100 Meters
100 Yards
FRIARS WALK
PARK AVE.
CLON ROAD
CLON ROADMOR
TRAIN & BUS STATION
To Craggaunowen Open-Air Folk Museum
R-469
To Limerick

housed separately; children over age three were expected to work. There were no common areas for mingling. Conditions were notoriously inhumane. Ironically, it was cheaper for landlords to pay for paupers' boat passage to North America than to keep them in workhouses (which were financed by a property tax).

Cost and Hours: €7, daily 9:30-17:00, closed Nov-Feb, St. Brigid's Road, Portumna, tel. 090/975-9200, www.irishworkhousecentre.ie. Helpful guides give 45-minute tours that add a human angle to the spartan buildings.

Getting There: The workhouse is about an hour east of Ennis or Kinvarra, located just over the border in County Galway. From Ennis, it's a winding one-hour drive—stay on R-352 the entire way. As you enter Portumna, turn left at Bank of Ireland, and continue to the workhouse (on your right).

Rick's Tip: *Skip the crowded* **Bunratty Castle and Folk Park** *near the Shannon Airport (past Limerick on the road to Ennis). Leave it to the jet-lagged, big-bus tour groups.*

Experiences

Ennis' modern **Glór Irish Music Centre** (*glór* is Irish for "sound") connects you with Irish culture. It's worth considering for traditional music, dance, or storytelling performances (€10-25, year-round usually at 20:00, 5-minute walk behind TI on Friar's Walk; ticket office open Mon-Sat 10:00-17:00, closed Sun; tel. 065/684-3103, www.glor.ie).

The original stage show housed in the local **Cois na hAbhna** (COSH-na-HOW-na) **Hall** is a fine way to spend an evening. Sponsored by Comhaltas, a nonprofit focused on Irish traditional music, it's a celebration of Irish performing arts presented in two parts. The first features great Irish music, song, and dance. After the break, you're invited to kick up your heels and take the floor as

Craggaunowen

the dancers teach some famous Irish set dances. Phone ahead to see if a *ceilidh* is scheduled on off nights (€10-15, generally May-Sept Wed and Fri at 20:30, call ahead to confirm, at edge of town on N-18 Galway road, tel. 065/682-4276, www.coisnahabhna.ie).

Live **traditional** music begins in pubs at about 21:30. The best is **Cruise's** on Abbey Street, with music nightly year-round and good food (bar is cheaper than restaurant, tel. 065/682-8963). Other pubs offering weekly traditional music nights (generally on weekends, but schedules vary) are **Quinn's** on Lower Market Street (tel. 065/682-8148), **Knox's** on Abbey Street (tel. 065/682-287), and **Brogan's** on O'Connell Street (tel. 065/682-9480). The **Old Ground Hotel** hosts live music year-round in its pub (Tue-Sun, open to anyone); although tour groups stay at the hotel, the pub is low-key and feels real, not staged.

Sleeping

$$$$ Old Ground Hotel is a stately, ivy-covered 18th-century minister's residence with 105 rooms and a family feel (four blocks from station at intersection of Station Road and O'Connell Street, tel. 065/682-8127, www.oldgroundhotelennis.com, reservations@oldgroundhotel.ie).

$$$$ Temple Gate Hotel's 70 rooms are more modern and less personal (breakfast extra, just off O'Connell Street, in courtyard with TI, tel. 065/682-

The Voyage of St. Brendan

It has long been part of Irish lore that St. Brendan the Navigator (AD 484-577) and 12 followers sailed from southwest Ireland to the "Land of Promise" (what is now North America) in a *currach*—a wood-frame boat covered with ox hide and tar. According to a 10th-century monk who poetically wrote of the journey, St. Brendan and his crew encountered a paradise of birds, were attacked by a whale, and suffered the smoke of a smelly island in the north before finally reaching their Land of Promise.

Parts of the tale hold up: The smelly island could well be the sulfuric volcanoes of Iceland. Other parts seem like devoted delirium: The holy monks claimed to have come upon Judas, chained to a rock in the middle of the ocean for all eternity.

A British scholar of navigation, Tim Severin, re-created the mythic journey in 1976-1977. He and his crew set out from Brendan Creek in County Kerry in a *currach*. Prevailing winds blew them to the Hebrides, the Faroe Islands, Iceland, and finally to Newfoundland. While this didn't prove that St. Brendan sailed to North America, it did prove that he could have. (You can visit Tim Severin's boat at the Craggaunowen open-air folk museum.)

According to his 10th-century biographer, "St. Brendan sailed from the Land of Promise home to Ireland. And from that time on, Brendan acted as if he did not belong to this world at all. His mind and his joy were in the delight of heaven."

3300, www.templegatehotel.com, info@templegatehotel.com).

$ Grey Gables B&B has 12 tastefully decorated rooms (cash only, wheelchair access, family rooms, parking, on Station Road 5 minutes from train station toward town center, tel. 065/682-4487, mobile 085-739-3793, www.greygables.ie, info@greygables.ie, Mary Keane).

¢ Rowan Tree Hostel is a well-run budget option with better-than-expected private rooms and tidy dorm rooms, centrally located beside the gurgling River Fergus. A grand old gentleman's club and a pleasant café/bar round out the complex (on Harmony Row next to the bridge, tel. 065/686-8687, www.rowantreehostel.ie, info@rowantreehostel.ie).

Eating

The Cloisters, next door to Ennis Friary, inhabits equally historic 800-year-old walls. Its steak, lamb, and fish dishes are the best in town and are served in a tasteful atmosphere, either in the upstairs **$$$$ restaurant** (Tue-Sun 17:30-21:00) or the downstairs **$$$ pub** (Tue-Sun 12:00-17:30, both sections closed Mon, Abbey Street, tel. 065/686-8198).

The Old Ground Hotel serves up hearty meals in its **$$$ Poet's Corner pub** (Mon-Sat 12:00-21:00, Sun from 16:00).

For better-than-average pub grub, I like **$ Knox's Pub** on Abbey Street (daily 12:00-21:00, tel. 065/682-287). Or try one of the other places mentioned under "Experiences," earlier.

The simple **$ Numero Uno Pizzeria** is good for an easy pub-free dinner (Mon-Sat 12:00-23:00, Sun from 15:00, on Old Barrack Street off Market Place, tel. 065/684-1740).

Transportation

Arriving and Departing

BY CAR

Day-trippers can park in one of several pay-and-display lots (enforced Mon-Sat 9:30-17:30, free on Sun). The centrally located multistory lot on Market Place Square charges €5 per day (Mon-Sat 7:30-19:30, closed Sun).

BY TRAIN OR BUS

The train and bus station is located southeast of town, a 15-minute walk from the center. To reach town, exit the station parking lot and turn left on Station Road, passing through a roundabout and past the recommended Grey Gables B&B. Turn right after the Old Ground Hotel onto O'Connell Street.

From Ennis by Train to: Galway (5/day, 1.5 hours), **Limerick** (9/day, 40 minutes), **Dublin** (10/day, 4 hours, change in Limerick, Limerick Junction, or Athenry). Train info: Tel. 065/684-0444, www.irishrail.ie.

From Ennis by Bus to: Galway (hourly, 1.5 hours), **Dublin** (almost hourly, 5 hours), **Limerick** (hourly, 1 hour), **Ballyvaughan** (1/day, 2.5 hours), **Tralee** (6/day, 3.5 hours, change in Limerick), **Doolin** (5/day, 2 hours). Bus info: Tel. 065/682-4177, www.buseireann.ie.

BY PLANE

Shannon Airport is about 15 miles south of Ennis. The major airport in western Ireland comes with far less stress than Dublin's overcrowded airport (code: SNN, www.shannonairport.ie). A taxi between the airport and Ennis should run about €35.

From Shannon Airport by Bus to: Ennis (bus #51 runs between the airport and the Ennis train station hourly, 20 minutes after the hour starting at 8:20, 30 minutes), **Galway** (bus #51, hourly, 2 hours), **Limerick** (at least 2/hour, 1 hour, can continue to Tralee—2 hours more, and Dingle—4/day, another 2 hours; bus tel. 061/313-333, www.buseireann.ie).

CLIFFS OF MOHER

A visit to the Cliffs of Moher (pronounced "MO-hur")—a ▲▲▲ sight—is one of Ireland's great natural thrills. For five miles, the dramatic cliffs soar as high as 650 feet above the Atlantic.

Getting There

The Cliffs of Moher are located on R-478, south of Doolin. The parking lot across the road from the visitors center is for the general public; pay the attendant as you drive in. The lot next to the visitors center is for tour buses and visitors with disabilities.

If you're without wheels, it's easiest to get here on a bus tour from Galway or Ennis; check the companies listed on page 217 (tours generally include the Burren). From Doolin, it's possible to hike to the cliffs, ride a shuttle bus, or take a boat cruise (see page 214).

Orientation

Cost: €8, €4 if you book online and visit before 11:00 or after 16:00, includes parking and admission to the visitors center and its exhibit. It's not worth the €2 to climb O'Brien's Tower.

Hours: Daily 8:00-19:00, gradually later closing times toward midsummer (as late as 21:00 May-Aug), Nov-Feb 9:00-17:00.

Information: Tel. 065/708-6141, www.cliffsofmoher.ie.

Services: You'll find an information desk and ATM in the visitors center—the Tolkienesque labyrinth tucked under the grassy hillside—flanked by six hobbit garages housing gift shops (across the street from the parking lot). **Cliffs View Café,** upstairs in the visitors center, serves coffee and substantial cafeteria-style hot

The Cliffs of Moher

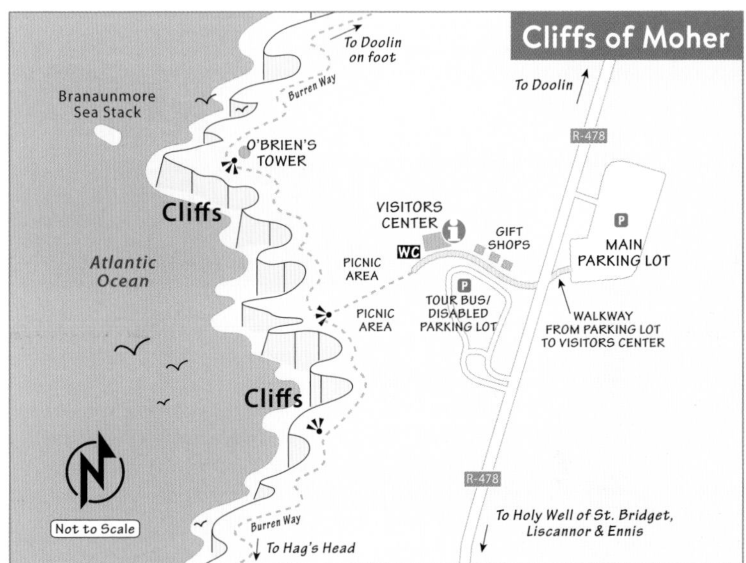

meals until 16:30. There's also the **Puffin's Nest,** a small sandwich café downstairs.

➔ Visiting the Cliffs

The visitors center is designed smartly to orient you to the cliffs experience, spiraling up and finally out onto the cliffs themselves in this order: entry (TI, shop, café); nature exhibit; short film in theater; main restaurant and WC; and outside to the cliffs. (While this is ideal, if the weather seems iffy and you see a sun break, you could do the cliff walk first.)

Visitors Center: The Atlantic Edge exhibit, downstairs, focuses mainly on natural and geological history, native bird and marine life, and virtual interactive exhibits aimed at children. You may even learn why the cliffs are always windy. A small theater shows *The Ledge Experience,* a film following a gannet as he flies along the cliffs and then dives underwater, encountering puffins, seals, and even a humpback whale along the way.

The Cliffs: After leaving the visitors center, walk 200 yards to the **cliff** edge. A protective wall of the slate (notice the squiggles made by worms, eels, and snails long ago) keeps visitors safely back from the cliff. You can walk behind the protective wall in either direction. The trail to the right (north, uphill toward the castle-like tower) is the most rewarding. **O'Brien's Tower,** built in 1835, marks the highest point of the cliffs (but isn't worth the fee to climb...30 feet up doesn't improve the views much). In the distance, on windy days, you can see the Aran Islands wearing their white necklace of surf.

Hike to Hag's Head: From the main viewpoint, look left (south) and spot the tiny tower in the far distance. Fit hikers can spend 2.5 hours (5 miles round-trip) following the up-and-down trail along the lip of the cliffs the whole way. Initially, you'll be slowed down by crowds, but after 500 yards, you'll leave them behind.

Nearby: Drivers can check out the **Holy Well of St. Bridget,** located beside the tall column about a half-mile (1 km) south of the cliffs on the main road to Liscannor. In the short hall leading into the hillside spring, you'll find a treasure of ex-votos (religious offerings) left behind by devoted visitors seeking cures and blessings. A trickle of water springs from the hillside at the far end. To the right of the simple hall entrance is a stairway heading up into a peaceful graveyard. Be sure to check out the wishing tree (sometimes called a fairy bush or rag tree) halfway up the left side of the stairway—offerings to saints.

DOOLIN

Rated ▲, Doolin had long been a mecca for Irish musicians, who came together here to play before a few lucky aficionados. Many music lovers would come here directly from Paris or Munich, as the town was on the tourist map for its traditional music. But now crowds have overwhelmed the musicians, and I prefer Dingle's richer music scene. Still, as Irish and European fans crowd the pubs, the *bodhrán* beat goes on.

Orientation

The "town" is just a few homes and shops strung out along a valley road from the tiny harbor. Residents generally divide the town into an Upper Village and Lower Village. The Lower Village is the closest thing to a commercial center (it has a couple of pubs and a couple of music shops).

Tourist Information: The Upper Village has two privately owned TIs that generally exist to book lodging and Aran Islands boat trips (closed in off-season, tel. 065/707-5642). You'll find a similar boat-booking outfit in the Lower Village.

Laundry: The Lodge Doolin offers **laundry** service (drop-off only, pick up clothes in 8 hours, daily 8:00-20:00).

Experiences

Traditional Music

Doolin is famous for three pubs, all featuring Irish folk music: Nearest the harbor, in the Lower Village, is **Gus O'Connor's Pub** (tel. 065/707-4168). A mile farther up the road, the Upper Village—straddling a bridge—is home to two other destination pubs: **McGann's** (tel. 065/707-4133) and

Doolin pub

McDermott's (tel. 065/707-4328). Music starts between 21:30 and 22:00, finishing at about midnight. Get there before 21:00 if you want a place to sit, or pop in later and plan on standing. The *craic* is great regardless. Pubs serve decent dinners before the music starts.

Cliffs of Moher Walks, Shuttle Bus, and Cruises

From Doolin, you can hike up the Burren Way along the coast to the Cliffs of Moher. Local guide and farmer Pat Sweeny operates **Doolin Cliff Walk,** leading walking tours that depart daily at 10:00 from O'Connor's Pub. The five-mile walk to the cliffs takes three hours and is not safe for kids under age 10; you catch the 13:30 bus back to Doolin (€10, May-Sept, tel. 065/707-4170, mobile 086-822-9913, www.doolincliffwalk.com, phone ahead to reserve and check weather/trail conditions).

The **Hop-on, Hop-off Coastal Shuttle Bus** (16 seats) stops throughout Doolin, along the Cliffs of Moher coastal walk, and in the town of Liscannor (€6, departs every 90 minutes starting at 9:00 from Doolin Park & Ride lot—next to R-478, down the hill halfway between N-67 and Doolin Pier, tel. 065/707-5599, mobile 087-775-5098, www.cliffsofmohercoastalwalk.ie).

Two companies offer one-hour boat cruises along the Cliffs of Moher: **Doolin2Aran Ferries** (tel. 065/707-5949, mobile 087-245-3239, www.doolin2aranferries.com) and **Doolin**

Ferry/O'Brien Line (tel. 065/707-5618, www.obrienline.com). Boats depart from the pier in Doolin €20, runs daily April-Oct, 3/day, weather and tides permitting, call or go online for sailing schedule and to reserve).

Sleeping

$$ Harbour View B&B offers six rooms in a fine modern house overlooking the coast a mile from the Doolin fiddles. Amy Lindner keeps the place immaculate (on main road halfway between Lisdoonvarna and Cliffs of Moher, next to Aran View Market and gas station, tel. 065/707-4154, www.harbourviewdoolin.com, clarebb@eircom.net).

$$ Half Door B&B is the coziest place around, with five woody rooms (thin walls) and a pleasant sun porch. It's just a short walk from the pubs in the Upper Village (cash only, family rooms, a keg's roll from McDermott's pub, tel. 085/864-2388, www.halfdoordoolin.com, ann@halfdoordoolin.com, Anne Hughes).

$ The Lodge Doolin is a modern compound of four stone buildings with 21 bright, airy, good-value rooms (located halfway between Upper and Lower Villages, tel. 065/707-4888, www.doolinlodge.com, info@doolinlodge.com). The lodge offers laundry service.

¢ Doolin Inn & Hostel, right in Doolin's Lower Village, caters creatively to the needs of backpackers in town for the music. Friendly Anthony and Dierdre are on top of the local scene. The upper house has the Inn, which offers good-value double rooms and a café. The lower house across the road is the hostel (tel. 065/707-4421, www.doolininn.ie, reservations@doolininn.ie).

Eating

Doolin's only option above pub grub or café fare is **$$$ Oar Restaurant & Rooms,** in the Upper Village, 50 yards behind Half Door B&B. Reservations are smart (good-value early-bird special, lamb and fish dishes, Wed-Sun 17:30-21:30, closed Mon-Tue, tel. 065/704-7990, https://oardoolin.ie/oar-restaurant).

The **$$ Ivy Cottage,** in the Lower Village just past the bridge, has a pleasant, leafy tea garden out front. They do a dish of the day as well as simple sandwiches, quiche, or chowder (daily 10:00-18:00, mobile 089-977-1873). You can order fish-and-chips to take away.

$$ The Cliff Coast Café, across the bridge in the Doolin Inn, serves dependable dishes (daily 11:00-21:00, shorter hours off-season, mobile 087-282-0587).

Doolin has earned a reputation for consistently good pub grub. In the Lower Village, try **$$ Gus O'Connor's Pub,** and in the Upper Village, give **$$ McGann's** a spin. **Mac's Daybreak** is the town market and gas station (daily 7:00-20:00, on R-478 above town next to the Harbour View B&B).

Transportation

From Doolin by Bus to: Galway (5/day, 1.5 hours), **Ennis** (5/day, 2 hours). Buses depart from Doolin's hostel.

From Doolin by Ferry to the Aran Islands: Doolin2Aran Ferries or Doolin Ferry/O'Brien Line both take you to the closest island, Inisheer (with time to explore), then back along the Cliffs of Moher (they also go to Inishmore, the farthest island; if doing that, it's best to spend the night on the island). For details, see the Aran Islands chapter.

THE BURREN

Literally the "rocky place," the Burren is just that. This 10-square-mile limestone plateau, a ▲▲ sight, is so barren that a disappointed Cromwellian surveyor of the 1650s described it as "a savage land, yielding neither water enough to drown a man, nor a tree to hang him, nor soil enough to bury him." But he wasn't much of a botanist, because the Burren is in fact a unique ecosystem, with flora that has managed to

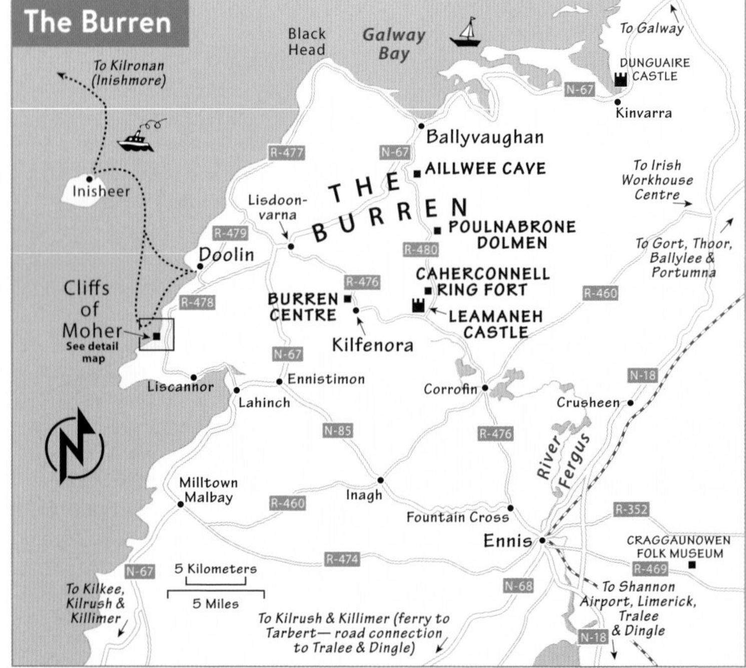

adapt since the last Ice Age, 10,000 years ago. It's also rich in prehistoric and early Christian sites, including dozens of Iron Age stone forts. When the first human inhabitants of the Burren came about 6,000 years ago, they cut down its trees with shortsighted slash-and-burn methods, which accelerated erosion of the topsoil (already scoured to a thin layer by glaciers)—making those ancient people partially responsible for the stark landscape we see today.

You can get a quick overview using my self-guided driving tour, or take your time and really get a feel for the land with a walking tour. Travelers without a car can see the Burren with a bus tour.

Tours

Walking Tours

Most travelers zip through the seemingly barren Burren without stopping, grateful for the soft soil they garden back home. But healthy hikers and armchair naturalists may want to slow down and take a closer look. Be sure to wear comfortable shoes for the wet, uneven, rocky bedrock. These guides can bring the harsh landscape to life.

From Ballyvaughan (at the northern entrance to the Burren): **Shane Connolly** leads in-depth, three-hour guided walking tours, explaining the region's history, geology, and flora, and the role humans have played in shaping this landscape. This proud farmer really knows his stuff (€15, daily at 10:00 and 15:00, call to book and confirm meeting place in Ballyvaughan, tel. 065/707-7168, mobile 086/265-4810, www.burrenhillwalks.ie).

From Carran (in the center of the Burren): **Tony Kirby** leads regularly scheduled 2.5-hour "Heart of Burren Walks" during the summer, and the rest of the year by appointment. His expertise peels back the rocky surface to reveal surprisingly fascinating natural and human history (€30, June-Aug Tue-Thu at 10:30, Fri

Cloudgazing in the Burren

at 14:15; meet opposite Cassidy's Pub in village of Carran, about seven miles east of Kilfenora; tel. 065/682-7707, mobile 087-292-5487, www.heartofburrenwalks.com, info@heartofburrenwalks.com).

Bus Tours

From Galway: Galway Tour Company's standard all-day bus tour of the Burren covers Kinvarra, Aillwee Cave, Poulnabrone Dolmen, and the Cliffs of Moher (€35, discounts if you book online, departs at 10:00, returns about 18:00, confirm schedule ahead). For €15 more, you can add a boat ride out from nearby Doolin to the Aran Island of Inisheer. **Lally Tours** and **Healy Tours** run similar day trips (see page 227 for contact information for all three companies).

➲ Burren Driving Tour

This drive from Kilfenora to Kinvarra offers the best quick swing through the historic Burren and covers about 30 miles from start to finish.

• *Begin in the town of Kilfenora, 8 kilometers (5 miles) southeast of Lisdoonvarna, at the T-intersection where R-476 meets R-481.*

Kilfenora

This town's hardworking, community-run **Burren Centre** shows an informative 10-minute video explaining the geology and botany of the region, and then ushers you into its enlightening museum exhibits (€6, daily June-Aug 9:30-17:30, mid-March-May and Sept-Oct 10:00-17:00, closed in winter, tel. 065/708-8030, www.theburrencentre.ie). You'll also see copies of a fine eighth-century golden collar and ninth-century silver brooch (originals in Dublin's National Museum).

The ruined **church** next door has a couple of 12th-century crosses, but there isn't much to see. Mass is still held in the church, which claims the pope as its bishop by papal dictate. As the smallest and poorest diocese in Ireland, Kilfenora was almost unable to function after the famine, so in 1866 Pope Pius IX supported the town as best he could—by personally declaring himself its bishop.

For lunch in Kilfenora, consider the cheap and cheery **Burren Centre Tea Room** (daily 9:30-17:30, located at far back of building) or the more atmospheric **Vaughan's Pub.** If you're spending the night in County Clare, make a real effort

Leamaneh Castle

to join the locals at the fun set-dancing get-togethers run by the Vaughans in the **Barn Pub,** adjacent to their regular pub. This local dance scene is a memorable treat (€5, Sun at 21:30, also Thu in July-Aug, call ahead to confirm schedule, tel. 065/708-8004).

• *To continue from Kilfenora into the heart of the Burren, head east out of town on R-476. After about 5 kilometers (3 miles), you'll come to the junction with northbound R-480. Take the sharp left turn onto R-480, and slow down to gaze up (on the left) at the ruins of...*

Leamaneh Castle

This ruined shell of a fortified house is closed to everyone except the female ghost that supposedly haunts it. From the outside, you can see how the 15th-century fortified tower house (the right quarter of the remaining ruin) was expanded 150 years later (the left three-quarters of the ruin). The castle evolved from a refuge into a manor, and windows were widened to allow for better views as defense became less of a priority.

• *From the castle, continue north on R-480 (direction: Ballyvaughan). After about 8 kilometers (5 miles), you'll hit the start of the real barren Burren. Keep an eye out for the next stop.*

Caherconnell (Cahercommaun) Ring Fort

Of many ring forts in the area, this one is the most accessible. You can see the low stone profile of Caherconnell to the left on the crest of a hill just off the road. You can park in the gravel lot and walk up to the small visitors center and handy café for an informative 20-minute film followed by a quick wander through the small fort. The fort sometimes features a sheepherding demo with dogs (generally at 12:00 and 15:00—call to confirm).

Cost and Hours: €6, €10 with sheepherding demo, daily 10:00-18:00, Easter-June and Sept-Oct 10:30-17:30, closed in winter, tel. 065/708-9999, www.caherconnell.com.

• *The stretch from the ring fort north to Ballyvaughan offers the starkest scenery. Soon you'll see a 10-foot-high stone structure a hundred yards off the road to the right (east, toward an ugly gray metal barn). Pull over for a closer look.*

Poulnabrone Dolmen

Poulnabrone Dolmen

While it looks like a stone table, this is a portal tomb. Two hundred years ago, locals called this a "druids' altar." Five thousand years ago, it was a grave chamber in a cairn of stacked stones. Amble over for a look. (It's crowded with tour buses at midday, but it's all yours early or late.)

Wander about for some quiet time with the wildflowers and try to think like a geologist. You're walking across a former seabed, dating from 250 million years ago when Ireland was at the equator (before continental drift nudged it north). Look for white smudges of fossils. Stones embedded in the belly of an advancing glacier ground the scratches you see in the rocks. The rounded boulders came south from Connemara, carried on a giant conveyor belt of ice and then left behind when the melting glaciers retreated north.

• *As you drive away from the dolmen (continuing north), look for the 30-foot-deep sinkhole beside the road on the right (a collapsed cave). From here, R-480 winds slowly downhill for about 6 kilometers (4 miles), eventually leaving the rocky landscape behind and entering a comparatively lush green valley. Eventually, on the right, you'll find the turn up to...*

Aillwee Cave

As this is touted as "Ireland's premier show cave," I couldn't resist a look. While fairly touristy and not worth the time or money if you've seen a lot of caves, it's the easiest way to sample the massive system of caves that underlies the Burren. Your guide walks you 300 yards into the plain but impressive cave, giving a serious 40-minute geology lesson.

Rick's Tip: *If you take the Aillwee Cave tour, also* **take a sweater:** *The cave is a constant 50°F.*

Just below the cave (and on the same property) is the **Burren Birds of Prey Centre,** which houses owls, eagles, hawks, and falcons (bird demonstrations May-Aug at 12:00, 14:00, and 16:00, Sept-April at 12:00 and 15:00—but call for daily schedule).

Adjacent to the cave, the **Hawk Walk** gets visitors face-to-beak with a Harris hawk, "the world's only social raptor."

Dunguaire Castle

After a brief training session, an instructor leads a small group on a one-hour hike up a nearby mountain trail. Those paying the stiff €95 fee get to launch and call the bird back to perch on their arm (limited slots, must reserve).

Cost and Hours: Cave-€15, bird center-€15, €22 combo-ticket includes both sights but not Hawk Walk; open daily at 10:00, last tour at 18:30 July-Aug, otherwise 17:30, Dec-Feb call ahead for limited tours; clearly signposted just south of Ballyvaughan, tel. 065/707-7036, www.aillweecave.ie.

• *Continuing on, our final destination is...*

Kinvarra

This tiny town, between Ballyvaughan and Galway, is waiting for something to happen in its minuscule harbor. It faces Dunguaire Castle, a four-story tower house from 1520 that stands a few yards out in the bay.

The touristy but fun **Dunguaire Castle medieval banquet** is Kinvarra's most worthy attraction (€63, cheaper if you book online, most evenings at 17:30 and sometimes at 20:30, mid-April-mid-Oct, reservations required, tel. 061/360-788, castle tel. 091/637-108, www.shannonheritage.com). **Warning:** The company also operates banquets at two other castles in the region, so be sure that you make your reservation for the correct castle.

The evening is as intimate as a gathering of 55 tourists under one time-stained, barrel-vaulted ceiling can be. You get a decent four-course meal with wine (or mead if you ask sweetly), served amid an entertaining evening of Irish tales and folk songs. Remember that in medieval times, it was considered polite to flirt with wenches. It's a small and multitalented cast: one harpist and three singer/actors who serve the "lords and ladies" between tunes. The highlight is the 40-minute stage show, which features songs and poems by local writers, and comes with dessert.

You can visit the castle itself by day without taking in an evening banquet (€8, daily 10:00-16:30).

Botany of the Burren in Brief

The Burren is a story of water, rock, geological force, and time. It supports the greatest diversity of plants in Ireland. Like nowhere else, Mediterranean and Arctic wildflowers bloom side by side in the Burren. It's an orgy of cross-pollination that attracts more insects than Doolin does music lovers—even beetles help out. Limestone, created from layers of coral, seashells, and mud, is the bedrock of the Burren. (The same formation resurfaces 10 miles or so out to sea to form the Aran Islands.)

Geologic forces in the earth's crust heaved up the land, and the glaciers swept it bare and shattered it like glass under their weight—dropping boulders as they receded. Rain, reacting naturally with the limestone to create a mild but determined acid, slowly drilled potholes into the surface. Rainwater cut through the limestone's weak zones, leaving crevices on the surface and one of Europe's most extensive systems of caves below. Algae grew in the puddles, dried into a powder, and combined with bug parts and rabbit turds (bunnies abound in the Burren) to create a very special soil. Plants and flowers fill the cracks in the limestone. Grasses and shrubs don't do well here, and wild goats eat any trees that try to grow, giving tender little blossoms a chance to enjoy the sun. Different blooms appear throughout the months, sharing space rather than competing. The flowers are best in June and July.

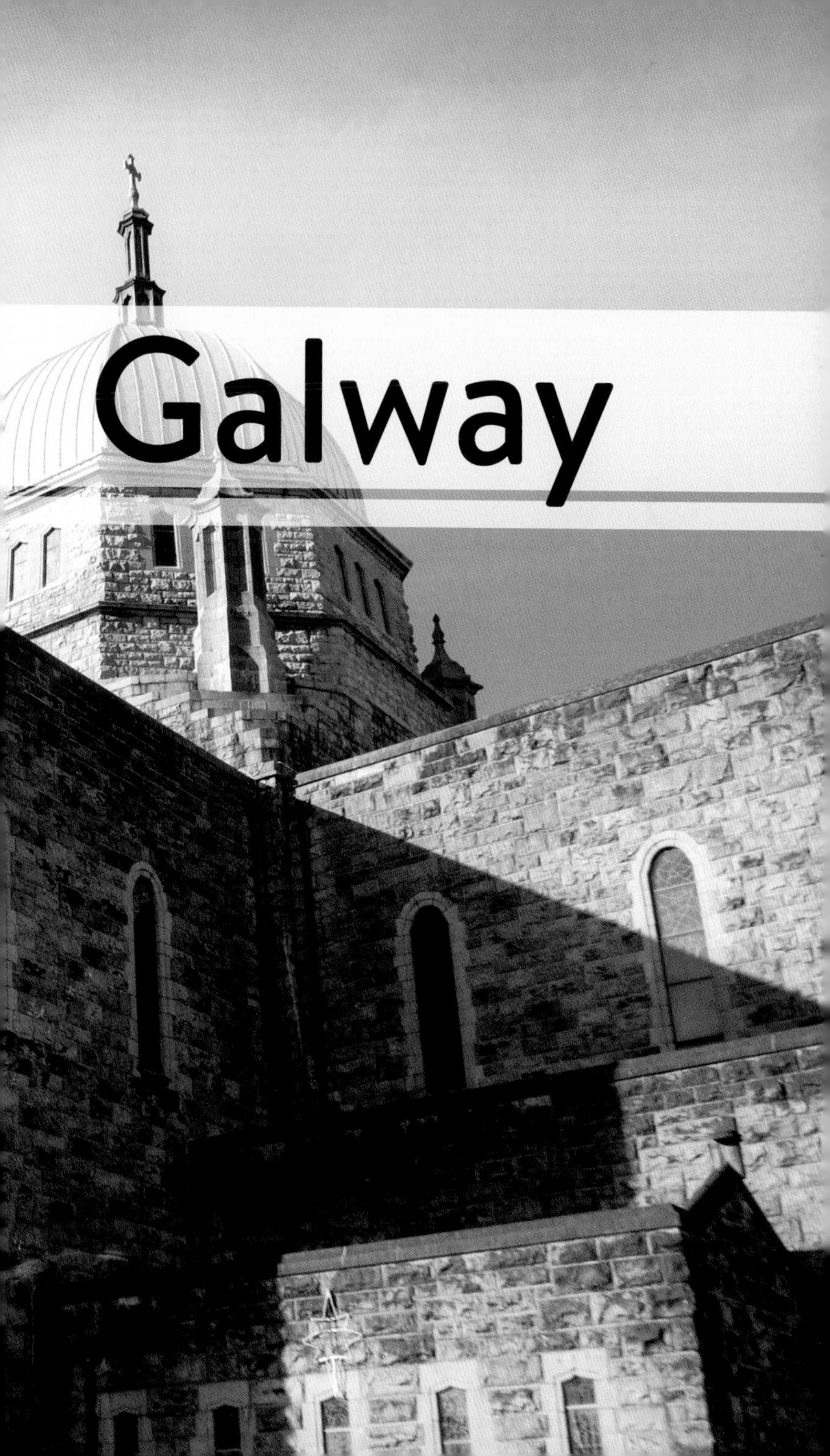

Galway

Galway offers the most easily accessible slice of Ireland's west coast. With 80,000 people, this is Galway County's main city, a lively university town, and the region's industrial and administrative center.

While Galway has a long and interesting history, precious little from old Galway survives. What does remain has the disadvantage of being built in the local limestone, which, even if medieval, looks like modern stone construction.

What Galway lacks in sights it makes up for in ambience. Spend an afternoon just wandering its medieval streets, with their delightful mix of colorful facades, labyrinthine pubs, weather-resistant street musicians, and steamy eateries. After dark, blustery Galway heats up, with a fine theater and a pub scene that attracts even Dubliners. Visitors mix with old-timers and students as the traditional music goes round and round.

Galway is well connected by train to Dublin. And it's a convenient jumping-off point for visiting the Aran Islands (a Gaelic cultural preserve), the Burren (an area of geologic and prehistoric interest, to the south), and the Connemara (a region steeped in Irish history, to the north).

GALWAY IN 1 DAY

The real joy of Galway is in its street scene. Although you could see the town's sights in a couple of hours, the best part of Galway is its nightlife—starring traditional music.

Here are efficient plans:

By Car: Spend two nights in Galway and the day visiting the Aran Islands. For example: If you're driving north from Dingle, visit the Cliffs of Moher and the Burren en route, and spend the night in Galway. In Galway, stroll from Eyre Square to Galway Bay, seeking out a pub with music. The next day, visit the Aran Islands (Inishmore), then return to Galway to enjoy another music-filled evening. Get an early start the next morning and drive through the Connemara region on your way to Northern Ireland.

By Public Transportation and Tour: Arrive in Galway by train or bus. Spend two nights there, and use your full day for a day trip to the Aran Islands (my top choice), the Burren and Cliffs of Moher, or the Connemara region. Tour companies make day trips to all three regions affordable and easy.

ORIENTATION

The center of Galway is Eyre (pronounced "air") Square. Within three blocks, you'll find the TI, Aran boat offices, a tour pickup point, and accommodations. The train and public bus stations butt up against The Hardiman, a huge gray railroad hotel dominating the square.

The coach station (for private buses) is a block away, just beyond the TI. From

GALWAY AT A GLANCE

▲**The Medieval "Latin Quarter"** Half-mile-long pub and shopping zone linking Eyre Square to Galway Bay, dotted with old Norman architecture and weatherproof street musicians. See page 227.

▲**Eyre Square** Grassy fair-weather community gathering spot, location of beloved JFK speech, and haven for Frisbee tossers and dog walkers. See page 227.

▲**Cathedral of St. Nicholas** Town's 50-year-old center of worship with richly appointed interior and quirky mosaic honoring JFK at the foot of Christ's Ascension. See page 232.

▲**Salthill** Unpretentious suburb with a popular swimming beach and waterfront promenade, fun for strollers, joggers, and cyclists. See page 233.

Galway bus tour

Eyre Square, Williams Gate leads a pedestrian parade right through the lively old town (changing street names several times) to Wolfe Tone Bridge. Nearly everything you'll see and do is within a few minutes' walk of this spine.

Tourist Information

The well-organized TI, located a block from the train/bus station, has regional as well as local information (Mon-Sat 9:00-17:00, closed Sun, Forster Street, tel. 091/537-700, www.discoverireland.ie).

Helpful Hints

Markets: On Saturdays year-round and Sundays in summer, a fun market clusters around the Collegiate Church of St. Nicholas (all day, best 9:00-14:00).

Laundry: You have two full-service drop-off options. **Prospect Hill Launderette** is beside the bike-rental shop a block north of Eyre Square (Mon-Fri 8:30-18:30, closed Sat-Sun, Prospect Hill Road, tel. 087/313-7715). **Sea Road Launderette** is three blocks west of Wolfe Tone Bridge (Mon-Sat 8:30-18:30, closed Sun, 4 Sea Road, tel. 091/584-524).

Bike Rental: On Yer Bike rents bikes to tool around flat Galway town. Consider a pleasant ride out to the end of Salthill's beachfront promenade and back (€15-20/day, Mon-Sat 9:00-19:00, Sun 12:00-18:00, shorter hours off-season, 42 Prospect Hill, tel. 091/563-393, mobile 087-942-5479, www.onyourbikecycles.com).

Taxi: Give **Big-O-Taxis** a try (tel. 091/585-858).

Rick's Tip: *Expect huge crowds—and much higher prices—during the* **Galway Arts Festival** *(mid-late July, www.galwayartsfestival.com) and* **Galway Oyster Festival** *(late Sept, www.galwayoysterfest.com).*

Tours

In Galway

▲**Hop-on, hop-off city bus tours** depart from the northwest end of Eyre Square (opposite end of the square from the huge Hardiman Hotel) and make the dozen most important stops, including the cathedral, Salthill, and the Spanish Arch. These large coaches can't penetrate some of the winding medieval back streets, but you can get off, explore, and hop back on later. **Galway City** buses are blue (€10, April-Sept daily at 10:30, 12:00, 14:00, and 15:30, tel. 091/770-066, www.galwaybustours.ie). **City Sightseeing** buses are red (€12, April-Sept daily at 10:30, 12:00, 13:30, and 15:00, tel. 091/562-905, www.lallytours.com).

City **walking tours** have flexible start times and location (call ahead to confirm). **Galway Walking Tours** are led by Fiona Brennan (leisurely 1.5 hours, €10, mobile 087-290-3499, www.galwaywalkingtours.com, feebrenn@iol.ie). **Liam Silke** comes from one of Galway's oldest families (1.5 hours, €10, departs from Brown's Doorway by flags on north side of Eyre Square, tel. 091/588-897, mobile 086-348-0958, www.walkingtoursgalway.com, info@walkingtoursgalway.com). **Galway Walk and Talk Tours** operates with the motto that "a walker has plenty of stories to tell" (€10, departs at 10:30 from TI, mobile 087-690-1452). **Great Guides of Galway** offers historical walking tours in the early evening (€10, departs from The Hardiman hotel steps; Mon, Wed, and Fri at 17:00, Sat at 14:00; mobile 086-727-4888, greatguidesofgalway@hotmail.com).

Galway Region

Good day-trip options from Galway include the Aran Islands, the Burren and Cliffs of Moher, and the Connemara region.

Faherty Tours visits Inishmore, the largest of the three Aran Islands, with a guide native to the island. Tours depart daily at 9:00 from the private coach station on Fairgreen Road—across from the TI—and return by 18:45 (€50, tel. 091/442-913, mobile 087/611-0913, www.fahertytours.com, fahertytours@gmail.com).

High King Tours takes a bite-sized chunk of Connemara focused on Cong and the last Irish King, Rory O'Connor. The tour follows a relaxed itinerary that includes Cong Abbey's ruins, the grounds of Ashford Castle, and a two-hour cruise on the River Corrib. Tours depart from the coach station at 9:00 and return by 18:00 (€70, tel. 091/398-116, www.highkingtours.ie, info@highkingtours.ie).

Galway Tour Company runs bus tours all over the region (office located just a few doors down Forster Street from TI, toward Eyre Square, tours depart from coach station, tel. 091/566-566, www.galwaytourcompany.com, info@galwaytourcompany.com). If Galway Tour Company is booked, try similar **Lally Tours** (tel. 091/562-905, www.lallytours.com) or **Healy Tours** (tel. 091/770-066, mobile 087-259-0160, www.healytours.ie). Drivers take cash only; to pay with a credit card, book in advance.

SIGHTS

The Medieval "Latin Quarter"

Walking from Eyre Square down the pedestrian (and tourist) spine of old Galway to the River Corrib takes you past the essential sights. I've connected these sights in an easy downhill stroll, worth ▲.

▲EYRE SQUARE

Galway is dominated by its main, parklike square. On a sunny day, Eyre Square is filled with people just hanging out. In the Middle Ages, it was a field right outside the town wall. The square is named for the mayor who gave the land to the city in 1710. It now contains John F. Kennedy Park—established in memory of the Irish American president's visit in 1963, when he filled this space with adoring Irish just a few months before his assassination (a JFK bust near the kids' play area commemorates his visit).

Walk to the rust-colored "Hooker" sculpture, built in 1984 to celebrate the 500th anniversary of the incorporation of the city. The sails represent Galway's square-rigged fishing ships ("hookers") and the vessels that made Galway a trading center so long ago. The Browne Doorway, from a 1627 fortified townhouse, is a reminder of the 14 family tribes that once

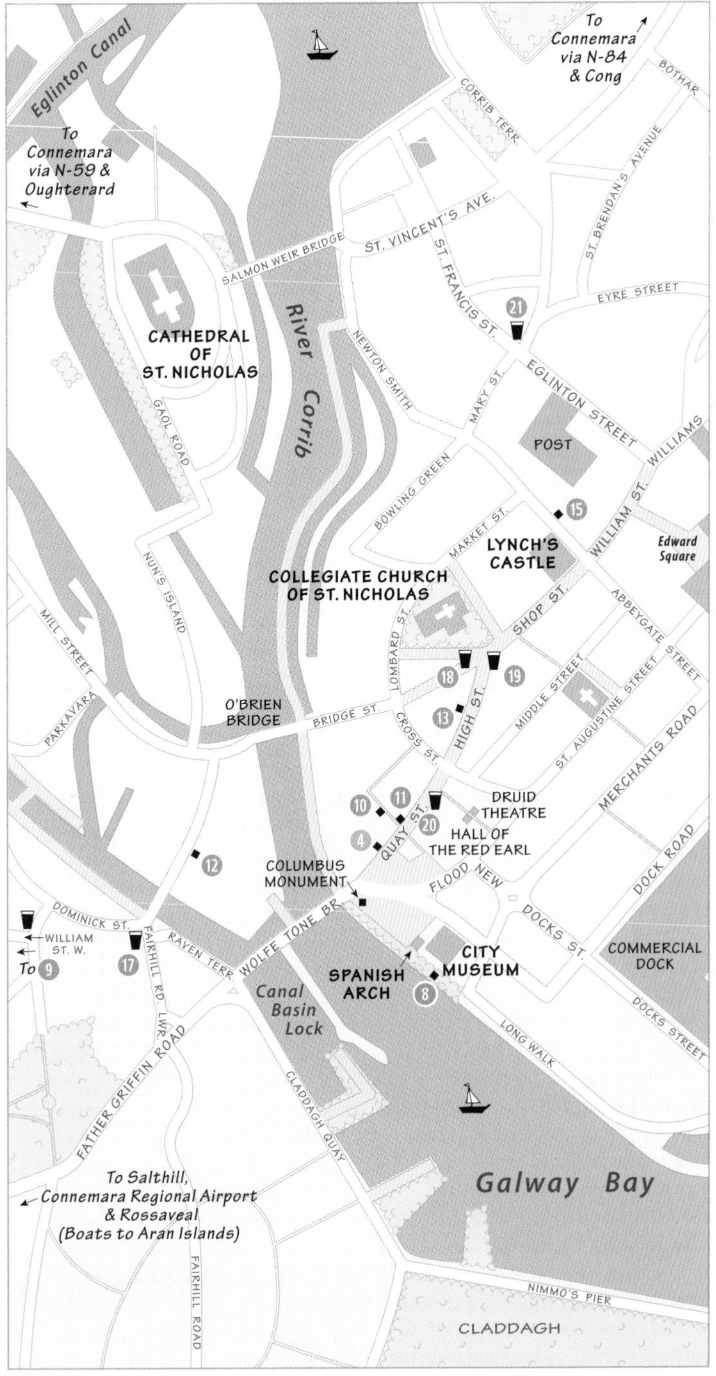
Eglinton Canal
To Connemara via N-84 & Cong
To Connemara via N-59 & Oughterard
BOTHAR
CORRIB TERR.
ST. BRENDAN'S AVENUE
ST. VINCENT'S AVE.
SALMON WEIR BRIDGE
ST. FRANCIS ST.
EYRE STREET
21
CATHEDRAL OF ST. NICHOLAS
River Corrib
NEWTON SMITH
MARY ST.
EGLINTON STREET
GAOL ROAD
POST
WILLIAMS
BOWLING GREEN
15
WILLIAM ST.
MARKET ST.
LYNCH'S CASTLE
Edward Square
NUN'S ISLAND
COLLEGIATE CHURCH OF ST. NICHOLAS
ABBEYGATE STREET
SHOP ST.
MILL STREET
LOMBARD ST.
18
19
MIDDLE STREET
ST. AUGUSTINE STREET
PARKAVARA
O'BRIEN BRIDGE
BRIDGE ST.
13
HIGH ST.
CROSS ST.
MERCHANTS ROAD
10
11
20
DRUID THEATRE
QUAY ST.
4
HALL OF THE RED EARL
DOCK ROAD
12
COLUMBUS MONUMENT
FLOOD NEW
DOMINICK ST.
WILLIAM ST. W.
To 9
17
FAIRHILL RD. LWR.
RAVEN TERR.
WOLFE TONE BR.
DOCKS ST.
CITY MUSEUM
COMMERCIAL DOCK
SPANISH ARCH
8
Canal Basin Lock
DOCKS STREET
LONG WALK
FATHER GRIFFIN ROAD
CLADDAGH QUAY
Galway Bay
To Salthill, Connemara Regional Airport & Rossaveal (Boats to Aran Islands)
FAIRHILL ROAD
NIMMO'S PIER
CLADDAGH

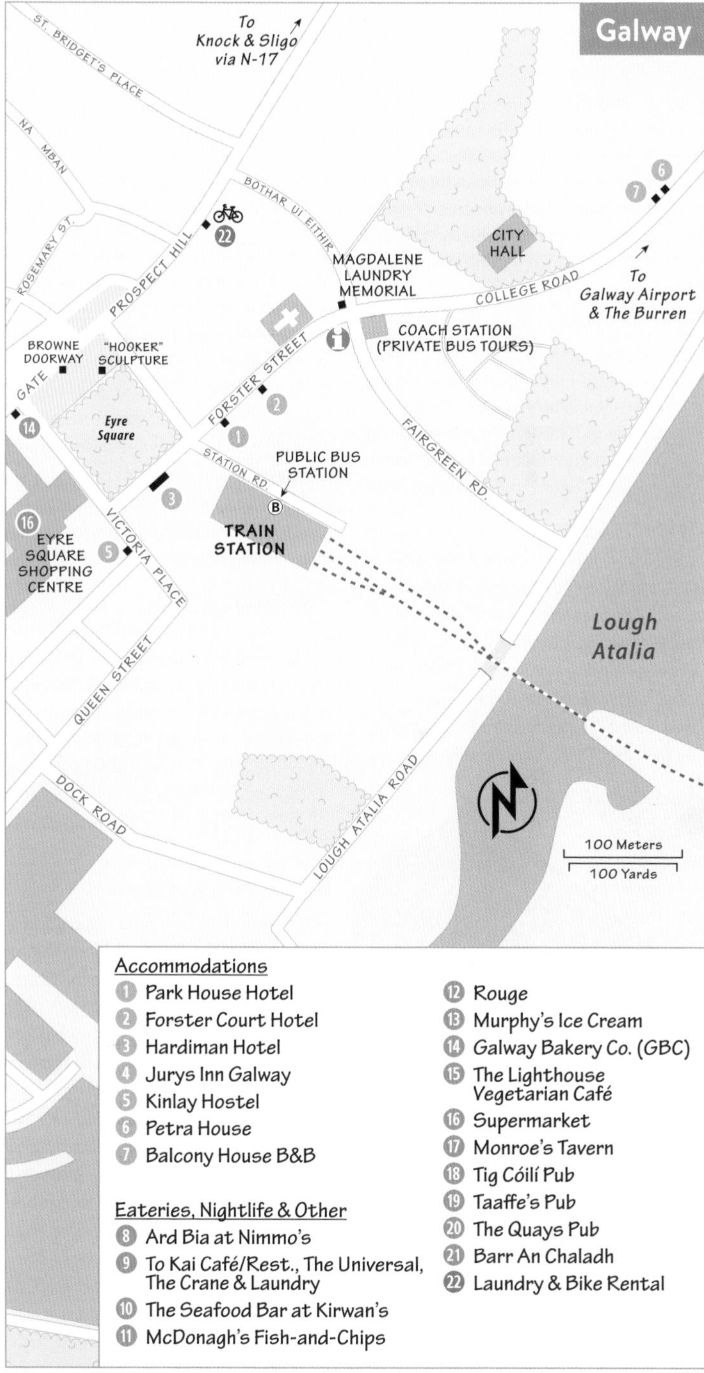
Galway
To Knock & Sligo via N-17
ST. BRIDGET'S PLACE
NA MBAN
BOTHAR UI EITHIR
ROSEMARY ST.
PROSPECT HILL
MAGDALENE LAUNDRY MEMORIAL
CITY HALL
COLLEGE ROAD
To Galway Airport & The Burren
COACH STATION (PRIVATE BUS TOURS)
BROWNE DOORWAY
"HOOKER" SCULPTURE
GATE
FORSTER STREET
Eyre Square
STATION RD.
PUBLIC BUS STATION
FAIRGREEN RD.
TRAIN STATION
EYRE SQUARE SHOPPING CENTRE
VICTORIA PLACE
Lough Atalia
QUEEN STREET
DOCK ROAD
LOUGH ATALIA ROAD
100 Meters
100 Yards
Accommodations
1 Park House Hotel
2 Forster Court Hotel
3 Hardiman Hotel
4 Jurys Inn Galway
5 Kinlay Hostel
6 Petra House
7 Balcony House B&B
Eateries, Nightlife & Other
8 Ard Bia at Nimmo's
9 To Kai Café/Rest., The Universal, The Crane & Laundry
10 The Seafood Bar at Kirwan's
11 McDonagh's Fish-and-Chips
12 Rouge
13 Murphy's Ice Cream
14 Galway Bakery Co. (GBC)
15 The Lighthouse Vegetarian Café
16 Supermarket
17 Monroe's Tavern
18 Tig Cóilí Pub
19 Taaffe's Pub
20 The Quays Pub
21 Barr An Chaladh
22 Laundry & Bike Rental

ruled the town (Lynch's Castle, nearby, gives you a feel for an intact townhouse). Each family tribe had a town castle—much like the towers that characterize the towns of Italy, with their feuding noble families. So little survives of medieval Galway that the town makes a huge deal of any remaining window or crest. Each of the 14 colorful flags lining the west end of the square represents a different original Norman founding tribe.

• *From the top of Eyre Square, walk down Williams Gate—a street named for the old main gate of the Norman town wall that once stood here. The road changes names several times as it leads downhill to the River Corrib. After about three blocks you'll see a bold limestone "town castle" on your right.*

LYNCH'S CASTLE

Now a bank, this limestone tower, Galway's best late-15th-century fortified townhouse, was the home of the Lynch family—the most powerful of the town's 14 tribes—and the only one of their mansions to survive. Most of the mayors who ruled Galway in the 16th and 17th centuries were from the Lynch family.

Lynch's Castle

• *Continuing another block downhill, you'll veer half a block to the right off the main pedestrian flow, to the big church.*

COLLEGIATE CHURCH OF ST. NICHOLAS

This church, the finest medieval building in town (1320), is dedicated to St. Nicholas of Myra, the patron saint of sailors. Columbus is said to have worshipped here in 1477, undoubtedly contemplating a scary voyage. Its interior is littered with obscure bits of town history. Consider attending an evening concert of traditional Irish music in this atmospheric venue (see "Nightlife," later). An open-air market surrounds the church most Saturdays year-round and also on Sundays in summer.

• *Returning to the pedestrian mall, carry on another block and a half downhill. Look for The Quays pub on your left.*

THE QUAYS

This pub was once owned by "Humanity Dick," an 18th-century Member of Parliament who was the original animal-rights activist. His efforts led to the world's first conviction for cruelty to animals in 1822. It's worth a peek inside for its lively interior.

• *Head down the lane just before the pub, about 50 yards, to the big glass windows on the right.*

HALL OF THE RED EARL

A big glass wall shows the excavation site of the Hall of the Red Earl. Wall diagrams and storyboards explain that these are the dusty foundations of Galway's oldest building, once the 13th-century hall of the Norman lord Richard de Burgo (free, closed Sun).

Across the lane is the **Druid Theatre.** This 100-seat venue offers top-notch contemporary Irish theater. Although the theater company is away on tour more often than not, it's worth checking their schedule online or dropping by to see if anything's playing (€20-30 tickets, Chapel Lane, tel. 091/568-660, www.druid.ie).

• *Finally, walk to the end of the pedestrian*

mall, cross the busy street, and follow it to Wolfe Tone Bridge, where you'll find two gray stone monuments (each about as tall as you are). Above the bridge, a sign says Welcome to Galway's West End. You just walked the tourist gauntlet. (Across the river and to the right is a trendy foodie zone.) Stand between the two stone monuments.

COLUMBUS MONUMENT

The monument (closest to the bridge) was given to Galway by the people of Genoa, Italy, to celebrate the 1477 visit here of Christopher Columbus—Cristoforo Colombo in Italian. (That acknowledgment, from an Italian town so proud and protective of its favorite son, helps to substantiate the famous explorer's legendary visit.) The other memorial is dedicated to sailors lost at sea.

• *Don't cross the bridge. Instead, stroll left downstream to the old fortified arch.*

SPANISH ARCH

Overlooking the River Corrib, this makes up the best remaining chunk of the old city wall. A reminder of Galway's former importance in trade, the arch (c. 1584) is the place where Spanish ships would unload their cargo (primarily wine).

• *Walk through the arch and take an immediate right. Go past the stone steps to the far corner of the embankment over the river.*

RIVER CORRIB SIGHTS

Enjoy this river scene. On either side is a park—a constant party on sunny days. (It's ideal for a picnic of fish-and-chips from the recommended McDonagh's chipper, near the end of the pedestrian mall.) Across the river is the modern housing project that replaced the original Claddagh in the 1930s. **Claddagh** was a picturesque, Irish-speaking fishing village with a strong tradition of independence—and open sewers. This gaggle of thatched cottages functioned as an independent community with its own "king" until the early 1900s, when it was torn down for health reasons.

The old Claddagh village is gone, but the tradition of its popular ring (sold all over town) lives on. The **Claddagh ring** shows two hands holding a heart that wears a crown. The heart represents love, the crown is loyalty, and the hands are

Galway's waterfront at Spanish Arch

Galway Legends and Factoids

Because of the dearth of physical old stuff, the town milks its legends. Here are a few that you'll encounter repeatedly:

- In the 15th century, the mayor, one of the Lynch tribe, condemned his son to death for the murder of a Spaniard. When no one in town could be found to hang the popular boy, the dad—who loved justice more than he loved his son—did it himself.
- Columbus is said to have stopped in Galway in 1477. He may have been inspired by tales of the voyage of St. Brendan, the Irish monk who is thought by some (mostly Irish) to have beaten Columbus to the New World by almost a thousand years.
- On the main drag, you'll find a pub called The King's Head. It was originally given to the man who chopped off the head of King Charles I in 1649. For his safety, he settled in Galway—about as far from London as an Englishman could get back then.
- William Joyce, born in America, spent most of his childhood in Galway and later was seduced by fascist ideology in the 1930s. He moved to Germany and became "Lord Haw-Haw," infamous as the radio voice of Nazi propaganda during World War II. After the war, he was hanged in London for treason. His daughter had him buried in Galway.

friendship. If the ring is worn with the tip of the heart pointing in, it signifies that the wearer is taken. However, if the tip of the heart points out, it means the wearer is available.

Survey the harbor. A few of Galway's famous square-rigged "hooker" fishing ships are often tied up and on display. Called "hookers" for their method of fishing with multiple hooks on a single line, these sturdy yet graceful boats were later used to transport turf from Connemara, until improved roads and electric heat made them obsolete.

More Sights

GALWAY CITY MUSEUM

Fragments of old Galway are kept in this modern museum. Check out the intact Galway "hooker" fishing boat hanging from the ceiling. The ground floor houses the archaeological exhibits: prehistoric and ancient Galway-related treasures such as medieval pottery, Iron Age ax heads, and Bronze Age thingamajigs. The first floor sheds light on Galway's role in the Irish struggle for independence in the early 1900s. The top floor is devoted to "sea science" (oceanography).

Cost and Hours: Free, Tue-Sat 10:00-17:00, Sun from 12:00, closed Sun Oct-March and Mon year-round, handy café with cheap lunches, tel. 091/532-460, www.galwaycitymuseum.ie.

▲CATHEDRAL OF ST. NICHOLAS

Opened by American Cardinal Cushing in 1965, this is one of the last great stone churches built in Europe. The interior is a treat and is worth a peek.

Cost and Hours: Free, open to visitors daily 8:30-18:30 as long as you don't interrupt Mass, church bulletins at doorway list upcoming Masses and concerts, located across Salmon Weir Bridge on outskirts of town, tel. 091/563-577.

Visiting the Cathedral: Inside, you'll see mahogany pews set on green Connemara marble floors under a Canadian

Magdalene Laundries Memorial

Documentaries and films such as *The Magdalene Sisters* and *Philomena* highlight the 20th-century practice of incarcerating unmarried, pregnant Irish women and forcing them to work doing laundry as virtual slaves. Viewing premarital pregnancy as one step short of prostitution, various Catholic orders operated these infamous "Magdalene laundries." (No such stigma applied to the men involved.) Across from the TI (at 47 Forster Street), a modest and easy-to-miss statue stands on the site of one such facility, operated by the Sisters of Mercy, which opened in 1824 with a capacity of 110 young women, and closed in 1984 with 18 inmates remaining. It's estimated that upwards of 10,000 women passed through the Magdalene laundry system. Magdalene survivors claim that they were held against their will, forced to work without pay, and physically abused...and their children were sold for adoption. The Irish government apologized in 2013 for turning a blind eye to the mistreatment of these "fallen women," who were imprisoned out of sight, often with the consent of their shamed families.

cedar ceiling. The acoustically correct cedar enhances the church's fine pipe organ. Two thousand worshippers sit on three sides facing the central altar. A Dublin woman carved the 14 larger-than-life stations of the cross. The carving above the chapel (left of entry) is from the old Collegiate Church of St. Nicholas. Explore the modern stained glass. Find the Irish Holy Family—with Mary knitting and Jesus offering Joseph a cup of tea. The window depicting the Last Supper is particularly creative—find the 12 apostles.

Next, poke your head into the side chapel with a mosaic of Christ's resurrection (if you're standing in the nave facing the main altar, it's on the left and closest to the front). Take a closer look at the profiled face in a circular frame, below and to the right of Christ—the one looking up while praying with clasped hands. It's JFK, nearly a saint in Irish eyes at the time this cathedral was built.

Outer Galway

▲SALTHILL

This small resort town packs pubs, nightclubs, a splashy water park, amusement centers, and a fairground up against a fine, mile-long beach promenade (Ireland's longest). Watch for local power walkers "kicking the wall" when they reach the western end of the promenade to emphasize that they've gone the entire distance.

At the **Atlantaquaria Aquarium,** which

The River Corrib glides through Galway.

features native Irish aquatic life and some Amazonian species, kids can help feed the fish at 13:00 (freshwater), 15:00 (big fish), 16:00 (small fish), and 17:00 (naughty kids fed to piranhas). They can cuddle the crustaceans anytime (€13, kids-€8.50, Mon-Fri 10:00-17:00, Sat-Sun until 18:00, touch tanks, The Promenade, tel. 091/585-100, www.nationalaquarium.ie).

For beach time, a relaxing sunset stroll, late-night traditional music, or later-night nightclub action, Salthill hops.

Getting There: To get to Salthill, catch bus #401 from Eyre Square in front of the AIB bank, next to the Hardiman Hotel (3/hour, €2).

EXPERIENCES

Nightlife

▲*Traditional Irish Music*

Galway, like Dingle and Doolin, is a mecca for good Irish music (nightly 21:30-23:30). But unlike Dingle and Doolin, this is a university town, and many pubs are often overrun with noisy students. Still, your chances of landing a seat close to a churning band surrounded by new Irish friends are good any evening of the year.

Across Wolfe Tone Bridge: A good place to start is at **Monroe's Tavern,** with its vast, music-filled interior (check website for trad-music schedule, Dominick Street, tel. 091/583-397, www.monroes.ie). **The Crane,** a couple blocks west of Monroe's, has trad sessions nightly at 21:30 downstairs, a variety of other music upstairs, and Celtic Tales storytelling sessions on Thursdays from April to October (€10 for storytelling at 20:00, other sessions free, 2 Sea Road, tel. 091/587-419, www.thecranebar.com).

On the Main Drag: Pubs known for Irish music include **Tig Cóilí,** featuring Galway's best trad sessions (Mon-Sat at 18:00 and 22:00, Sun at 14:00 and 21:00, corner of Main Guard Street and High Street, tel. 091/561-294); **Taaffe's** (nightly music sessions at 17:30 and 21:30, Shop Street, across from St. Nicholas Church, tel. 091/564-066); and **The Quays** (trad music most nights at 21:30, sporadic schedule, young scene, Quay Street, tel. 091/568-347). A bit off the main drag, **Barr An Chaladh** is a scruffy little place offering nightly trad or ballad sessions

Trad music in Galway

and more locals (3 Daly's Place, tel. 091/895-762).

Performances

Trad on the Prom: This fine, traditional, music-and-dance troupe was started by Galway-born performers who returned home after years of touring with *Riverdance* and the Chieftains. Their show is a great way to enjoy live step dancing and accomplished musicians in a fairly intimate venue (€32-59, mid-May-mid-Oct only, shows at 20:30 on Tue, Thu, and Sun—call to confirm, and best to reserve ahead online; at Leisureland Theatre beside Salthill Park, 30-minute walk west of town along the Salthill promenade or short ride on bus #401 from Eyre Square; tel. 091/582-860, mobile 087-674-1877, www.tradontheprom.com).

Celtic Dream is an Irish music-and-dance show hosted by Monroe's Tavern with an option to grab a pub-grub dinner before the performance (€30, €5 discount off pub meal if booked for performance, May-Sept Mon-Wed at 20:00, 14 Dominick Street Upper, tel. 085/842-9912, www.monroes.ie/events).

Tunes in the Church: The Collegiate Church of St. Nicholas is a mellow, medieval venue with great acoustics, hosting a lineup of accomplished trad musicians. The 1.5-hour concerts are fun for early birds who don't want to stay up late (€15; June-Aug Mon-Fri at 20:00, where High Street and Shop Street intersect, mobile 087-962-5425, www.tunesinthechurch.com).

SLEEPING

Hotels

$$$$ Park House Hotel, a plush, business-class hotel, offers the best value for a fancy place. Ideally located a block from the train station and Eyre Square, it has 84 spacious rooms and all the comforts you'd expect (expensive full Irish breakfast, elevator, pay parking, great restaurant, helpful staff, Forster Street, tel. 091/564-924, www.parkhousehotel.ie, reservations@parkhousehotel.ie).

$$$$ Forster Court Hotel has a quiet and professional vibe with 50 uncluttered and refined rooms a half-block from Eyre Square (elevator, Forster Street, tel. 091/564-111, www.theforstercourt.ie, reservations@theforstercourt.ie).

$$$$ Hardiman Hotel (formerly Hotel Meyrick), filled with palatial Old World elegance and 97 rooms, marks the end of the Dublin-Galway train line and the beginning of Galway. Since 1845, it has been Galway's landmark hotel...JFK stayed here in 1963 when it was The Great Southern (elevator, at the head of Eyre Square, tel. 091/564-041, www.thehardiman.ie, info@thehardiman.ie).

Rick's Tip: *With easy train access from Dublin, Galway is a popular weekend destination for rambunctious stag and hen parties. If you want a good night's sleep on a Friday or Saturday,* **steer clear of hotels with bars** *downstairs or nearby.*

$$$$ Jurys Inn Galway has 130 American-style rooms in a modern hotel, centrally located where the old town hits the river. The big, bright rooms have double beds and huge modern bathrooms (breakfast extra, elevator, lots of tour groups, pay parking, Quay Street, tel. 091/566-444, US tel. 800-423-6953, www.jurysinns.com, jurysinngalway@jurysinns.com).

¢ Kinlay Hostel is a no-nonsense place just 100 yards from the train station, with 224 beds in bare, clean, and simple rooms, including 15 doubles/twins. Easygoing people of any age feel welcome here, but if you want a double, book well ahead—several months in advance for weekends (private rooms available, elevator, baggage storage, laundry service, on Merchants Road just off Eyre Square, tel. 091/565-244, www.kinlaygalway.ie, info@kinlaygalway.ie).

B&Bs in Town

A 10-minute walk from Eyre Square, these homey B&Bs are reasonably priced, have parking, and serve a full "Irish fry" breakfast.

$$ Petra House is Galway's best lodging value. Consistently helpful and attentive owners Frank and Joan Maher maintain a peaceful-feeling brick building with nine fresh, homey rooms (family rooms, elegant sitting room, 29 College Road, tel. 091/566-580, mobile 087-451-1711, www.petrahousegalway.net, petrahouse@eircom.net).

$$ Balcony House B&B rents eight pleasant, large rooms (family rooms, 27 College Road, tel. 091/563-438, www.balconyhouse.ie, info@aaabalconyhouse.ie, Teresa Coyne).

B&Bs in Salthill

A 30-minute walk (or short ride on bus #401) west of town, these are at the western end of the beach community of Salthill.

$$ Marless House is a fine traditional B&B with six large, tastefully furnished rooms a block from the beach (cash only, family rooms, parking, 8 Threadneedle Road, tel. 091/523-931, www.marlesshouse.com, info@marlesshouse.com, Mary Geraghty).

$$ Coolin House has three comfy rooms in a modern home with all the standard amenities (cash only, family room, parking, Threadneedle Road, tel. 091/523-411, www.coolinhousesalthill.com, coolinhouse@eircom.net, Marion Coyne).

EATING

Near the Bottom of the Old Town

$$$ Ard Bia at Nimmo's fills an old stone warehouse behind the Spanish Arch. It's rustically elegant, with beautifully presented dishes from a farm-to-table menu (daily, café lunches 12:00-15:30, fancier dinners 18:00-21:30, Long Walk Street, tel. 091/561-114 or 091/539-897, run by Aoibheann—pronounced "aye-von").

$$$ Kai Café and Restaurant is a stylish little place with a candlelit, stone-and-hardwood ambience. A café at lunch and a restaurant at dinner, it serves local foodies quirky, contemporary Irish cuisine (daily 12:00-15:00 & 18:30-21:30, reservations required for dinner, 20 Sea Road, tel. 091/526-003, www.kaicaferestaurant.com).

$$$ The Universal gastropub is another hit with Galway foodies. This feels more like a food-lover's pub with an open kitchen, stools at the bar, and eight little tables. Choose tapas or full plates of creative, ingredient-driven cuisine (craft beers on tap, food served Tue-Sat 18:00-22:00, 9 William Street West, tel. 091/728-271).

$$$ The Seafood Bar at Kirwan's is a good place in the touristy center for quality seafood in a romantic setting (Mon-Sat 12:30-14:30 & 18:00-22:00, Sun 18:00-22:00, Kirwan's Lane, tel. 091/568-266, www.kirwanslane.ie).

$ McDonagh's Fish-and-Chips is a favorite among residents. It has a fast, cheap, all-day **chipper** on one side and a more expensive sit-and-stay-awhile dinner-only **restaurant** on the other. Both have a couple of outdoor tables right in the Quay Street action (chipper Mon-Sat 12:00-23:00, Sun 14:00-21:00; restaurant Mon-Sat 17:00-22:00, closed Sun; 22 Quay Street, tel. 091/565-001).

$$$ Rouge is a French splurge with leather couches and live jazz or mellow music almost nightly. Instead of à la carte, you'll choose between two set menus (daily 18:00-24:00, reservations wise, 38 Lower Dominick Street, tel. 091/530-681, www.rougegalway.com).

Dessert: For ice cream, try **Murphy's,** made from locally sourced, homemade ingredients. While you'll pay a premium for even a small cup, it's worth it for flavors like Dingle sea salt (hand harvested) and caramelized brown bread (daily 12:00-22:30, 12 High Street).

Galway's "Latin Quarter"

Near Eyre Square

$$ Galway Bakery Company (GBC) is a popular, basic place for a quick Irish meal with a self-serve buffet line (daily 8:00-18:00, later in summer, 7 Williams Gate, near Eyre Square, tel. 091/563-087). They have a simple, good-value restaurant upstairs (open later).

$$ The Lighthouse Vegetarian Café is a calm and cozy little vegetarian haven (lunch only) with creative, well-presented plates and fresh-baked goods, just steps behind Lynch's Castle (Mon-Sat 10:00-17:30, Sun 11:00-16:00, 8 Abbeygate Street Upper, mobile 087-352-0198).

Supermarket: Dunnes is tucked in the Eyre Square Shopping Centre (Mon-Sat 9:00-19:00, Thu-Fri until 21:00, Sun 11:00-19:00, supermarket in basement). Smaller grocery shops are scattered throughout town.

TRANSPORTATION

Arriving and Departing

By Train and Bus

Trains and most buses share the same station, virtually on Eyre Square (which has the nearest ATMs). The train station can store your bag (Mon-Fri 8:00-18:00, closed Sat-Sun). To get from the station to the TI, go left on Station Road as you exit the station (toward Eyre Square), and then turn right on Forster Street.

Don't confuse the public bus station (in same building as the train station) with the coach station (a block away, just beyond the TI), which handles privately owned coaches. Citylink buses from Dublin and Dublin's airport, as well as regional day-tour buses, also use the coach station.

From Galway by Train to: Dublin (nearly hourly, 2.5 hours), **Limerick** (6/day, 2 hours), **Ennis** (5/day, 1.5 hours). For **Belfast** and **Tralee,** you'll change in or near Dublin. Train info: Tel. 091/561-444, www.irishrail.ie.

From Galway by Bus to: Dublin (hourly, 3.5 hours; also see Citylink, later), **Kilkenny** (3/day, 5 hours), **Cork** (hourly, 4.5 hours), **Ennis** (hourly, 1.5 hours), **Shannon Airport** (hourly, 2 hours), **Cliffs of Moher** (8/day in summer, some with change in Ennis, 2 hours), **Doolin** (5/day, 1.5 hours), **Limerick** (hourly, 2 hours), **Dingle** (5/day, 6 hours), **Tralee** (8/day, 4 hours), **Westport** (6/day, 2-4 hours), **Belfast** (every 2 hours, 6 hours, change in Dublin), **Derry** (6/day, 5.5 hours). Bus info: Tel. 091/562-000, www.buseireann.ie.

Citylink runs cheap and fast **bus** service from the coach station near the TI to **Dublin** (arriving at Bachelor's Walk, a block from Tara Street DART station; hourly, 2.5 hours), **Dublin Airport** (hourly, 3 hours), and **Cork Airport** (6/day, 4 hours). Bus info: Tel. 091/564-164, www.citylink.ie.

By Car

Drivers staying overnight at a College Road B&B can park there for free (each has a small lot in front). For daytime parking, the handiest and most central parking garage is under the recommended Jurys Inn Galway in the town center (€2.20/hour, €30/24 hours, Mon-Sat 8:00-1:00 in the morning, Sun 9:00-18:00). Otherwise, you buy a pay-and-display ticket and put it on your dashboard (€2, 2-hour maximum).

BEST OF THE REST

Connemara

If you have a car, consider spending a day exploring the wild western Irish fringe known as Connemara. Drop in at a Westport pub owned by a member of The Chieftains, the popular traditional Irish music group. Hike the peak of Croagh Patrick, the mountain from which St. Patrick supposedly banished the snakes from Ireland. Pass through the desolate Doo Lough Valley on a road stained with tragic famine history. Bounce on a springy peat bog. This beautiful area also claims a couple of towns—Cong and Leenane—as well as the photogenic Kylemore Abbey.

Day Plan

By Car: The Connemara area makes a satisfying day trip from Galway. I've listed the region's prime towns and sights in a loop that starts and ends in Galway (driving north, then back south). Drivers who are aiming for Northern Ireland from Galway can easily modify the loop route by stopping only in Cong and Westport on the way north. With more time, visit the described sights in this order: Cong, then across the Maam Valley to Leenane, and up to Louisburgh and Murrisk on the way to Westport (consider spending the night). From there you can head northeast to Sligo, Donegal, and across the border into Northern Ireland.

Without a Car: Three Galway-based companies—Galway Tour Company, Lally Tours, and Healy Tours—run efficient all-day **bus tours** of nearby regions; see page 226 for contact information). For a more intimate experience, consider a private **driver/guide.** Try Neal Doherty (€300/half-day, €500/full day, www.alchemytours.ie).

➲ *Connemara Loop Drive*

With a long and well-organized day, you can loop around from Galway and enjoy the most important sights of Connemara (5 hours of driving and 200 miles). Pick up

Monks' stone house

Ashford Castle, home of the Ireland School of Falconry

a good map before departing. For maximum coverage, lace together the sights described in this chapter in a route that goes in this order: Cong, Westport, Murrisk, Louisburgh, through the Doo Lough Valley to Leenane, then on to Clifden (passing Kylemore Abbey and Connemara National Park), along the coast to Roundstone, and finally back to Galway.

CONG

The town of Cong offers a fascinating mix of attractions: a medieval ruined abbey, a modern church with exquisite stained-glass windows, and a falconry experience on the grounds of the extravagant Ashford Castle. Everything is within a short walk of the parking lot in front of the abbey. The **TI,** where you can pick up a handy map, is across from the entrance to Cong Abbey. Fuel up at **$$ The Crowe's Nest** (daily, in Ryan's Hotel on Main Street). The **Spar Market** meets the town's grocery needs (daily, Main Street).

Cong Abbey: The ruins of Cong Abbey (free and always open) are the main attraction in town. Construction on the abbey began in the early 1100s in Romanesque style and continued into the Gothic age.

Take a walk through the cloister and down the gravel path behind the abbey. From a little bridge you'll see the **monks' stone house.** It was designed so part of the stream would flow directly under it. The monks simply lowered a net through the floor and attached a bell to the rope; whenever a fish was netted, the bell would ring.

Next to the abbey's cemetery is the modern, concrete, bunker-like **Church of St. Mary of the Rosary** (free, daily 8:00-22:00). Drop in to marvel at its three exquisite windows, made by Irish artist Harry Clarke in 1933.

▲▲Ireland School of Falconry: If you've never experienced falconry, this is a great chance. Animal lovers, aviation engineers, and wannabe medieval hunters will thrill to this hour-long experience. You must reserve ahead (€95 for one person, €75/person for two, on the grounds of Cong's Ashford Castle, tel. 094/954-6820, mobile 087-297-6092, www.falconry.ie, info@falconry.ie).

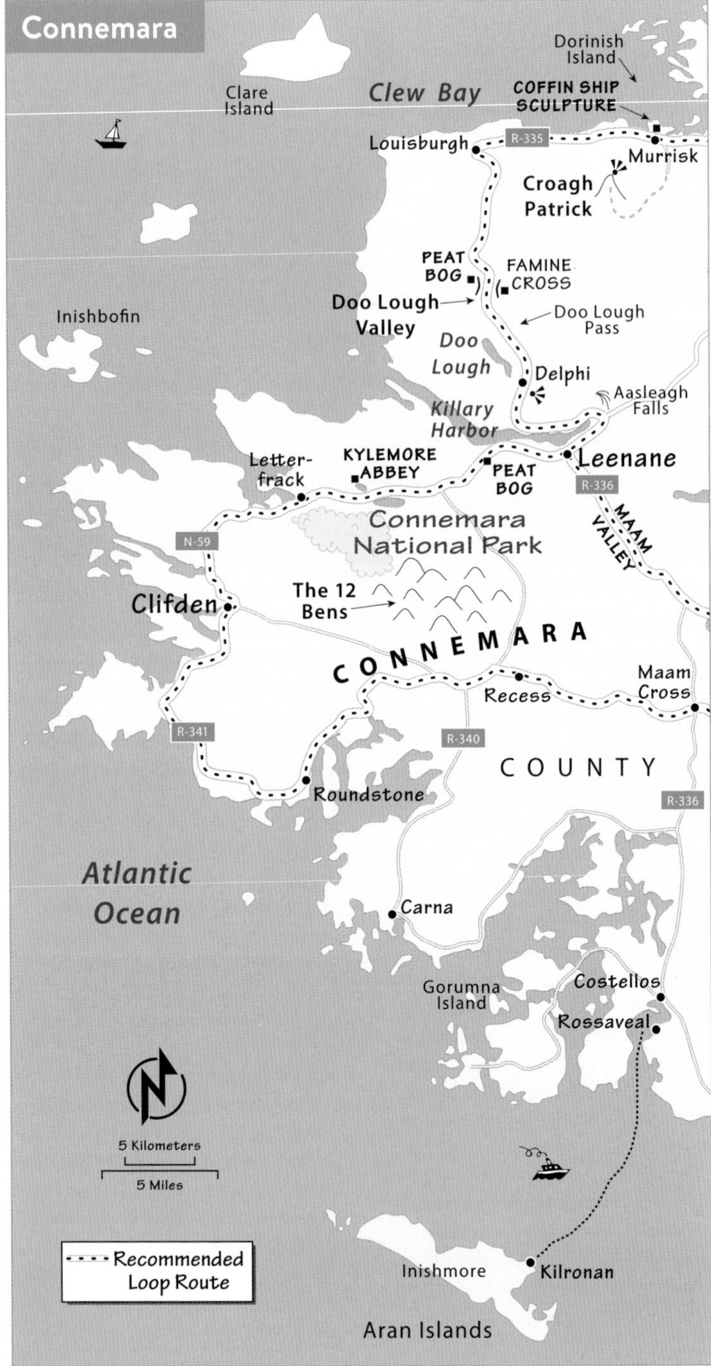
Connemara
Clare Island
Clew Bay
Dorinish Island
COFFIN SHIP SCULPTURE
Louisburgh
R-335
Murrisk
Croagh Patrick
PEAT BOG
FAMINE CROSS
Doo Lough Valley
Doo Lough Pass
Inishbofin
Doo Lough
Delphi
Aasleagh Falls
Killary Harbor
Letter-frack
KYLEMORE ABBEY
PEAT BOG
Leenane
R-336
MAAM VALLEY
N-59
Connemara National Park
The 12 Bens
Clifden
CONNEMARA
Maam Cross
Recess
R-341
R-340
COUNTY
Roundstone
R-336
Atlantic Ocean
Carna
Gorumna Island
Costellos
Rossaveal
5 Kilometers
5 Miles
Recommended Loop Route
Inishmore
Kilronan
Aran Islands

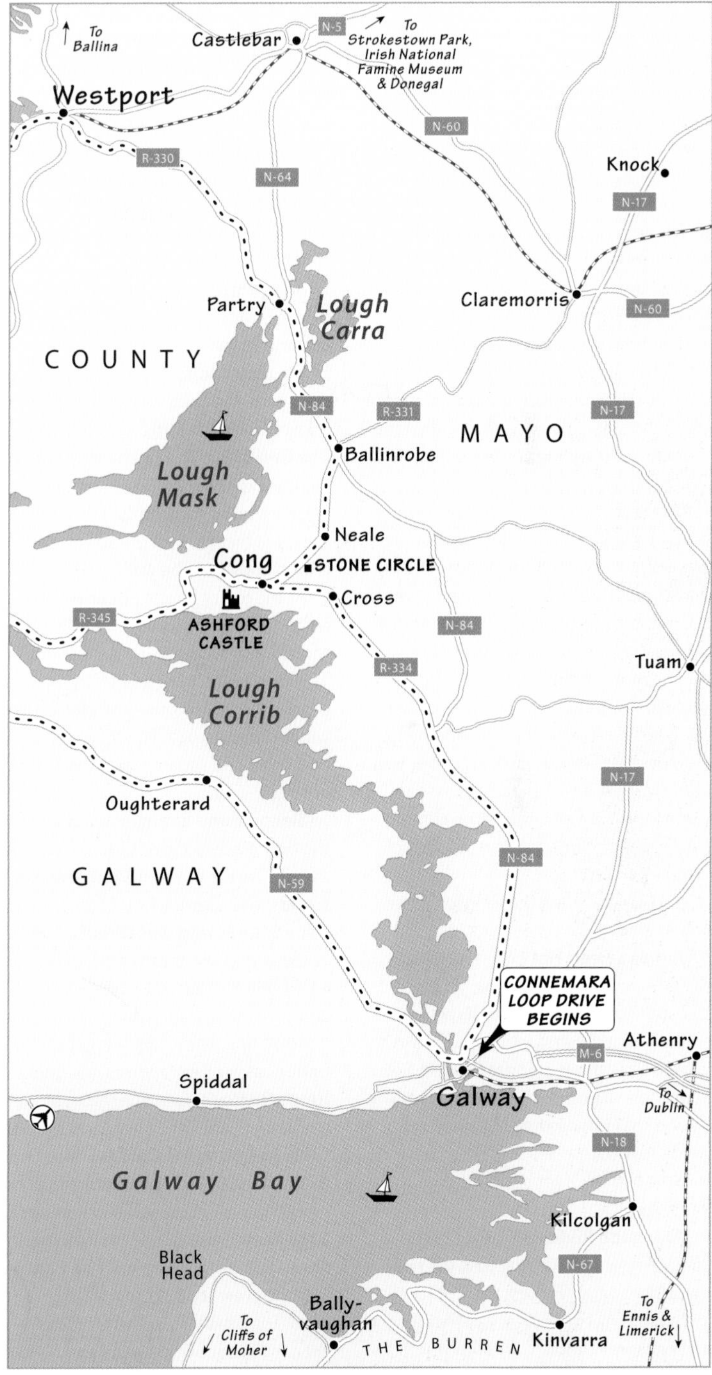
To Ballina
Castlebar
N-5
To Strokestown Park, Irish National Famine Museum & Donegal
Westport
N-60
R-330
N-64
Knock
N-17
Partry
Lough Carra
Claremorris
N-60
COUNTY
N-84
R-331
N-17
MAYO
Ballinrobe
Lough Mask
Neale
Cong
STONE CIRCLE
Cross
R-345
ASHFORD CASTLE
N-84
R-334
Tuam
Lough Corrib
N-17
Oughterard
N-84
GALWAY
N-59
CONNEMARA LOOP DRIVE BEGINS
Athenry
M-6
Spiddal
Galway
To Dublin
N-18
Galway Bay
Kilcolgan
Black Head
N-67
Bally-vaughan
To Cliffs of Moher
THE BURREN
Kinvarra
To Ennis & Limerick

WESTPORT

Westport, with just 9,000 people, is "the big city" in this part of Ireland. While other villages seem organic and grown out of the Middle Ages, this is a planned town. It was built in the late 1700s with a trendy-back-then Georgian flair by celebrated architect James Wyatt, who designed it to support the adjacent estate of the English Lord Browne. The **TI** (called the "Discover Ireland Centre") is on Bridge Street (closed Sun).

This little self-guided town walk—almost a complete loop—will acquaint you with Westport's charms, beginning at the eight-sided main "square" called the Octagon and ending at the clock tower on Bridge Street.

Octagon: Surrounded by 30 townhouses, this was the centerpiece of the planned town back in the 1760s. The big limestone structure with the clock was the old **market house,** where trade was organized, and taxes and customs paid.

The **monument** in the center of the Octagon was built in 1843 to honor Lord Browne's banker, George Glendenning. But the statue of the English banker was shot to pieces by Irish patriots in 1922, during the civil war (notice the gunfire-pocked column). Today, St. Patrick perches on top.

• *Stroll downhill from the Octagon along James Street.*

James Street: Notice a few things. First, there are no stop signs. That's because traffic is supposed to be so friendly that drivers yield to anyone in a crosswalk without being reminded. Second, there are no chain stores. The town council has not allowed big chains to open in the town center.

• *At the bottom of James Street, stand at the bridge.*

Along the River: Look over at the fancy Anglican church across the river (wealthy English Protestants). Rather than crossing the bridge, we'll head right, to the more humble Catholic church. In front of the church, by the water, is a bust of Westport-born **Major John MacBride,** one of the more colorful rebels of the 1916 Easter Rising. MacBride joined a band of insurgents marching into Dublin at the start of the rebellion, and was among the 14 men executed at Kilmainham Gaol after its failure.

• *At the next bridge, turn right and go uphill on Westport's main street.*

Bridge Street to the Clock Tower: Bridge Street is lined by some of the finest old storefronts in Ireland. Farther up the street, **Matt Molloy's Pub** is the biggest draw in town—famous because its namesake owner is the flutist for the trad group The Chieftains. You can hear music here nightly. Explore the pub during the day when it's quiet and empty. The back room is a small theater with photos of celebrated guests on the wall.

At the top of Bridge Street you'll reach the classic storefront of **Thomas Moran**—so classic it's on an Irish stamp. Tidy flower patches (tended by an army of volunteers) surround the **clock tower,** which dates to 1947. The tower marks the town's second square—and the end of our walk.

Sleeping and Eating: Westport is the best place along this route to spend a night. Try the modern **$$$ Clew Bay Hotel** (www.clewbayhotel.com), good-value **$ Boulevard Guesthouse** (www.boulevard-guesthouse.com), or budget **¢ Old Mill Hostel** (www.oldmillhostel.com).

You'll find plenty of **$** budget eating options along Bridge Street, including **Ring's Bistro** (closed Sun-Mon, hidden up Market Lane off Bridge Street) and **Chilli Restaurant & Coffee Shop.** These **$$$** places serve contemporary Irish cuisine (dinners only, reservations smart): **Sage Restaurant** (daily, 10 High Street, www.sagewestport.ie) and **The Pantry & Corkscrew** (daily in summer, closed Mon-Tue off-season, The Octagon, www.thepantryandcorkscrew.com).

MURRISK

In the tiny town of Murrisk you'll find the trailhead for the long hike up Croagh Patrick and a monument remembering the famine.

Croagh Patrick: This fabled mountain-pilgrimage destination rises 2,500 feet above the bay from Murrisk. St. Patrick is said to have fasted on its summit for the 40 days of Lent in the fifth century. It's from here that he supposedly rang his bell, driving all the snakes from Ireland. From the trailhead at Murrisk (where you'll find a big pay-and-display parking lot and a visitors center), you can see the ruddy trail worn down by a thousand years of pilgrims heading up the hill and along the northeast ridge to the summit. Fit hikers should allow three hours to reach the top and two hours to get back down (wear good shoes—solid boots if you have them, and bring rain gear, sunscreen, and plenty of water). The first half of the trail is easy to follow, but the upper half of the mountain is a steep slope of loose, shifting scree. I highly advise buying or renting a walking stick in nearby Westport. There's a primitive WC near the summit.

Coffin-Ship Sculpture: Across the street from the Croagh Patrick trailhead is a modern bronze ship sculpture. A memorial to the famine, it depicts a "coffin ship," like those of the late 1840s that carried the sick and starving famine survivors across the ocean in hope of a new life. Weak from starvation, the desperate emigrants were vulnerable to "famine fever," which they spread to others in the barely seaworthy ships' putrid, cramped holds. Pause a moment to look at the silent skeletons swirling around the ship's masts.

DOO LOUGH VALLEY

The Doo Lough Valley, unfolding between Louisburgh and Delphi (on R-335), is some of the most desolate country in Ireland. Signs of human habitation vanish from the bog land, and it seems ghosts might appear beside the road. Stop at the summit (north end of the valley, about 13 kilometers south of Louisburgh) when you see a simple gray stone cross memorializing famine victims. The lake below is Doo Lough (Irish for "Black Lake").

County Mayo's rural folk were the hardest hit when the Great Potato Famine came in 1845. In the winter of 1849, about 600 starving Irish walked 12 miles from Louisburgh over this summit and south to Delphi Lodge, hoping to get food from their landlord. But they were turned away. Almost 200 of them died along the side of this road. Today an annual walk commemorates the tragedy.

KILLARY HARBOR AND AASLEAGH FALLS

As you drive toward the town of Leenane, you'll skirt along Killary Harbor. The rows of blue floats in the harbor mark mussel farms, with the mollusks growing on hanging nets in the cold seawater.

At the east end of Killary Harbor, stop to enjoy the scenic Aasleagh Falls. In late

Coffin ship sculpture

Doo Lough Valley

Kylemore Abbey, a Connemara landmark

May, the banks below the falls explode with lush, wild, purple rhododendron blossoms.

LEENANE

The "town" of Leenane (just a crossroads) is a good place for a break. Drop into the Leenane Sheep and Wool Centre to see interesting wool-spinning and weaving demonstrations (€7, daily 9:30-18:00, closed Nov-March; demos run June-Aug at 10:00, 12:00, 14:00, and 16:00; café, tel. 095/42323, www.sheepandwoolcentre.com).

Bog Fun: About eight kilometers west of Leenane, you'll spot areas on the south side of the road that offer a good, close look at a turf cut in a peat bog. Be sure to get out and frolic in the peat fields... with decent footwear and an eagle eye for mushy spots.

Walk a few yards onto the spongy green carpet. Find a dry spot and jump up and down to get a feel for it. Have your companion jump; you'll feel the vibrations 30 feet away.

These bogs once covered almost 20 percent of Ireland. As the climate got warmer at the end of the last Ice Age, plants began growing along the sides of the many shallow lakes and ponds. When the plants died in these waterlogged areas, there wasn't enough oxygen for them to fully decompose. Over the centuries, the moss built up, layer after dead layer, helping to slowly fill in the lakes.

It's this wet, oxygen-starved ecosystem that has preserved ancient artifacts so well, many of which can be seen in Dublin's National Museum. Most bizarre are the wrinkled bog mummies that are occasionally unearthed. These human remains (many over 2,000 years old) are so incredibly intact that their eyelashes, hairstyles, and the last meal in their stomachs can be identified. They were likely sacrificial offerings to the pagan gods of Celtic times.

People have been cutting, drying, and burning peat as a fuel source for more than a thousand years. The cutting usually begins in April or May, when drier weather approaches. You'll probably see stacks of "turf" piled up to dry along recent cuts. In the past few decades, bogs have been recognized as a rare habitat, and conservation efforts have been encouraged. These days, the sweet, nostalgic smell of burning peat is becoming increasingly rare.

Coastal Connemara

KYLEMORE ABBEY

This Neo-Gothic country house was built by the wealthy English businessman Mitchell Henry in the 1860s, after he and his wife had honeymooned in the area. After World War I, refugee Benedictine nuns from Ypres, Belgium, took it over and ran it as an exclusive girls' boarding school. The nuns still live upstairs, but you can visit the half-dozen open rooms downstairs that display the Henry family's cushy lifestyle. Hourly tours of the abbey and gardens are so-so; it's best just to enjoy the setting (€14 combo-ticket for abbey and gardens; daily 9:00-18:00, July-Aug until 19:00, www.kylemoreabbeytourism.ie).

CONNEMARA NATIONAL PARK

This park encompasses almost 5,000 acres of wild bog and mountain scenery. The visitors center (just outside Letterfrack) displays worthwhile exhibits of local flora and fauna, which are well explained in the 15-minute *Man and the Landscape* film that runs every half-hour (free; park open daily year-round; visitors center open daily 9:00-17:30, closed Nov-Feb; tel. 095/41054, www.connemaranationalpark.ie). For a quick visit, take a nature walk along the boardwalk raised above the bog. Nature lovers may want to join a two-hour walking tour with a park naturalist (July-Aug, Wed and Fri at 11:00, departs from visitors center). Call ahead to confirm walking-tour schedules, and bring rain gear and hiking shoes.

COASTAL CONNEMARA

If you're short on time, you can connect Clifden and Galway with the fast main road (N-59). But the slower coastal loop along R-341 rewards drivers with great scenery. The essence of scenic Connemara—rocky yet seductive—is captured in this neat little 38-kilometer stretch. The 12 Bens (peaks) of Connemara loom deeper inland. In the foreground, broad shelves of bare bedrock are netted with stone walls, which interlock through the landscape. The ocean slaps the hardscrabble shore. Fishermen cast into their favorite little lakes, and ponies trot in windswept fields. Abandoned, roofless stone cottages stand mute. While the loop is desolate, Roundstone is a perfect place to stop for a cup of coffee to fuel your ride back to Galway.

Aran Islands

Strewn like limestone chips hammered off the jagged west coast, the three Aran Islands—Inishmore, Inishmaan, and Inisheer—confront the wild Atlantic with stubborn grit. The largest, Inishmore, is my island of choice. Inisheer, the smallest, is worth considering for travelers with less time. Snoozing between them is Inishmaan, with little tourism infrastructure (not covered in this chapter).

The landscape of all three islands is harsh. Craggy, vertical cliffs fortify their southern flanks. Windswept rocky fields, stitched together by stone walls, blanket the interiors. And the islands' precious few sandy beaches hide in coves that dimple their northern shores. During the winter, severe gales sweep through; because of this, most settlements on the islands are found on the more sheltered northeastern side.

In the past, people made a precarious living here from fishing and farming. The scoured bedrock offered little in the way of topsoil, so over centuries the islanders created it by layering seaweed with limestone sand and animal dung. Fields are small, divided by several thousand miles of "dry stone" wall (made without mortar).

Nowadays, tourism boosts the islands' economy. The 800 people of Inishmore greet as many as 2,000 visitors a day, mostly day-trippers. But an overnight on either Inishmore or Inisheer is a memorable low-stress treat.

INISHMORE IN 1 DAY

Most travelers visit Inishmore (Inis Mór) as a day trip by boat from Rossaveal, near Galway. Here's a good framework: Leave Galway at 9:00 by car or shuttle bus to Rossaveal, where you'll catch the 10:30 boat. Arriving in Kilronan about 11:15, arrange minivan transport or rent a bike. Visit the Iron Age fort of Dun Aengus, and grab a bite at a simple café near the base of the fort trail (or bring a picnic). Explore

ARAN ISLANDS AT A GLANCE

Inishmore (best reached from Galway)

▲▲▲**Dun Aengus** Remote 2,000-year-old Iron Age ring fort, perched on a cliff with breathtaking coastal views and surrounded by a defensive ring of sharp stones. **Hours:** Daily March-Oct 9:30-18:00, off-season until 16:00, closed Mon-Tue in Jan-Feb. See page 253.

▲▲**Island Minivan Tours** Dependable, weatherproof transport between the island's sights, driven by gift-of-gab locals who contribute random, humorous, and occasionally factual commentary en route. See page 252.

Seven Churches and St. Enda's Church Ruins of two separate early Christian communities at opposite ends of the island, both reachable by minivan, bike, or pony trap. See page 253.

Black Fort, St. Benen's Church, and the Worm Hole Three separate, isolated ancient sites scattered across the island, offering dramatically windswept vistas reachable only by rocky and rewarding hikes. See page 255.

Inisheer (best reached from Doolin)

Small, quiet-island alternative to Inishmore's hectic day-tripper scene, featuring modest sights including the ruins of O'Brien's Castle, the sand-sunken St. Cavan's Church, and the beached An Plassy shipwreck. See page 257.

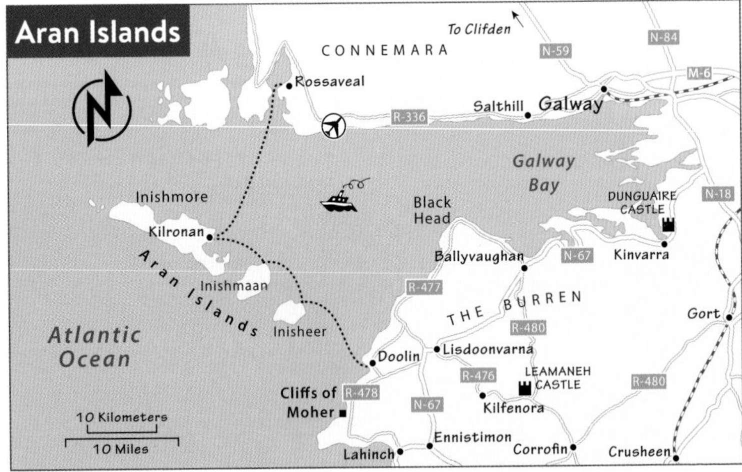

the island during low tide, and depart on the boat when high tides return between 16:00 and 18:00. Return to Galway by car or shuttle bus.

Staying Overnight: If you're spending the night, plan your time around the crush of day-trippers, who make a beeline straight off the boat to Dun Aengus. Upon arrival, head first in the opposite direction to check out the subtle charms of the less-visited eastern end of the island. Buy a picnic at the supermarket in Kilronan. Then walk to either the ruins of tiny St. Benen's Church (an 45-minute hike one-way from Kilronan) or the rugged Black Fort ruins (a rocky one-hour scramble one-way from Kilronan). Save Dun Aengus for later in the afternoon, after the midday crowds have subsided. Enjoy an evening in the pubs and take a no-rush midmorning boat trip or flight back to the mainland the next day.

INISHMORE

The largest of the Aran Islands has a blockbuster sight: the striking Dun Aengus fort, set on a sheer cliff. Everyone arrives at Kilronan, the Aran Islands' biggest town, though it's just a village. Groups of backpackers wash ashore with the docking of each ferry. Minivans, bike shops, and a few men in pony carts sop up the tourists.

Orientation

Your first stop on Inishmore is the town of Kilronan, huddling around the pier. There are a half-dozen shops, a scattering of B&Bs, a few restaurants, and a couple of bike-rental huts. A few blocks inland up the high road, you'll find the best folk-music pub (Joe Watty's), a post office, and a tiny bank (open one day a week) across from the roofless Anglican church ruins.

The friendly Man of Aran café/shop lurks on the back side of the stony Aran Sweater Market building, across from the high cross (daily 10:00-20:00, shorter hours off-season; sells hiking maps, offers Irish lessons, and shows the 1934 documentary film *Man of Aran*). Public WCs are 100 yards beyond the TI on the harbor road.

The huge Spar supermarket, two blocks inland from the harbor, has the island's only ATM.

Rick's Tip: *Bring* **cash** *or get it when you arrive. Most B&Bs and quite a few other businesses don't accept credit cards.*

Tourist Information: Facing the harbor, Kilronan's TI is helpful (daily 10:00-17:00, may close during lunch, shorter hours in winter, tel. 099/20862). The free map given out by the TI or ferry operator is all

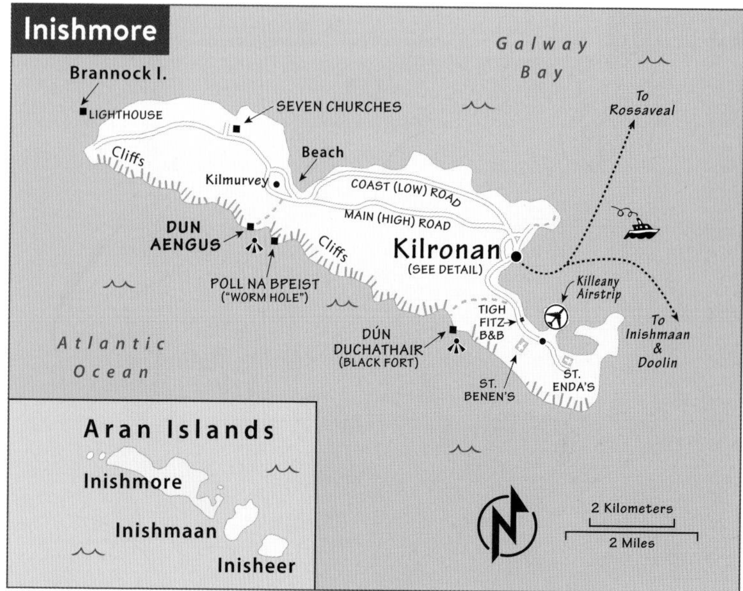

the average day-tripper or leisure biker will need. Serious hikers will want to invest in the detailed Ordnance Survey map (€13.50, sold at the Man of Aran shop).

Audioguides: Mobile phone-size audioguides, with informative commentary and a color-coded map, are useful for bikers and hikers (€8/day, rent from Rustic Rock Restaurant facing harbor).

Getting Around

Just about anything on wheels functions as a taxi here. A shared minivan trip from Kilronan to Dun Aengus to the Seven Churches and back to Kilronan costs €15 per person. Pony carts cost about €25 per person for a trip to Dun Aengus and back.

Biking here is great. You can rent a bike at huts near the pier (daily 9:00-17:00, regular 21-speed bikes about €10/day plus €10 deposit, electric bikes €25/day plus €20 deposit).

Figure 30 minutes to ride from Kilronan to the start of the trailhead up to Dun Aengus. Cyclists should take the high road over and the low road back—you'll encounter fewer hills, scenic shoreline, and at low tide, a dozen seals basking in the sun. Novice bikers should be aware that the terrain is hilly and there are occasional headwinds and unpredictable showers.

Keep a sharp lookout along the roadside for handy, modern limestone signposts (with distances in kilometers) that point the way to important sights. They're in Irish, but you'll be clued in by the small metal depictions of the sights.

Biking outside Kilronan

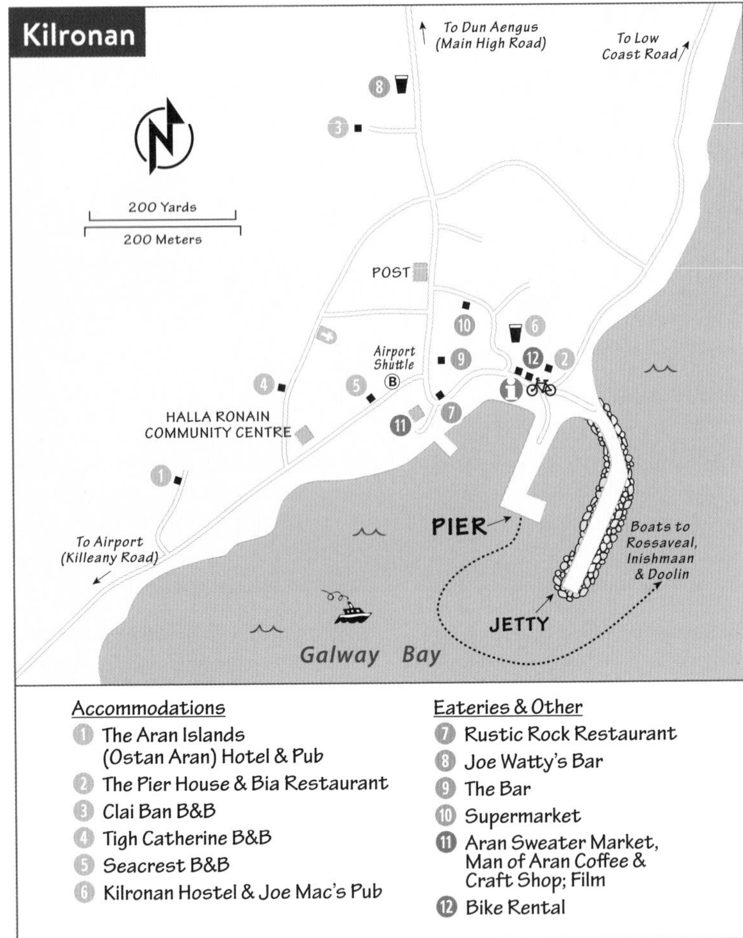

Tours

▲▲ISLAND MINIVAN TOURS

A line of vans (seating 8-18 passengers) awaits the arrival of each ferry, offering €15 island tours. They're basically a shared taxi service that will take you to the various sights, drop you off, and return at an agreed time to take you to the next attraction.

Chat with a few drivers to find one who likes to talk. The tour zips you to the end of the island for a quick stroll in the desolate fields, gives you 15 minutes to wander through the historic but visually unimpressive Seven Churches, and then drops you off for two hours at Dun Aengus (30 minutes to hike up, 30 minutes at the fort, 20-minute hike back down, 40 minutes in café for lunch or shopping at drop-off point) before running you back to Kilronan. (These sights can be linked in various sequences, but the trailhead crossroads below Dun Aengus—with two cafés—makes the best lunch stop.) Ask your driver to take you back along the smaller coastal road (scenic beaches and well-camouflaged sunbathing seals at low tide).

▲WALKING & BIKE TOURS

Cyril O'Flaherty leads tours (on foot or by bike) that take the navigational hassle out of reaching the Worm Hole, the Black Fort, or St. Benen's Church, while adding rich insights on local history, wildlife, language, and culture (mobile 087-688-0688, www.aranwalkingtours.com, info@aranwalkingtours.com).

Sights

▲▲▲DUN AENGUS (DÚN AONGHASA)

The stone fortress hangs spectacularly and precariously on the edge of a cliff 200 feet above the Atlantic. The crashing waves seem to say, "You've come to the end of the world." Gaze out to sea and consider this: Off this coast, Hy-Brasil—a phantom island cloaked in mist—was said to pop into view once every seven years. This mythical place appeared on maps as late as the mid-1800s.

Little is known about this 2,000-year-old Iron Age fort. Its concentric walls are 13 feet thick and 10 feet high. As an added defense, the fort is ringed with a commotion of spiky stones, sticking up like lances, called *chevaux-de-frise* (literally, "Frisian horses," named for the Frisian soldiers who used pikes to stop charging cavalry). Slowly, as the cliff erodes, hunks of the fort fall into the sea.

Dun Aenghus

Dun Aengus gets crowded after 11:00. If you can, get there early or late. A small visitors center (housing the ticket office and controlling access to the trail) displays aerial views of the fort and tells the story of its inhabitants. Trail access to the fort is open and free when the visitors center is closed.

Cost and Hours: €5; daily 9:30-18:00, off-season until 16:00, closed Mon-Tue in Jan-Feb, last entry one hour before closing; during June-Aug guides at the trailhead answer questions and can sometimes give free tours up at the fort if you call ahead; 5.5 miles from Kilronan, tel. 099/61008.

Warnings: Rangers advise visitors to wear sturdy walking shoes and watch kids closely; there's no fence between you and a crumbling 200-foot cliff overlooking the sea. Also, be wary of unexpected gusts of wind and uncertain footing near the edge. The Irish don't believe in litigation, just natural selection.

SEVEN CHURCHES (NA SEACHT TEAMPAILL)

Close to the western tip of the island, this gathering of ruined chapels, monastic houses, and fragments of a high cross dates from the 8th to 11th century. Inishmore is dotted with reminders that Christianity was brought to the islands in the fifth century by St. Enda, who established a monastery here. Many great monks studied under Enda. Among these "Irish apostles" who started Ireland's "Age of Saints and Scholars" (AD 500-900) was Columba (Colmcille in Irish), the founder of a monastery on the island of Iona in Scotland—home of the Irish monks who produced the Book of Kells. Check out the ornate gravestones (best detail on sunny days) of the "seven Romans," located in the slightly elevated back corner of the graveyard, farthest from the road. These

Seven Churches

pilgrims came here from Rome in the ninth century, long after the fall of the Roman Empire.

KILMURVEY

The island's second-largest village nestles below Dun Aengus. More a simple crossroads than a village, it sports two soup-and-sandwich cafés, a gaggle of homes, and a great sheltered swimming beach with a blue flag. Throughout Ireland, "blue flag" beaches proclaim clean water, safe currents, and the color of your toes when you shiver back to your towel.

THE WORM HOLE (POLL NA BPEIST)

Off the beaten path and accessible only by hiking, this site (also called the "Serpent's Lair") takes the "logic" out of geo-*logic.* It's a large, perfectly rectangular, 40-by-100-foot seawater-filled pool (60 feet deep) that was cut by nature into the flat coastal bedrock. You'd swear that God used a cake knife to cut out this massive slab—just to mess with us. The Worm Hole was formed when the roof of the hidden cave underneath (cut by tidal action) collapsed just so.

Boulder-hopping your way across the narrowest section of the island, you'll find the Worm Hole beneath the island's southern cliffs, one mile straight south of Kilmurvey's fine beach. It's signposted from the Main Road as *Pol na bPeist,* but the detailed Ordnance Survey map (available at the Man of Aran Coffee & Craft Shop) is handy for navigating here.

ANCIENT SITES NEAR KILLEANY

The quiet eastern end of Inishmore offers ancient sites in evocative settings for overnight visitors with more time, or for those seeking rocky hikes devoid of crowds. Before heading out, get the detailed Ordnance Survey map (available at the Man of Aran Coffee & Craft Shop) and consider assembling a picnic. Ask the folks in town for directions (almost always a memorable experience in Ireland).

Closest to the road, amid the dunes one mile past the Tigh Fitz B&B and just south of the airport, is the eighth-century **St. Enda's Church** (Teaghlach Einne). Protected from wave erosion by a stubborn breakwater, it sits half-submerged in a sandy graveyard, surrounded by a sea of sawgrass and peppered with tombstones. St. Enda is said to be buried here, along with 125 other saints who flocked to Inishmore in the fifth century to learn from him.

St. Benen's Church (Teampall Bheanáin) perches high on a desolate ridge opposite the Tigh Fitz B&B. Walk up

St. Benen's Church

Currach and Navogue Boats

These are the traditional fishing boats of the west coast of Ireland—lightweight and easy to haul. In your coastal travels, you'll see a few actual *currach* or *navogue* boats—generally retired and stacked. The *currach* is native to the Aran Islands, while the *navogue* is native to the Dingle Peninsula. A fisherman would build a boat to suit his needs: a higher bow to deal with more surf, higher sides to lean over when pulling up lobster pots, a flat stern, etc. Few raw materials were needed to make the boats: a wooden frame with canvas (originally cowhide) and paint with tar. A disadvantage was their fragility when hauling anything other than men or fish. When transporting sheep, farmers would lash each sheep's pointy little hooves together and place it carefully upside-down in the *currach*—so it wouldn't kick a hole in the little craft's thin canvas skin.

the stone-walled lane, passing a holy well and the stubby remains of a round tower. Then take another visual fix on the church's silhouette on the horizon, and zigzag up the stone terraces to the top. The 30-minute hike up from the B&B pays off with a great view. Dedicated to St. Benen, a young disciple of St. Patrick, this tiny (12-by-6-foot) 10th-century oratory is aligned north-south (instead of the usual east-west) to protect the doorway from prevailing winds.

About a five-minute walk past the Tigh Fitz B&B (on your left as you head toward the airport), you'll notice an abandoned stone pier and an adjacent, modest medieval ruin. This was **Arkin Fort,** built by Cromwell's soldiers in 1652 using cut stones taken from the round tower and the monastic ruins that once stood below St. Benen's Church. The fort was used as a prison for outlawed priests before English authorities sent them to the West Indies to be sold into slavery.

Hidden on a remote, ragged headland an hour's walk from Kilronan to the south side of the island, you'll find the **Black Fort** (Dún Duchathair). After Dun Aengus, this is Inishmore's most dramatic fortification, built on a promontory with cliffs on three sides. Its defenders would have held out behind dry-stone ramparts, facing the island's interior attackers. The Ordnance Survey map is essential to navigate here. Watch your step on the uneven ground and be ready to course-correct as you go, and chances are you'll have this windswept ruin all to yourself. Imagine the planning and cooperative effort that went into building these life-saving structures 2,000 years ago.

Experiences

Pub Music

Kilronan's pubs offer music sporadically on summer evenings. Ask at your B&B or look for posted notices in front of the supermarket or post office. **Joe Watty's Bar,** on the high road 100 yards past the post office, is worth the 10-minute walk from the dock. Its appealing front porch goes great with a pint, and live music warms the interior most nights. The more central **Joe Mac's Pub** (next to the hostel) and **The Bar** (next to the high cross at the base of the high road) are also possibilities.

Events

The three-day **Patrún** celebration during the last weekend of June includes *currach* boat races, Galway "hooker" boat races, and a fun run. June 23 is **St. John's Eve Bonfire Night,** a Christian/pagan tradition held the night before St. John's Day, close to (but not on) the summer solstice. Each community stokes a raging fire around dusk, and dozens are visible not only on the island but also on the distant shore of Connemara.

Sleeping

The following places are in Kilronan. Remember, this is a rustic island. Many rooms are plain, with simple plumbing. Luxury didn't make the leap from the mainland.

$$$ The Aran Islands (Ostan Aran) Hotel is the most modern option. Its 20 rooms (four with large harbor-facing porches) have the comforts you'd expect. An additional dozen boxy "chalets" cascade down the slope beside the hotel. Beware of loud weekend stag/hen parties drawn to their downstairs pub (tel. 099/61104, 10-minute walk east of the dock on the coast road heading toward Killeany, www.aranislandshotel.com, info@aranislandshotel.com).

$$ The Pier House stands solidly 50 yards from the pier, offering 12 decent rooms, a good restaurant downstairs, and harbor views from many of its rooms (tel. 099/61417, www.pierhousearan.com, pierhousearan@gmail.com).

$$ Clai Ban, the only really cheery place in town, is run by friendly Marion and Bartley Hernon. Their six rooms and warm hospitality are worth the 10-minute uphill walk from the pier (cash only, family rooms, walk past bank out of town and up the 50-yard-long lane on left, tel. 099/61111, claibanhouse@gmail.com).

$ Tigh Catherine is a well-kept B&B with four homey rooms overlooking the harbor (cash only, on Church Road up behind the Halla Ronain community center, tel. 099/61464, mobile 087-980-9748, catherineandstiofain@gmail.com, Catherine Mulkerrin).

$ Seacrest B&B offers six uncluttered rooms in a central location behind the Aran Sweater Market (cash only, tel. 099/61292, mobile 087-161-6507, seacrestaran@gmail.com, Geraldine and Tom Faherty).

¢ Kilronan Hostel, overlooking the harbor near the TI, is cheap but noisy above Joe Mac's Pub (tel. 099/61255, www.kilronanhostel.com, kilronanhostel@gmail.com).

The Black Fort

Eating

$$ Rustic Rock Restaurant, standing proudly beside the high cross, is the island's most central and stylish (a relative term) option (daily 12:00-21:00, mobile 086-792-9925).

$$ Joe Watty's Bar, up the hill, has a friendly vibe and tasty grub (daily April-Oct 12:30-15:30 & 17:00-21:00, tel. 099/20892, pleasant front-porch seating).

$$ The **Aran Islands Hotel pub** is a modern place serving simple lunches and hot dinners (daily 12:00-21:00, tel. 099/61104).

$$$ Bia Restaurant, on the ground floor of The Pier House guesthouse, is dependable (daily May-Sept 11:00-21:30, tel. 099/61811).

Supermarket: The **Spar** has all the groceries you'll need (Mon-Sat 9:00-18:00, July-Aug until 19:00, Sun 10:00-17:00).

INISHEER

The roughly circular little island of Inisheer (Inis Oírr) has less than a quarter of the land area and population of Inishmore. But Inisheer's proximity to the mainland makes it an easy 35-minute boat journey from Doolin and a good option for those with limited time who aren't going north to Galway. Inisheer, just 1.5 miles square, offers a vivid glimpse of Aran Island culture and has an engaging smorgasbord of salty but modest sights.

Orientation

You'll dock on the north side of the island in its only settlement. Facing inland with your back to the pier, you'll be able to spot nearly all of the island's landmarks. Although some pony carts and minivan drivers meet you at the pier, I'd rely on them only on a rainy day (€10).

For me, the joy of compact Inisheer is seeing it on a bike ride or a long breezy walk. The bike-rental outfit is right at the base of the pier (€10/2 hours, €12/day, tel. 099/75049, www.rothai-inisoirr.com, no deposit necessary "unless you look suspicious"). Any of the boat operators can give you a free map of the island showing Inisheer's primitive road network. That's all you'll need to navigate.

There are three pubs on the island, one small grocery store, and no ATMs. All the sights, with the exception of the lonely lighthouse on the southern coast, are concentrated on the northern half.

Sleepy Inisheer

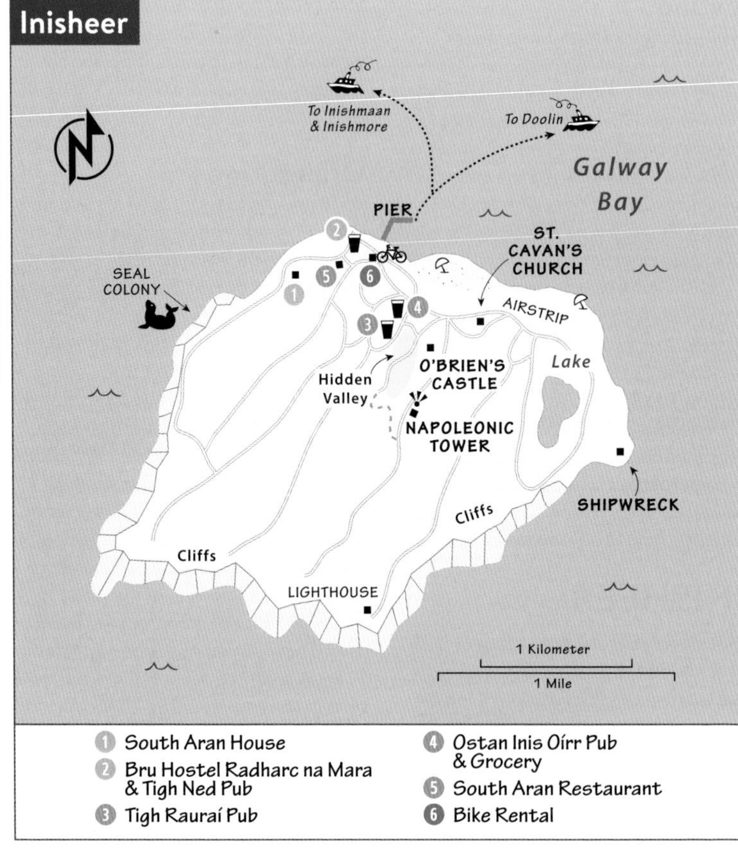

Sights

The following sights are free and open all the time. See them in the order listed, from west to east, across the northern half of the island. If you bike, be prepared to walk the bike up (or down) short, steep hills.

O'BRIEN'S CASTLE (CAISLEAN UI BHRIAIN)

The ruins of this castle dominate the hilltop and are visible from almost anywhere on the northern half of the island. It's a steep 20-minute walk from the pier up to the castle ruins. The small castle was built as a tower-house refuge around 1400 by the O'Brien clan from nearby County Clare. It sits inside a low wall of a much older Iron Age ring fort. Cromwell's troops destroyed the castle in 1652, leaving the evocative ruins you see today.

If you've made it up to O'Brien's Castle, go another easy five minutes to the **Napoleonic Tower** (An Tur Faire), which was built in the early 1800s to watch for a feared French invasion that never took place. The views from this highest point on the island are worth it.

• *Consult your map and continue (south) on the paved road into the heart of the island. Take your first right turn, roughly 100 yards after the Napoleonic Tower, onto a rocky, grassy cow lane that zigzags downhill into a lush* ***hidden valley,*** *displaying the prettiest mosaic of ivy-tangled rock walls and small green fields I've seen anywhere on the Aran Islands.*

O'Brien's Castle

The wreck of the An Plassy

Once you've wound your way back down to the main north-shore road again, turn right and continue east with the airstrip on your left. On your right, you'll soon see a time-passed graveyard up atop a sandy hill. Hike the 50 yards up into the graveyard to find...

ST. CAVAN'S CHURCH (TEAMPALL CHAOMHAIN)

St. Cavan was the brother of St. Kevin, who founded the monastery at Glendalough in the Wicklow Mountains. In the middle of the graveyard is a sunken sandpit holding the rugged, roofless remains of an 11th-century church. The shifting sand dunes almost buried it before sawgrass stabilized the hill. St. Cavan's reputed gravesite is protected by a tiny modern structure worth poking your head into for its candlelit atmosphere. Local folklore held that if you spent a night sleeping on the tomb lid, your particular illness would be cured.

• *Head back down to the north-shore road and head out on the coast road (to the southeast) 30 minutes to the remote...*

SHIPWRECK OF THE *AN PLASSY*

This freighter was wrecked offshore on Finn's Rock in 1960. But islanders worked with the coastal patrol to rescue the crew with no loss of life. A couple of weeks later the unmanned ship was washed high up onto the rocky shore, where it still sits today, a rusty but fairly intact ghost ship with a broken back. The fierce winter winds and record-breaking waves of 2013 shifted the wreck, further weakening it, and discussions are under way to remove it as it deteriorates. A local told me, "We may have to go out some night with lanterns to bring in a new shipwreck."

Beware of unstable footing on the rounded cobbles thrown up by the surf near the wreck.

• *With more time, consult your map and seek out the remaining intimate little church ruins and holy wells that the island has to offer. Or head back to town for a beverage while you await the return ferry.*

Sleeping

$ South Aran House is a quiet, well-run place with five spic-and-span, black-and-white rooms. Humorous Enda and friendly Maria Conneely are generous with local tips and also run the nearby South Aran Restaurant, where you'll have breakfast (easy 10-minute walk west of pier on north-shore road, call ahead with your ferry arrival time so they can meet you with keys, tel. 099/75073, mobile 087-340-5687, www.southaran.com, info@southaran.com). Their small rental cottage sleeps two.

¢ Bru Hostel Radharc na Mara is a simple 40-bed option just 100 yards west of the pier, next to Tigh Ned Pub. They also offer five basic doubles in their adjacent

B&B directly behind (includes continental breakfast, open mid-March-Oct, tel. 099/75024, radharcnamara@hotmail.com).

Eating

Inisheer's three main pubs offer decent pub grub (usually 12:30-20:30). **$$ Tigh Rauraí Pub** (House of Rory) is the epicenter of island social life (from the pier, head east to the edge of the beach and turn right—inland—up a narrow lane for 100 yards). **$$ Ostan Inis Oírr Pub** (Hotel Inisheer), closer to the beach, sports a colorful collage of international flags draping the pub's ceiling and stag/hen parties on weekends. **$$$ Tigh Ned Pub** (House of Ned) is right next door to the hostel, near the pier on the north-shore road. Sit outside at their appealing front tables on a summer evening, enjoying a pint in the salt air.

If you overnight here, **$$ South Aran Restaurant,** a five-minute walk west of the pier on the north-shore road, is a good choice for a mellow evening meal (daily 18:00-21:00, tel. 099/75073, mobile 087-340-5687).

Picnic lovers flock to the small Siopa XL **grocery,** behind Ostan Inis Oírr Pub and below Tigh Rauraí Pub (Mon-Sat 9:00-18:00, Sun 10:00-14:00).

TRANSPORTATION

Arriving and Departing

By Ferry

FROM ROSSAVEAL (NEAR GALWAY)

Island Ferries sails to Inishmore from the port of Rossaveal, 20 miles west of Galway. In peak season (mid-April-Sept), ferries depart from Rossaveal at 10:30, 13:00, and 18:30; from Inishmore at 8:15 (9:00 on Sun), 12:00, and 17:00 (also at 16:00 in June and 18:30 in July-Aug; confirm schedule online). They also run a shuttle bus from Galway to the Rossaveal dock (3/day in peak season, bus ride and ferry crossing each take 45 minutes; coming from Galway, allow 2 hours total; €25 round-trip boat crossing plus €9 round-trip for shuttle bus, 10 percent discount if you book online). Catch shuttle buses from Galway on Queen Street, a block behind the Kinlay Hostel (check-in 1.5 hours before sailing); shuttles return to Galway immediately after each boat arrives. Island Ferries has two offices in Galway: on Forster Street across from the TI and at 19 Eyre Square (tel. 091/568-903, after-hours tel. 091/572-273, www.aranislandferries.com).

Note: The boat you take out to the islands may not be the same as the one you come back on. And sometimes you'll board by walking up the gangplank of one boat and walking across its deck to another boat docked beside or behind it.

Parking in Rossaveal: Drivers should go straight to the ferry landing in Rossaveal, passing several ticket agencies and pay parking lots. At the boat dock, you'll find a convenient €8/day lot and an office that sells tickets for Island Ferries (with better WCs than on the ferry).

FROM DOOLIN

Boats from Doolin sail to all three Aran Islands but make the most sense if you're day-tripping to Inisheer or overnighting on Inishmore. (While it's possible to travel from Doolin to Inishmore and back in one day, it's a 75-minute trip each way, leaving less time ashore; sail from Rossaveal instead).

Buying Tickets: The scene at the Doolin ferry dock is a confusing mosh pit of competition. Two ferry companies operate from three ticket huts with one thing in mind: snaring your business. They have similar schedules and prices. It's smart to check online for discounts. It's also important to double-check schedules and arrive at least 15 minutes early. Be patient: Boats can be 30 minutes late...or 10 minutes early. You're on Irish time.

Doolin2Aran Ferries is run by the Garrihy family (to Inisheer: €20 same-day round-trip, 30 minutes, departs Doolin at 10:00, 11:00, 16:00, and 17:30, departs Inisheer at 8:30, 10:20, 11:20, 12:15, 13:45, and 16:45; to Inishmore: €25 round-trip, 75 minutes, generally departs Doolin at 10:00, 11:00, and 13:00, departs Inishmore at 11:30 and 16:00). Their fun €30 triangular day trip takes you from Doolin to Inisheer, drops you off on Inisheer for about 3.5 hours, then sails along the base of the Cliffs of Moher before docking back in Doolin (departs at 10:00 and 11:00, returns to Doolin by 16:45, runs March-Oct, tel. 065/707-5949, mobile 087-245-3239, www.doolin2aranferries.com).

Doolin Ferry/O'Brien Line, run by Bill O'Brien, has been at it the longest, with similar schedules and occasionally cheaper prices. They also offer a cruise along the base of the Cliffs of Moher that includes a stop at Inisheer (tel. 065/707-5618, mobile 087-958-1465, www.obrienline.com).

Parking in Doolin: With a car, Doolin is easy to reach; without one, it's better to go to Inishmore from Rossaveal. Parking at the Doolin dock is pay-and-display (€1/2 hours, €5 overnight). Give yourself enough time to deal with parking and the line of visitors waiting to pay at the single machine. For details on Doolin, see page 214.

By Plane

Aer Arann Islands, a friendly and flexible little airline, flies daily from Connemara Regional Airport, serving all three islands (3/day, up to 11/day in peak season, €25 one-way, €49 round-trip, 10-minute flight, tel. 091/593-034, www.aerarannislands.ie, info@aerarannislands.ie). The eight-seat planes get booked up—reserve as soon as you are sure of your dates. Note that the baggage weight limit is 50 pounds total.

Chartered sightseeing-only Aer Arann flights leave from the same airport (by reservation only). Cruising at 500 feet, you'll fly above all three Aran Islands with an extra swoop past the Cliffs of Moher (€960 for seven-passenger aircraft, 35 minutes).

Getting to and from the Airports: Connemara Regional Airport is 20 slow miles west of Galway—allow 45 minutes for the drive, plus 30 minutes to check in before the scheduled departure. A minibus shuttle—€5 one-way—runs from Victoria Hotel off Eyre Square in Galway an hour before each flight. Be sure to reserve a space on the shuttle bus at the same time you book your flight. The Kilronan airport on Inishmore is minuscule. A minibus shuttle (€3 one-way, €5 round-trip) travels the two miles between the airport and Kilronan (stop is behind the Aran Sweater Market).

Northern

Northern Ireland is a different country than the Republic—both politically (it's part of the United Kingdom) and culturally (a combination of Irish, Scottish, and English influences). Occupying the northern one-sixth of the island of Ireland, it's only about 13 miles from Scotland at the narrowest point of the North Channel, and bordered on the south and west by the Republic.

When you leave the Republic of Ireland and enter Northern Ireland, you are crossing an international border. (For years, the border has been almost invisible, without passport checks, though Brexit, the UK's withdrawal from the EU, could potentially change the way the border is handled in the future.)

You won't use euros here; Northern Ireland issues its own Ulster pound, which, like the Scottish pound, is interchangeable with the English pound (€1=about £0.90; £1=about $1.30). Price differences create a lively daily shopping trade for those living near the border. Some establishments near the border may take euros, but at a lousy exchange rate. Keep any euros for your return to the Republic, and get pounds from an ATM inside Northern Ireland instead. And, if you're heading to Britain next, it's best to change your Ulster pounds into English ones (free at any bank in Northern Ireland, England, Wales, or Scotland).

But some differences between Northern Ireland and the Republic are disappearing: Following the Republic's lead,

Ireland

Northern Ireland legalized same-sex marriage and decriminalized abortion in 2019 (also bringing its legislation more in line with rest of the United Kingdom).

A generation ago, Northern Ireland was a sadly contorted corner of the world. On my first visit, I remember thinking that even the name of this region sounded painful ("Ulster" seemed to me like a combination of "ulcer" and "blister"). But today, Northern Ireland has emerged from the dark shadow of the decades-long political strife and violence known as the Troubles.

While not as popular among tourists as its neighbor to the south, Northern Ireland offers plenty to see and do... and learn.

It's important for visitors to Northern Ireland to understand the ways in which its population is segregated along political, religious, and cultural lines. Roughly speaking, the eastern seaboard is more Unionist, Protestant, and of English-Scottish heritage, while the south and west (bordering the Republic of Ireland) are Nationalist, Catholic, and of indigenous Irish descent. Cities are often clearly divided between neighborhoods of one group or the other. Early in life, locals learn to identify the highly symbolic (and highly charged) colors, jewelry, sports jerseys, music, names, accents, and vocabulary that distinguish the cultural groups.

Northern Ireland Almanac

Official Name: Northern Ireland (pronounced "Norn Iron" by locals). Some call it Ulster (although historically that term included three counties that today lie on the Republic's side of the border), while others label it the Six Counties.

Size: 5,400 square miles (about the size of Connecticut), constituting a sixth of the island. With 1.8 million people, it's the smallest of the four United Kingdom countries (the others are England, Wales, and Scotland).

Geography: Northern Ireland is shaped roughly like a doughnut, with the UK's largest lake in the middle (Lough Neagh, 150 square miles and a prime eel fishery). Gently rolling hills of green grass rise to the 2,800-foot Slieve Donard. The weather is temperate, cloudy, moist, windy, and hard to predict.

Latitude and Longitude: 54°N and 5°W (as far north as parts of the Alaskan panhandle).

Biggest Cities: Belfast, the capital, has 300,000 residents. A half-million people—nearly one in three Northern Irish—inhabit the greater Belfast area. Derry (called Londonderry by Unionists) has 95,000 people.

Economy: Northern Ireland's economy is more closely tied to the UK than to the Republic of Ireland, and is subsidized by the UK. Traditional agriculture (potatoes and grain) is fading, but Northern Ireland remains a major producer of sheep, cows, and grass seed. Modern software and communications companies are replacing traditional manufacturing. Once proud shipyards are rusty relics, and the linen industry is now threadbare.

Government: Northern Ireland is not a self-governing nation, but is part of the UK, ruled from London by Queen Elizabeth II and Prime Minister Boris Johnson, and represented by 18 elected Members of Parliament. For 50 years (1922-1972), Northern Ireland was granted a great deal of autonomy and self-governance, known as "Home Rule." Today some decisions are delegated to a National Assembly (90-seat Parliament), but political logjams often render it ineffective.

Flag: The official flag of Northern Ireland is the Union flag of the UK. But you'll also see the green, white, and orange Irish tricolor (waved by Nationalists) and the Northern Irish flag (white with a red cross and a red hand at its center), which is used by Unionists.

The roots of Protestant and Catholic differences date back to the time when Ireland was a colony of Great Britain. Four hundred years ago, Protestant settlers from England and Scotland were strategically "planted" in Catholic Ireland to help assimilate the island into the British economy. In 1620, the dominant English powerbase in London felt entitled to call both islands—Ireland as well as Britain—the "British Isles" on maps. These Protestant settlers established their own cultural toehold on the island, laying claim to the most fertile land. Might made right, and God was on their side. Meanwhile, the underdog Catholic Irish held strong to their Gaelic culture on their ever-diminishing, boggy, rocky farms.

Over the last century, the conflict between these two groups has not been solely about faith. Heated debates today are usually about politics: Will Northern Ireland stay part of the United King-

dom (Unionists), or become part of the Republic of Ireland (Nationalists)?

By the beginning of the 20th century, the sparse Protestant population could no longer control the entire island. When Ireland won its independence in 1921 (after a bloody guerrilla war against British rule), 26 of the island's 32 counties became the Irish Free State, ruled from Dublin with dominion status in the British Commonwealth—similar to Canada's level of sovereignty. In 1949, these 26 counties left the Commonwealth altogether and became the Republic of Ireland, severing all political ties with Britain. Meanwhile, the six remaining northeastern counties—the only ones with a Protestant majority who considered themselves British—chose not to join the Irish Free State and remained part of the UK.

But within these six counties—now joined as the political entity called Northern Ireland—was a large, disaffected Irish (mostly Catholic) minority who felt marginalized by the drawing of the new international border. This sentiment was represented by the Irish Republican Army (IRA), who wanted all 32 of Ireland's counties to be united in one Irish nation—their political goals were "Nationalist." Their political opponents were the "Unionists"—Protestant British eager to defend the union with Britain.

In the Republic of Ireland, where the population was 94 percent Catholic and only 6 percent Protestant, there was a clearly dominant majority. But in Northern Ireland, Catholics were a sizable 35 percent of the population—enough to demand attention when they exposed anti-Catholic discrimination on the part of the Protestant government. It was this discrimination that led to the Troubles, the conflict that filled headlines from the late 1960s to the late 1990s.

Partly inspired by Martin Luther King,

Jr. and the civil rights movement in America, in the 1960s the Catholic minority in Northern Ireland began a nonviolent struggle to end discrimination, advocating for better jobs and housing. Extremists polarized issues, and once-peaceful demonstrations became violent.

Unionists were afraid that if the island became one nation, the relatively poor Republic of Ireland would drag down the comparatively affluent North, and feared losing political power to a Catholic majority. As the two sides clashed in 1969, the British Army entered the fray. Their role, initially a peacekeeping one, gradually evolved into acting as muscle for the Unionist government. In 1972, more than 500 people died as combatants moved from petrol bombs to guns, and a new, more violent IRA emerged. In the 30-year (1968-1998) chapter of the struggle for an independent and united Ireland, more than 3,000 people died.

Nationalist mural in Belfast

In the 1990s—with the UK (and Ireland's) membership in the EU, the growth of its economy, and the weakening of the Catholic Church's authority—the Republic of Ireland's influence became less threatening to the Unionists. Optimists hailed the signing of a breakthrough peace plan in 1998, called the "Good Friday Peace Accord" by Nationalists, or the "Belfast Agreement" by Unionists. This led to the release of political prisoners on both sides in 2000—a highly emotional event.

British Army surveillance towers in Northern Ireland's cities were dismantled in 2006, and the army formally ended its 38-year-long Operation Banner campaign in 2007. In 2010, the peace process was jolted forward by a surprisingly forthright apology offered by then-British Prime Minister David Cameron. The apology was prompted by the Saville Report—the results of an investigation conducted by the UK government as part of the Good Friday Peace Accord. It found that the 1972 shootings of Nationalist civil-rights marchers—known as Bloody Sunday—by British soldiers was "unjustified" and the victims innocent (vindication for the victims' families, who had fought since 1972 to clear their loved ones' names).

Major hurdles to a lasting peace persist. Occasionally backward-thinking extremists ape the brutality of their grandparents' generation. And as the UK leaves the European Union, many worry that tensions between the Republic and Northern Ireland will flare up. But the downtown checkpoints are long gone, replaced by a forest of construction cranes, especially in rejuvenated Belfast.

You're safer in Belfast than in many UK cities—and far safer, statistically, than in most major US cities. Just don't seek out spit-and-sawdust pubs in working-class neighborhoods and spew simplistic opinions about sensitive local topics. Tourists notice lingering tension mainly during the "marching season" (Easter-Aug, peaking in early July). July 12—"the Twelfth"—is

Northern Ireland Terminology

You may hear Northern Ireland referred to as **Ulster**—the traditional name of Ireland's ancient northernmost province. When the Republic of Ireland became independent in 1922, six of the nine counties of Ulster elected to form Northern Ireland, while three counties joined the Republic.

The mostly Protestant **Unionist** majority—and the more hardline, working-class **Loyalists**—want the North to remain in the UK. The **Ulster Unionist Party** (UUP) is the political party representing moderate Unionist views (Nobel Peace Prize co-winner David Trimble led the UUP from 1995 to 2005). The **Democratic Unionist Party** (DUP) takes a harder stance in defense of Unionism. The Ulster Volunteer Force (UVF), the **Ulster Freedom Fighters** (UFF), and the **Ulster Defense Association** (UDA) are Loyalist paramilitary organizations: All three are labeled "proscribed groups" by the UK's 2000 Terrorism Act.

The mostly Catholic **Nationalist** minority—and the more hardline, working-class **Republicans**—want a united and independent Ireland ruled by Dublin. The **Social Democratic Labor Party** (SDLP), founded by Nobel Peace Prize co-winner John Hume, is the moderate political party representing Nationalist views. **Sinn Féin** takes a harder stance in defense of Nationalism. The **Irish Republican Army** (IRA) is the now-disarmed Nationalist paramilitary organization historically linked with Sinn Féin.

The **Alliance Party** wants to bridge the gap between Unionists and Nationalists.

The long-simmering struggle to settle Northern Ireland's national identity precipitated the **Troubles,** the violent, 30-year conflict (1968-1998) between Unionist and Nationalist factions. To gain more insight into the complexity of the Troubles, the 90-minute documentary *Voices from the Grave* provides an excellent overview (easy to find on YouTube). Also check out the University of Ulster's informative and evenhanded Conflict Archive at https://cain.ulster.ac.uk.

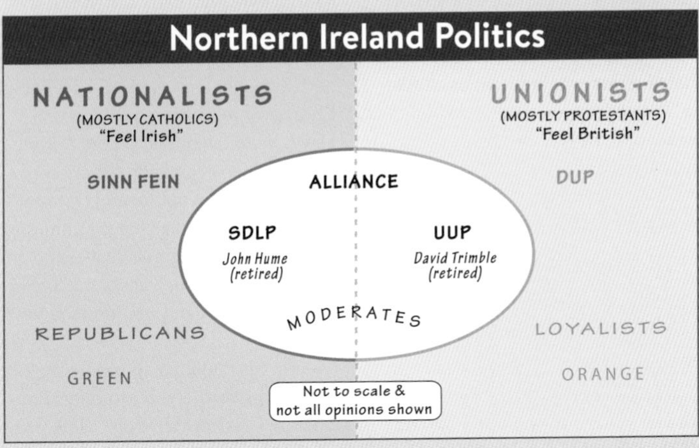

Visitors are drawn by the geologic formations of the Giant's Causeway.

traditionally the most confrontational day of the year in the North, when proud Protestant Unionist Orangemen march to celebrate their Britishness (often through staunchly Nationalist Catholic neighborhoods—it's still good advice to lie low if you stumble onto any big Orange parades).

As the less-fractured Northern Ireland enters the 21st century, one of its most valuable assets is its industrious people (the "Protestant work ethic"). When they emigrated to the US, they became known as the Scots-Irish and played a crucial role in our nation's founding. They were signers of our Declaration of Independence, a dozen of our presidents (think tough-as-nails "Old Hickory" Andrew Jackson as a classic example), and the ancestors of Davy Crockett and Mark Twain.

Northern Irish workers have a proclivity for making things that go. They've produced far-reaching inventions like Dunlop's first inflatable tire. The Shorts aircraft factory (in Belfast) built the Wright Brothers' first aircraft for commercial sale and the world's first vertical takeoff jet. The *Titanic* was the only flop of Northern Ireland's otherwise successful shipbuilding industry. The once-futuristic DeLorean sports car was made in Belfast.

Notable people from Northern Ireland include musicians Van Morrison and James Galway, and actors Liam Neeson, Roma Downey, Ciarán Hinds, and Kenneth Branagh. The North also produced Christian intellectual and writer C. S. Lewis, Victorian physicist Lord Kelvin, engineer Harry Ferguson (inventor of the modern farm tractor and first four-wheel-drive Formula One car), and soccer-star playboy George Best—who once famously remarked, "I spent most of my money on liquor and women...and the rest I wasted."

As in the Republic, sports are big in the North. Northern-born golfers Rory McIlroy, Graeme McDowell, and Darren Clarke have won a fistful of majors, filling local hearts with pride. With close ties to Scotland, many Northern Irish fans follow

the exploits of Glasgow soccer teams—but which team you root for betrays which side of the tracks you come from. Those who cheer for Glasgow Celtic (green and white) are Nationalist and Catholic; those waving banners for the Glasgow Rangers (blue with red trim) are Unionist and Protestant. To maintain peace, some pubs post signs on their doors banning patrons from wearing sports jerseys. Luckily, sports with no sectarian history are now being introduced, such as the Belfast Giants ice hockey team—a hit with both communities.

The North is affordable, the roads are great, and it's small enough to get a real feel for the place on a short visit. Fishers flock to the labyrinth of lakes in County Fermanagh, hikers seek out County Antrim coastal crags, and those of Scots-Irish descent explore their ancestral farmlands (some of the best agricultural land on the island). Today, more tourists than ever are venturing north to Belfast and Derry, and cruise-ship crowds disembark in Belfast to board charter buses that fan out to visit the Giant's Causeway and Old Bushmills Distillery.

As you travel through Northern Ireland today, you'll encounter a fascinating country with a complicated, often tragic history—and a brightening future.

Belfast

Seventeenth-century Belfast was just a village. With the influx of English and Scottish settlers—and the subjugation of the Irish—the character of the place changed. Spurred by the success of the local linen, rope-making, and especially shipbuilding industries, Belfast blossomed. The Industrial Revolution took root here with a vengeance, earning the city its nickname ("Old Smoke").

Belfast is the birthplace of the *Titanic* (and many other ships that didn't sink). In 2012, to mark the 100th anniversary of the *Titanic* disaster, a modern new attraction launched in Belfast's shipyard, telling the ill-fated ship's fascinating and tragic story. Nearby, two huge, mustard-colored cranes (nicknamed Samson and Goliath) stand idle, but serve as a reminder of this town's former shipbuilding might...strategic enough to be the target of Luftwaffe bombing raids in World War II.

At the beginning of the 21st century, the peace process began to take root. It's hard to believe that the bright and bustling pedestrian center was once a subdued, traffic-free security zone. These days, both Catholics and Protestants root for the Belfast Giants ice hockey team. Aggressive sectarian murals are slowly being repainted with scenes celebrating heritage pride...less carnage, more culture. It feels like a new morning in Belfast.

BELFAST IN 1 DAY

Belfast makes a pleasant overnight stop, with plenty of inexpensive accommodations, weekend hotel deals, and a relaxed neighborhood with B&Bs 30 minutes away in Bangor.

With one day in Belfast, browse the pedestrian zones around City Hall, take the City Hall tour (first tour at 10:00, 12:00 on Sat-Sun), have lunch, and ride a shared black taxi up Falls Road. Visit the Titanic Belfast Museum after midday crowds subside. Stroll the Golden Mile.

In the evening, choose among these options: Make reservations for a memorable splurge meal at the Merchant Hotel, have dinner at a pub, or rub elbows with the locals in the historic Crown Liquor Saloon. See what's on at the Opera House.

With Extra Time: With a second day, take the City Sightseeing bus tour in the morning, then visit Carrickfergus Castle in the afternoon—or check out more of Belfast's sights, such as the Ulster Folk Park and Transport Museum.

If Day-Tripping from Dublin: Using

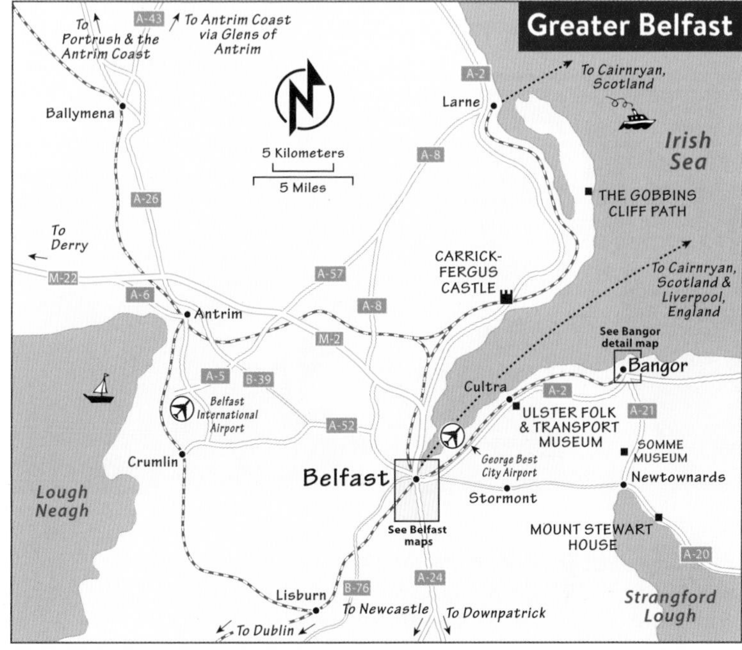

the handy, two-hour Dublin-Belfast train (get "day return" tickets), you could make Belfast a day trip (this plan works best weekdays): Catch the 7:35 train from Dublin's Connolly Station (arriving in Belfast's Layton Place/Central Station at 9:45). Take the City Hall tour weekdays at 11:00, browse the pedestrian zone, have lunch, ride a black taxi up Falls Road, and visit Titanic Belfast (or the Ulster Folk Park and Transport Museum). Have dinner near City Hall or in the Cathedral Quarter and return to Dublin in the evening (last train departs Belfast Mon-Sat at 20:00).

ORIENTATION

Belfast is flat and spread out. When planning, think of it as having four sightseeing zones: Central Belfast (government center, shopping and restaurant district, trendy nightlife), West Belfast (both Republican and Loyalist sectarian neighborhoods), the Titanic Quarter (superstar museum and riverside walk), and South Belfast (college vibe, good hotels and B&Bs, gardens and history museum).

Tourist Information

The modern TI (look for *Visit Belfast* sign) faces City Hall and has a courteous staff and baggage storage (Mon-Sat 9:00-17:30, June-Sept until 19:00, Sun 11:00-16:00 year-round; 9 Donegall Square North, tel. 028/9024-6609, http://visitbelfast.com). City walking tours depart from the TI (see "Tours," later).

Helpful Hints

Belfast Visitor Pass: This pass combines sightseeing discounts with iLink smartcards for free bus, rail, and tram rides within the Belfast Visitor Pass Zone (downtown Belfast as far out as the Ulster Folk Park and Transport Museum in Cultra, but not as far as Carrickfergus or Bangor). You'll save money with the one-day pass if you visit the Titanic Belfast Museum (£3 discount) and the Ulster Folk Park and Transport Museum (30 percent discount)

BELFAST AT A GLANCE

▲▲▲**Titanic Belfast Museum** Excellent high-tech exhibit covering the famously infamous ship and local shipbuilding, in a stunning structure on the site where the Titanic was built. **Hours:** Daily June-Aug 8:30-19:00, April-May and Sept 9:00-18:00; Oct-March 10:00-17:00. See page 290.

▲▲▲**Sectarian Neighborhoods Taxi Tours** Local cabbies drive visitors through West Belfast's Falls Road and Shankill Road neighborhoods, offering personal perspectives on the slowly fading Troubles. See page 284.

▲▲**City Hall** Central Belfast's polished and majestic celebration of Victorian-era pride built with industrial wealth. **Hours:** Daily 8:00-17:00. See page 280.

▲**HMS *Caroline*** WWI battleship that looks just like it did at the Battle of Jutland in 1916. **Hours:** Daily 10:00-17:00. See page 291.

▲**Ulster Museum** Mixed bag of local artifacts, natural history, and coverage of political events; a good rainy-day option near Queen's University. **Hours:** Tue-Sun 10:00-17:00, closed Mon. See page 291.

▲**Botanic Gardens** Belfast's best green space, featuring the Palm House loaded with delicate tropical vegetation. **Hours:** Gardens daily 7:30 until dusk; Palm House daily 10:00-17:00, Oct-March until 16:00. See page 292.

Near Belfast

▲▲**Ulster Folk Park and Transport Museum** A glimpse into Northern Ireland's hardworking heritage, split between a charming re-creation of past rural life and halls of vehicular innovation (8 miles east of Belfast). **Hours:** March-Sept Tue-Sun 10:00-17:00; Oct-Feb Tue-Fri 10:00-16:00, Sat-Sun from 11:00; closed Mon year-round. See page 292.

▲**Carrickfergus Castle** Northern Ireland's first and most important fortified refuge for invading 12th-century Normans (14 miles northeast of Belfast). **Hours:** Daily 9:00-17:00, Oct-March until 16:00. See page 294.

▲**The Gobbins** Rugged, unique, wave-splashed hiking trail cut into coastal rock, accessible by guided tour (34 miles northeast of Belfast). **Hours:** Visitors center daily 9:30-17:30, guided hikes about hourly in good weather. See page 294.

Near Bangor

▲**Mount Stewart House** Fine 18th-century manor house displaying ruling-class affluence, surrounded by lush and calming gardens (18 miles east of Belfast). **Hours:** Daily 11:00-17:00, closed Nov-Feb. See page 301.

Belfast's Troubled History

Seventeenth-century Belfast was just a village. With the influx, or "plantation," of mostly Scottish settlers—and the subjugation of the native Irish—Belfast blossomed, spurred by the success of local industries. The city built many of the world's biggest and finest ships. And when the American Civil War shut down the US cotton industry, the linen mills of Belfast were beneficiaries. In fact, Belfast became known as "Linen-opolis."

The year 1888 marked the birth of modern Belfast. After Queen Victoria granted Belfast city status, it boomed. The population (only 20,000 in 1800) reached 350,000 by 1900. And its citizens built Belfast's centerpiece—its grand City Hall. Belfast was also busy building ships, from transoceanic liners like the ill-fated *Titanic* to naval vessels during the world wars.

Of course, the sectarian Troubles ravaged Belfast along with the rest of Northern Ireland from 1969 to 1998—a time when downtown Belfast was ringed with security checks and nearly shut down at night. There was almost no tourism for two decades (and only a few pubs downtown). Thankfully, at the beginning of the 21st century, the peace process began to take root, and investments from south of the border—the Republic of Ireland—injected new life into the dejected shipyards where the *Titanic* was built.

Still, it's a fragile peace. Hateful bonfires, built a month before they're set ablaze, still scorch the pavement in working-class Protestant neighborhoods each July. Pubs with security gates are reminders that the island is still split—and 900,000 Protestant Unionists in the North prefer it that way.

and connect them by train or bus (free with pass). Buy it at the TI, any train station, either airport, Europa Bus station, or online (1-day pass-£6, 2 consecutive days-£11, 3 days-£14.50, tel. 028/9066-6630, www.translink.co.uk).

Laundry: Globe Launderers has both self-serve and drop-off service (Mon-Fri 8:00-21:00, Sat until 18:00, Sun 12:00-18:00, 37 Botanic Avenue, tel. 028/9024-3956). **Whistle Cleaners** is handy to hotels south of the university (drop-off service, Mon-Fri 8:30-18:00, Sat 9:00-17:30, closed Sun, 160 Lisburn Road, at intersection with Eglantine Avenue, tel. 028/9038-1297). For locations, see the map on page 293.

Tours

Beyond the tours listed next, I highly recommend visiting the **sectarian neighborhoods** in West Belfast on a taxi or walking tour (see "Touring the Sectarian Neighborhoods" on page 281).

LOCAL GUIDES

Dee Morgan grew up on Falls Road and can tailor your tour to history, food, politics, or music (£180/half-day, info@deetoursireland.com). **Susie Millar** is a sharp former BBC TV reporter with family connections to the *Titanic* tragedy. She can also take you farther afield by car (yours or hers, 3-hour tour-£30/person, mobile 078-5271-6655, www.titanictours-belfast.co.uk). **Lynn Corken** has a passion for her hometown, politics, history, and Van Morrison (on foot or with her car, £100/half-day, £200/day, mobile 077-7910-2448, lynncorken@hotmail.co.uk).

WALKING TOURS

Free tours are actually "pay what you think it's worth" tours, led by locals who spin a good yarn. These tours leave from in front of City Hall and the TI (daily in season at 11:00 and 14:30, just show up, www.belfastfreewalkingtour.com).

Experience Belfast Tours, a step up, introduces you to the city's 300-year history. Their "Hidden Belfast" tour includes City Hall, the Cathedral Quarter, and the Linen Hall Library (£10, 1 hour, daily at 11:00 and 13:00). Their "Troubles" tour covers everything on the "Hidden" tour plus the River Lagan and Belfast's political murals (£15, 2.5 hours, daily at 10:00). Both meet in front of the City Hall main gate facing Donegall Square North (mobile 077-7164-0746, https://experiencebelfast.com).

Belfast Hidden Tours focuses on trade and industry with a sprinkling of rebel sedition and Luftwaffe destruction, while leading visitors to less obvious corners of the city (£10, 1 hour; March-Oct daily at 10:00, 12:00, and 14:00; meet at TI, mobile 079-7189-5746, www.belfasthiddentours.com).

Tour guide in Belfast

▲HOP-ON, HOP-OFF BUS TOURS

City Sightseeing offers the best quick introduction to the city's political and social history. Their open-top, double-decker buses link major sights and landmarks, including the Catholic and Protestant working-class neighborhoods, the Stormont Parliament building, Titanic Belfast Museum, and City Hall. Pay cash on the bus (£12.50/24 hours, £14/48 hours, 2/hour, fewer in winter, daily 10:00-16:00, 20 stops, 1.5-hour loop; departs from Castle Place on High Street, 2 blocks west of Albert Memorial Clock Tower; tel. 028/9032-1321, http://belfastcitysightseeing.com).

City Tours offers a route with more than 20 stops. It starts on High Street (near Albert Clock), then veers westward to take in Falls and Shankill roads (£11/24 hours, £12.50/72 hours, pay cash on bus or book in advance, 2/hour, daily 9:45-16:45, tel. 028/9032-1912, www.citytoursbelfast.com).

COUNTRYSIDE BUS TOURS

McComb's offers several big-bus tours, day-tripping out of Belfast to distant points. Their "Giant's Causeway Tour" visits Carrickfergus Castle (photo stop), the Giant's Causeway, Dunluce Castle (photo stop), and Carrick-a-Rede Rope Bridge (£25, daily depending on demand, book through and depart from Belfast International City Hostel, pickup around 9:00, back to Belfast by 19:00). Their "*Game of Thrones* Tour" visits many of the sites where the hit TV series was filmed (£35, pickup at 8:30, return by 19:00, tel. 028/9031-5333, www.mccombscoaches.com).

HARBOR TOURS

The **Lagan Boat Company** offers a one-hour tour with an entertaining guide showing the shipyards, the fruits of the city's £800 million investment in its harbor, and the rusty *Titanic* heritage (£12; April-Oct daily sailings at 12:30, 14:00, and 15:30; fewer off-season, tel. 028/9024-0124, www.laganboatcompany.com, Joyce). Tours depart from near the Lagan Weir just past the Albert Clock Tower.

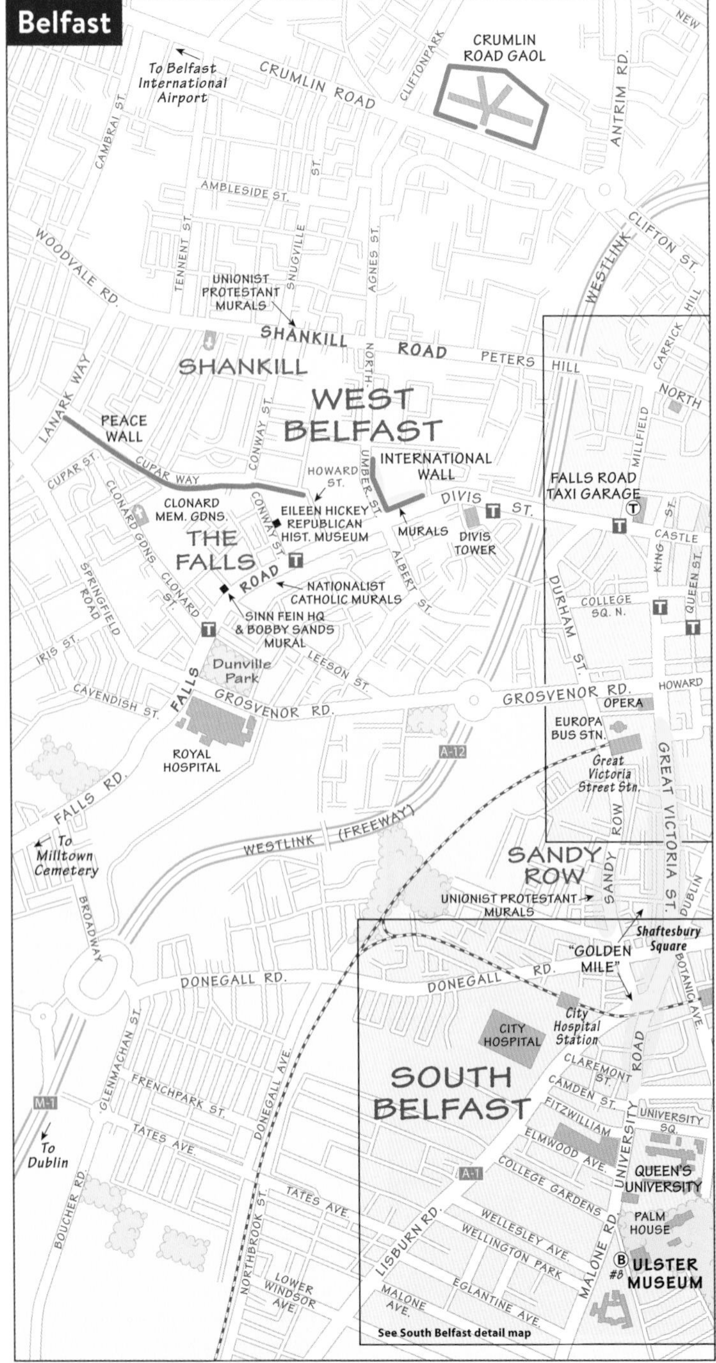

Belfast
To Belfast International Airport
CRUMLIN ROAD
CRUMLIN ROAD GAOL
CLIFTONPARK
ANTRIM RD.
NEW
CAMBRAI ST.
AMBLESIDE ST.
ST.
TENNENT ST.
SNUGVILLE
AGNES ST.
WOODVALE RD.
CLIFTON ST.
WESTLINK
CARRICK HILL
UNIONIST PROTESTANT MURALS
SHANKILL ROAD
PETERS HILL
SHANKILL
WEST BELFAST
NORTH
LANARK WAY
PEACE WALL
CONWAY ST.
NORTH-
MILLFIELD
CUPAR WAY
CUPAR ST.
HOWARD ST.
UMBER. ST.
INTERNATIONAL WALL
FALLS ROAD TAXI GARAGE
CLONARD MEM. GDNS.
CLONARD GDNS.
CONWAY ST.
EILEEN HICKEY REPUBLICAN HIST. MUSEUM
DIVIS ST.
MURALS
DIVIS TOWER
KING ST.
CASTLE
QUEEN ST.
THE FALLS
ROAD
NATIONALIST CATHOLIC MURALS
ALBERT ST.
DURHAM ST.
COLLEGE SQ. N.
SPRINGFIELD ROAD
CLONARD ST.
SINN FEIN HQ & BOBBY SANDS MURAL
IRIS ST.
Dunville Park
LEESON ST.
CAVENDISH ST.
FALLS
GROSVENOR RD.
GROSVENOR RD.
HOWARD
OPERA
EUROPA BUS STN.
ROYAL HOSPITAL
A-12
Great Victoria Street Stn.
GREAT VICTORIA ST.
FALLS RD.
WESTLINK (FREEWAY)
ROW
To Milltown Cemetery
SANDY ROW
SANDY
UNIONIST PROTESTANT MURALS
DUBLIN
BROADWAY
Shaftesbury Square
"GOLDEN MILE"
BOTANIC AVE.
DONEGALL RD.
DONEGALL RD.
City Hospital Station
CITY HOSPITAL
ROAD
GLENMACHAN ST.
CLAREMONT ST.
SOUTH BELFAST
CAMDEN ST.
FRENCHPARK ST.
FITZWILLIAM
UNIVERSITY SQ.
M-1
DONEGALL AVE.
TATES AVE.
ELMWOOD AVE.
UNIVERSITY
To Dublin
A-1
COLLEGE GARDENS
QUEEN'S UNIVERSITY
BOUCHER RD.
NORTHBROOK ST.
TATES AVE.
WELLESLEY AVE.
PALM HOUSE
LISBURN RD.
WELLINGTON PARK
MALONE RD.
ULSTER MUSEUM
#8
LOWER WINDSOR AVE.
MALONE AVE.
EGLANTINE AVE.
See South Belfast detail map

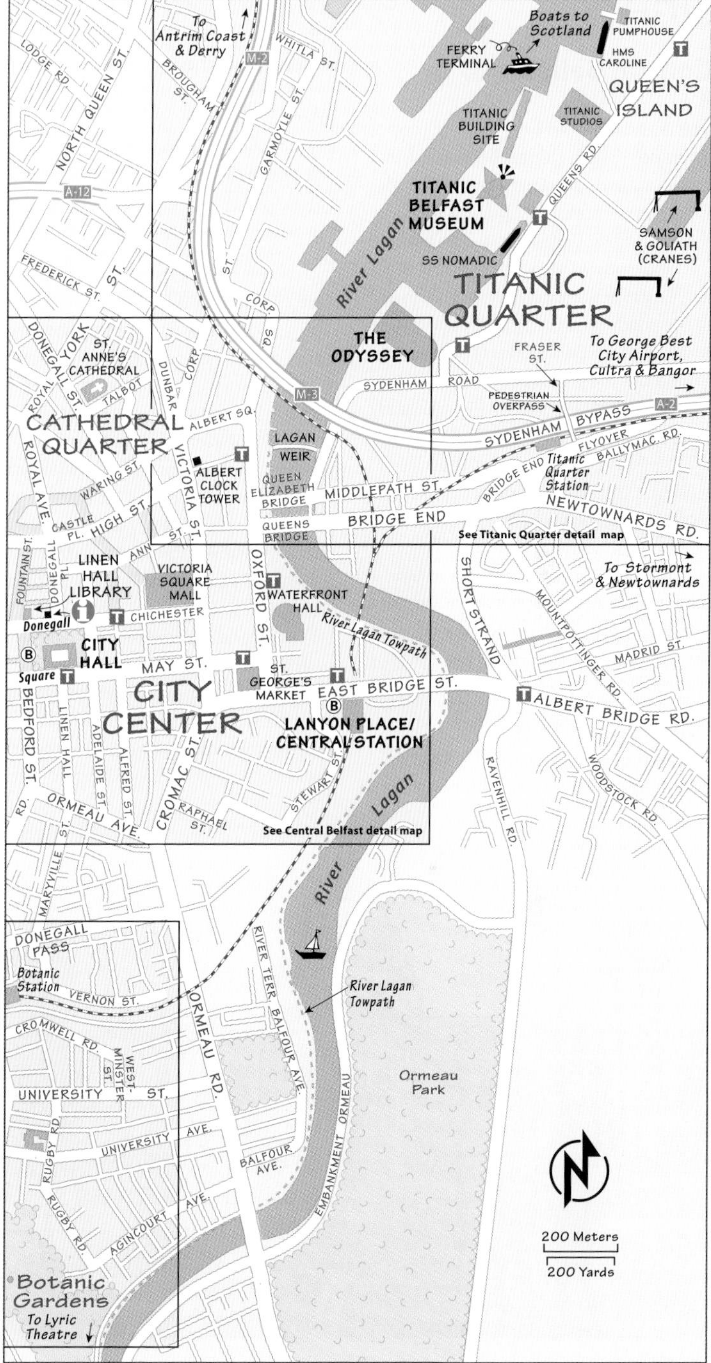
To Antrim Coast & Derry
Boats to Scotland
FERRY TERMINAL
TITANIC PUMPHOUSE
HMS CAROLINE
QUEEN'S ISLAND
TITANIC STUDIOS
TITANIC BUILDING SITE
TITANIC BELFAST MUSEUM
SS NOMADIC
SAMSON & GOLIATH (CRANES)
TITANIC QUARTER
River Lagan
THE ODYSSEY
To George Best City Airport, Cultra & Bangor
FRASER ST.
PEDESTRIAN OVERPASS
ST. ANNE'S CATHEDRAL
CATHEDRAL QUARTER
LAGAN WEIR
ALBERT CLOCK TOWER
QUEEN ELIZABETH BRIDGE
QUEENS BRIDGE
Titanic Quarter Station
See Titanic Quarter detail map
To Stormont & Newtownards
LINEN HALL LIBRARY
VICTORIA SQUARE MALL
WATERFRONT HALL
River Lagan Towpath
Donegall Square
CITY HALL
ST. GEORGE'S MARKET
CITY CENTER
LANYON PLACE/ CENTRAL STATION
See Central Belfast detail map
River Lagan
Botanic Station
River Lagan Towpath
Ormeau Park
Botanic Gardens
To Lyric Theatre
200 Meters
200 Yards
LODGE RD.
NORTH QUEEN ST.
WHITLA ST.
BROUGHAM ST.
GARMOYLE ST.
QUEENS RD.
FREDERICK ST.
YORK ST.
CORP. SQ.
DONEGALL ST.
ROYAL AVE.
TALBOT
DUNBAR
ALBERT SQ.
SYDENHAM ROAD
SYDENHAM BYPASS
FLYOVER
BALLYMAC. RD.
BRIDGE END
WARING ST.
VICTORIA ST.
MIDDLEPATH ST.
NEWTOWNARDS RD.
CASTLE PL.
HIGH ST.
ANN ST.
OXFORD ST.
SHORT STRAND
MOUNTPOTTINGER RD.
MADRID ST.
FOUNTAIN ST.
CHICHESTER
MAY ST.
EAST BRIDGE ST.
ALBERT BRIDGE RD.
BEDFORD ST.
LINEN HALL
ADELAIDE ST.
ALFRED ST.
CROMAC ST.
STEWART ST.
RAVENHILL RD.
WOODSTOCK RD.
ORMEAU AVE.
RAPHAEL ST.
MARYVILLE ST.
DONEGALL PASS
VERNON ST.
RIVER TERR.
ORMEAU RD.
BALFOUR AVE.
CROMWELL RD.
WEST-MINSTER ST.
UNIVERSITY ST.
ORMEAU EMBANKMENT
RUGBY RD.
UNIVERSITY AVE.
AGINCOURT AVE.

SIGHTS

Central Belfast

▲▲CITY HALL

This grand structure's 173-foot-tall copper dome dominates Donegall Square at the center of town. Built between 1898 and 1906, with its statue of Queen Victoria scowling down Belfast's main drag and the Neoclassical dome looming behind her, City Hall is a stirring sight. Free tours of the building run daily, and the worthwhile 16-room Belfast History and Culture exhibit fills the ground floor.

Cost and Hours: City Hall—free, daily 8:00-17:00; Belfast History and Culture exhibit—free, daily 9:00-17:00; audioguide-£3.50; Bobbin coffee shop on ground floor, tel. 028/9032-0202, www.belfastcity.gov.uk/cityhall.

Tours: Free 45-minute tours run Mon-Fri at 10:00, 11:00, 14:00, 15:00, and 16:00; Sat-Sun at 12:00, 14:00, 15:00, and 16:00 (fewer off-season); drop by, call, or check online to confirm schedule and book a spot.

LINEN HALL LIBRARY

Across the street from City Hall, the 200-year-old Linen Hall Library welcomes guests. Described as "Ulster's attic," the library takes pride in being a neutral space where anyone trying to make sense of the sectarian conflict can view the "Troubled Images," a historical collection of engrossing political posters.

Cost and Hours: Free, Mon-Fri 9:30-17:30, closed Sat-Sun, 45-minute tours (£5) run daily at 10:30, 17 Donegall Square North, tel. 028/9032-1707, www.linenhall.com.

THE GOLDEN MILE

The "Golden Mile" is the overstated nickname of a Belfast entertainment zone with a few interesting sights on Great Victoria Street, just southwest of City Hall.

The **Presbyterian Assembly Building,** a fine example of Scottish Baronial architecture, has a welcoming little visitor exhibition that tells the story of the Presbyterians in Northern Ireland (free, Mon-Fri 9:30-17:00, closed Sat-Sun, across from Jury's Inn at 2 Fisherwick Place).

The **Grand Opera House,** originally built in 1895, bombed and rebuilt in 1991, and bombed and rebuilt again in 1993, is extravagantly Victorian and *the* place to take in a concert, play, or opera (ticket office open Mon-Sat 10:00-17:00,

City Hall

Crown Liquor Saloon

closed Sun; ticket office to right of main front door on Great Victoria Street, tel. 028/9024-1919, www.goh.co.uk). The nearby **Hotel Europa,** considered to be the most-bombed hotel in the world (33 times during the Troubles), actually feels pretty laid-back today.

The Crown Liquor Saloon is the ultimate gin palace. Built in 1849, its mahogany, glass, and marble interior is a trip back into the days of Queen Victoria. Wander through and imagine the snugs (booths designed to provide a little privacy for un-Victorian behavior) before the invasion of selfie-snapping tourists. Upstairs, the recommended Crown Dining Room serves pub grub and is decorated with historic photos.

CATHEDRAL QUARTER

Tucked between St. Anne's Cathedral and the River Lagan, this rejuvenating district is busy with shoppers by day and clubbers by night. And, being the oldest part of Belfast, it's full of history. Before World War I, this was the whiskey warehouse district—at time when the Belfast region produced about half of all Irish whiskey. While today's Cathedral District has a few minor sights, the big attraction is its nightlife—restaurants, clubs, and pubs. For the epicenter of this zone, head for the intersection of **Hill Street and Commercial Court** and peek into nearby breezeways. As you explore, you'll find a maze of narrow streets, pubs named for the colorful characters that gave the city its many legends, and creative street-art murals that hint at the artistic spirit and still-feisty edginess of Belfast.

The Cathedral Quarter extends to the old merchant district, with its Victorian-era **Customs House** backed up to the river. Nearby, at the intersection of High Street and Victoria Street, is Belfast's "Little Big Ben," the **Albert Memorial Clock Tower.** The tower was built in 1870 to honor to Queen Victoria's beloved Prince Albert, nine years after he died. The clock tower is the start of my "Titanic Quarter Walk" (see page 287).

Sectarian Neighborhoods in West Belfast

This slowly rejuvenating section of gritty West Belfast is home to two sectarian communities, living along the main roads to either side of a peace wall: Unionist/Loyalists/Protestants along Shankill Road and Republicans/Nationalists/Catholics along Falls Road.

There's plenty to see in the sectarian hoods—especially murals. While you could simply (and safely) walk through these districts on your own, you'd be missing an easy opportunity to employ working-class locals who'd love to give you their firsthand, personal take on the Troubles from the perspective of their communities.

Touring the Sectarian Neighborhoods

You can visit with a shared taxi, a private taxi tour, or on foot (with a guide, or your own—using cabs as you go). Hop-on, hop-off bus tours also drive these roads, but are

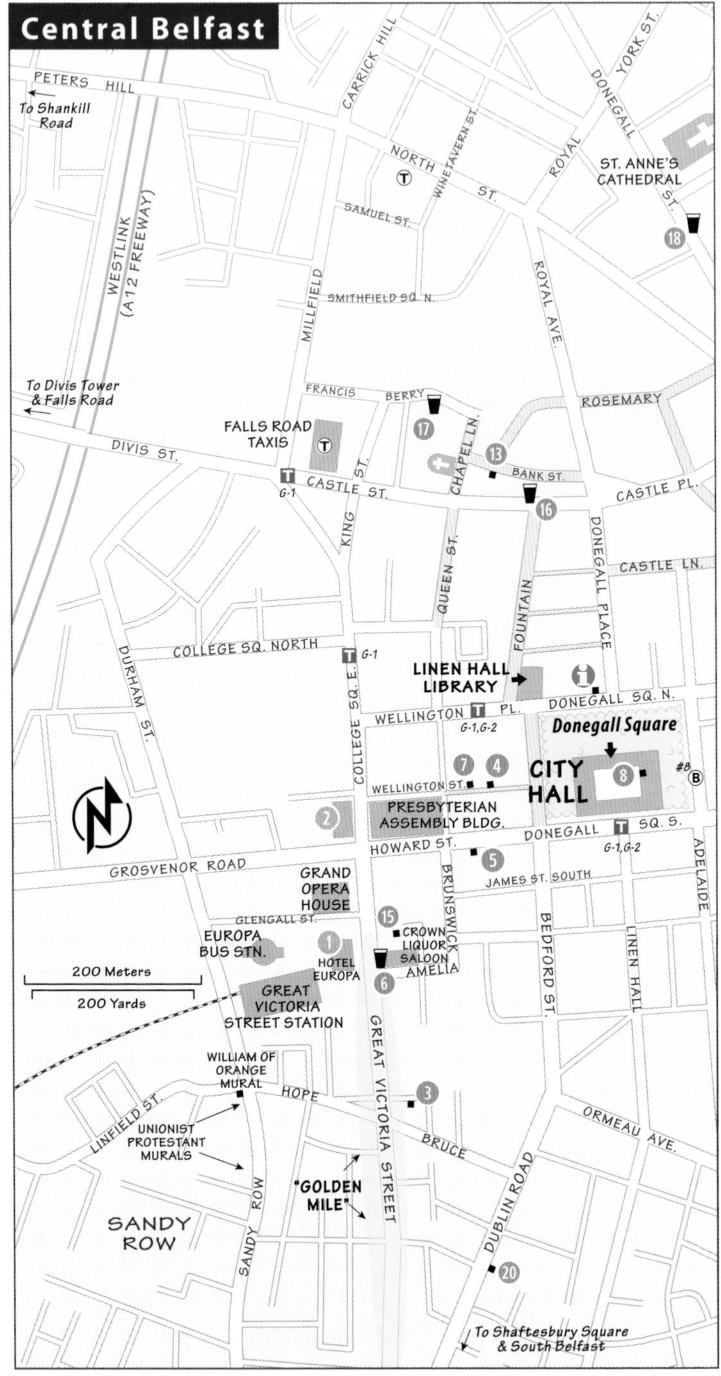
Central Belfast
Peters Hill
To Shankill Road
Carrick Hill
York St.
Donegall St.
North St.
Winetavern St.
Royal Ave.
St. Anne's Cathedral
Samuel St.
Westlink (A12 Freeway)
Millfield
Smithfield Sq. N.
To Divis Tower & Falls Road
Francis
Berry
Rosemary
Falls Road Taxis
Divis St.
Chapel Ln.
Bank St.
Castle St.
Castle Pl.
King St.
Queen St.
Fountain
Donegall Place
Castle Ln.
College Sq. North
Durham St.
Linen Hall Library
Wellington Pl.
Donegall Sq. N.
Donegall Square
College Sq. E.
City Hall
Wellington St.
Presbyterian Assembly Bldg.
Donegall Sq. S.
Howard St.
Grosvenor Road
Grand Opera House
James St. South
Adelaide
Glengall St.
Brunswick
Bedford St.
Linen Hall
Europa Bus Stn.
Crown Liquor Saloon
Hotel Europa
Amelia
200 Meters
200 Yards
Great Victoria Street Station
William of Orange Mural
Hope
Great Victoria Street
Linfield St.
Unionist Protestant Murals
Bruce
Ormeau Ave.
"Golden Mile"
Dublin Road
Sandy Row
To Shaftesbury Square & South Belfast

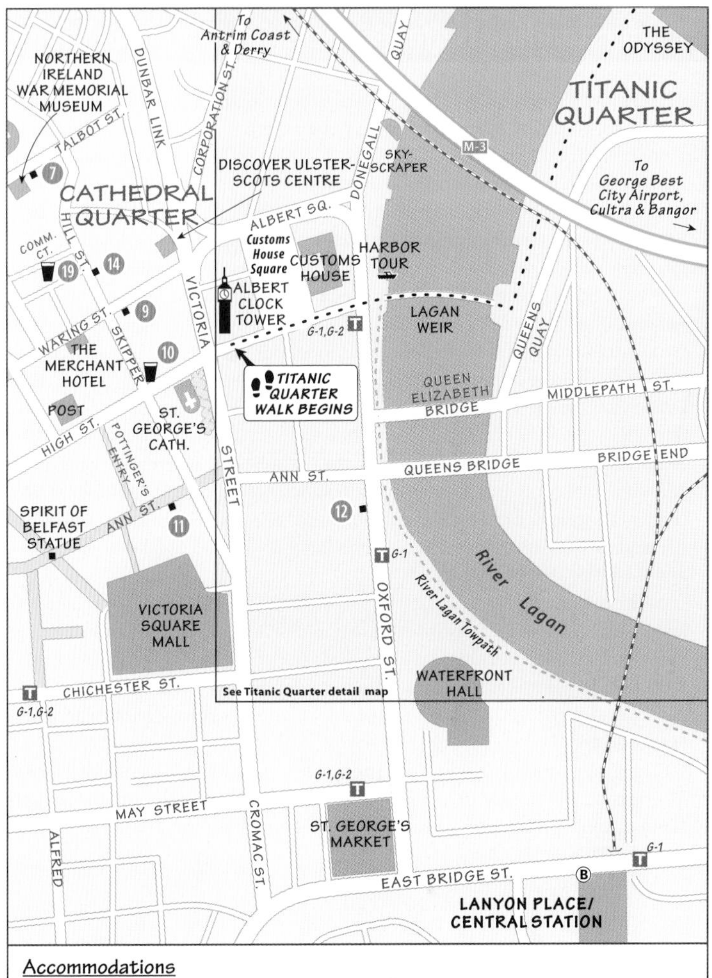

<u>Accommodations</u>

1 Hotel Europa
2 Jurys Inn

<u>Eateries</u>

3 The Ginger Bistro
4 Yügo Asian Fusion Food
5 Deanes Love Fish & Deanes Meatlocker
6 Crown Liquor Saloon & Dining Room
7 Made in Belfast (2)
8 The Bobbin Café
9 The Merchant Hotel (Afternoon Tea)
10 Bert's Jazz Bar
11 Fish City
12 Ox Cave
13 Mourne Seafood Bar
14 The Yardbird & The Dirty Onion
15 Grocery

<u>Nightlife & Other</u>

16 Kelly's Cellars
17 Madden's Pub (Belfast Story)
18 The John Hewitt
19 The Duke of York
20 The Points Whiskey & Alehouse

Understanding Belfast's Sectarian Neighborhoods

For centuries, Ireland has lived with tensions between Loyalists (also called Unionists, generally Protestants, who want to remain part of the United Kingdom, ruled from London) and Republicans (also called Nationalists, generally Roman Catholics, who want to be part of a united Ireland, independent from Great Britain). The Catholic Irish are the indigenous Irish and the Protestant loyalists are later arrivals, mostly "Scotch Irish," planted by London from Scotland in the north of Ireland.

A flare-up of violence in 1969 between these two communities led to a spontaneous mass reshuffling of working-class people in Belfast. Those who were minorities decided it was too dangerous to stay in the "wrong" sectarian neighborhood and moved into districts where they would be among their "tribe." Protestants left the Falls Road area for the Shankill Road area and Catholics left the Shankill Road area for the Falls Road area.

It's said that in these neighborhoods, the Catholics became more Irish than the Irish and the Protestants became more British than the British. Fighting between the two districts led the British army to build "peace walls" to keep them apart. Paramilitary organizations on each side incited violence, and what came to be known as the Troubles began.

With two newly created ghettos dug in, it was a sad and bloody time that lasted until the Good Friday peace agreement in 1998. Since then, the bombings, assassinations, and burnings have stopped, and peace has had the upper hand.

But Belfast is still segregated. The two groups have no trouble working or even socializing together downtown, but at night they retreat back to their separate enclaves.

The peace walls no longer stops projectiles, and their gates are mostly open. There is peace. But there is no forgiveness: Murderers still cross paths with their victims' loved ones. Locals say it'll take another generation to be truly over the Troubles.

impersonal and keep you at a distance. Skip them in favor of one of these options.

▲▲▲SECTARIAN NEIGHBORHOOD TAXI TOURS

Taxi tours are easy, inexpensive, and, for me, the most interesting 90 minutes you can have in Belfast. Quiz the cabbie (who grew up here) and pull over for photos. You'll get honest (if biased) viewpoints on the Troubles and local culture, see the political murals, and visit the many Troubles-related sights.

Falls Road Shared Taxi Service: The **West Belfast Taxi Association** (WBTA), run by a group of local Falls Road men, is located in the Castle Junction Car Park at the intersection of Castle and King streets. On the ground floor of this nine-story parking garage, a passenger terminal (entrance on King Street) connects travelers with old black cabs—and the only Irish-language signs in downtown Belfast.

These shared black cabs efficiently shuttle residents from outlying neighborhoods up and down Falls Road and to the city center. All shared cabs go up Falls Road, past Sinn Féin headquarters and lots of murals, to the Milltown Cemetery (sit in front and talk to the cabbie). Shared taxi cars have their roof sign removed and no meters. You'll pay £2/ride. You can get a cab at the Castle Junction Car Park, or anywhere along Falls Road, where easy-to-flag-down cabs run every minute or so in each direction. Just flag one down to stop it, and rap on the window to exit. Hop in and out. You can also hire a cab for a private 90-minute tour (see next).

Black Taxi Tours of Falls Road: Nearly any of the WBTA cabs described above are ready and able to give private tours (£45 for 3 people, more for up to 6, 90 minutes). While the drivers are Republican, these days they venture into the Loyalist zone as well. Three is comfortable in a cab. More than that and you'll have a hard time seeing. Just drop into the WBTA Passenger Terminal and they'll set you up (Taxi Trax Black Taxi Tours, tel. 028/9031-5777, mobile 078-9271-6660, www.taxitrax.com).

Rick's Tip: *Taxi tours work great* **in the rain,** *as the cabbie just parks and talks while you look out the window.*

Cab Tours Belfast: This group of driver/guides from both communities (Catholic and Protestant) has teamed up and is committed to giving unbiased dual-narrative tours. Their "Belfast Murals Tour" covers both neighborhoods and is a fascinating 90 minutes. As their £35 price covers two people and includes free pick up and drop-off within central Belfast, this can work very efficiently with your sightseeing day (mobile 077-1364-0647, www.cabtoursbelfast.com).

SECTARIAN NEIGHBORHOOD WALKING TOURS

On your own, get a map and lace together the sights along Falls Road by walking the street. Walking mixes well with hopping into shared taxis (described earlier) that go up and down constantly. Or consider one of the following **walking-tour companies:**

Coiste Irish Political Tours offers the Republican/Catholic community perspective on an extended, two-hour "Falls Road Murals" walking tour. Led by former IRA prisoners, you'll visit murals, gardens of remembrance, and peace walls, and get to know the community. Tours meet beside the Divis Tower (the solitary, purple 20-story apartment building at the east end of Divis Road) and end at Milltown Cemetery. Afterwards, you're invited for a complimentary glass of Guinness at the Felons Club Pub—run by former IRA prisoners (£10; Tue, Thu, and Sat at 10:00; Sun at 14:00; best to book in advance, tel. 028/9020-0770, www.coiste.ie).

Belfast Political Tours runs a unique tour called "Conflicting Stories" in which former combatants from each side show and tell their story: a Republican for Falls Road sights and then a Unionist for Shankill Road sights (£18, 3 hours, most days at 9:30 and 14:30, departs from Divis Tower, mobile 073-9358-5531, www.belfastpoliticaltour.com).

Sandy Row Walking Tours provides the Unionist/Loyalist point of view during 90-minute walks centering on Sandy Row, Belfast's oldest residential neighborhood. Tours go beyond the Troubles to cover the city's industrial heritage, the Orange Order, both world wars, and historic local churches. They depart from the William of Orange mural at the intersection of Sandy Row and Linfield Road (£7.50; most days at 10:00, 12:00, and 14:00; call to book, mobile 079-0925-4849, www.historicsandyrow.co.uk).

Sights in the Sectarian Neighborhoods

The sectarian neighborhoods are known for their murals. But with more peaceful times, the character of these murals is slowly changing. The government is helping fund programs that replace aggressive murals with positive ones. Paramilitary themes are gradually being covered over with images of pride in each neighborhood's culture.

SHANKILL ROAD

In the Loyalist Shankill Road area there are plenty of vivid murals and lots of red, white, and blue. You'll see fields where bonfires are built, with piles of wood awaiting the next Orange Day, July 12—when Protestants march and burn huge fires (and when Catholics choose to leave town on vacation). There is a particularly interesting series of murals at Lower Shankill Estate.

PEACE WALL

This sad, corrugated structure, known as a peace wall, runs a block or so north of Falls Road (along Cupar Way) separating the Catholics from the Protestants in the Shankill Road area. The wall has five gates that open each day from about 8:00 to 18:00. On the Protestant side there is a long stretch where tour groups stop to write peaceful and hopeful messages.

The first cement wall was 20 feet high—it was later extended another 10 feet by a solid metal addition, and then another 15 feet with a metal screen. Seemingly high enough now to deter a projectile being lobbed over, this is one of many such walls erected in Belfast during the Troubles. Meant to be temporary, these barriers stay up because of old fears among the communities on both sides.

INTERNATIONAL WALL

Just past the gate on Townsend Street on the Republican side stretches the colorful, so-called "International Wall"—

Shankill Road

Falls Road

an L-shaped, two-block-long series of political murals that shows solidarity with other oppressed groups. (For example, Catholics in Ulster have a natural affinity with Basques in Spain and Palestinians in Israel). Along the Falls Road section of the International Wall are "current events" murals as up-to-date as last month.

FALLS ROAD AND NEARBY

In the Catholic Falls Road area, you'll notice that the road signs are in two languages (Irish first). Sights include the many political murals, neighborhood memorial gardens, and Bombay Street, which the Protestants burned in 1969, igniting the Troubles.

Sinn Féin Press Office: Near the bottom of Falls Road, at #51, is the press center for the hardline Republican party, Sinn Féin. While the press office is not open to the public, the adjacent **bookstore** (with an intriguing gift shop) is welcoming and worth a look. Around the corner is a big and bright mural remembering **Bobby Sands,** a member of parliament who led a hunger strike in prison with fellow inmates and starved himself to death to very effectively raise awareness of the Republican concerns.

Eileen Hickey Republican History Museum: This volunteer-run museum, tucked away in a residential complex, has a clear mission: "For Republican history to be told by Republicans. To educate our youth so they may understand why Republicans fought, died, and spent many years in prison for their beliefs." This is an unforgettable museum, with real (if totally biased) history shown and told by people who played a part in it (free, Tue-Sat 10:00-14:00, closed Sun-Mon, two blocks from Sinn Féin Press Office at 5 Conway Place, tel. 028/9024-0504, www.eileenhickeymuseum.com).

Bombay Street and Clonard Memorial Garden: About a 10-minute walk from the Sinn Féin Press Office is Bombay Street and the Clonard Memorial Garden. On August 15, 1969, Loyalists set fire to the Catholic homes and a monastery on this street. In the violence, a Republican teenager was killed. The burning of this Catholic street led to the "sorting out" of the communities and the building of a peace wall. Today you'll see Bombay Street nicely rebuilt, photos of the terrible event, and a peaceful memorial garden against the wall.

Milltown Cemetery: To reach the cemetery, take a taxi or the #G1 Glider tram to the Falls Park stop; it's too far to walk (cemetery open daily 9:00-16:00, 546 Falls Road, tel. 028/9061-3972). This burial site for Republican martyrs can be a pilgrimage for some. You'll walk past all the Gaelic crosses down to the far right-hand corner (closest to the highway), where little green railings set apart the IRA Roll of Honor from the thousands of other graves.

SANDY ROW

To the southwest of City Hall, Sandy Row is a smaller Unionist, Protestant working-class street just behind Hotel Europa that offers a cheap and easy way to get a dose of a sectarian neighborhood. A stop in a Unionist memorabilia shop, a pub, or one of the many cheap eateries here may give you an opportunity to talk to a local. Along the way you'll see murals filled with Unionist symbolism.

Titanic Quarter

To mark the 100th anniversary of the *Titanic* disaster in 2012, Belfast opened the Titanic Belfast Museum, a phenomenally popular exhibition about the ill-fated ship. Today, the entire eastern bank of the River Lagan is a delightful promenade nicknamed "the Maritime Mile."

While you can just go to the Titanic Belfast Museum, if you have time, see the museum as part of the following walk. The slick new Glider tram #G2 from City Hall makes stops all along the way, including at the Titanic Belfast Museum and the HMS *Caroline.*

➲ *Titanic Quarter Walk*

This self-guided walk, rated ▲▲, takes about an hour, not including visits to its two major stops: the Titanic Belfast Museum and the HMS *Caroline.*

• *Belfast's leaning* ❶ ***Albert Memorial Clock Tower*** *marks the start of this walk (for more about the clock tower, see page 281). From there, head for the River Lagan, where you'll find the...*

❷ **Lagan Weir:** The first step in rejuvenating a derelict riverfront is to tame the river, get rid of the tides, and build modern embankments. The star of that major investment is the Lagan Weir, the

Modern Belfast

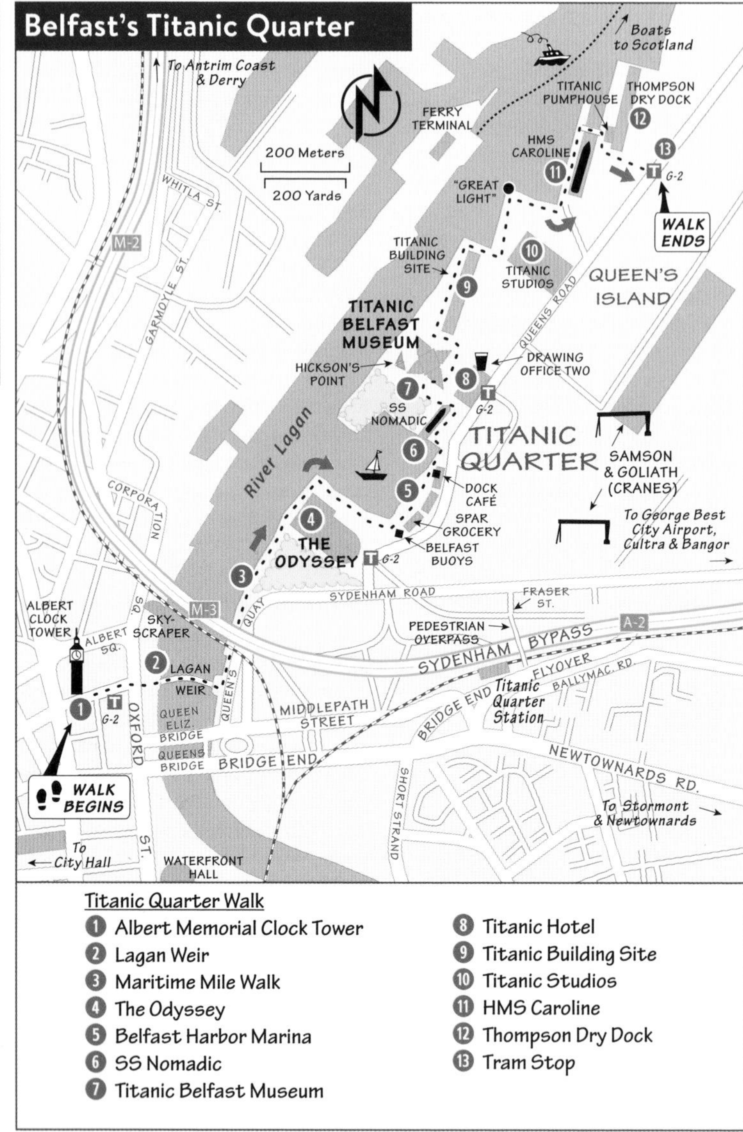

people-friendly gateway to the Titanic Quarter. Built in 1994, the weir is made up of four large pier houses and five giant gates that divide freshwater from saltwater and control the river's flow—no more flooding. You can walk across the weir on a curving pedestrian footbridge (added in 2015). On the other side, a popular riverside walk goes scenically inland from here 14 miles along the old tow path.

• *Cross the weir and turn left.*

❸ **Maritime Mile Walk:** This parklike promenade laces together several sights along the riverbank. It's lined with historic photo plaques that tell the story of this industrial river. The far side of the river was busy with trade (importing and exporting) and this side was all about shipbuilding. All along the way you'll get glimpses (to the right) of the city's iconic and giant yellow cranes. Find a *Game of Thrones* stained-glass window. You'll see a couple of these on this walk. (Belfast has six, commemorating the TV series filmed here that gave tourism in Northern Ireland a nice bump.)

• *Continue walking until you reach the Odyssey arena complex.*

❹ **The Odyssey:** This huge millennium-project complex offers a food pavilion, bowling alley, 12-screen cinema, and the **W5 science center** with interactive, educational exhibits for youngsters (£10, Mon-Sat 10:00-18:00, Sun from 12:00, 2 Queen's Quay, tel. 028/9046-7790, www.w5online.co.uk).

There's also the 12,000-seat **SSE Odyssey Arena,** where the Belfast Giants professional hockey team skates.

• *Turning inland, you come to the* ❺ ***Belfast Harbor Marina*** *with an arc of shops and condos. On the corner are three huge buoys (buoy is pronounced "boy" in Britain). "The Belfast Buoys" (fondly called Tom, Dick, and Harry here) are described on info boards.*

At the far end of the arc of shops, find the **Dock Café,** *a welcoming, convivial, and homey spot. There's soup and bread at lunch time (Mon-Sat 11:00-17:00, closed Sun).*

• *Ahead looms the superstar of the Titanic Quarter, the Titanic Belfast Museum, as tall as the mighty ship itself. As you approach, you'll pass a big ship that was just the tender (the shuttle dinghy) for the* Titanic.

❻ **SS Nomadic:** This ship once ferried first-class passengers between the dock and the *Titanic.* Sitting in the dry dock where it was built, it's restored to appear as it was in 1912 when it ferried Benjamin Guggenheim, John Jacob Astor, Molly Brown, and Kate Winslet to that fateful voyage (50 yards south of the Titanic Belfast Museum, same hours and ticket as the museum).

• *Now is a good time to tour the* ❼ ***Titanic Belfast Museum*** *(see listing later in this section). Afterwards walk across the plaza to the...*

❽ **Titanic Hotel:** Housed in the former Harland and Wolff shipyard headquarters (known as the Drawing Office), this new hotel was permitted on condition that the public would be allowed to wander through its historic spaces. For 150 years, many of the largest and finest ships in the world were designed here. Pick up an info sheet at the reception and treat the place like a free museum. The well-lit central space, now the Drawing Office Two pub, is where the plans for the *Titanic* were drawn.

• *Head for the river to see the place where the* Titanic *was actually built.*

❾ ***Titanic*** **Building Site:** A big, stylized **map** in the pavement shows the route of the *Titanic*'s one and only voyage. The brown benches are long and short—set up in dots and dashes to represent the Morse code distress transmissions sent on that fateful day. Just beyond two dashes, a few steps to the left, find the symbolic steel tip of the ship in the pavement and stand there looking out. This was where the bow was; the lampposts (stretching 300 yards before you) mark the size of the ship built here. Fifty yards ahead is a memorial with the names of all who perished.

• *Walk to what would have been the stern of the* Titanic.

❿ **Titanic Studios:** The *Game of Thrones* stained-glass window here features the

Game of Thrones stained glass

Iron Throne. (You've just got to get a selfie.) The giant warehouse-like building to your right was once the shipyard's Paint Hall, and is now Titanic Studios (not open to public)—the soundstage where much of *Game of Thrones* was filmed.

• *Continue walking up the promenade to the...*

⑪ **HMS *Caroline:*** A WWI battleship that fought in the 1916 Battle of Jutland, the HMS *Caroline* is one of only three surviving Royal Navy ships from that war, and well worth exploring (see listing, later).

• *Walking from the HMS* Caroline *away from the river toward the tram stop you'll pass the...*

⑫ **Thompson Dry Dock:** This is the massive dry dock where the *Titanic* last rested on dry land. It's here that the final outfitting was completed, adding extra weight before the final watertight launch. You can pay to go inside the pump room and descend into the dry dock to walk in the *Titanic*'s massive footprint (£5, daily 10:00-17:00, café, tel. 028/9073-7813, www.titanicsdock.com).

• *Across the street is a* ⑬ ***tram stop.*** *From here you can catch the Glider tram #G2 back to City Hall.*

Rick's Tip: *Go early or late as big bus-tour or cruise-ship crowds can clog the* **Titanic Belfast Museum** *exhibits from 10:00 to 15:00.* **Book ahead online** *to get the entry time you want.*

Titanic Quarter Sights

▲▲▲TITANIC BELFAST MUSEUM

This £97 million attraction stands right next to the original slipways where the *Titanic* was built. Creative displays tell the tale of the famous ocean liner, proudly heralded as the largest man-made moving object of its time. The sight has no actual artifacts from the underwater wreck (out of respect for the fact that it's a mass grave). The artifacts on display are from local shipbuilding offices and personal collections.

Cost and Hours: £19, £11.50 Late Saver Ticket sold one hour before closing; daily June-Aug 8:30-19:00, April-May and Sept 9:00-18:00, Oct-March 10:00-17:00; audioguide-£4, but you get plenty of info without it; tel. 028/9076-6399, www.titanicbelfast.com. Early Riser Tickets for some morning slots (book online) can save up to 30 percent.

Getting There: From the Albert Memorial Clock Tower at the edge of the Cathedral Quarter, it's a 10-minute walk: Follow my "Titanic Quarter Walk." From Donegall Square, take the Glider tram (#G2, 6/hour) or go by taxi (about £6).

Tours: The **Discovery Tour** explains the striking architecture of the Titanic Belfast Museum building and the adjacent slipways where the ship was built (£9, 1 hour, call ahead for tour times).

Visiting the Museum: The spacey architecture of the Titanic Belfast Museum building is a landmark on the city's skyline. Six stories tall, it's clad in more than 3,000 sun-reflecting aluminum panels. Its four corners represent the bows of the many ships (most of which didn't sink) that were

Titanic Belfast Museum

built in these yards during the industrial Golden Age of Belfast.

You'll follow a one-way route through the exhibit's nine galleries on six floors. Helpful "crew" (museum staff) are posted throughout to answer questions. The "shipyard ride" near the beginning is a fun (if cheesy) five-minute experience. Six people share a gondola as you glide through a series of vignettes that attempt to capture what it was like to be a worker building the ship. (There can be a 20-minute wait—if in a hurry, I'd skip it and use my time more productively in the fascinating displays that follow.)

Continuing on, you'll find a big window overlooking the actual construction site (which you can visit after leaving the building). Next, you'll see exhibits on the construction, historic photographs, proud displays of the opulence on board, a recounting of the disaster (with Morse code transmissions sent after the ship hit the iceberg) and, in the 200-seat Discovery Theatre, the seven-minute *Titanic Beneath* video, with eerie footage of the actual wreckage sprouting countless "rusticles"

Replica Titanic *lifeboat*

12,000 feet down on the ocean floor. Don't miss the see-through floor panels at the foot of the movie screen where the wreck passes slowly under your feet. The last escalator leaves you on the ground floor facing the back door of the center.

And what do the people of Belfast have to say about the ship they built that sank on her first voyage? "She was OK when she left."

▲HMS *CAROLINE*

Launched in 1914, the HMS *Caroline* is the sole surviving ship of the greatest naval battle of World War I—the Battle of Jutland in the North Sea. Despite being the bloodiest day in British naval history, it's regarded as a victory over the German Navy, which never challenged Britain again. Follow the one-way route with the included audioguide. You'll start with a fascinating exhibit about the ship, which includes a 10-minute *Jutland Experience* video. Then you'll enter the actual ship, restored as if time stopped in 1916 (dinner is still on the table), and are free to explore from the torpedo exhibit to the thunderous engine room.

Cost and Hours: £13.50, daily 10:00-17:00; walk around the ship to the adjacent building—the old pump house for the Thompson Dry Dock—for tickets; Alexandra Dock, Queen's Road, www.nmrn.org.uk.

South Belfast

▲ULSTER MUSEUM

This is Belfast's most venerable museum. It offers an earnest and occasionally thought-provoking look at the region's history, with a cross-section of local artifacts.

Cost and Hours: £5 suggested donation; Tue-Sun 10:00-17:00, closed Mon; south of downtown, in the Botanic Gardens on Stranmillis Road, tel. 028/9044-0000, www.nmni.com.

Visiting the Museum: The five-floor museum is pretty painless. Ride the elevator to the top floor and follow the spiraling

Palm House in Botanic Gardens

Ulster Folk Park and Transport Museum

exhibits downhill through various zones. The top two floors are dedicated to rotating art exhibits, the next floor down covers local nature, and the two below that focus on history. The ground floor covers the Troubles, and has a coffee shop and gift shop.

In the delicately worded History Zone, a highlight is the wall covered with antique text. On the left is the Ulster Covenant (1912), signed in blood by Unionist Protestants to resist incorporation into an independent Irish state. On the right is the Irish Proclamation of the Republic (1916), dear to Nationalist Catholic hearts as the moral compass of the Easter Uprising. Compare the passion of these polar opposite points of view.

Then continue through the coverage of the modern-day Troubles as this museum strives for balanced and thought-provoking reflections. It's encouraging to see: When I first came to the North over 40 years ago, institutions like this would have only presented one point of view.

▲BOTANIC GARDENS

This is the backyard of Queen's University, and on a sunny day, you couldn't imagine a more relaxing park setting. On a cold day, step into the Tropical Ravine for a jungle of heat and humidity. Take a quick walk through the Palm House, reminiscent of the one in London's Kew Gardens, but smaller. The Ulster Museum is on the garden's grounds.

Cost and Hours: Free; gardens daily 7:30 until dusk; Palm House daily 10:00-17:00, Oct-March until 16:00; tel. 028/9031-4762, www.belfastcity.gov.uk/parks.

Beyond Belfast

▲▲ULSTER FOLK PARK AND TRANSPORT MUSEUM

This sprawling 180-acre, two-museum complex straddles the road and rail line at Cultra, midway between Bangor and Belfast (8 miles east of town). Allow three hours, and expect lots of walking. Most people will spend an hour in the Transport Museum and a couple of hours at the Folk Park.

Cost and Hours: £9 for each museum, £11 combo-ticket for both, £29 for families; March-Sept Tue-Sun 10:00-17:00; Oct-Feb Tue-Fri 10:00-16:00, Sat-Sun 11:00-16:00; closed Mon year-round; check the schedule for the day's special events, tel. 028/9042-8428, www.nmni.com.

Getting There: From Belfast, you can reach Cultra by taxi (£15), bus #502 (2/hour, 30 minutes, from Laganside Bus Centre), or train (2/hour, 15 minutes, from any Belfast train station or from Bangor). Buses stop right in the park, but schedules are skimpy on Saturday and Sunday. Train service is more dependable (and more frequent on the weekend): Get off at the Cultra stop.

Visiting the Museums: The **Transport Museum** consists of three buildings. Start at the bottom and trace the evolution of

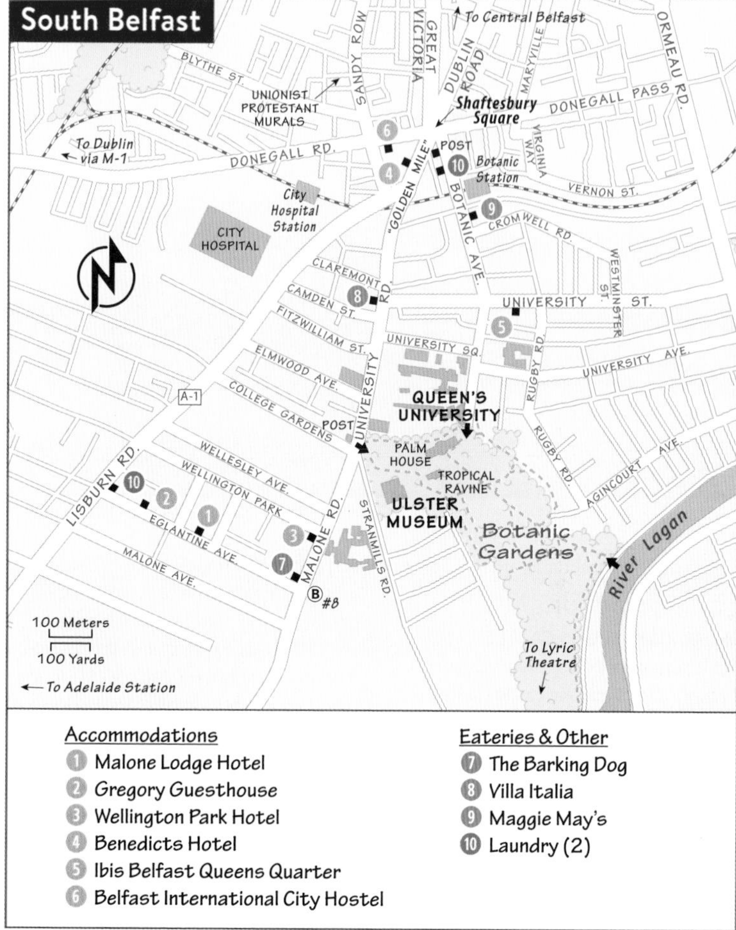

transportation from 7,500 years ago—when people first decided to load an ox—to the first vertical takeoff jet. In 1909, the Belfast-based Shorts Aviation Company partnered with the Wright brothers to manufacture the first commercially available aircraft. The middle building holds an intriguing section on the sinking of the *Titanic.* The top building covers the history of bikes, cars, and trains. The car section rumbles from the first car in Ireland (an 1898 Benz), through the "Cortina Culture" of the 1960s, to the local adventures of controversial automobile designer John DeLorean and a 1981 model of his sleek sports car.

The **Folk Park,** an open-air collection of 34 reconstructed buildings from all over the nine counties of Ulster, showcases the region's traditional lifestyles. After wandering through the old-town site (church, print shop, schoolhouse, humble Belfast row house, silent movie theater, and so on), you'll head off into the country to nip into cottages, farmhouses, and mills. Some houses are warmed by a wonderful peat fire and a friendly attendant. Your visit can be dull or vibrant, depending

Carrickfergus Castle

upon whether attendants are available to chat. Drop a peat brick on the fire.

▲CARRICKFERGUS CASTLE

Built during the Norman invasion of the late 1100s, this historic castle stands sentry on the shore of Belfast Lough. William of Orange landed here in 1690, when he began his Irish campaign against deposed King James II. In 1778, the American privateer ship *Ranger* (the first ever to fly the Stars and Stripes), under the command of John Paul Jones, defeated the HMS *Drake* just up the coast. These days the castle feels a bit sanitized and geared for kids, but it's an easy excursion if you're seeking a castle experience near the city.

Cost and Hours: £5.50; daily 9:00-17:00, Oct-March until 16:00; tel. 028/9335-1273.

Getting There: It's a 20-minute train ride from Belfast (on the line to Larne). Turn left as you exit the train station and walk straight downhill for five minutes—all the way to the waterfront—passing under the arch of the old town wall en route. You'll find the castle on your right.

▲THE GOBBINS CLIFF PATH

The Gobbins Cliff Path is an Edwardian adventure with birds, beautiful scenery, and occasional rogue waves. Located 20 miles northeast of Belfast, beyond Carrickfergus, this complex path is a mix of tunnel bridges, railings, and steps carved, hammered, or fastened to the cliff. It takes two to three hours to hike, and is awkward and steep in places, but not terribly strenuous.

Cost and Hours: £10, visitors center open daily 9:30-17:30, required guided hikes generally hourly (weather permitting), book in advance as tours can fill up, tel. 028/9337-2318, 68 Middle Road, Islandmagee, www.thegobbinscliffpath.com.

Getting There: By car, take the A-2 from Belfast to Larne, turn right on B-90, and follow signs to *Islandmagee* and *The Gobbins.* Without a car, take a train to Ballycarry (on the Larne line) and either walk a mile to the visitors center, or take a taxi (Ballycarry Cabs, tel. 028/9303-8131). McCombs Coach Tours may offer summer excursions here from Belfast—check their offerings by phone or online (tel. 028/9031-5333, www.mccombscoaches.com, info@mccombscoaches.com).

EXPERIENCES

Shopping

On Friday, Saturday, and Sunday, the Victorian confines of **St. George's Market** are a commotion of commerce with an arts, crafts, and flea market—it's also a people-watching delight. If you're looking for a shopping mall, **Victoria Square** is a glitzy American-style mall where you can find whatever you need (3 blocks east of City Hall—bordered by Chichester, Victoria, Ann, and Montgomery streets; www.victoriasquare.com).

Nightlife

TRADITIONAL MUSIC AND DANCE

Belfast Story features former *Riverdance* musicians and dancers in an energetic hour-long performance celebrating the people, poetry, and music of Belfast. It's held in a characteristic and recommended pub—with the local crowd on the ground floor and tourists packed into a tiny performance room upstairs (£25; May-Oct Fri-Sat at 20:00, upstairs in Madden's Pub at 74 Berry Street, mobile 079-7189-5746, www.belfasthiddentours.com, Conner Owens).

MUSICAL PUB CRAWL

Belfast Trad Trail Tours is led by two local musicians. You'll walk to three fun drinking establishments in the Cathedral Quarter, where they play and explain traditional Irish music. It's a great intro to Irish music and Belfast's pulsing evening scene (£15, 2.5 hours, mid-May-Aug Sat at 16:00, meet at Dirty Onion Pub, 3 Hill Street, tel. 028/9028-8818, www.tradtrail.com).

▲▲LIVE MUSIC

A great way to connect with the people and culture of Belfast is over a beer in a pub. Those listed here have music—mostly traditional Irish (a.k.a. trad)—nearly every night. Check pub websites to see what's on when you're in town.

Kelly's Cellars, once a rebel hangout (see plaque above door), still has a very gritty Irish feel. It's 300 years old, has a great fun-loving energy inside, and a lively terrace (Mon-Sat 11:30-24:00, Sun 13:00-23:30; live music nightly at 21:30, trad music Tue-Thu and Sat-Sun at 21:30; 32 Bank Street, 100 yards behind Tesco supermarket, access via alley on left side when facing Tesco, tel. 028/9024-6058, www.facebook.com/kellys.cellars).

Madden's Pub is wonderfully characteristic, with a local crowd and trad music every night from 21:00 (no food, also hosts the "Belfast Story" described earlier, 2 blocks from Kelly's Cellars at 74 Berry Street, tel. 028/9024-4114).

The John Hewitt is committed to the local arts scene—giving both musicians and artists a platform. They don't serve food but they do dish up live music almost nightly from 21:30 (trad music Tue and Sat-Sun, rock on Fri, folk and acoustic on Mon and Thu, closed Wed, 51 Donegall Street, tel. 028/9023-3768, www.thejohnhewitt.com).

The Duke of York is noisy for both eyes and ears—jammed with vintage mirrors and memorabilia, it feels like a drunken lamps-and-lighting store. They have live music nightly (from 21:30, often just one guitarist hollering above the din) to crank up the volume even more. It's on Commercial Court, the noisiest and most trendy/touristy street for nightlife in Belfast (7 Commercial Court, tel. 028/9024-1062, www.dukeofyorkbelfast.com).

The Points Whiskey and Alehouse is an authentic Belfast pub, famed for its music—trad and Irish rock on two stages nightly after 22:00. It's near Hotel Europa at 44 Dublin Road. They offer more music in the quieter and adjacent **An Síbín pub** (tel. 028/9099-4124, www.thepointsbelfast.com).

Bert's Jazz Bar, at the Merchant Hotel, is good if you're in the mood for a cocktail in a plush, velvety Art Deco lounge with live jazz (from 21:00 nightly, 16 Skipper Street, tel. 028/9026-2713).

SLEEPING

Central Belfast

$$$$ Hotel Europa is Belfast's landmark hotel—fancy, comfortable, and central—with four stars and lower weekend rates. Modern yet elegant, this place is the choice of visiting diplomats (breakfast extra, Great Victoria Street, tel. 028/9027-1066, www.hastingshotels.com, res@eur.hastingshotels.com).

$$$ Jurys Inn, an American-style hotel that rents 190 identical modern rooms, is perfectly located two blocks from City Hall (breakfast extra, Fisherwick Place, tel. 028/9053-3500, www.jurysinns.com, jurysinnbelfast@jurysinns.com).

Rick's Tip: *For* **cozy B&Bs,** *check out the Queen's University area or the nearby seaside town of Bangor.*

South Belfast

South of Queen's University

Many of Belfast's best budget beds cluster in a comfortable, leafy neighborhood just south of Queen's University (near the Ulster Museum). The Botanic, Adelaide, and City Hospital **train stations** are nearby (I find Botanic the most convenient), and buses zip down Malone Road every 20 minutes. Any **bus** on Malone Road goes to Donegall Square East. **Taxis** take you downtown for about £6 (your host can call one).

$$$$ Malone Lodge Hotel, by far the classiest listing in this neighborhood, provides slick, business-class comfort in 119 spacious rooms on a quiet street (elevator, restaurant, parking, 60 Eglantine Avenue, tel. 028/9038-8000, www.malonelodgehotel.com, info@malonelodgehotel.com).

$$$$ Gregory Guesthouse, with its stately red brick, ages gracefully behind a green lawn with 15 large, fresh rooms. Prices are soft, so it can be a good value with its subtle charm on a quiet street (family room, parking, 32 Eglantine Avenue, tel. 028/9066-3454, www.thegregorybelfast.com, info@thegregorybelfast.com).

$$ Wellington Park Hotel is a dependable, if unimaginative, chain-style hotel with 75 rooms. It's predictable but in a good location (pay parking, 21 Malone Road, tel. 028/9038-1111, www.wellingtonparkhotel.com, info@wellingtonparkhotel.com).

Between Queen's University and Shaftesbury Square

$$$ Benedicts Hotel has 32 rooms in a good location at the northern fringe of the Queen's University district. Its popular bar is a maze of polished wood and can be loud on weekend nights (elevator, 7 Bradbury Place, tel. 028/9059-1999, www.benedictshotel.co.uk, info@benedictshotel.co.uk).

$$ Ibis Belfast Queens Quarter, part of a major European hotel chain, has 56 practical rooms in a convenient location. It's a great deal if you're not looking for cozy character (breakfast extra, elevator, a block north of Queen's University at 75 University Street, tel. 028/9033-3366, https://ibis.accorhotels.com, h7288@accor.com).

¢ Belfast International City Hostel, big and creatively run, provides the best value among Belfast's hostels. It's near Botanic Station, in the heart of the lively university district, and has 24-hour reception. Paul, the manager, is a veritable TI, with a passion for his work (private rooms available, 22 Donegall Road, tel. 028/9031-5435, www.hini.org.uk, info@hini.org.uk).

EATING

Near City Hall

$$$ The Ginger Bistro serves a smart local crowd Irish/Asian cuisine with special attention to vegetarian and fish dishes. The casual front is for walk-ins, and the quieter, more romantic back is for those with reservations (Tue-Sat 12:00-22:00, closed Sun-Mon, early-bird specials Tue-Fri until 18:45, 68 Great Victoria Street, tel. 028/9024-4421, www.gingerbistro.com).

$$$ Yügo Asian Fusion Food is a foodie fave, trendy but with no pretense and lots of booze. The small dining room is tight with a dozen tables; eating at the bar gets you a fun view of the open kitchen. While they have main courses, their small plates—£5-10 each—are designed to be eaten tapas style (vegetarian-friendly, Tue-Sat 12:00-15:00 & 17:00-22:00, closed Sun-Mon, reservations smart, 3 Wellington Street, tel. 028/9031-9715, www.yugobelfast.com).

$$$ Deanes Love Fish and **Deanes Meatlocker** are side-by-side sister places run by the powerhouse restaurateur of Deanes Eipic, a Michelin-star place next door. Each has a confident, impersonal vibe with good-value meals in a classy atmosphere; the lunch and pre-theater specials are especially economic. I prefer the Loves Fish place with its minimalist, nautical feel. The Meatlocker is more for red meat and romance (Mon-Sat 12:00-15:00 & 17:00-22:00, closed Sun, one block from City Hall at 28 Howard Street, tel. 028/9033-1134, www.michaeldeane.co.uk).

$$ Crown Liquor Saloon and Dining Room is a dazzling gin palace on every sightseers list. The ground floor pub is a mesmerizing mishmash of mosaics and shareable snugs (booths—best to reserve), topped with a smoky tin ceiling. The dining room upstairs is similarly elegant but much quieter. Both serve the same pub grub but upstairs seating comes with table service (downstairs 11:30-20:00, upstairs 12:30-22:00, across from Hotel Europa at 46 Great Victoria Street, tel. 028/9024-3187, www.nicholsonspubs.co.uk).

$$ Made in Belfast has a crazy, fake-bohemian dining room with a creative and fun-loving menu. While exciting a decade ago, it's a bit tired now, but I find the food inviting, the spacious seating enjoyable, and the lunch/early-bird specials (until 18:00) a good value (daily, on Wellington Street a block from City Hall, tel. 028/9024-6712). A second location with similar vibes and menu is in the Cathedral Quarter (facing the cathedral at 23 Talbot Street, tel. 028/9545-8120).

Cheap Lunches in City Hall: $ The Bobbin Café at City Hall is a good, cheap, and cheery little cafeteria serving soups, sandwiches, and hot dishes (daily 9:00-17:00, tel. 028/9050-2068). A nonprofit, they employ young people with learning disabilities.

Groceries: The **Tesco Express** across from Hotel Europa is open very late and seems equipped for the hungry traveler.

Cathedral Quarter

$$$$ The Merchant Hotel presents its afternoon tea in an expensive ritual. You'll enjoy velvety Victorian splendor under an opulent dome with a piano accompaniment. Sit under the biggest chandelier in Northern Ireland as you dine in the great hall of a former bank headquarters. If you've got a little money to burn, consider dressing up the best you can and indulging. You'll go home with a fancy box of leftovers (£30/person, daily 12:30-16:30, reservations smart, 35 Waring Street, tel. 028/9023-4888, www.themerchanthotel.com). Dinner is less expensive (daily 17:30-21:45, mod Irish/French cuisine).

$$$ Bert's Jazz Bar, also at the Merchant Hotel, is a fine option if you're looking for French cuisine served with jazz. Their early-bird special is a good value (daily generally 17:00-22:00, 16 Skipper Street, tel. 028/9026-2713).

$$ Fish City is a simple, peaceful dining room with an open kitchen, attentive service, spacious seating with nautical decor, and a focus on quality. Their seafood is caught under high environmental standards (daily 12:00-21:00, 33 Ann Street, tel. 028/9023-1000, Grace).

$$$ Ox Cave is a sleek and mod place with aproned French elegance. It was designed by the owners of the adjacent Michelin-starred Ox restaurant to entertain diners with wine and cheese as they wait for their table. But with charming Alain as your host, you could settle in here to make a meal from their charcuterie and cheese plates and exciting wines. Have fun with their wine matrix—lots of vintages by the glass at the same price (Tue-Sat 16:00 until late, closed Sun-Mon, 3 Oxford Street, tel. 028/9023-2567).

$$$ Mourne Seafood Bar is my choice for seafood in an elegant setting with a fun staff and smart clientele. It's run by a marine biologist and a great chef—no gimmicks, just top-quality seafood (daily 12:00-21:30, reservations smart, 34 Bank Street, tel. 028/9024-8544, www.mourneseafood.com). As it's next to Kelly's Cellars (described earlier under "Experiences"), consider dining here and then enjoying the music next door.

$ The Yardbird, rough and spacious, is housed in an open-beam attic and serves a down-and-dirty menu of ribs and wings. It's known for its cheap and tasty rotisserie chicken (daily 12:00-22:00, 3 Hill Street, tel. 028/9024-3712). The **Dirty Onion** (downstairs) is a popular pub that spills suds and live music into its packed outer courtyard on summer nights.

Near Queen's University

$$$ The Barking Dog, elegant and inviting, serves small plates to be enjoyed family style, along with pastas and burgers. It's closest to my cluster of accommodations south of the university (daily 12:00-14:30 & 17:00-22:00, near corner of Eglantine Avenue at 33 Malone Road, tel. 028/9066-1885).

$$ Villa Italia packs in crowds hungry for linguini and *bistecca.* Huge and family-friendly, with checkered tablecloths and a wood-beamed ceiling draped with grape leaves, it's a little bit of Italy in Belfast (Mon-Sat 17:00-23:00, Sun 12:30-21:30, three long blocks south of Shaftesbury Square, at intersection with University Street, 39 University Road, tel. 028/9032-8356).

$$ Maggie May's serves hearty, simple, affordable meals in a tight and cheery little bistro room (Sun-Thu 8:00-22:00, Fri-Sat until 23:00, one block south of Botanic Station at 50 Botanic Avenue, tel. 028/9032-2662).

TRANSPORTATION

Getting Around Belfast

If you line up your sightseeing logically, you can do most of this flat city on foot. But for more far-flung sights, the train, bus, or tram can be useful. If you plan to use public transit, consider the Belfast Visitor Pass (see "Helpful Hints," earlier).

By Train, Bus, or Tram: Translink operates Belfast's system of trains, buses, and trams (tel. 028/9066-6630, www.translink.co.uk).

At any **train** station, ask about iLink smartcards, which cover one day of unlimited train, tram, and bus travel. The Zone 1 card (£6) covers the city center, Cultra (Ulster Folk Park and Transport Museum), and George Best Belfast City Airport. The handy Zone 2 card (£11) adds Bangor and Carrickfergus Castle. The Zone 3 card (£14.50) is only useful for reaching Belfast's distant international airport. Zone 4 (£17.50) gets you anywhere in Northern Ireland, including Portrush and Derry.

Pink-and-white city **buses** go from Donegall Square East to Malone Road and my recommended accommodations (any #8 bus, 3/hour, covered by iLink smartcards, otherwise £2.40, £4.20 all-day pass, cheaper after 9:30 and on Sun). Sunday service is less frequent.

The slick two-line Glider **tram** system connects East and West Belfast (line #G1) and downtown with the Titanic Quarter (line #G2). Rides cost £2 (6/hour, ticket machines at each stop, covered by iLink smartcards). The #G2 is particularly handy for travelers connecting City Hall with all the Titanic area sights.

By Taxi: Taxis are reasonable (£3 drop charge plus £1.60/ mile)—but can be hard to flag down. Locals routinely call for a cab, as do restaurants and hotels for their guests. Try **Valu Cabs** (tel. 028/9080-9080). If you're going up Falls Road, ride a shared cab (explained earlier, under "Touring the Sectarian Neighborhoods"). Uber is nicknamed "Uber Expensive" here—it doesn't work well.

Arriving and Departing

By Plane

Belfast has two airports. **George Best Belfast City Airport** (code: BHD, tel. 028/9093-9093, www.belfastcityairport.com) is a five-minute, £8 taxi ride from town (near the docks) or a £2.60 ride on the Airport Express bus #600 (hourly from Europa Bus Centre). **Belfast International Airport** (code: BFS, tel. 028/9448-4848, www.belfastairport.com) is 18 miles west of town—an £8 ride on the Airport Express bus #300 (hourly from Europa Bus Centre next to Hotel Europa).

To get to Belfast directly from **Dublin Airport,** the **Aircoach** express bus runs through the night in each direction (hourly, 2 hours). It stops at both Dublin Airport terminals and in downtown Belfast on Glengall Street (next to the Europa Hotel and Great Victoria Street station). With this service you can spend your last night in Belfast and fly out of Dublin in the morning (£14 from Belfast, €17 from Dublin, tel. 028/9033-0655, www.aircoach.ie). For Dublin Airport details, see page 93.

By Train and Bus

Arriving by train at Belfast's **Lanyon Place/ Central Station,** take the Centrelink bus to Donegall Square, where you'll find City Hall and the TI (4/hour, free with any train or bus ticket, the stop is out the station and 50 yards to the right). Allow £6 for a taxi to Donegall Square or the Titanic Belfast Museum; £10 to my accommodation listings south of the university.

Slower trains arc through the city, stopping at several downtown stations, including Great Victoria Street Station (most central, near Donegall Square and most hotels) and Botanic Station (close to the university, Botanic Gardens, and some recommended lodgings). It's easy and cheap to connect stations by train (£1.50).

If day-tripping into Belfast from Bangor, use the station closest to your targeted sights. Note that trains cost the same from Bangor to all three Belfast stations (Lanyon Place/Central, Great Victoria Street, and Botanic).

If arriving by bus, the **Europa Bus Centre** is downtown behind Hotel Europa.

TRAIN AND BUS CONNECTIONS

For schedules and prices for trains and buses in Northern Ireland, check with Translink (tel. 028/9066-6630, www.translink.co.uk). Note that service is less frequent on Sundays.

By Train to: Dublin (8/day, 2 hours), **Derry** (10/day, 2.5 hours), **Larne** (hourly, 1 hour), **Portrush** (15/day, 2 hours, transfer in Coleraine), **Bangor** (2/hour, 30 minutes).

By Bus to: Portrush (12/day, 2 hours; scenic-coast route, 2.5 hours), **Derry** (hourly, 2 hours), **Dublin** (hourly, most via Dublin Airport, 3 hours), **Galway** (every 2 hours, 5 hours, change in Dublin).

By Car

Driving in Belfast is a pain. Avoid it if possible. Street parking in the city center is geared for short stops (use pay-and-display machines, £0.30/15 minutes, one-hour maximum, Mon-Sat 8:00-18:00, free in evenings and on Sun).

NEAR BELFAST

Bangor

To stay in a laid-back seaside hometown—with more comfort per pound—sleep 12 miles east of Belfast in Bangor (BANG-grr). It's a handy alternative for travelers who find Belfast booked up by occasional conventions and conferences. Formerly a Victorian resort and seaside escape from the big city nearby, Bangor now has a sleepy residential feeling.

Day Plan

Most of your sightseeing time will be spent in Belfast. But if you have time to burn in Bangor, enjoy the waterfront **Coastal Path,** which leads west out of town from the marina. A pleasant three-mile level walk along the water leads you to Crawfordsburn Country Park in the suburb of Helen's Bay. With a car, you'll find two worthwhile sights near Bangor: the Somme Museum and Mount Stewart House (see below).

Orientation

With elegant old homes facing its spruced-up harbor and not even a hint of big-city Belfast, this town has appeal.

Arrival in Bangor: Catch the train to Bangor from Belfast's Lanyon Place/Central or Great Victoria Street stations (2/hour, 30 minutes, go to the end of the line—don't get off at Bangor West).

Tourist Information: Bangor's TI is in a stone tower house (from 1637) on the harborfront, a 10-minute walk from the train station (Mon-Fri 9:15-17:00, Sat from 10:00, Sun from 13:00 except closed Sun Sept-April, 34 Quay Street, tel. 028/9127-0069, www.discovernorthernireland.com, search for "Bangor Visitor Information Centre").

Local Taxis: For taxi service try **Kare Cabs** (tel. 028/9145-6777) or **Bangor Cabs** (tel. 028/9145-6456).

Mount Stewart House

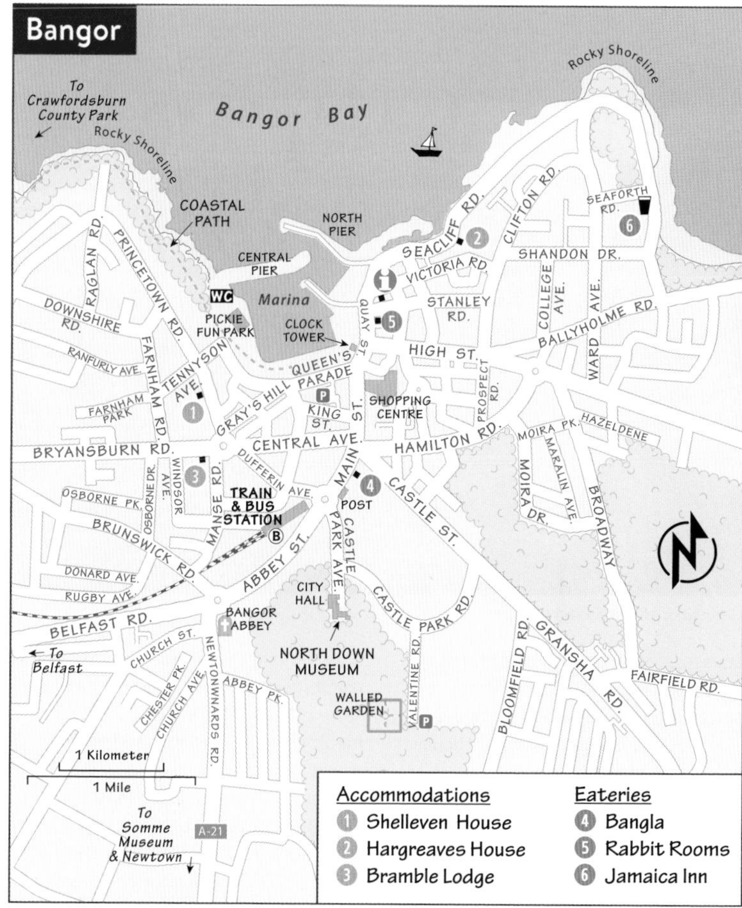

Sights near Bangor

The eastern fringe of Northern Ireland is populated mostly by people who consider themselves true-blue British citizens with a history of loyalty to the Crown that goes back more than 400 years. Two sights within reach by car from Bangor highlight this area's firm roots in British culture: the Somme Museum and Mount Stewart House.

Getting There: I'd rent a car at nearby George Best Belfast City Airport, which is only 15 minutes by train from Bangor or 10 minutes from Belfast's Lanyon Place/ Central Station. Bus service from Bangor to these sights is patchy (15 minutes to Somme Museum, one hour to Mount Stewart House with transfer, best to check schedule with Bangor TI or www.translink.co.uk).

▲MOUNT STEWART HOUSE

No manor house in Ireland better illuminates the affluent lifestyle of the Protestant ascendancy than this lush estate. After the defeat of James II (the last Catholic king of England) at the Battle of the Boyne in 1690, the Protestant monarchy was in control—and the privileged status of landowners of the same faith was assured. In the 1700s, Ireland's many Catholic rebellions seemed finally to be

Gardens of Mount Stewart House

squashed, so Anglican landlords felt safe flaunting their wealth in manor houses surrounded by utterly perfect gardens. The Mount Stewart House in particular was designed to dazzle.

Cost and Hours: £10.45 for house and gardens; house open daily 11:00-17:00, gardens from 10:00, closed Nov-Feb; 8 miles south of Bangor, just off A-20 beside Strangford Lough, tel. 028/4278-8387, www.nationaltrust.org.uk/mount-stewart.

Visiting the House: In the **manor house,** you'll glimpse the cushy life led by the Marquess of Londonderry and his heirs over the past three centuries. The main entry hall is a stunner, with a black-and-white checkerboard tile floor, marble columns, classical statues, and pink walls supporting a balcony with a domed ceiling and a fine chandelier. In the dining room, you'll see the original seats occupied by the rears of European heads of state, brought back from the Congress of Vienna after Napoleon's 1815 defeat. A huge painting of Hambletonian, a prize-winning racehorse, hangs above the grand staircase, dwarfing a portrait of the Duke of Wellington in a hall nearby. The heroic duke (worried that his Irish birth would be seen as lower class by British blue bloods) once quipped in Parliament, "Just because one is born in a stable does not make him a horse." Irish emancipator Daniel O'Connell retorted, "Yes, but it could make you an ass."

Afterward, wander the expansive manicured **gardens.** The fantasy life of parasol-toting, upper-crust Victorian society seems to ooze from every viewpoint. Fanciful sculptures of extinct dodo birds and monkeys holding vases on their heads set off predictably classic Italian and Spanish sections. An Irish harp has been trimmed out of a hedge a few feet from a flowerbed shaped like the Red Hand of Ulster. Swans glide serenely among the lily pads on a small lake.

SOMME MUSEUM

World War I's trench warfare was a meat grinder. More British soldiers died in the last year of that war than in all of World

War II. Northern Ireland's men were not spared—especially during the bloody Battle of the Somme in France, starting in July 1916. Among the Allied forces was the British Army's 36th Ulster Division, which drew heavily from this loyal heartland of Northern Ireland. The 36th Ulster Division suffered brutal losses at the Battle of the Somme—of the 760 men recruited from the Shankill Road area in Belfast, only 10 percent survived.

Exhibits portray the battle experience through a mix of military artifacts, photos, historical newsreels, and life-size figures posed in trench warfare re-creations. To access the majority of the exhibits, it's essential to take the one-hour guided tour (leaving hourly, on the hour). Visiting this place is a moving experience, but it can only hint at the horrific conditions endured by these soldiers.

Cost and Hours: £8.50; July-Aug Mon-Sat 10:00-17:00, Sept-June Mon-Thu 10:00-16:00, Feb-Nov Sat from 11:00; closed Fri-Sat Sept-June, Mon-Fri Feb-Nov, plus Sun year-round; last tour one hour before closing, 3 miles south of Bangor just off A-21 at 233 Bangor Road, tel. 028/9182-3202, www.irishsoldier.org.

Sleeping and Eating

$$$ Shelleven House is an old-fashioned, well-kept, stately place with 13 prim rooms (RS%, family rooms, 61 Princetown Road, www.shellevenhouse.com). **$$ Hargreaves House,** a homey Victorian waterfront refuge with three cozy, refurbished rooms, is Bangor's best value (RS%, 78 Seacliff Road, www.hargreaveshouse.com). **$ Bramble Lodge** offers three inviting and spotless rooms (1 Bryansburn Road, tel. 028/9145-7924, jacquihanna_bramblelodge@yahoo.co.uk).

Most restaurants in town stop seating at about 20:30. **$$$ Bangla** serves fine Indian cuisine with attentive service (open daily 12:00-14:00 for lunch, 16:30-23:00 for dinner, 115 Main Street). **$$ The Rabbit Rooms** serves hearty Irish food (daily, live music Mon and Thu-Sat, near the harbor at 33 Quay Street). The **$$ Jamaica Inn** offers pleasant pub grub and a breezy waterfront porch (daily, 188 Seacliff Road).

Portrush & the Antrim Coast

The Antrim Coast is one of the most interesting and scenic coastlines in Ireland. Portrush, a faded but charming seaside resort town, is an ideal base for exploring the highlights of the Antrim Coast: evocative castle ruins, the world's oldest whiskey distillery, a bouncy rope bridge, and the famous Giant's Causeway.

PORTRUSH & THE ANTRIM COAST IN 1 DAY

You need a full day to explore the Antrim Coast by car, so allow two nights in Portrush (see "Getting Around the Antrim Coast" for other transportation options).

Advance planning is important for these popular sights. Book a timed-entry ticket online to cross the Carrick-a-Rede Rope Bridge. Arrive early for the Giant's Causeway (book a guided hike a day in advance or hike on your own with no reservation). For sights that can't be reserved, pick the one that most interests you and visit it first, then take your chances with the rest. Visit Dunluce Castle last; it's the least crowded of the main choices.

My ideal day would start with the Giant's Causeway, arriving by 9:00, when crowds are lightest. Follow this with a tour of Old Bushmills Distillery. For lunch, bring a picnic or eat cheaply at the causeway visitors center or the Old Bushmills hospitality room. After lunch, drive to Carrick-a-Rede (about 20 minutes from the distillery). Without a ticket, you can still enjoy the scenic cliff-top trail hike all the way to the bridge, as well as the nearby viewpoint for dramatic views of the bridge. From here, hop in your car and double back west to cliff-perched Dunluce Castle for a late-afternoon tour. The castle is a five-minute drive from Portrush.

Getting Around the Antrim Coast

By Car: A car is the best way to explore the charms of the Antrim Coast. Distances are short and parking is easy.

By Bus: In peak season, an all-day bus pass helps you get around the region economically. The **Causeway Rambler** links Portrush to Old Bushmills Distillery, the Giant's Causeway, and the Carrick-a-Rede Rope Bridge (stopping at the nearby town of Ballintoy). The bus journey from Portrush to Carrick-a-Rede takes 45 minutes (£7.50/day, runs roughly 10:00-18:00, hourly May-Sept, fewer off-season). Pick up a Rambler bus schedule at the TI, and buy the ticket from the driver (in Portrush, the Rambler stops at Dunluce Avenue, next to public WC, a 2-minute walk from TI; operated by Translink, tel. 028/9066-6630, www.translink.co.uk).

By Bus Tour: From Belfast, you can visit most Antrim Coast sights with a **McComb's** tour (see page 277). Those based in Derry can get to the Giant's Causeway and Carrick-a-Rede Rope Bridge with City Sightseeing (see page 320).

By Taxi: Groups (up to four) can reasonably visit most sights by taxi (except the more distant Carrick-a-Rede). Approximate one-way prices

PORTRUSH & THE ANTRIM COAST AT A GLANCE

▲▲**Giant's Causeway** Otherworldly coastline of quirky geologic formations, breezy hikes, and mythological confrontations between Celtic giant rivals. **Hours:** Visitors center open daily 9:00-18:00, June-Sept until 19:00, Nov-March until 17:00; causeway always open for hiking. See page 312.

▲▲**Old Bushmills Distillery** The oldest whiskey distillery in the world (over 400 years old), where connoisseurs tour the production process and debate the merits of triple distilling. **Hours:** Tours go on the half-hour Mon-Sat at 9:30-16:00 (last tour), Sun from 12:00; shorter hours Nov-March. See page 316.

▲▲**Carrick-a-Rede Rope Bridge** Spectacular terminus of scenic coastal hike, drawing photographers, bird watchers, and thrill seekers. **Hours:** Daily 9:30-18:00, June-Aug until 20:00; Nov-Feb until 15:30; book online in advance. See page 316.

▲**Dunluce Castle** Historic and haunted Irish-Scottish hybrid fortification clinging to the peak of a sea stack while daring attack from any side. **Hours:** Daily 10:00-17:00, winter until 16:00. See page 317.

Portrush Victorian-age working-class beach getaway and regional sightseeing base, complete with old-time arcade and world-famous Royal Portrush links golf course. See page 308.

from Portrush: £12 (Dunluce Castle), £15 (Old Bushmills Distillery), £23 (Giant's Causeway). Try **Andy Brown's Taxi** (tel. 028/7082-2223), **Hugh's Taxi** (mobile 077-0298-6110), or **North West Taxi** (tel. 028/7082-4446).

PORTRUSH

Homey Portrush used to be known as "the Brighton of the North." It first became a resort in the late 1800s, as railroads expanded to offer the new middle class a weekend by the shore. Victorians believed that swimming in saltwater would cure many common ailments.

While it's seen its best days, Portrush retains the atmosphere and architecture of a genteel seaside resort. Its peninsula is filled with lowbrow, family-oriented amusements, fun eateries, and B&Bs. Summertime fun seekers promenade along the tiny harbor and tumble down to the sandy beaches, which extend in sweeping white crescents on either side.

Students from nearby University of Ulster at Coleraine give the town a little more personality. Along with the usual arcade amusements, there are nightclubs, restaurants, summer theater productions, and convivial pubs that attract customers all the way from Belfast.

Orientation

Portrush's pleasant and easily walkable town center features sea views in every direction. On one side are the harbor and most of the restaurants, and on the other are Victorian townhouses and vast, salty vistas. The tip of the peninsula is filled with tennis courts, lawn-bowling greens, putting greens, and a park.

Tourist Information: The TI is located underneath the very central, red-brick Town Hall (Mon-Sat 9:00-17:00, Sun 11:00-16:00, shorter hours off-season and closed Oct-March; Kerr Street, tel. 028/7082-3333). Consider the Collins Ireland Visitors Map (£9), the free *Visitor Guide* brochure, and, if needed, a free Belfast map.

Rick's Tip: *Avoid visiting on crowded* **Easter weekend**, *and during the* **Northwest 200 Race** *in mid-May—when thousands of die-hard motorcycle fans converge here (accommodations book up a year ahead; www.northwest200.org).*

Laundry: Full service is available at **Causeway Laundry** (Mon-Tue and Thu-Fri 9:00-16:30, Wed and Sat until 13:00, closed Sun, 68 Causeway Street, tel. 028/7082-2060).

Sights

BARRY'S OLD-TIME AMUSEMENT ARCADE

This fun arcade is bigger than it looks and offers a chance to see Northern Ireland at play. Older locals visit for the nostalgia, as many of the rides and amusements go back 50 years. Ride prices are listed at the door. Everything runs with tokens (£0.50 each or £10/24, buy from coin-op machines). Located just below the train station on the harbor, Barry's is filled with "candy floss" (cotton candy) and crazy "scoop treats" (daily 12:30-22:00 in summer, weekends only Easter-May, closed Sept-Easter, www.barrysamusements.com).

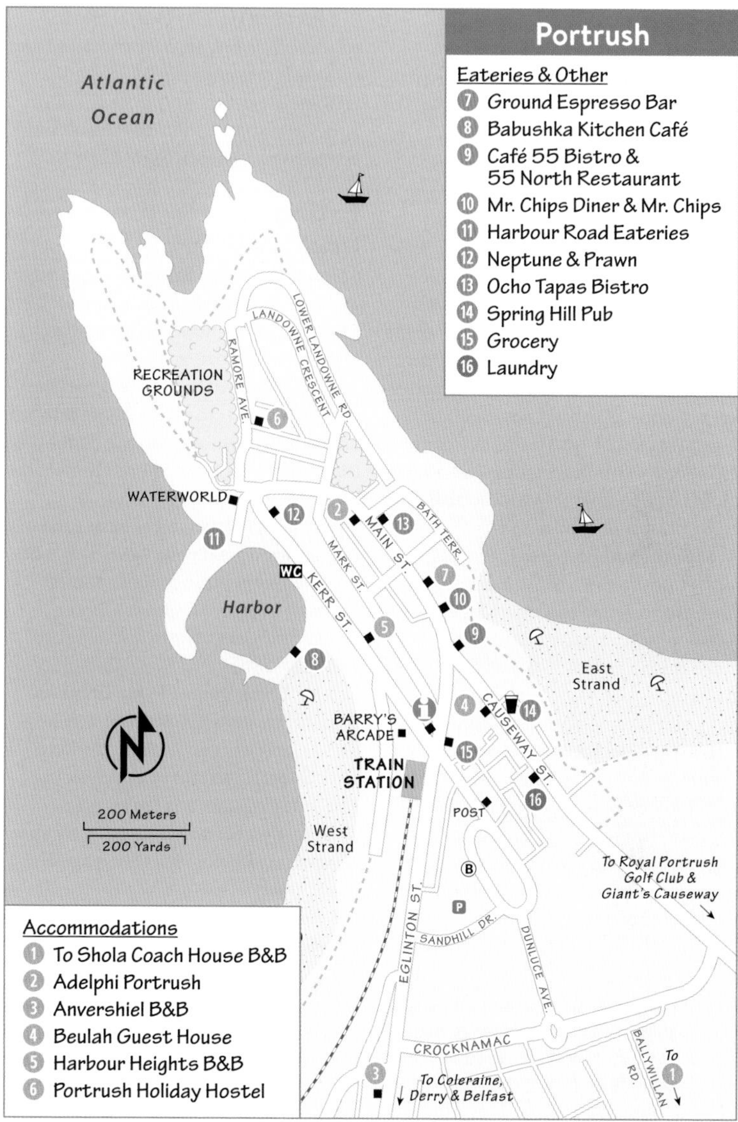

ROYAL PORTRUSH GOLF CLUB

Irish courses, like those in Scotland, are highly sought after for their lush greens in glorious settings. Serious golfers can get a tee time at the Royal Portrush, a links course that hosted the British Open in 1951 and then again in 2019. Check out the trophy case and historic photos in the clubhouse (green fees generally £220, less most days in off-season). The adjacent, slightly shorter Valley Course is more budget-friendly (green fees £50, 10-minute walk from station, tel. 028/7082-2311, www.royalportrushgolfclub.com).

Sleeping

August and Saturday nights can be crowded (and loud) with young party groups. Most places listed have lots of stairs. Parking is easy.

$$$ Shola Coach House is a memorable treat. About 1.5 miles south of town, it's easiest for drivers (otherwise it's a 30-minute uphill walk or £5 taxi ride). The secluded, 170-year-old, renovated stone structure once housed the coaches and horses for a local landlord. The decor of the four rooms is tasteful, the garden patio is delightful, and Sharon and David Schindler keep it spotless (parking, no kids under 18, 2-night minimum, 110A Gateside Road at top of Ballywillan Road, tel. 028/7082-5925, mobile 075-6542-7738, www.sholabandb.com, sholabandb@gmail.com).

$$$ Adelphi Portrush is the best large hotel in town, with 28 tastefully furnished modern rooms, an ideal location, and a hearty bistro downstairs (family rooms, 67 Main Street, tel. 028/7082-5544, www.adelphiportrush.com, stay@adelphiportrush.com).

$ Anvershiel B&B, with seven nicely refurbished rooms, is a great value (RS%, family rooms, parking, 10-minute walk south of train station, 16 Coleraine Road, tel. 028/7082-3861, www.anvershiel.com, enquiries@anvershiel.com, Alan and Janice Thompson).

$ Beulah Guest House is a traditional, old-fashioned place. It's centrally located and run by cheerful Helen and Charlene McLaughlin, with 11 prim rooms (parking at rear, 16 Causeway Street, tel. 028/7082-2413, www.beulahguesthouse.com, stay@beulahguesthouse.com).

$ Harbour Heights B&B rents nine retro-homey rooms. It has an inviting guest lounge overlooking the harbor. Friendly South African hosts Sam and Tim Swart manage the place with a light hand (family rooms, 17 Kerr Street, tel. 028/7082-2765, mobile 078-9586-6534, www.harbourheightsportrush.com, info@harbourheightsportrush.com).

¢ Portrush Holiday Hostel offers clean, well-organized, economical lodging (private rooms available, tel. 028/7082-1288, mobile 078-5037-7367, 24 Princess Street, www.portrushholidayhostel.com, portrushholidayhostel@gmail.com).

Eating

Lunch Spots

$ Ground Espresso Bar makes fresh sandwiches and panini, soup, and great coffee (daily 9:00-17:00, July-Aug until 22:00, 52 Main Street, tel. 028/7082-5979).

$ Babushka Kitchen Café serves fresh sandwiches and creative desserts with an unbeatable view—actually out on the pier (daily 9:15-17:00, West Strand Promenade, tel. 077-8750-2012).

$$ Café 55 Bistro serves basic sandwiches with a great patio view (daily 9:00-17:00, longer hours in summer, shorter hours off-season, 1 Causeway Street, beneath fancier 55 North restaurant, tel. 028/7082-2811).

$ Mr. Chips Diner and **Mr. Chips** are the local favorites for cheap, quality fish-and-chips (daily 12:00-22:00, 12 and 20 Main Street). Both are mostly takeout, while the diner also has tables.

Groceries: For picnic supplies, try **Spar Market** (across from Barry's Arcade on Main Street).

Harbour Road Eateries

A lively cluster of restaurants overlooks the harbor. With the same owner, they all have a creative and fun energy, and are generally open from about 17:00 to 22:00.

$$ Ramore Wine Bar is a salty, modern place, with an inviting menu ranging from steaks to vegetarian items (open daily for lunch and dinner, tel. 028/7082-4313).

$$ The Tourist is a hit for its pizza, tacos, burritos, and burgers (daily, tel. 028/7082-3311).

$$$ Harbour Bistro is dark, noisy, and sprawling with a sloppy crowd enjoying chargrilled meat and fish (daily, no kids after 20:00, tel. 028/7082-2430).

Dining in Portrush

$$ Mermaid Kitchen & Bar is all about fresh fish dishes with a Spanish twist and great harbor views (closed Mon-Tue, no kids under 18, tel. 028/7082-6969).

$$$ Neptune & Prawn (just across the inlet from the others) is the most yacht-clubby of the bunch. Serving Asian and other international food with a fancy presentation, this place is noisy and high-energy, with rock music playing (daily, no kids under 18, tel. 028/7082-2448).

Other Dining Options off the Harbor

$$$ 55 North (named for the local latitude) has the best sea views in town, with windows on three sides. The filling pasta-and-fish dishes, along with some Asian plates, are a joy. Their lunch and early-bird special (order by 18:45) is three courses at the cost of the entrée (daily 12:30-14:00 & 17:00-21:00, 1 Causeway Street, tel. 028/7082-2811).

$$ Ocho Tapas Bistro brings sunny Spanish cuisine to the chilly north, featuring a great early-bird menu (Tue-Fri 17:00-21:30, Sat-Sun 12:30-14:30 & 17:00-22:00, closed Mon, 92 Main Street, tel. 028/7082-4110).

Pubs

Harbour Bar is an old-fashioned pub next to the Harbour Bistro (see above). **Harbour Gin Bar** (above Harbour Bar) is romantic and classy—a rustic, spacious, and inviting place with live acoustic folk music from 20:30 (almost nightly) and a fun selection of 45 gins.

Neptune & Prawn Cocktail Bar (above the restaurant by the same name; see listing above) has great views over the harbor and is the most classy-yet-inviting place in town for a drink.

Spring Hill Pub is a good bet for its friendly vibe and occasional live music, including traditional sessions Thursdays at 21:30 (17 Causeway Street).

Transportation

Arriving and Departing

BY TRAIN OR BUS

The train tracks stop at the base of the tiny peninsula that Portrush fills (no baggage storage at station). The bus stop is two blocks from the train station.

Day Pass: Consider a £17.50 Zone 4 iLink smartcard, good for all-day Translink train and bus use in Northern Ireland

(£16.50 top-up for each additional day, tel. 028/9066-6630, www.translink.co.uk).

From Portrush by Train to: Coleraine (hourly, 12 minutes), **Belfast** (15/day, 2 hours, transfer in Coleraine), **Dublin** (7/day, 5 hours, transfer in Belfast). Note that on Sundays, service is greatly reduced.

From Portrush by Bus to: Belfast (12/day, 2 hours; scenic coastal route, 2.5 hours), **Dublin** (4/day, 5.5 hours).

BY CAR

If driving on to Belfast from Portrush, consider the slower but scenic coastal route via the Glens of Antrim.

ANTRIM COAST

The craggy 20-mile stretch of the Antrim Coast extending eastward from Portrush to Ballycastle rates second only to the tip of the Dingle Peninsula as the prettiest chunk of coastal Ireland. From your base in Portrush, you have a grab bag of sightseeing choices: Giant's Causeway, Old Bushmills Distillery, Dunluce Castle, and Carrick-a-Rede Rope Bridge.

It's easy to weave these sights together by car, but bus service is viable only in summer, and taxi fares are reasonable only for the sights closest to Portrush.

Sights

▲▲GIANT'S CAUSEWAY

This five-mile-long stretch of coastline is famous for its bizarre basalt columns. The shore is covered with largely hexagonal pillars that stick up at various heights. It's as if the earth were offering God a choice of 37,000 six-sided cigarettes.

Geologists claim the Giant's Causeway was formed by volcanic eruptions more than 60 million years ago. As the surface of the lava flow quickly cooled, it contracted and crystallized into columns (resembling the caked mud at the bottom of a dried-up lakebed, but with far deeper cracks). As the rock later settled and eroded, the columns broke off into the many stair-like steps that now honeycomb the Antrim Coast.

Of course, in actuality, the Giant's Causeway was made by a giant Ulster warrior named Finn MacCool who knew of a rival giant living across the water in Scotland. Finn built a stone bridge to Scotland to spy on his rival, and found

Giant's Causeway, along the Antrim Coast

The Scottish Connection

The Romans called the Irish the "Scoti" (meaning pirates). When the Scoti crossed the narrow Irish Sea and invaded the land of the Picts 1,500 years ago, that region became known as Scoti-land. Ireland and Scotland were never conquered by the Romans, and they retained similar clannish Celtic traits. Both share the same Gaelic branch of the linguistic tree.

On clear summer days from Carrick-a-Rede, the island of Mull in Scotland—only 17 miles away—is visible. Much closer on the horizon is the boomerang-shaped Rathlin Island, part of Northern Ireland. Rathlin is where Scottish leader Robert the Bruce (a compatriot of William "Braveheart" Wallace) retreated in 1307 after defeat at the hands of the English. Legend has it that he hid in a cave on the island, where he observed a spider patiently rebuilding its web each time a breeze knocked it down. Inspired by the spider's perseverance, Robert gathered his Scottish forces once more and finally defeated the English at the decisive Battle of Bannockburn.

Flush with confidence from his victory, Robert the Bruce opened a second front against the English...in Ireland. In 1315, he sent his brother Edward over to enlist their Celtic Irish cousins in an effort to thwart the English. After securing Ireland, Edward hoped to move on and enlist the Welsh, thus cornering England with their pan-Celtic nation. But Edward's timing was bad—Ireland was in the midst of famine. The Scots quickly wore out their welcome, and Edward the Bruce was eventually killed in battle near Dundalk in 1318.

This was not the only time in history that Ireland was used as a pawn by England's enemies. Spain and France saw Ireland as the English Achilles' heel, and both countries later attempted invasions of the island. The English Tudor and Stuart royalty countered these threats in the 16th and 17th centuries by starting the "plantation" of loyal subjects in Ireland. The only successful long-term settlement by the English was here in Northern Ireland, which remains part of the United Kingdom today.

It's interesting to imagine how things might be different today if Ireland and Scotland had been permanently welded together as a nation 700 years ago. You'll notice the strong Scottish influence in this part of Ireland when you ask a local a question and he answers, "Aye, a wee bit." The Irish joke that the Scots are just Irish people who couldn't swim home.

out that the Scottish giant was much bigger. Finn retreated to Ireland and had his wife dress him as a sleeping infant, just in time for the rival giant to come across the causeway to spy on Finn. The rival, shocked at the infant's size, fled back to Scotland in terror of whoever had sired this giant baby. Breathing a sigh of relief, Finn tore off the baby clothes and prudently knocked down the bridge. Today, proof of this encounter exists in the geologic formation that still extends undersea and surfaces in Scotland (at the island of Staffa).

Cost and Hours: The Giant's Causeway is free and always open. But in practice, anyone parking there needs to pay £12.50/adult. This includes an audioguide (or one-hour guided walk; leaves regularly with demand), a map, and entrance to the

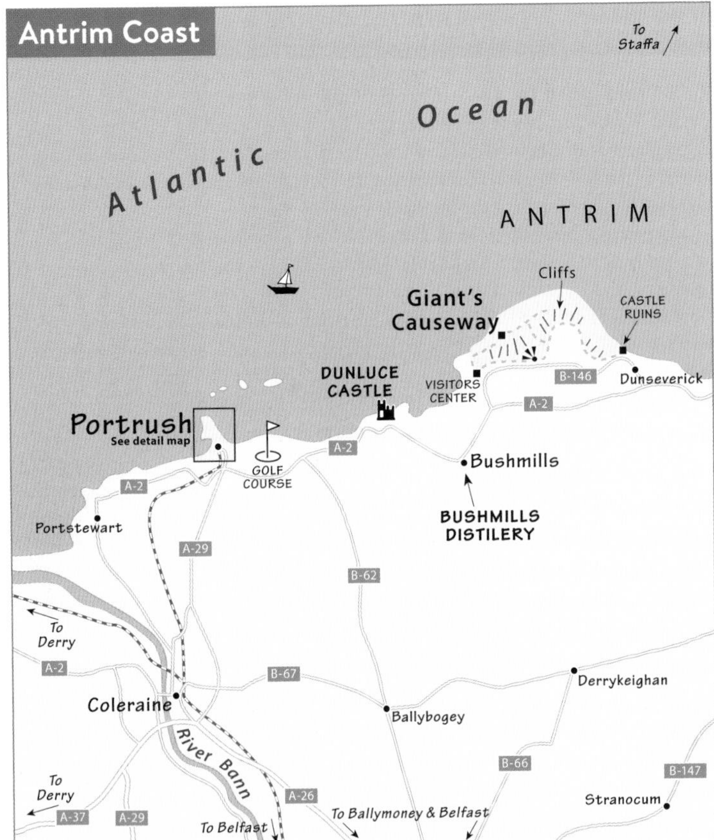

visitors center (daily 9:00-18:00, June-Sept until 19:00, Nov-March until 17:00, tel. 028/2073-1855, www.nationaltrust.org.uk/giantscauseway).

Visiting the Causeway: For cute variations on the Finn story, as well as details on the ridiculous theories of modern geologists, start in the **Giant's Causeway Visitor Centre.** It's filled with kid-friendly interactive exhibits giving a worthwhile history of the Giant's Causeway, with a regional overview. On the far wall opposite the entrance, check out the interesting three-minute video showing the evolution of the causeway from molten lava to the geometric, geologic wonderland of today. The large 3-D model of the causeway offers a bird's-eye view of the region. There's also an exhibit about the history of tourism here from the 18th century.

The **causeway** itself is the highlight of the entire coast. The audioguide and map feature 15 stops. From the visitors center, you have several options:

Short and Easy: A **shuttle bus** (4/hour from 9:00, £1 each way) zips tourists a half-mile from the visitors center down a paved road to the causeway. This standard route (the blue dashed line on your map) offers the easiest access and follows the stops on your audioguide. Many choose to walk down and then take the shuttle back up.

Mid-Level Hike: For a longer hike and a more varied dose of causeway views, consider the cliff-top trail (red dashed line on

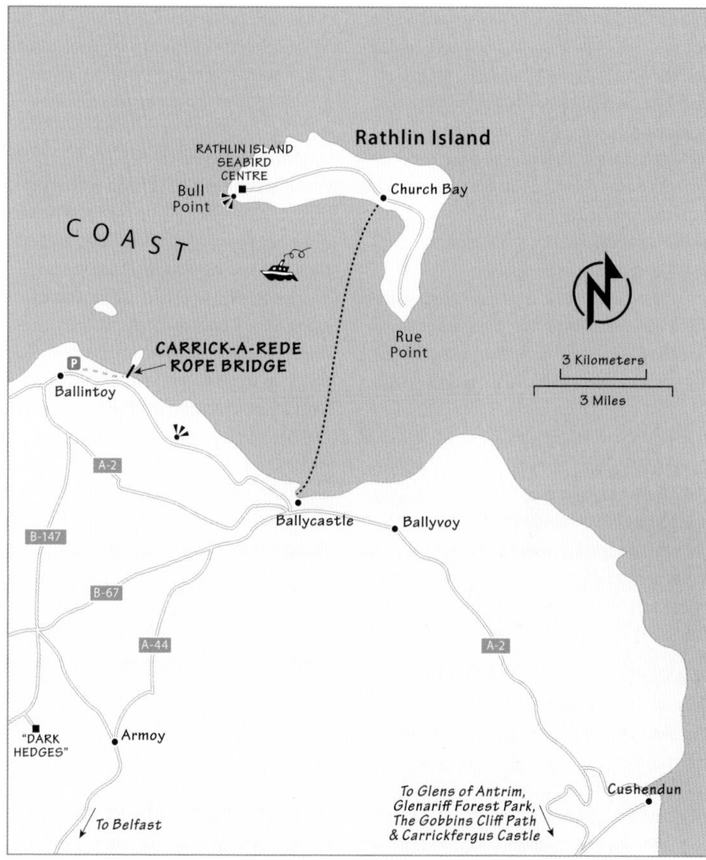

your map). Take the easy-to-follow trail uphill from the visitors center 10 minutes to Weir's Snout, the great fence-protected precipice viewpoint. Then hike 15 minutes farther (level) to reach the Shepherd's Steps. Grab the banister on the steep (and slippery-when-wet) stairs that zigzag down the switchbacks toward the water. At the T-junction, go 100 yards right, to the towering rock pipes of "the Organ." (You can detour another 500 yards east around the headland, but the trail dead-ends there.) Now retrace your steps west on the trail (don't go up the steps again), continuing down to the tidal zone, where the "Giant's Boot" (6-foot boulder, on the right) provides some photo fun. Another 100 yards farther is the dramatic point where the causeway meets the sea. Just beyond that, at the asphalt turnaround, is the shuttle bus stop.

Return to the visitors center by hiking up the paved lane. Or, from the turn-around, you can catch the shuttle bus back to the visitors center.

Longer Hike: Hardy hikers and avid photographers can join the guided **Clifftop Experience** trek exploring the trail that runs along a five-mile section of the Causeway Coast, starting at the meager ruins of Dunseverick Castle—east of Giant's Causeway on B-146 (yellow dashed line on your map). The hike is led by a naturalist, who ventures beyond the crowds to explore the rugged rim of this most-scenic section of the Antrim Coast.

Expect undulating grass and gravel paths with no WC options and no shelter whatsoever from bad weather (£35, includes parking; daily at 12:15, Nov-Feb at 10:15, must book online by 16:00 a day ahead; allow 3.5 hours, no kids under 12, meet at visitors center and bus to Dunseverick trailhead, tel. 028/2073-3419, www.giantscausewaytickets.com, northcoastbookings@nationaltrust.org.uk).

The hike can also be done on your own. Take the Causeway Rambler bus (see "Getting Around the Antrim Coast," earlier) or a taxi from Portrush to Dunseverick Castle and hike to the visitors center (there's also limited parking at the Dunseverick Castle trailhead). From the castle, hike west, following the cliff-hugging contours of Benbane Head back to the visitors center. For more info on hiking the route without a naturalist, see www.visitcausewaycoastandglens.com and search for "North Antrim Cliff Path."

▲▲OLD BUSHMILLS DISTILLERY

Bushmills claims to be the world's oldest distillery. Though King James I (of Bible translation fame) only granted Bushmills its license to distill "Aqua Vitae" in 1608, whiskey has been made here since the 13th century. Distillery tours waft you through the process, making it clear that Irish whiskey is triple distilled—and therefore smoother than Scotch whisky (distilled merely twice).

Cost and Hours: £9 for 45-minute tour followed by a tasting; tours go on the half-hour Mon-Sat 9:30-16:00 (last tour), Sun from 12:00; shorter hours Nov-March; tours are limited to 18 people and can fill up (only groups of 15 or more can reserve ahead); tel. 028/2073-3218, www.bushmills.com.

Old Bushmills Distillery

Visiting the Distillery: Tours start with the mash pit, which is filled with a porridge that eventually becomes whiskey. (The leftovers of that porridge are fed to the county's particularly happy cows.) You'll see a huge room full of whiskey aging in oak casks—casks already used to make bourbon, sherry, and port. Whiskey picks up its color and personality from this wood (which breathes and has an effective life of 30 years).

To see the distillery at its lively best, visit when the 100 workers are staffing the machinery—Monday morning through Friday noon. (The still is still on weekends and in July.) The finale, of course, is the opportunity for a sip in the 1608 Bar—the former malt barn. Visitors get a single glass of their choice. Hot-drink enthusiasts might enjoy a cinnamon-and-cloves hot toddy. Teetotalers can just order tea. After the tour, you can get a decent lunch in the hospitality room.

▲▲CARRICK-A-REDE ROPE BRIDGE

For 200 years, fishermen hung a narrow, 90-foot-high bridge (planks strung between wires) across a 65-foot-wide chasm between the mainland and a tiny island. Today, the bridge (while not the original version) gives access to the sea stack where salmon nets were set (until 2002) during summer months to catch the fish turning and hugging the coast's corner. (The complicated system is described at the gateway.) A pleasant, 30-minute, one-mile walk from the parking lot takes you down to the rope bridge. Cross over to the island for fine views and great seabird-watching.

Cost and Hours: £9 trail and bridge fee, book online in advance; daily 9:30-18:00, June-Aug until 20:00, Nov-Feb until 15:30, last entry 45 minutes before closing; tel. 028/2076-9839, www.nationaltrust.org.uk.

Carrick-a-Rede Rope Bridge

Dunluce Castle

A coffee shop and WCs are near the parking lot.

Advance Tickets Recommended: Buying a timed-entry ticket in advance will save you time and possibly the frustration of not getting a ticket at all (available at http://carrickaredetickets.com; can sell out up to 4 months in advance). Without an advance ticket, arrive as early as possible.

Nearby Viewpoint: If you have a car and a picnic lunch, don't miss the terrific coastal scenic rest area one mile steeply uphill and east of Carrick-a-Rede (on B-15 to Ballycastle). This grassy area offers one of the best picnic views in Northern Ireland (tables but no WCs). Feast on bird's-eye views of the rope bridge, nearby Rathlin Island, and the not-so-distant Island of Mull in Scotland.

▲DUNLUCE CASTLE

These romantic ruins, perched dramatically on the edge of a rocky headland, are a testimony to this region's turbulent past. During the Middle Ages, the castle was a prized fortification. But on a stormy night in 1639, dinner was interrupted as half of the kitchen fell into the sea, taking the servants with it. That was the last straw for the lady of the castle. The countess of Antrim packed up and moved inland, and the castle "began its slow submission to the forces of nature."

Cost and Hours: £5.50, daily 10:00-17:00, winter until 16:00, tel. 028/2073-1938.

Visiting the Castle: While it's one of the largest castles in Northern Ireland and is beautifully situated, there's precious little left to see. Look for distinctively hexagonal stones embedded in the castle walls, plucked straight from the nearby Giant's Causeway.

Before entering, catch the eight-minute video about the history of the castle (across from the ticket desk). The ruins themselves are dotted with plaques that show interesting artists' renditions of how the place would have looked 400 years ago.

The 16th-century expansion of the castle was financed by treasure salvaged from a shipwreck. In 1588, the Spanish Armada's *Girona*—overloaded with sailors and the valuables of three abandoned sister ships—sank on her way home after the aborted mission against England. More than 1,300 drowned, and only five survivors washed ashore. The shipwreck was more fully excavated in 1967, and a bounty of golden odds and silver ends wound up in Belfast's Ulster Museum.

BEST OF THE REST

Derry

No city in Ireland connects the kaleidoscope of historical dots more colorfully than Derry. From a leafy monastic hamlet to a Viking-pillaged port, from a cannonball-battered siege survivor to an Industrial Revolution sweatshop, from an essential WWII naval base to a wrenching flashpoint of sectarian Troubles...Derry has seen it all.

When Ireland was being divvied up, the River Foyle was the logical border between the North and the Republic. But, for sentimental and economic reasons, the North kept Derry, which is otherwise on the Republic's side of the river. Consequently, this predominantly Catholic-Nationalist city was much contested throughout the Troubles.

While most of its population, its city council, and this book call it "Derry," some maps, road signs, and all UK train schedules use "Londonderry," the name on its 1662 royal charter and the one favored by Unionists.

The past 15 years have brought some refreshing changes. Most British troops finally departed in 2007, after 38 years in Northern Ireland. In 2011, a curvy pedestrian bridge across the River Foyle was completed. Locals dubbed it the Peace Bridge because it links the predominantly Protestant Waterside (east bank) with the predominantly Catholic Cityside (west bank). Today, you can feel comfortable wandering the streets and enjoying this underrated city.

Day Plan

It takes a few hours to see the essential Derry sights: Visit the Tower Museum and catch some views from the town wall. With more time, spend a night in Derry, so you can see the powerful Bogside murals and take a walking tour around the town walls.

Orientation

The River Foyle flows north, slicing Derry into eastern and western chunks. The old town walls and almost all worthwhile sights are on the west side. (The tiny train station and Ebrington Square—at the

Derry

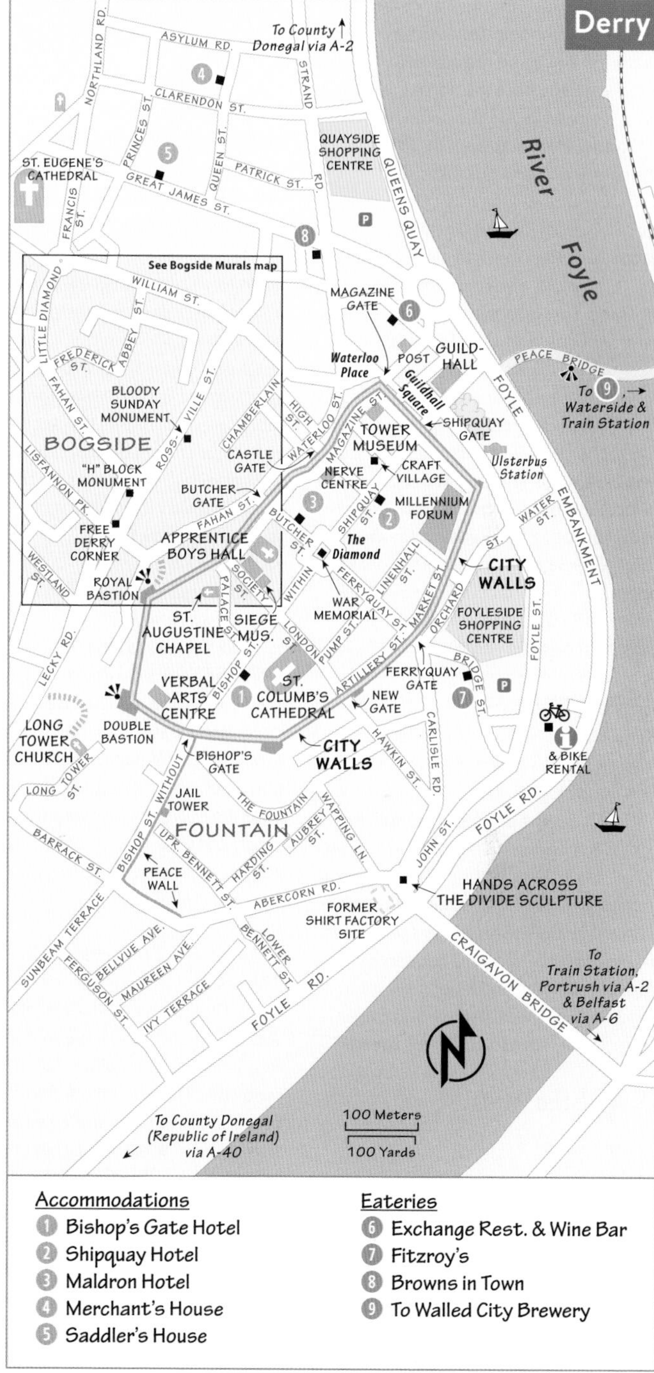
Derry
River Foyle
To County Donegal via A-2
ASYLUM RD.
NORTHLAND RD.
CLARENDON ST.
STRAND RD.
PRINCES ST.
QUEEN ST.
PATRICK ST.
QUAYSIDE SHOPPING CENTRE
QUEENS QUAY
ST. EUGENE'S CATHEDRAL
FRANCIS ST.
GREAT JAMES ST.
See Bogside Murals map
WILLIAM ST.
LITTLE DIAMOND
ABBEY ST.
FREDERICK ST.
MAGAZINE GATE
Waterloo Place
POST
GUILD-HALL
Guildhall Square
PEACE BRIDGE
To 9, Waterside & Train Station
BLOODY SUNDAY MONUMENT
ROSSVILLE ST.
FAHAN ST.
CHAMBERLAIN
HIGH ST.
WATERLOO ST.
MAGAZINE ST.
TOWER MUSEUM
SHIPQUAY GATE
FOYLE
BOGSIDE
CASTLE GATE
CRAFT VILLAGE
NERVE CENTRE
Ulsterbus Station
"H" BLOCK MONUMENT
LISFANNON PK.
BUTCHER GATE
SHIPQUAY ST.
MILLENNIUM FORUM
WATER ST.
EMBANKMENT
FAHAN ST.
BUTCHER ST.
The Diamond
FREE DERRY CORNER
APPRENTICE BOYS HALL
SOCIETY ST.
WITHIN
LINENHALL ST.
CITY WALLS
WESTLAND ST.
ROYAL BASTION
PALACE ST.
FERRYQUAY ST.
WAR MEMORIAL
MARKET ST.
ORCHARD ST.
FOYLESIDE SHOPPING CENTRE
FOYLE ST.
ST. AUGUSTINE CHAPEL
SIEGE MUS.
LONDON ST.
PUMP ST.
LECKY RD.
BISHOP ST.
ARTILLERY ST.
FERRYQUAY GATE
BRIDGE ST.
VERBAL ARTS CENTRE
ST. COLUMB'S CATHEDRAL
NEW GATE
LONG TOWER CHURCH
DOUBLE BASTION
CITY WALLS
BISHOP'S GATE
HAWKIN ST.
CARLISLE RD.
& BIKE RENTAL
LONG TOWER ST.
BISHOP ST. WITHOUT
JAIL TOWER
THE FOUNTAIN
WAPPING LN.
FOYLE RD.
FOUNTAIN
AUBREY ST.
BARRACK ST.
UPR. BENNETT ST.
HARDING ST.
JOHN ST.
PEACE WALL
ABERCORN RD.
HANDS ACROSS THE DIVIDE SCULPTURE
FORMER SHIRT FACTORY SITE
SUNBEAM TERRACE
BELLVUE AVE.
FERGUSON ST.
MAUREEN AVE.
LOWER BENNETT ST.
CRAIGAVON BRIDGE
To Train Station, Portrush via A-2 & Belfast via A-6
IVY TERRACE
FOYLE RD.
To County Donegal (Republic of Ireland) via A-40
100 Meters
100 Yards
Accommodations
1 Bishop's Gate Hotel
2 Shipquay Hotel
3 Maldron Hotel
4 Merchant's House
5 Saddler's House
Eateries
6 Exchange Rest. & Wine Bar
7 Fitzroy's
8 Browns in Town
9 To Walled City Brewery

end of the Peace Bridge—are the main reasons to spend time on the east side.) Waterloo Place and the adjacent Guildhall Square, just outside the north corner of the old city walls, are the pedestrian hubs.

Tourist Information: The TI sits on the riverfront and rents bikes, and can book bus and walking tours (Mon-Fri 9:00-17:30, Sat-Sun 10:00-17:00, closes earlier in off-season; 44 Foyle Street, tel. 028/7126-7284, www.visitderry.com).

Tours: For walking tours, consider **McCrossan's City Tours** (£4; tel. 028/7127-1996, mobile 077-1293-7997, www.derrycitytours.com) or **Bogside History Tours** (£6; mobile 077-3145-0088 or 078-0056-7165, www.bogsidehistorytours.com). **Game of Thrones Tours** brings you to locations used in the TV show (£40, tel. 028/9568-0023, www.gameofthronestours.com). **City Sightseeing**'s double-decker buses are a good option for an overview (£12.50, tel. 028/7137-0067, www.citysightseeingderry.com).

Getting There

Derry is an hour's drive from Portrush; the Foyleside parking garage across from the TI is handy for drivers.

If you're using public transportation, consider a Zone 4 iLink smartcard, good for all-day train and bus use in Northern Ireland (see page 298). Derry's little end-of-the-line train station (next to the river on the east side of town) has service to Portrush, Belfast, and Dublin. All intercity buses stop at the Ulsterbus Station, on Foyle Street close to Guildhall Square.

➲ *Walk the Walls*

• *This walk, lasting about an hour, focuses on Derry's early days. It starts on the old city walls and ends near St. Columb's Cathedral, and can be linked with my Bogside Murals Walk.*

Old City Walls: Squatting determinedly in the city center, Derry's ▲▲ old city walls (built 1613-1618 and still intact) hold an almost mythic place in Irish history.

It was here in 1688 that a group of brave apprentice boys made their stand, slamming the city gates shut in the face of the approaching Catholic forces of deposed King James II. With this act, the boys galvanized the city's indecisive Protestant defenders inside the walls. Months of negotiations and a grinding 105-day siege followed. The sacrifice and defiant survival of the city turned the tide in favor of newly crowned Protestant King William of Orange, who arrived in Ireland soon after and defeated James at the pivotal Battle of the Boyne.

Almost 20 feet high and at least as thick, the walls form a mile-long oval loop. The most interesting section is the half-circuit facing the Bogside, starting at Magazine Gate (stairs face the Tower Museum Derry inside the walls) and finishing at Bishop's Gate.

• *Enter the walls at Magazine Gate and find the stairs opposite the Tower Museum. Once atop the walls, head left.*

Walk the wall as it heads uphill, snaking along the earth's contours. In the row of buildings on the left (just before crossing over Castle Gate), you'll see an arch entry into the **Craft Village,** an alley lined with a cluster of cute shops and cafés that showcase the economic rejuvenation of Derry (Mon-Sat 9:30-17:30, closed Sun).

• *After crossing over Butcher Gate, stop in front of the grand building with the four columns to view the...*

First Derry Presbyterian Church: This stately Neoclassical, red-sandstone church was finished in 1780. It was eventually closed due to dry rot and Republican firebombings. But in 2011, the renovated church reopened to a chorus of cross-community approval (one more sign of the slow reconciliation taking place in Derry). The **Blue Coat School** exhibit behind the church highlights the important role of Presbyterians in local history (free but donation encouraged, closed Sat-Tue in summer and Oct-April).

• *Just up the block is the...*

Apprentice Boys Memorial Hall: Built

in 1873, this houses the private lodge and meeting rooms of an all-male Protestant organization. The group is dedicated to the memory of the original 13 apprentice boys who saved the day during the 1688 siege. Each year, on the Saturday closest to the August 12 anniversary date, the modern-day Apprentice Boys Society celebrates the end of the siege with a controversial march atop the walls. The **Siege Museum** stands behind the hall, giving a narrow-focus Unionist view of the siege (£4, closed Sun, 18 Society Street).

Next, you'll pass a large, square pedestal on the right atop Royal Bastion. It once supported a column in honor of Governor George Walker, the commander of the defenders during the siege. In 1972, the IRA blew up the column, which had 105 steps to the top (one for each day of the siege).

• *Opposite the empty pedestal is the small Anglican...*

St. Augustine Chapel: Set in a pretty graveyard, this Anglican chapel is where some believe the original sixth-century monastery of St. Columba stood. The quaint grounds are open to visitors (closed Sun except for worship).

As you walk, you'll pass a long wall (on the left)—all that's left of a former **British Army base,** which stood here until 2006. Two 50-foot towers used to loom out of it, bristling with cameras and listening devices. Its dismantling—as well as the removal of most of the British Army from Northern Ireland—is a positive sign in cautiously optimistic Derry.

Stop at the **Double Bastion** fortified platform that occupies this corner of the city walls. The old cannon is nicknamed "Roaring Meg" for the fury of its firing during the siege.

From here, you can see across the Bogside to the not-so-far-away hills of County Donegal in the Republic.

Directly below and to the right are Free Derry Corner and Rossville Street, where the tragic events of Bloody Sunday took place (see sidebar on page 323).

Down on the left is the 18th-century **Long Tower** Catholic church, named after the monk-built round tower that once stood in the area.

• *Head to the grand brick building behind you. This is the...*

Siege-defending cannons atop Derry's walls

Bishop's Gate

Verbal Arts Centre: A former Presbyterian school, this center promotes the development of local literary arts in the form of poetry, drama, writing, and storytelling. Drop in to check the events schedule (closed Sun, www.verbalartscentre.co.uk).

• *Go another 50 yards around the corner to reach...*

Bishop's Gate: From here, look up Bishop Street Within (inside the walls). This was the site of a British Army surveillance tower that overlooked the neighborhood until 2006. Now look in the other direction to see Bishop Street Without (outside the walls). You'll spot a modern wall topped by a high mesh fence, running along the left side of Bishop Street Without.

This is a so-called **"peace wall,"** built to ensure the security of the Protestant enclave living behind it in when the Troubles reignited over 50 years ago. The stone tower halfway down the peace wall is all that remains of the old jail that briefly held rebels after a 1798 revolt against the British.

• *To do the Bogside Murals Walk from here, backtrack along the walls to head through Butcher Gate and down the long flight of stairs (see next).*

➲ *Bogside Murals Walk*

The Catholic Bogside area was the tinderbox of the modern Troubles in Northern Ireland, and the site of Bloody Sunday, a terrible confrontation during a march that occurred nearly 50 years ago. Today, the ▲▲ murals of the Bogside give visitors an accessible glimpse of this community's passionate perception of those events.

Getting There: The events are memorialized in 12 murals painted on the ends of residential flats along a 200-yard stretch of Rossville Street and Lecky Road, where the march took place. For the purposes of this walk, you can reach them from Waterloo Place via William Street. They are also accessible from the old city walls at Butcher Gate via the long set of stairs extending below Fahan Street on the grassy hillside.

The Artists: Two brothers, Tom and William Kelly, and their childhood friend Kevin Hasson are known as the Bogside Artists. They grew up in the Bogside and witnessed the tragic events that took place there, which led them to begin painting the murals in 1994.

The Murals: Start out at the roundabout intersection of Rossville and William streets.

The Bogside murals face different directions (and some are partially hidden by buildings), so they're not all visible from a single viewpoint. Plan on walking three

Peace *mural in Bogside*

Bloody Sunday

In the mid-1960s, inspired by civil rights protests in the US, the Prague Spring uprising, and student strikes in Paris, civil rights groups became more outspoken in Northern Ireland. Initially, their goals were to gain better housing, secure fair voting rights, and end employment discrimination for Catholics in the North. Tensions mounted, and clashes with the predominantly Protestant Royal Ulster Constabulary police force became frequent. Eventually, the British Army was called in to keep the peace.

On January 30, 1972, about 10,000 people protesting internment without trial held an illegal march sponsored by the Northern Ireland Civil Rights Association. British Army barricades kept them from the center of Derry, so they marched through the Bogside neighborhood.

That afternoon, some youths rioted on the fringe of the march. Shooting broke out, and after 25 minutes, 13 marchers were dead and 13 were wounded (one of the wounded later died). The soldiers claimed they came under attack from gunfire and nail-bombs. The marchers said the army shot indiscriminately at unarmed civilians.

The clash, called "Bloody Sunday," uncorked pent-up frustration and gave birth to a flood of fresh IRA volunteers. An investigation at the time exonerated the soldiers, but the relatives of the victims called it a whitewash and insisted on their innocence.

In 1998, the British government began a new inquiry into the events. The Saville Report, released in 2010, determined that the Bloody Sunday civil rights protesters were innocent.

In a dramatic 2010 speech in the House of Commons, then-British Prime Minister David Cameron apologized to the people of Derry. "What happened on Bloody Sunday was both unjustified and unjustifiable. It was wrong," he declared. Cheers rang out in Derry's Guildhall Square, where thousands had gathered to watch the televised speech. After 38 years, Northern Ireland's bloodiest wound started healing.

long blocks along Rossville Street (which becomes Lecky Road) to see them all.

From William Street, walk south along the right side of Rossville Street toward Free Derry Corner. The murals will all be on your right.

The first mural you'll walk past is the colorful ❶ ***Peace,*** showing the silhouette of a dove in flight (left side of mural) and an oak leaf (symbol of Derry; right side of mural), both created from a single ribbon.

❷ ***The Hunger Strikers*** features two Derry-born participants of the 1981 Maze Prison hunger strike, as well as their mothers, who sacrificed and supported them in their fatal decision (10 strikers died).

Smaller and easy to miss (above a ramp with banisters) is ❸ ***John Hume.*** It's actually a collection of four faces (clockwise from upper left): Nationalist leader John Hume, Martin Luther King, Jr., Nelson Mandela, and Mother Teresa. The Brooklyn Bridge in the middle symbolizes the long-term bridges of understanding that the work of these four Nobel Peace Prize-winning activists created.

Now look for ❹ ***The Saturday Matinee,*** which depicts an outgunned but

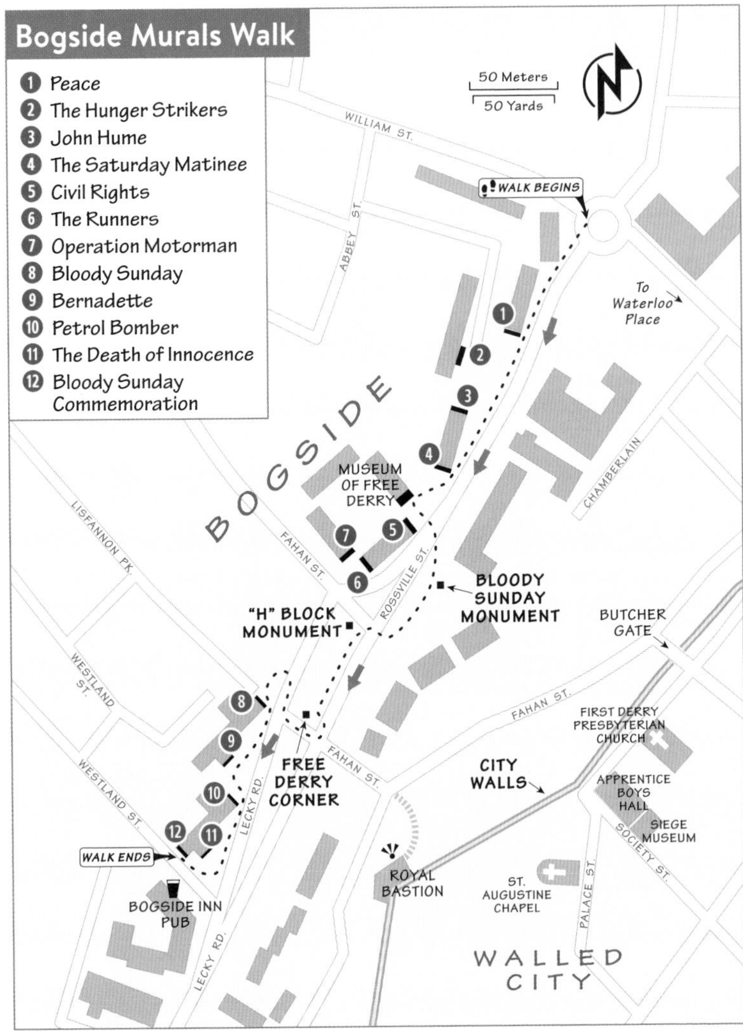

undaunted local youth behind a shield. He holds a stone, ready to throw, while a British armored vehicle approaches. Why *Saturday Matinee?* It's because the weekend was the best time for locals to engage in a little "recreational rioting." The "MOFD" at the bottom of this mural stands for the nearby Museum of Free Derry.

Nearby is 5 ***Civil Rights,*** showing a marching Derry crowd carrying an anti-sectarian banner. In the building behind this mural, you'll find the intense **Museum of Free Derry** (£6, open Mon-Fri 9:30-16:00 year-round, also open April-Sept Sat-Sun 13:00-16:00, 55 Glenfada Park, www.museumoffreederry.org).

Cross over to the other side of Rossville Street to see the **Bloody Sunday Monument.** This small, fenced-off stone obelisk lists the names of those who died that day, most within 50 yards of this spot. Take a look at the map pedestal by the

Political Murals

The dramatic and emotional murals you'll encounter in Northern Ireland will likely be one of your trip's most enduring travel memories. During the 19th century, Protestant neighborhoods hung flags and streamers each July to commemorate the victory of King William of Orange at the Battle of the Boyne in 1690. Modern murals evolved from these colorful annual displays.

Unionist murals were created during the extended Home Rule political debate that eventually led to the partitioning of the island in 1921 and the creation of Northern Ireland. Murals that expressed opposing views in Nationalist Catholic neighborhoods were outlawed. The ban remained until the eruption of the modern Troubles, when staunchly Nationalist Catholic communities isolated themselves behind barricades, gaining freedom to express their pent-up passions. In Derry, this form of resistance first appeared in 1969 with the simple "You are now entering Free Derry" message that you'll still see painted on the surviving gable wall at Free Derry Corner.

Found mostly in working-class neighborhoods of Belfast and Derry, today's political murals blur the line between art and propaganda, giving visitors a striking glimpse of each community's history, identity, and values.

monument, which shows how a rubble barricade was erected to block the street.

Cross back again, this time over to the grassy median strip that runs down the middle of Rossville Street. At this end stands a granite letter ***H*** inscribed with the names of the IRA hunger strikers who died (and how many days they starved) in the H-block of Maze Prison.

From here, as you look across at the corner of Fahan Street, you get a good view of two murals. In ❻ ***The Runners*** (right), four rioting youths flee tear gas from canisters used by the British Army to disperse hostile crowds. Meanwhile, in ❼ ***Operation Motorman*** (left), a British soldier wields a sledgehammer to break through a house door.

Walk down to the other end of the median strip where the white wall of **Free Derry Corner** announces "You are now entering Free Derry." This was the gabled end of a string of houses that stood here almost 50 years ago. During the Troubles, it became a traditional meeting place for speakers to address crowds.

Cross back to the right side of the street (now Lecky Road) to see ❽ ***Bloody Sunday,*** in which a small group of men carry a body from that ill-fated march. It's based on a famous photo of Father Edward Daly that was taken that day.

Bernadette Devlin mural in Bogside

Operation Motorman *mural*

Near it is a mural called ⑨ ***Bernadette.*** The woman with the megaphone is Bernadette Devlin McAliskey, an outspoken civil rights leader, who, at age 21, became the youngest elected member of British Parliament.

⑩ ***Petrol Bomber,*** showing a teen wearing an army-surplus gas mask, captures the Battle of the Bogside, when locals barricaded their community, effectively shutting out British rule.

In ⑪ ***The Death of Innocence,*** a young girl stands in front of bomb wreckage. She is Annette McGavigan, a 14-year-old who was killed on this corner by crossfire in 1971. She was the 100th fatality of the Troubles, which eventually took more than 3,000 lives (and she was also a cousin of one of the artists). The broken gun beside her points to the ground, signifying that it's no longer being wielded. The large butterfly above her shoulder symbolizes the hope for peace. For years, the artists left the butterfly an empty silhouette until they felt confident that the peace process had succeeded. They finally filled in the butterfly with optimistic colors in the summer of 2006.

Finally, around the corner, you'll see a circle of male faces: ⑫ ***Bloody Sunday Commemoration***, painted in 1997 to observe the 25th anniversary of the tragedy, shows the 14 victims.

Across the street, drop into the **Bogside Inn** for a beverage and check out the black-and-white photos of events in the area during the Troubles. This pub has been here through it all, and lives on to tell the tale.

While these murals preserve the struggles of the late 20th century, today sectarian violence has given way to a settlement that seems to be working.

Sights

▲▲TOWER MUSEUM DERRY

This well-organized museum combines modern audiovisual displays with historical artifacts to tell Derry's story from a skillfully unbiased viewpoint, sorting out some of the tangled history of Northern Ireland's Troubles. Occupying a modern reconstruction of a fortified medieval tower house, it provides an excellent introduction to the city. The museum is divided into two sections: the Story of Derry (on the ground floor) and the Spanish Armada (on the four floors of the tower).

Cost and Hours: £4, includes audioguide for Armada exhibits, daily 10:00-17:30, last entry at 16:00, Union Hall Place, tel. 028/7137-2411, www.derrystrabane.com/towermuseum.

Sleeping and Eating

$$$$ Bishop's Gate Hotel is Derry's top lodging option (fine bar, 24 Bishop Street, www.bishopsgatehotelderry.com). **$$$$** The **Shipquay Hotel** rents 21 rooms with stylish minimalist comfort (15 Shipquay Street, www.shipquayhotel.com). **$$ Maldron Hotel** features 93 modern and large rooms (Butcher Street, www.maldronhotelderry.com). **$ Merchant's House** is a fine Georgian townhouse (16 Queen Street, www.thesaddlershouse.com); **$ Saddler's House** is a charming Victorian townhouse (36 Great James Street, www.thesaddlershouse.com).

The trendy **$$$ Exchange Restaurant and Wine Bar** offers lunches and quality dinners in a central location near the river behind Waterloo Place (Queen's Quay). Busy **$$$ Fitzroy's,** tucked below Ferryquay Gate and stacked with locals, serves good lunches and dinners (2 Bridge Street). **$$ Browns in Town** is a casual, friendly lunch or dinner option (21 Strand Road). **$$ Walled City Brewery,** across the Peace Bridge, is a fun change of pace (70 Ebrington Square).

Irish History & Culture

Ireland is rich with history, culture, and language.

IRISH HISTORY

Prehistory

Ireland became an island when rising seas covered the last land bridge (7000 BC), a separation from Britain that the Irish would fight to maintain for the next 9,000 years. (Snakes were too slow to migrate before the seas cut Ireland off, despite later legends about St. Patrick banishing them.) By 6000 BC, Stone Age hunter-fishers had settled on the east coast, followed by Neolithic farmers from the island of Britain. These early inhabitants left behind impressive but mysterious funeral mounds (passage graves) and large Stonehenge-type stone circles.

The Celts (500 BC-AD 450)

More an invasion of ideas than of armies, the Celtic culture from Central Europe settled in Ireland, where it would dominate for a thousand years. There were more than 300 *tuatha* (kingdoms) in Ireland, each with its own *rí* (king), who would've happily chopped the legs off anyone who called him "petty." The island was nominally ruled by a single *Ard Rí* (high king) at the **Hill of Tara** (north of Dublin), though there was no centralized nation.

In 55 BC, the Romans conquered the Celts in England, but they never invaded Ireland. Irish history forever skewed in a different direction—Gaelic, not Latin. The Romans called Ireland **Hibernia,** meaning Land of Winter; it was apparently too cold and bleak to merit an attempt at colonization.

The Age of Saints and Scholars (AD 450-800)

When Ancient Rome fell and took the Continent—and many of the achievements of Roman culture—with it, Gaelic Ireland was unaffected. There was no Dark Age here, and the island was a beacon of culture for the rest of Europe. Ireland (population c. 750,000) was still a land of many feuding kings, but the culture was stable.

Christianity and Latin culture arrived first as a trickle from trading contacts with Christian Gaul (France), then more emphatically in AD 432 with **St. Patrick,** who persuasively converted the sun- and nature-worshipping Celts. Legends say he drove Ireland's snakes (symbolic of pagan beliefs) into the sea and explained the Trinity with a shamrock—three leaves on one stem.

Later monks continued Christianizing the island. They flocked to scattered, isolated monasteries, living in stone igloo beehive huts, translating and illustrating manuscripts. Perhaps the greatest works of art from all of Dark Age Europe are these manuscripts, particularly the ninth-century Book of Kells (in Dublin).

By 800, **Charlemagne** was importing educated and literate Irish monks to help organize and run his Frankish kingdom. Meanwhile, Ireland remained a relatively cohesive society based on monastic settlements rather than cities. Impressive round towers from those settlements still dot the Irish landscape—silent reminders of this scholarly age.

Viking Invasion
(800-1100)

In 795, Viking pirates from Norway invaded, first testing isolated island monasteries, then boldly sailing up Irish rivers into the country's interior. The many raids wreaked havoc on the monasteries and continued to shake Irish civilization for two chaotic centuries. In 841, a conquering Viking band decided to winter in Ireland. The idea caught on as subsequent raiders eventually built the island's first permanent walled cities, Dublin and Waterford. The Viking raiders slowly evolved into Viking traders. They were the first to introduce urban life and commerce to Ireland.

Anglo-Norman Arrival
(1100-1500)

The Normans were Ireland's next aggressive guests. In 1169, a small army of well-armed soldiers of fortune invaded Ireland under the pretense of helping a deposed Irish king regain his lands. This was the spearhead of a century-long invasion by the so-called Anglo-Normans—the French-speaking rulers of England, descended from William the Conqueror and his troops.

By 1250, the Anglo-Normans occupied two-thirds of the island. But when the **Black Death** came in 1348, it spread rapidly and fatally in the tightly packed Norman settlements. The plague, along with Normans intermarrying with Gaels, eventually diluted Norman identity and shrank English control. But even as Anglo-Norman power eroded, the English kings considered Ireland theirs.

The End of Gaelic Rule
(1500s)

Martin Luther's **Reformation** split the Christian churches into Catholic and Protestant, making Catholic Ireland a hot potato for newly Protestant England to handle. In 1534, angered by **Henry VIII** and his break with Catholicism, the **earls of Kildare** (father, then son) led a rebellion. Henry crushed the revolt, executed the earls, and confiscated their land. Henry's daughter, **Elizabeth I,** gave the land to English Protestant colonists (called "planters"). The next four centuries would see a series of rebellions by Gaelic-speaking Irish-Catholic farmers fighting to free themselves from rule by English-speaking Protestant landowners.

Hugh O'Neill (1540-1616), a Gaelic chieftain angered by planters and English abuses, led a Gaelic revolt in 1595. At the Battle of Yellow Ford (1598), guerrilla tactics brought about an initial Irish victory. But after the disastrous **Battle of Kinsale** (1601), O'Neill ceded a half-million acres to England, signaling the end of Gaelic Irish rule.

English Colonization and Irish Rebellions
(1600s)

By 1641, 25,000 Protestant English and Scottish planters had settled into the confiscated land, making Ulster (in the northeast) the most English area of the island.

Then, **Oliver Cromwell**—who had pulled off a *coup d'état* in England—invaded and conquered Ireland (1649-1650) with a Puritanical, anti-Catholic zeal. Cromwell confiscated 11 million additional acres of land from Catholic Irish landowners to give to English Protestants.

In 1688-1689, Irish rebels rallied around Catholic **King James II,** who had been deposed by the English Parliament. He wound up in Ireland, where he formed an army to retake the crown. The showdown came at the massive **Battle of the Boyne** (1690), north of Dublin. James and his 25,000 men were defeated by the troops of Protestant **King William III** of Orange. From this point on, the color orange became a symbol in Ireland for pro-English, pro-Protestant forces.

Protestant Rule

(1700s)

During the 18th century, urban Ireland thrived economically, and even culturally, under the English. Dublin in the 1700s (pop. 50,000) was Britain's second city, and one of Europe's wealthiest and most sophisticated.

But beyond Dublin, rebellion continued to brew. Irish nationalists were inspired by budding democratic revolutions in America (1776) and France (1789). Increasingly, the issue of Irish independence was less a religious question than a political one.

England tried to solve the Irish problem politically by forcing Ireland into a "Union" with England as part of a "United Kingdom" (**Act of Union,** 1801). The 500-year-old Irish Parliament was dissolved, with its members becoming part of England's Parliament in London. From then on, "Unionists" have been those who oppose Irish independence, wanting to preserve the country's union with England.

Votes, Violence, and the Famine

(1800s)

Irish politicians lobbied in the British Parliament for Catholic rights, reform of absentee-landlordism, and for **Home Rule.** But any hope of an Irish revival was soon snuffed out by the biggest catastrophe in Irish history: The **Great Potato Famine** (1845-1849). Legions of people (between 500,000 and 1.1 million) starved to death or died of related diseases. Another 1 to 2 million emigrated.

Ireland was ruined. Many of the best and brightest fled, and the island's economy—and spirit—took generations to recover. And culturally, old Gaelic, rural Ireland was being crushed under the Industrial Revolution and the political control wielded by Protestant England.

Easter Rising and War of Independence

(1900-1920)

As the century turned, Ireland prepared for the inevitable showdown with Britain. On Easter Monday, April 24, 1916, Irish nationalists marched on Dublin and proclaimed Ireland an independent republic. British troops struck back and, in just one week, suppressed the insurrection. When the British government swiftly executed the ringleaders, Ireland resolved to win its independence at all costs.

In the 1918 elections, the separatist Sinn Féin party (meaning "Ourselves") won big, but these new members of Parliament refused to go to London. Instead, they formed their own independent Irish Parliament in Dublin. Then Irish rebels began ambushing policemen—seen as the eyes and ears of British control—sparking the **War of Independence** in 1919. The fledgling Irish Republican Army faced 40,000 British troops. A thousand people died in this multiyear guerrilla war of street fighting, sniper fire, jailhouse beatings, terrorist bombs, and reprisals.

Partition and Civil War

(1920-1950)

Finally, Britain agreed to Irish independence. But Ireland itself was a divided nation—the southern three-quarters of the island was mostly Catholic, Gaelic, rural, and for Home Rule; the northern quarter was Protestant, English, industrial, and Unionist. The solution? In 1921, the British Parliament partitioned the island into two independent, self-governing countries within the British Commonwealth: **Northern Ireland** and the **Irish Free State.**

Ireland's various political factions wrestled with this compromise solution, and the island plunged into a **Civil War** (1922-1923). The hardline IRA opposed the partition. Dublin and the southeast were ravaged in a year of bitter fighting before the Irish Free State emerged victorious. The IRA went underground, moving its fight north and trying for the rest of the century to topple the government of Northern Ireland.

In 1949, the Irish Free State left the Commonwealth and officially became the **Republic of Ireland.**

Troubles in the North

(1950-2000)

The Republic moved toward prosperity in the second half of the century, but Northern Ireland—with a slight Protestant majority and a large, disaffected Catholic minority—was plagued by the **Troubles.** In 1967, organized marches and demonstrations demanded equal treatment for Catholics. Protestant **Unionist Orangemen** countered by marching through Catholic neighborhoods, provoking riots. In 1969, Britain sent troops to help Northern Ireland keep the peace.

From the 1970s to the 1990s, the North was a low-level battlefield, with the IRA using terrorist tactics to advance their political agenda. The Troubles, which claimed some 3,000 lives, continued with bombings, marches, hunger strikes, rock-throwing, and riots (notably Derry's **Bloody Sunday** in 1972).

Finally, after a string of failed peace agreements, came the watershed 1998 settlement known as the **Good Friday Accord** (to pro-Irish Nationalists) or the **Belfast Agreement** (to pro-British Unionists).

Global Nations

(2000 and Beyond)

After years of negotiation, in 2005 the IRA formally announced an end to its armed campaign, promising to pursue peaceful, democratic means. In 2007, London returned control of Northern Ireland to the popularly elected Northern Ireland Assembly. Perhaps most important, after almost 40 years, the British Army withdrew 90 percent of its forces from Northern Ireland that summer.

Now it's up to Northern Ireland to keep the peace. The 1998 peace accord gives Northern Ireland the freedom to leave the UK if ever the majority of the population approves a referendum to do so. At the same time, the Republic of Ireland withdrew its constitutional claim to the entire island of Ireland. Northern Ireland now has limited autonomy from London, with its own democratically elected, power-sharing government.

Britain's decision to leave the European Union (Brexit) has brought new uncertainties to Ireland. The stakes are high: Even with an open border between Northern Ireland (part of the UK) and the Republic of Ireland (a separate country and EU member), political or economic instability could inflame tensions in these divided communities.

IRISH CULTURE

Irish Art

Megalithic tombs, ancient gold and metalwork, illuminated manuscripts, high crosses carved in stone, paintings of rural Ireland, and provocative political murals—

Ireland comes with some fascinating art. Here are a few highlights.

Megalithic Period: During the Stone Age, 5,000 years ago, farmers living in the **Boyne Valley,** north of Dublin, built a "cemetery" of approximately 40 **burial mounds.** The most famous of these mound tombs is the passage tomb at Newgrange, part of Brú na Bóinne, which also features some of Europe's best examples of megalithic (big rock) art.

The Age of Saints and Scholars: Christianity grew in Ireland from St. Patrick's first efforts in the fifth century AD. During this "Golden Age" of Irish civilization, monks, along with metalworkers and stonemasons, created imaginative designs and distinctive stylistic motifs for **manuscripts, metal objects,** and **crosses.**

Monks wrote out and richly decorated manuscripts of the Gospels. The most beautiful and imaginative of these illuminated manuscripts is the **Book of Kells** (c. AD 800). Crafted by Irish monks at a monastery on the Scottish island of Iona, the book was brought to Ireland for safekeeping from rampaging Vikings. Many consider this book the finest piece of art from Europe's Dark Ages (now at Dublin's Trinity College Library).

The monks used Irish high crosses to celebrate the triumph of Christianity and to educate the illiterate masses through simple stone carvings of biblical themes. The **Cross of Murdock** (Muiredach's Cross, AD 923) is 18 feet tall, towering over the remains of the monastic settlement at Monasterboice. It is but one of many monumental crosses in Ireland.

Native Irish Art: The English suppressed Celtic Irish culture, replacing native styles with English traditions in architecture, painting, and literature. But in the late 19th century, revivals in Irish language, folklore, music, and art began to surface. **Jack B. Yeats** (1871-1957, brother of the poet W. B. Yeats), Belfast-born painter **Paul Henry** (1876-1958), and **Sean Keating** (1889-1977) were among the painters who looked to traditional Irish subjects for inspiration, focusing on

Trinity Library in Dublin

Church of St. Mary of the Rosary, Cong

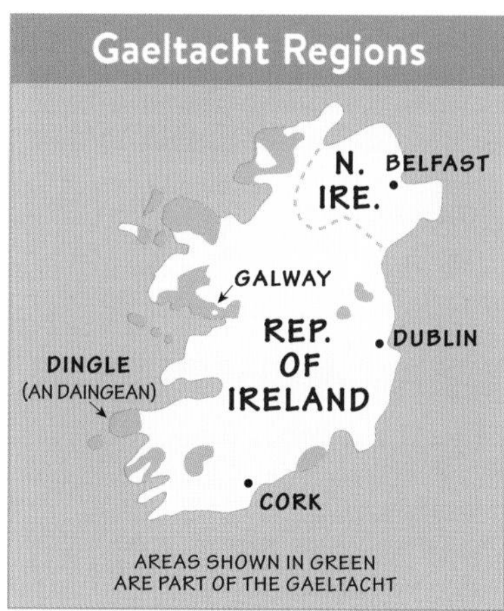

Ireland's people, the country's rugged beauty, and its struggle for independence.

Irish Literature

Since the Book of Kells, Ireland's greatest contributions to the world of art have been through words. After Christianity transformed Ireland into a refuge of literacy (while the rest of Europe crumbled into the Dark Ages), Charlemagne's imported Irish monks invented "minuscule," which became the basis of the lowercase letters we use in our alphabet today. The cultural importance placed on the word (spoken, and, for the past 1,500 years, written) is today reflected in the rich output of modern Irish writers.

William Butler Yeats' early poems and plays are filled with fairies and idyllic rural innocence, while his later poems reflect Ireland's painful transition to independence. Yeats' Nobel Prize for literature (1923) was eventually matched by three later, Nobel-winning Irish authors: **George Bernard Shaw** (1925), **Samuel Beckett** (1969), and **Seamus Heaney** (1995).

Dublin-born **Oscar Wilde** wowed London with his quick wit, outrageous clothes, and flamboyant personality. Wilde wrote the darkly fascinating *Picture of Dorian Gray* (1890) and skewered upper-class Victorian society in witty comedic plays such as *The Importance of Being Earnest* (1895). Meanwhile, **Bram Stoker** was conjuring up a Gothic thriller called *Dracula* (1897). Most inventive of all, perhaps, was **James Joyce,** who captured literary lightning in a bottle with his modern, stream-of-consciousness *Ulysses,* set on a single day in Dublin (June 16, 1904).

In recent decades, the bittersweet Irish literary parade has been inhabited by tragically volcanic characters like **Brendan Behan,** who exclaimed, "I'm a drinker with a writing problem." Bleak poverty experienced in childhood was the catalyst for **Frank McCourt**'s memorable *Angela's Ashes.* Among the most celebrated of today's Irish writers is **Roddy Doyle,** whose feel for working-class Dublin resonates in his novels of contemporary life (such as *The Commitments*).

Irish Language

The Irish have a rich oral tradition that goes back to their ancient fireside storytelling days. Part of the fun of traveling here is getting an ear for the way locals express themselves.

Irish Gaelic is one of four surviving Celtic languages, along with Scottish Gaelic, Welsh, and Breton. Some proud Irish choose to call their native tongue

Irish Words

Irish	English
Pleasantries	
Fáilte. (FAHLT-chuh or FAHLT-uh)	Welcome.
Conas tá tú? (CONN-us A-ta too)	How are you?
Go raibh maith agat. (guh rov mah UG-ut)	Thank you.
Slán. (slawn)	Bye.
Slainte! (SLAWN-chuh)	Cheers! (To your health!)
Useful Words	
alt (ahlt)	cliff
an lár (ahn lar)	city center
ard (ard)	high, height, hillock
baile (BALL-yah)	town, town land
beag (beg)	little
bearna (bar-na)	gap
boireann (burr-en)	large rock, rocky area
bóthar (boh-er)	road
bun (bun)	end, bottom
caiseal (CASH-el)	circular stone fort
caisleán (cash-LAWN)	castle
cathair (CAHT-her)	circular stone fort, city
cill (kill)	church
craic (crack)	fun atmosphere, good conversation
droichead (DROCKH-ed)	bridge
drumlin (DRUM-lin)	small hill
dún (doon)	fort
fír (fear)	men's room
gaeltacht (GAIL-takt)	Irish language district
gall (gaul)	foreigner
garda (gar-dah)	police officer
gort (gort)	field
inis (in-ish)	island
lei thras (LEH-hrass)	toilets
mileac (MIL-yach)	low marshy ground
mná (min-AW)	women's room
mór (mor)	large
oifig an phoist (UFF-ig un fusht)	post office
poll (poll)	hole, cave
rath (rath)	ancient earthen fort
ros (ross)	wood or headland
sí (shee)	fairy mound, bewitching
slí (slee)	route, way
sliabh (sleeve)	mountain
sráid (shrayd)	street
trá (traw)	beach, strand

"Irish" instead of "Gaelic" to ensure that there is no confusion with the language spoken in parts of Scotland.

Only 165 years ago, the majority of the Irish population spoke Irish Gaelic. But most of the speakers were of the poor laborer class that either died or emigrated during the famine. After the famine, parents and teachers understood that their children would be better off speaking English if they emigrated to the US, Canada, Australia, or England. Children in schools wore a tally stick around their necks, and teachers cut a notch each time a child was caught speaking Irish. At the end of the day, the child received a whack for each notch in the stick. It wasn't until a resurgence of cultural pride in the late 19th century that an attempt was made to promote the language again.

These days, less than 5 percent of the Irish population is fluent in their native tongue. However, it's taken seriously enough that all national laws must first be written in Irish, then translated into English. Irish Gaelic can be heard most often in the western counties of Kerry, Galway, Mayo, and Donegal. You'll know you're entering an Irish Gaelic-speaking area when you see a sign saying Gaeltacht (GAIL-takt).

Irish Gaelic has no "th" sound—which you can hear today when an Irish person says something like "turdy-tree" (thirty-three). There are also no equivalents of the simple words "yes" and "no." Instead, answers are given in an affirmative or negative rephrasing of the question. For example, a question like "Did you mail the letter today?" would be answered with "I did (mail the letter)," rather than a simple "yes." Or "It's a nice day today, isn't it?" would be answered with "It is," or "'Tis."

Practicalities

TOURIST INFORMATION

Before your trip, scan the two government-funded tourist websites (Republic of Ireland, www.discoverireland.ie; Northern Ireland, www.discovernorthernireland.com).

In Ireland, a good first stop in any town is generally the tourist information office—abbreviated **TI** in this book. (The general nationwide tourist-information phone number for travelers calling from within Ireland is 1-850-230-330.) Avoid ad agencies masquerading as TIs, especially in Dublin—use the official TI. Swing by to pick up a city map and get information on public transit, walking tours, special events, and nightlife.

HELP!

Travel Advisories: For updated health and safety conditions, including any restrictions for your destination, consult the US State Department's international travel website (travel.state.gov).

Emergency and Medical Help: For any emergency service—ambulance, police, or fire—call **112** from a mobile phone or landline. If you get sick, do as the locals do and go to a pharmacist for advice. Or ask at your hotel for help—they'll know the nearest medical and emergency services.

Theft or Loss: To replace a passport, you'll need to go in person to an embassy (see next). If your credit and debit cards disappear, cancel and replace them (see "Damage Control for Lost Cards" on

Finding Your Irish Roots

Lots of travelers come to the Emerald Isle intent on tracing their Irish ancestry. But too few give it enough thought before they set foot on the old sod, and instead head straight to what they think might be the right town or region to start "asking around." While this approach may bear fruit (or at least give you an opportunity to meet nice Irish people), a bit of preparation can save time and increase your chances of making a real connection to your Celtic bloodlines.

First, a common false assumption: Many novice root-searchers think their Irish ancestors were from County Cork, because Cobh is listed as their emigration departure port. But Cobh was the primary departure port for the vast majority of Irish emigrants—regardless of where they had resided in Ireland. An even earlier wave of Irish emigrants (mostly Scots-Irish from Ulster) sailed from the port of Derry (the second busiest emigration port).

If you have an idea of what town your ancestors hailed from, search for its location (www.google.com/maps is a good starting point). Correct spelling is essential: Ballyalloly is up north in County Down while Ballyally is down south in County Cork. Just as there's a Springfield in almost every state in the Union, the same goes for some common Irish town names: There's a town named Kells in four different Irish counties.

Fáilte Ireland, the official government-sponsored Irish tourist board, is a safe bet for reputable genealogy sources (www.discoverireland.ie). Some websites to consider browsing are www.irishgenealogy.ie or www.ancestry.com. Online access to both the 1901 and 1911 Irish censuses has been a boon (www.census.nationalarchives.ie). However, many precious birth records (some dating back to the 1200s) were destroyed by a fire in 1922.

Before you get to Ireland, contact the **Genealogy Advisory Service** at the **National Library** in Dublin (tel. 01/603-0213, www.nli.ie, genealogy@nli.ie). It's also helpful to contact in advance the genealogy search service in Cobh (tel. 021/481-3591, www.cobhheritage.com/genealogy, genealogy@cobhheritage.com).

If you think your heritage might be Scots-Irish, check the **Discover Ulster-Scots Centre** in Belfast (tel. 028/9043-6710, http://discoverulsterscots.com, discoverulsterscots@gmail.com). Also consider the **Mellon Centre for Migration Studies,** near Omagh in Northern Ireland (tel. 028/8225-6315, www.qub.ac.uk/cms, mcms@librariesni.org.uk).

Another option is to hire a qualified expert to assist you in drilling deeper and navigating obstacles; Fáilte Ireland may be able to give you a recommendation. This kind of help doesn't come cheap, but if you're willing to invest in an experienced researcher, you may get better results. One worth considering is Sean Quinn of **My Ireland Heritage** (tel. 01/689-0213, www.myirelandheritage.com, sean@myirelandheritage.com, based near Dublin in Trim, County Meath, but able to work across Ireland).

With a few emails, phone calls, and internet searches, you may just end up having a pint with someone in Ireland who looks a lot like you.

page 340). File a police report, either on the spot or within a day or two; you'll need it to submit an insurance claim for lost or stolen rail passes or electronics, and it can help with replacing your passport or credit and debit cards. For more information, see RickSteves.com/help.

US Embassies: Dublin—42 Elgin Road, tel. 01/630-6200, http://ie.usembassy.gov; **Belfast**—Danesfort House, 223 Stranmillis Road, tel. 028/9038-6100, after-hours emergency mobile 012-5350-1106, http://uk.usembassy.gov/embassy-consulates/belfast.

Canadian Embassies: Dublin—7 Wilton Terrace, tel. 01/234-4000, www.canada.ie; **Belfast**—tel. 028/9754-2405, this office does not offer passport services; instead contact the Canadian High Commission in London (www.unitedkingdom.gc.ca).

TRAVEL TIPS

Time Zones: Ireland is five/eight hours ahead of the East/West coasts of the US—and one hour earlier than most of continental Europe. The exceptions are the beginning and end of Daylight Saving Time: Europe "springs forward" the last Sunday in March (two weeks after most of North America) and "falls back" the last Sunday in October (one week before North America). For a handy time converter, use the world clock app on your phone or download one (see www.timeanddate.com).

Business Hours: In Ireland, most stores are open Monday through Saturday from roughly 10:00 to 17:30, with a late night on Wednesday or Thursday (until 19:00 or 20:00). Saturdays are virtually weekdays, with earlier closing hours and no rush hour (though transportation connections can be less frequent). Sightseeing attractions are generally open on Sundays (with limited hours), while banks and many shops are closed. Friday and Saturday evenings are rowdy; Sunday evenings are quiet.

Watt's Up? Europe's electrical system is 220 volts, instead of North America's 110 volts. Most electronics (laptops, phones, cameras) and hairdryers convert automatically, so you won't need a converter, but you will need an adapter plug with three square prongs, sold inexpensively at travel stores in the US.

Discounts: Discounts for sights (called "concessions" in Ireland) are generally not listed in this book. However, seniors (age 60 and over), youths under 18, and students and teachers with proper identification cards (www.isic.org) can get discounts at many sights—always ask.

MONEY

Here's my basic strategy for using money in Europe:

- Upon arrival, head for a cash machine (ATM) at the airport and withdraw some local currency, using a debit card with low international transaction fees.
- In general, pay for bigger expenses with a credit card and use cash for smaller purchases. Use a debit card only for cash withdrawals.
- Keep your cards and cash safe in a money belt.

What to Bring

I pack the following and keep it all safe in my money belt.

Debit Card: Use at ATMs to withdraw cash.

Credit Card: Handy for bigger transactions (at hotels, shops, restaurants, car-rental agencies, and so on), payment machines, and online purchases.

Backup Card: Some travelers carry a third card (debit or credit; ideally from a different bank), in case one gets lost, demagnetized, eaten by a temperamental machine, or simply doesn't work.

A Stash of Cash: I carry US $100-200 as a cash backup, which comes in handy in an emergency (such as if your ATM card gets eaten by the machine).

What NOT to Bring: Resist the urge

Exchange Rate

1 euro (€) = **about** $1.20

1 British pound (£) = **about** $1.30

Republic of Ireland: To convert prices in euros to dollars, add about 20 percent: €20 = about $24, €50 = about $60. Just like the dollar, one euro (€) is broken down into 100 cents.

Northern Ireland: To convert prices in pounds to dollars, add 30 percent: £20 = about $26, £50 = about $65. The British pound (£, also called a "quid") is broken into 100 pence (p).

Check Oanda.com for the latest exchange rates.

to buy euros and pounds before your trip or you'll pay the price in bad stateside exchange rates. I've yet to see a European airport that didn't have plenty of ATMs.

Before You Go

Know your PIN. Make sure you know the numeric, four-digit PIN for all your cards, both debit and credit. Request it if you don't have one, as it may be required for some purchases in Europe.

Report your travel dates. Let your bank know that you'll be using your debit and credit cards in Europe, and when and where you're headed.

Adjust your ATM withdrawal limit. Find out how much you can take out daily and ask for a higher daily withdrawal limit if you want to get more cash at once. Note that European ATMs will withdraw funds only from checking accounts; you're unlikely to have access to your savings account.

Ask about fees. For any purchase or withdrawal made with a card, you may be charged a currency conversion fee (1-3 percent) and/or a Visa or MasterCard international transaction fee (less than 1 percent).

Rick's Tip: *Looking to upgrade your European* **travel skills?** *You'll find plenty of practical info at RickSteves.com/travel-tips.*

In Europe

Using Cash Machines: European cash machines work just like they do at home—except they spit out local currency instead of dollars, calculated at the day's standard bank-to-bank rate.

In most places, ATMs are easy to locate. When possible, withdraw cash from a bank-run ATM located just outside that bank. If your debit card doesn't work, try a lower amount—your request may have exceeded your withdrawal limit or the ATM's limit.

Avoid "independent" ATMs, such as Travelex, Euronet, Moneybox, Your Cash, Cardpoint, and Cashzone. These have high fees, can be less secure than a bank ATM, and may try to trick users with "dynamic currency conversion" (see later).

Exchanging Cash: Avoid exchanging money in Europe; it's a big rip-off. Banks do not exchange money unless you have an account with them. In most Irish countryside towns, the post office is your only option. In a pinch you can always find exchange desks at major train stations or airports—convenient but with crummy rates.

Using Credit Cards: Despite some differences between European and US cards, there's little to worry about: US credit cards generally work fine in Europe. I've been inconvenienced a few times by unattended payment machines (transit-ticket kiosks, parking, self-service gas stations, toll booths) where US cards may not work. Carry cash as a backup.

Dynamic Currency Conversion: If merchants offer to convert your purchase price into dollars (called dynamic currency conversion, or DCC), refuse this "service." You'll pay extra for the expen-

ATMs are easy to find.

sive convenience of seeing your charge in dollars. If an ATM offers to "lock in" or "guarantee" your conversion rate, choose "proceed without conversion." Other prompts might state, "You can be charged in dollars: Press YES for dollars, NO for euros." Always choose the local currency.

Security Tips: Pickpockets target tourists. Keep your cash, credit cards, and passport secure in your money belt, and carry only a day's spending money in your front pocket or wallet.

Damage Control for Lost Cards: If you lose your credit or debit card, report the loss immediately to the respective global customer-assistance centers. With a mobile phone, call these 24-hour US numbers: Visa (tel. +1 303/967-1096), MasterCard (tel. +1 636/722-7111), and American Express (tel. +1 336/393-1111). From a landline, you can call these US numbers collect by going through a local operator. European toll-free numbers (listed by country) can be found at the websites for Visa and MasterCard. You can generally receive a temporary card within two or three business days in Europe (see RickSteves.com/help).

Tipping

Tipping in Ireland is appreciated, but not expected. As in the US, the proper amount depends on your resources, tipping philosophy, and the circumstances, but some general guidelines apply.

Restaurants: At a pub or restaurant with waitstaff, check the menu or your bill to see if the service is included; if not, tip about 10 percent. At pubs where you order food at the counter, a tip is not expected but is appreciated.

Taxis: For a typical ride, round up your fare a bit (for instance, if the fare is €9, give €10).

Getting a VAT Refund

Wrapped into the purchase price of your Irish souvenirs is a value-added tax (VAT); it's 23 percent in the Republic and 20 percent in Northern Ireland. You're entitled to get most of that tax back if you purchase more than €30/£30 (about $36/$42) worth of goods at a store that participates in the VAT-refund scheme.

Get the paperwork. Have the merchant completely fill out the necessary refund document. You'll have to present your passport. Get the paperwork done before you leave the store to ensure you'll have everything you need (including your original sales receipt).

Get your stamp at the border or airport. Process your VAT document at your last stop in the European Union (such as at the airport) with the customs agent who deals with VAT refunds. Some customs desks are positioned before airport security; confirm the location before going through security.

Collect your refund. You can claim your VAT refund from refund companies such as Global Blue or Planet with offices at major airports, ports, or border crossings. These services (which extract a 4 percent fee) can refund your money in cash immediately or credit your card.

Customs for American Shoppers

You can take home $800 worth of items per person duty-free, once every 31 days. Many processed and packaged foods are allowed, including vacuum-packed cheeses, dried herbs, jams, baked goods, candy, chocolate, oil, vinegar, mustard, and honey. Fresh fruits and vegetables and most meats are not allowed, with exceptions for some canned items. As for alcohol, you can bring in one liter duty-free.

To bring alcohol (or liquid-packed foods) in your carry-on bag on your flight home, buy it at a duty-free shop at the airport. You'll increase your odds of getting it onto a connecting flight if it's packaged in a "STEB"—a secure, tamper-evident bag.

For details on allowable goods, customs rules, and duty rates, visit http://help.cbp.gov.

SIGHTSEEING

Sightseeing can be hard work. Use these tips to make your visits to Ireland's finest sights meaningful, fun, efficient, and painless.

Plan Ahead

Set up an itinerary that allows you to fit in all your must-see sights. Confirm open hours, and don't put off visiting a must-see sight—you never know when a place will close unexpectedly for a holiday, strike, or restoration. Many museums are closed or have reduced hours at least a few days a year. A list of holidays is on page 358; check for possible closures during your trip.

Reservations, Advance Tickets, and Passes

Given how precious your vacation time is, I recommend getting reservations for any must-see sight that offers them. Many popular sights sell advance tickets that guarantee admission at a certain time of day, or allow you to skip entry lines. Either way, it's worth giving up some spontaneity to book in advance. For popular sights, you may need to book weeks or even months in advance. As soon as you're ready to commit to a certain date, book it.

Heritage Card Pass: This pass gets you into nearly 100 historical monuments, gardens, and parks in the Republic of Ireland. It generally pays off if you visit at least eight included sights (valid one year, includes handy map and list of sights' hours and prices, purchase at first Heritage sight you visit, some sights take cash only, tel. 01/647-6592, www.heritageireland.ie, heritagecard@opw.ie).

At Sights

Here's what you can typically expect:

Entering: You may not be allowed to enter if you arrive too close to closing time. And guards start ushering people out well before the actual closing time, so don't save the best for last.

Many sights have a security check. Allow extra time for these lines. Some sights require you to check daypacks and coats.

Photography: If the museum's photo policy isn't clearly posted, ask a guard. Generally, taking photos without a flash or tripod is allowed. Some sights ban selfie sticks; others ban photos altogether.

Audioguides and Apps: Many sights rent audioguides with recorded descriptions. Museums and sights often offer free apps that you can download to your mobile device (check their websites).

Expect Changes: Artwork can be on tour, on loan, out sick, or shifted at the whim of the curator. Pick up a floor plan as you enter, and ask museum staff if you can't find a particular item.

SLEEPING

Extensive and opinionated listings of good-value rooms are a major feature of this book's Sleeping sections. Rather than list accommodations scattered throughout a town, I choose hotels in my favorite neighborhoods that are convenient to your sightseeing.

Rates and Deals

I've categorized my recommended accommodations based on price, indicated with a dollar-sign rating (see sidebar). The price ranges suggest an estimated cost for a one-night stay in high season in a standard double room with a private toilet and shower, include a hearty breakfast, and assume you're booking directly with the hotel (not through a booking site, which extracts a commission).

Booking Direct: Once your dates are set, compare prices at several hotels. You can do this by checking Hotels.com, Booking.com, and hotel websites. Then book directly with the hotel itself. Contact small family-run hotels directly by phone or email. When you go direct, the owner avoids the commission paid to booking sites, thereby leaving enough wiggle room to offer you a discount, a nicer room, or a free breakfast (if it's not already included). If you prefer to book online or are considering a hotel chain, it's to your advantage to use the hotel's website.

Getting a Discount: Some hotels extend a discount to those who pay cash or stay longer than three nights. And some accommodations offer a special discount for Rick Steves readers, indicated in this guidebook by the abbreviation **"RS%."** Discounts vary: Ask for details when you reserve.

Lodging Vouchers: Many US travel agents sell vouchers for lodging in Ireland. I don't recommend buying these; the voucher program is just an expensive middleman between you and the innkeeper.

Sleep Code

Hotels are categorized according to the average price of a standard en suite double room with breakfast in high season.

$$$$	**Splurge:** Most rooms over €170/£140
$$$	**Pricier:** €130–170/£110-140
$$	**Moderate:** €90–130/£80-110
$	**Budget:** €50–90/£50-80
¢	**Backpacker:** Under €50/£50
RS%	**Rick Steves discount**

Unless otherwise noted, credit cards are accepted and free Wi-Fi is available. Comparison-shop by checking prices at several hotels (on each hotel's own website, on a booking site, or by email). For the best deal, book directly with the hotel. Ask for a discount if paying in cash; if the listing includes **RS%,** request a Rick Steves discount.

Friendly hotel staff

Using Online Services to Your Advantage

From booking services to user reviews, online businesses play a greater role in travelers' planning than ever before. Take advantage of their pluses—and be wise to their downsides.

Booking Sites

Booking websites Booking.com and Hotels.com offer one-stop shopping for hotels. To be listed, a hotel must pay a sizable commission. When you use an online booking service, you're adding a middleman. To support small, family-run hotels, which have a world that is more difficult than ever, book direct.

Short-Term Rental Sites

Rental juggernaut Airbnb and other short-term rental sites allow travelers to rent rooms and apartments directly from locals. Airbnb fans appreciate feeling part of a real neighborhood as "temporary Europeans."

Critics view Airbnb as creating unfair competition for established guesthouse owners. As a lover of Europe, I share the worry of those who see residents nudged aside by tourists. But as an advocate for travelers, I appreciate the value and cultural intimacy Airbnb provides.

User Reviews

User-generated review sites and apps such as Yelp and TripAdvisor can give you a consensus of opinions about everything from hotels and restaurants to sights and nightlife. But a user-generated review is based on the limited experience of one person, while a guidebook is the work of a trained researcher who visits many restaurants and hotels year after year.

Both types of information have their place, and in many ways, they're complementary. If something is well reviewed in a guidebook and it also gets good online reviews, it's likely a winner.

Accommodations

Hotels

Ireland offers a wide variety of hotels: homey guesthouses, traditional old hotels, impersonal business-class chains, and chic boutiques. Wherever possible, I opt for a family-run hotel. Note that to be called a "hotel" in Ireland, a place must have certain amenities, including a 24-hour reception (though this rule is loosely applied).

Arrival and Check-In: Hotels (and B&Bs) are sometimes located on the higher floors of a multipurpose building with a secured door. In that case, look for your hotel's name on the buttons by the main entrance. When you ring the bell, you'll be buzzed in.

Hotel elevators are common, though some older buildings still lack them. You may have to climb a flight of stairs to reach the elevator (if so, you can ask the front desk for help carrying your bags up). Elevators are typically very small—you may need to send your bags up without you.

The EU requires that hotels collect your name, nationality, and ID number. When you check in, the receptionist will normally ask for your passport and may keep it for anywhere from a couple of

Making Hotel Reservations

Requesting a Reservation: For family-run hotels, it's generally best to book your room directly via email or phone. For business-class and chain hotels, or if you'd rather book online, reserve directly through the hotel's official website (not a booking website).

Here's what the hotelier wants to know:

- Type(s) of rooms you want and size of your party
- Number of nights you'll stay
- Your arrival and departure dates, written European-style as day/month/year (18/06/22 or 18 June 2022)
- Special requests (en suite bathroom, cheapest room, twin beds vs. double bed, quiet room)
- Applicable discounts (such as a Rick Steves reader discount, cash discount, or promotional rate)

Confirming a Reservation: Most places will request a credit-card number to hold your room. If you're using an online reservation form, make sure it's secure by looking for *https* or a lock icon at the top of your browser. If the website isn't secure, it's best to share that confidential info via a phone call.

Canceling a Reservation: If you must cancel, do so with as much notice as possible, especially for smaller family-run places. Cancellation policies can be strict; read the fine print before you book. Many discount deals require prepayment, with no cancellation refunds.

Reconfirming a Reservation: Always call or email to reconfirm your room reservation a few days in advance. For B&Bs or very small hotels, I call again on my day of arrival to tell my host what time to expect me (especially important if arriving late—after 17:00).

Phoning: For tips on how to call hotels overseas, see page 348.

minutes to a couple of hours. If you're not comfortable leaving your passport at the desk for a long time, ask when you can pick it up. Or, if you packed a color copy of your passport, you can generally leave that rather than the original.

Small Hotels and B&Bs

Bed-and-breakfast places give you double the cultural intimacy for half the price. B&Bs range from small homes renting out a couple of spare bedrooms to large guesthouses with 10-15 rooms. A "townhouse" or "house" is like a big B&B or a small family-run hotel—with fewer amenities but more character than a hotel.

Short-Term Rentals

A short-term rental—whether an apartment, house, or room in a local's home—is an increasingly popular alternative, especially if you plan to settle in one location for several nights. For stays longer than a few days, you can usually find a rental that's comparable to—and cheaper than—a hotel room with similar amenities. Websites such as Airbnb, FlipKey, Booking.com, and the HomeAway family of sites (HomeAway, VRBO, and VacationRentals) let you browse a wide range of properties. Alternatively, rental agencies such as InterhomeUSA.com or RentaVilla.com, which list more carefully

Cozy B&B bedroom

selected accommodations that might cost more, can provide more personalized service.

Other Options: Swapping homes with a local works for people with an appealing place to offer (don't assume where you live is not interesting to Europeans). Good places to start are HomeExchange.com and LoveHomeSwap.com. To sleep for free, Couchsurfing.com is a vagabond's alternative to Airbnb. It lists millions of outgoing members, who host fellow "surfers" in their homes.

Hostels

A hostel provides cheap beds in dorms where you sleep alongside strangers for about €30 per night. Travelers of any age are welcome if they don't mind dorm-style accommodations and meeting other travelers. Most hostels offer kitchen facilities, guest computers, Wi-Fi, and a self-service laundry. Family and private rooms are often available.

Independent hostels tend to be easygoing, colorful, and informal (no membership required, www.hostelworld.com). You may pay slightly less by booking directly with the hostel. Independent Holiday Hostels (www.hostels-ireland.com) is a network of independent hostels, requiring no membership. **Official hostels** are part of Hostelling International (HI) and share an online booking site (www.hihostels.com). HI hostels typically require that you be a member or else pay a bit more per night.

EATING

You'll find modern Irish cuisine delicious and varied. Irish beef, lamb, and dairy products are among the EU's best. And there are streams full of trout and salmon and a rich ocean of fish and shellfish right offshore. While potatoes remain staples, they're often replaced with rice or pasta in many dishes. Modern foodie places almost always have a serious vegetarian main dish. Try the local specialties wherever you happen to be eating.

Breakfast

The traditional breakfast, the "Irish Fry" (known in the North as the "Ulster Fry"), is a hearty way to start the day—with juice, tea or coffee, cereal, eggs, bacon, sausage, a grilled tomato, sautéed mushrooms, and optional black pudding (made from pigs' blood). Toast is served with butter and marmalade. Home-baked Irish soda bread can be an ambrosial eye-opener for those of us raised on Wonder Bread. This meal tides many travelers over until dinner.

Picnics

Picnicking saves time and money. Try boxes of orange juice (pure, by the liter), fresh bread (especially Irish soda bread), tasty Cashel blue cheese, meat, a tube of mustard, local-eatin' apples, bananas, small tomatoes, a small tub of yogurt (it's drinkable), rice crackers, trail mix or nuts, plain digestive biscuits (the chocolate-covered ones melt), and any local specialties. At open-air markets and supermarkets, you can get produce in small quantities. Supermarkets often have good deli sections, packaged sandwiches, and sometimes salad bars. If you're driving, pull over and grab a healthy snack at a roadside stand (Ireland's climate is ideal for strawberries).

Pubs

Pubs are a basic part of the Irish social scene, and whether you're a teetotaler or a beer-guzzler, they should be a part of your Ireland experience. Whether in rural villages or busy Dublin, a pub (short for "public house") is an extended living room where, if you don't mind the stickiness, you can feel the pulse of Ireland. You'll find the most traditional and atmospheric pubs in Ireland's countryside and smaller towns.

Smart travelers use pubs to eat, drink, get out of the rain, watch the latest sporting event, and make new friends. You're a guest on your first night; after that, you're a regular. *Craic* (pronounced "crack"), Irish for "fun" or "a good laugh," is the sport that accompanies drinking in a pub. To encourage conversation, stand or sit at the bar, not at a table.

It's a tradition to buy your table a round, and then for each person to reciprocate. If an Irishman buys you a drink, thank him by saying, *"Go raibh maith agat"* (guh rov mah UG-ut). Offer him a toast in Irish—*"Slainte"* (SLAWN-chuh, the equivalent of "cheers").

Pubs are generally open daily from 11:00 to 23:30 and Sunday from noon to 22:30. There's seldom table service; order at the bar. Pay as you order, and only tip (by rounding up to avoid excess coinage) if you like the service. Children are generally welcome before 20:00; you must be at least 18 to order a beer. All pubs in the

A new generation of Irish food

A hearty Irish dinner

Republic are smoke-free, but have covered smoking patios.

Pub Grub: Pub grub gets better every year—it's Ireland's best eating value. Pubs that are attached to restaurants are more likely to have fresh food. But don't expect high cuisine; this is, after all, comfort food. For about $20, you'll get a basic hot meal in friendly surroundings.

Pub menus offer a hearty assortment of traditional dishes, such as Irish stew (mutton with mashed potatoes, onions, carrots, and herbs), soups and chowders, coddle (bacon, pork sausages, potatoes, and onions stewed in layers), fish-and-chips, collar and cabbage (boiled bacon coated in bread crumbs and brown sugar, then baked and served with cabbage), boxty (potato pancake filled with fish, meat, or vegetables), and champ (potato mashed with milk and onions). Irish soda bread nicely rounds out a meal. In coastal areas, try seafood, such as mackerel, mussels, and Atlantic salmon.

Beer: The Irish take great pride in their beer. Guinness is the default beer in an Irish pub, known for its dark color and creamy white head. The color and slightly burnt flavor come from roasting the barley before the beer is brewed. Traditionally, Guinness is served at a slightly warmer temperature than most ales and lagers. If you think you don't like Guinness, try it in Ireland: It doesn't travel well and tastes better in its homeland.

For a small beer, ask for a glass, which is a half-pint. Stout is dark and more bitter, like Guinness (Murphy's is a very good one, a bit smoother and milder than Guinness). For a cold, refreshing, basic, American-style beer, ask for a lager, such as Harp. The ales vary from sweet to bitter, and often have a hoppy or nutty flavor (I swear by Smithwick's). Caffrey's is a satisfying cross between stout and ale. Craft beer microbrews are making inroads in Ireland (check www.beoir.org for options). Try the draft cider (sweet or dry)...carefully. The most common spirit is triple-distilled Irish whiskey. Teetotalers can order a soft drink.

STAYING CONNECTED

One of the most common questions I hear from travelers is, "How can I stay connected in Europe?" The short answer is: more easily and cheaply than you might think.

The simplest solution is to bring your own device—mobile phone, tablet, or laptop—and use it just as you would at home (following the money-saving tips below). For more details, see RickSteves.com/phoning. For a very practical one-hour talk covering tech issues for travelers, see RickSteves.com/mobile-travel-skills.

Because dialing instructions vary between the Republic and Northern Ireland, carefully read "How to Dial," on the next page.

Using a Mobile Phone in Europe

Sign up for an international plan. To stay connected at a lower cost, sign up for an international service plan through your carrier. Most providers offer a simple bundle that includes calling, messaging, and data. Your normal plan may already include international coverage (T-Mobile's does).

Use free Wi-Fi whenever possible. Unless you have an unlimited-data plan, it's best to save most of your online tasks for Wi-Fi. You can access the internet, send texts, and even make voice calls over Wi-Fi

Minimize the use of your cellular network. The best way to make sure you're not accidentally burning through data is to put your device in "airplane" mode (which also disables phone calls and texts), turn your Wi-Fi back on, and connect to networks as needed. When you need to get online but can't find Wi-Fi, simply turn on your cellular network (or turn off airplane mode) just long enough for the task

How to Dial

To make an international call, follow the dialing instructions below. Drop an initial zero, if present, when dialing a European phone number—except when calling Italy. I've used the telephone number of one of my recommended Dublin hotels as an example (tel. 01/679-6500).

From a Mobile Phone

It's easy to dial with a mobile phone. Whether calling from the US to Europe, country to country within Europe, or from Europe to the US—it's all the same. Press zero until you get a + sign, enter the country code (353 for the Republic of Ireland, 44 for Northern Ireland), then dial the phone number.

► To call the Dublin hotel from any location, dial +353 1 679 6500.

From a US Landline to Europe

Dial 011 (US/Canada access code), country code (353 for the Republic of Ireland, 44 for Northern Ireland), and phone number.

► To call the Dublin hotel from your home phone, dial 011 353 1 679 6500.

From a European Landline to the US or Europe

Dial 00 (Europe access code), country code (1 for the US, 353 for the Republic of Ireland, 44 for Northern Ireland), and phone number.

► To call my US office from the Republic of Ireland, dial 00 1 425 771 8303.

► To call the Republic of Ireland hotel from Germany, dial 00 353 1 679 6500.

For a complete list of European country codes and more phoning help, see HowToCallAbroad.com.

at hand. Disable automatic updates so your apps will update only when you're on Wi-Fi.

Use Wi-Fi calling and messaging apps. Skype, WhatsApp, FaceTime, and Google Hangouts are great for making free or low-cost calls or sending texts over Wi-Fi worldwide. Just log on to a Wi-Fi network, then connect with any of your friends or family members who use the same service.

Buy a European SIM card. If you anticipate making a lot of local calls, need a local phone number, or your provider's international data rates are expensive, consider buying a SIM card in Europe to replace the one in your (unlocked) US phone or tablet.

SIM cards are sold at department-store electronics counters, some newsstands, and vending machines. If you need help setting it up, buy one at a mobile-phone shop (you may need to show your passport). There are no roaming charges when using a European SIM card in other EU countries, though to be sure you get this "roam-like-at-home" pricing, ask if this feature is included when you buy your SIM card.

TRANSPORTATION

Figuring out how to get around in Europe is one of your biggest trip decisions. **Cars** work well for two or more traveling together (especially families with small

Tips on Internet Security

Make sure that your device is running the latest versions of its operating system, security software, and apps. Next, ensure that your device and key programs (like email) are password-protected. On the road, use only secure, password-protected Wi-Fi. Ask the hotel or café staff for the specific name of their network, and make sure you log on to that exact one.

If you must access your financial info online, use a banking app rather than accessing your account via a browser, and use a cellular connection, not Wi-Fi. Never log on to personal finance sites on a public computer. If you're very concerned, consider subscribing to a VPN (virtual private network).

kids), those packing heavy, and those delving into the countryside. **Trains** and **buses** are best for solo travelers, blitz tourists, city-to-city travelers, and those who want to leave the driving to others. Smart travelers can use short-hop **flights** within Europe to creatively connect the dots on their itineraries.

If your itinerary mixes cities and countryside, my advice is to connect cities by train (or bus) and to explore rural areas by rental car. Arrange to pick up your car in the last big city you'll visit, then use it to lace together small towns and explore the countryside.

Ireland has a good train-and-bus system, though departures are not as frequent as the European norm. Most rail lines spoke outward from Dublin, so you'll need to mix in bus transportation to bridge the gaps.

The best overall source of schedules for public transportation in the Republic of Ireland as well as Northern Ireland—including rail, cross-country and city buses, and Dublin's LUAS transit—is www.discoverireland.ie (select "Getting Around" near the bottom of the home page). For more detailed information on transportation throughout Europe, see RickSteves.com/transportation.

Trains

For travelers ready to lock in dates and times weeks or months in advance, buying nonrefundable tickets online can cut costs in half. To research rail connections in the Republic of Ireland, visit www.irishrail.ie; for Northern Ireland, use www.translink.co.uk (trains between Dublin and Belfast are the only city pair on both websites). For train schedules on the rest of the European continent, check www.bahn.com (Germany's excellent Europe-wide timetable).

Rail Passes: For most travelers in Ireland, a rail pass is not very useful. But if a pass works for your itinerary, keep in mind that Eurail passes cover all trains in both the Republic and Northern Ireland, and give a 30 percent discount on standard foot-passenger fares for some international ferries. Irish Rail also offers a pass covering five days of travel within a 15-day period in the Republic only (purchase at any major rail station in Ireland, www.irishrail.ie). For advice on figuring out the smartest train-ticket or rail-pass options for your trip, visit the Trains & Rail Passes section of my website at RickSteves.com/rail.

Ireland's Public Transportation

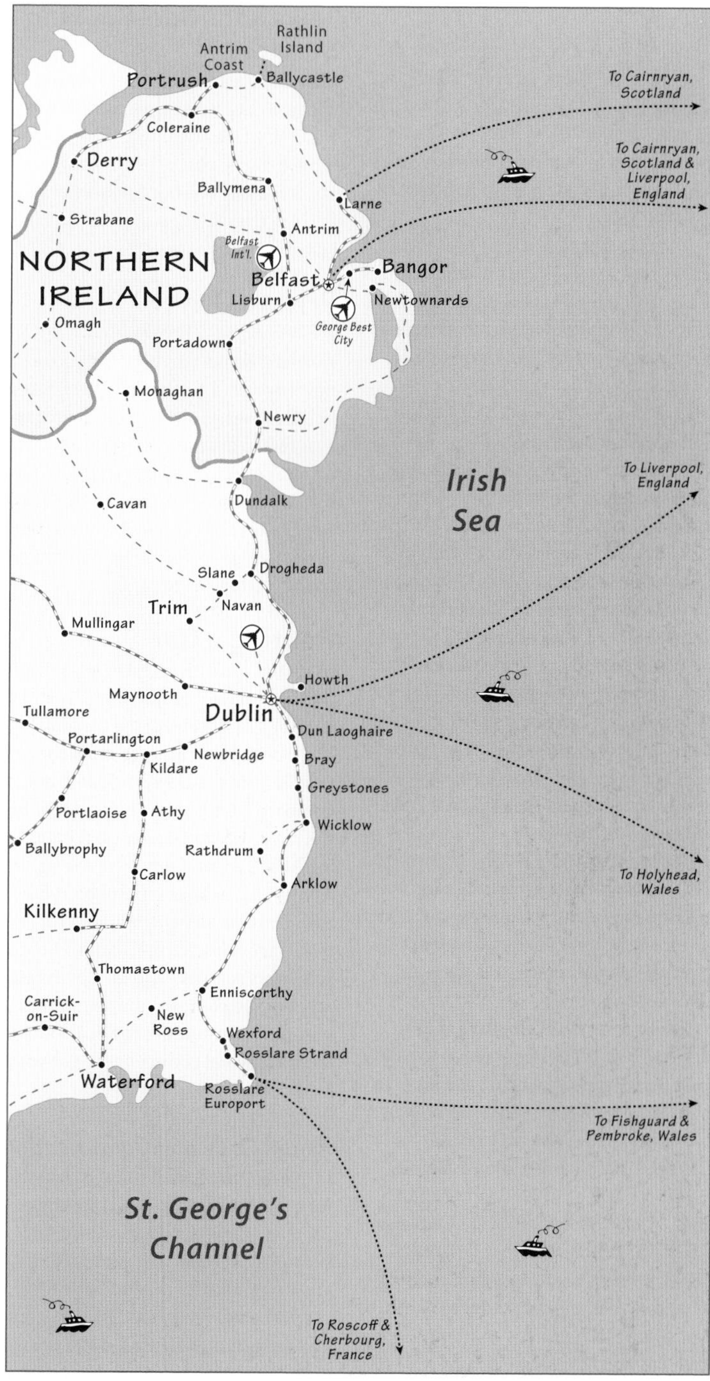
Rathlin Island
Antrim Coast
Portrush
Ballycastle
Coleraine
Derry
Ballymena
Larne
Strabane
Antrim
Belfast Int'l.
NORTHERN IRELAND
Belfast
Bangor
Lisburn
Newtownards
George Best City
Omagh
Portadown
Monaghan
Newry
Cavan
Dundalk
Irish Sea
Slane
Drogheda
Navan
Trim
Mullingar
Howth
Maynooth
Dublin
Tullamore
Dun Laoghaire
Portarlington
Newbridge
Kildare
Bray
Greystones
Portlaoise
Athy
Wicklow
Ballybrophy
Rathdrum
Carlow
Arklow
Kilkenny
Thomastown
Enniscorthy
Carrick-on-Suir
New Ross
Wexford
Rosslare Strand
Waterford
Rosslare Europort
St. George's Channel
To Cairnryan, Scotland
To Cairnryan, Scotland & Liverpool, England
To Liverpool, England
To Holyhead, Wales
To Fishguard & Pembroke, Wales
To Roscoff & Cherbourg, France

Buses

Public transit (especially cross-country Irish buses) will likely put your travels in slow motion. Although buses are about a third slower than trains, they're also a lot cheaper, and can be more direct. A combination of train and bus works best for many routes.

The Irish distinguish between "buses" (for in-city travel with lots of stops) and "coaches" (long-distance cross-country runs). Note that some rural coach stops are by "request only." This means the coach will drive right on by unless you flag it down by extending your arm straight out, with your palm open.

Bus Éireann Expressway is the main bus company in the Republic (www.buseireann.ie); **Translink** serves Northern Ireland (www.translink.co.uk). **Dublin Coach** covers Dublin, Ennis, Killarney, Tralee, Kildare, Kilkenny, Waterford, and Belfast (www.dublincoach.ie).

Travel Pass: Bus Éireann's **Open Road** tourist travel passes can be a good option for nondrivers. Coverage starts from three travel days in a six-day period and goes up to 15 days out of 30 (www.buseireann.ie, select "Tickets" and then "Tourist Travel Passes").

Discounts: Students can use their ISIC (international student identity card, www.isic.org) to get up to 50 percent discounts on cross-country coaches. Children 5-15 pay half-price on trains, and wee ones under age 5 go free.

Backpacker Bus Circuits: For a hop-on, hop-off bus ride geared to thrifty hostelers, **Paddy Wagon** offers three- to nine-day "tours" that can be combined into a comprehensive trip connecting Dublin, Cork, Killarney, Dingle, Galway, Westport, Donegal, Derry, and Belfast (May-Oct, 5 Beresford Palace, Dublin, tel. 01/823-0822, toll-free from UK tel. 0800-783-4191, www.paddywagontours.com). They also offer day tours to the Giant's Causeway, Belfast, Cliffs of Moher, Glendalough, and Kilkenny.

Taxis and Ride-Booking Services

Most European taxis are reliable and cheap. In many cities, two people can travel short distances by cab for little more than the cost of bus or subway tickets. If you like ride-booking services such as Uber, their apps usually work in Europe just like they do in the US.

Private Driver

While not cheap, hiring a private driver can make sense, particularly if you're traveling with a group. Consider **Fitzpatrick Coaches,** based in Monaghan but available to drive anywhere in Ireland (tel. 047/82331, mobile 087/273-1396, www.fitzpatrickcoaches.com). The three main vehicle size choices are SUV (3 passengers), van (up to 7 passengers), or small coach (up to 17 passengers).

Renting a Car

In Ireland you'll drive on the left side of the road—take it easy and you'll get the hang of it by the end of the first day.

It's cheaper to arrange most car rentals from the US, so research and compare rates before you go. Most of the major US rental agencies (including Avis, Budget, Enterprise, Hertz, and Thrifty) have offices throughout Europe. Also consider the two major Europe-based agencies, Europcar and Sixt. Consolidators such as Auto Europe (www.autoeurope.com—or the sometimes cheaper www.autoeurope.eu) compare rates at several companies to get you the best deal.

Rental Costs and Considerations

In midsummer expect to pay at least $250 for a one-week rental of a basic compact-size car with minimum insurance (not including fuel, tolls, and parking). You'll pay more for an automatic or for supplemental insurance. Smaller economy-size cars cost about $50 less per week.

Minibuses are a good, budget way to go for larger groups (five to nine people). To save money on fuel, request a diesel car.

Manual vs. Automatic: Almost all rental cars in Europe are manual by default—and cars with a stick shift are generally cheaper. If you need an automatic, request one in advance. An automatic makes sense for most American drivers: With a manual transmission in Ireland, you'll be sitting on the right side of the car and shifting with your left hand...while driving on the left side of the road.

Age Restrictions: Some rental companies impose minimum and maximum age limits. In the Republic of Ireland, you generally can't rent a car if you're 75 or older, and you'll usually pay an extra €25 per day insurance surcharge if you're 70-74. Some companies in Northern Ireland won't rent to anyone over 69.

Choosing Pickup/Drop-off Locations: Always check the hours of the locations you choose: Many rental offices close from midday Saturday until Monday morning and, in smaller towns, at lunchtime. You can drive your rental car from the Republic of Ireland into Northern Ireland, but will pay a drop-off charge (as much as $200) if you return it in the North. You'll pay a smaller drop-off charge (as much as $100) for picking up and returning the car from different locations within the same country, even within the same city.

Picking Up Your Car: Before driving off in your rental car, check it thoroughly and make sure any damage is noted on your rental agreement. Rental agencies in Europe tend to charge for even minor damage, so be sure to mark everything. Find out how your car's gearshift, lights, turn signals, wipers, radio, and fuel cap function, and know what kind of fuel the car takes (diesel vs. unleaded). When you return the car, make sure the agent verifies its condition with you. Some drivers take pictures of the returned vehicle as proof of its condition.

Car Insurance Options

When you rent a car in Europe, the price typically includes liability insurance, which covers harm to other cars or motorists—but not the rental car itself. To limit your financial risk in case of damage to the rental, choose one of these options: Buy a Collision Damage Waiver (CDW) with a low or zero deductible from the car-rental company (roughly 30-40 percent extra), get coverage through your credit card (more complicated, and few credit cards now offer free coverage in Ireland), or get collision insurance as part of a larger travel-insurance policy.

For more on car-rental insurance, see RickSteves.com/cdw.

Navigation Options

Your Mobile Phone: If you'll be navigating using your phone, remember to bring a car charger and device mount. Driving all day can burn through a lot of very expensive data. The economical work-around is to use map apps that work offline. By downloading in advance from Google Maps, City Maps 2Go, Apple Maps, Here WeGo, or Navmii, you can still have turn-by-turn voice directions and maps that recalibrate even when they're offline.

You must download your maps before you go offline—and it's smart to select large regions. Then turn off your data connection so you're not charged for roaming. This option is great for navigating in areas with poor connectivity.

GPS Devices: If you want the convenience of a dedicated GPS unit, consider renting one with your car ($10-30/day). These units offer real-time turn-by-turn directions and traffic without the data requirements of an app.

Paper Maps and Atlases: Even when navigating primarily with a mobile app or GPS, I always make it a point to have a paper map, ideally with a big, detailed regional road map. It's invaluable for getting the big picture, understanding alternate routes, and filling in if my phone runs out of juice. It's smart to buy a road atlas that covers all of Ireland; Ordnance Survey atlases are best (€11 in gas stations and bookstores). Drivers, hikers, and cyclists may want more detailed maps for Dingle, Connemara, the Antrim Coast, the Ring of Kerry, and the Boyne Valley (easy to buy locally at bookstores or gas stations).

Driving

Motorways link most major cities, but many smaller towns and rural sights

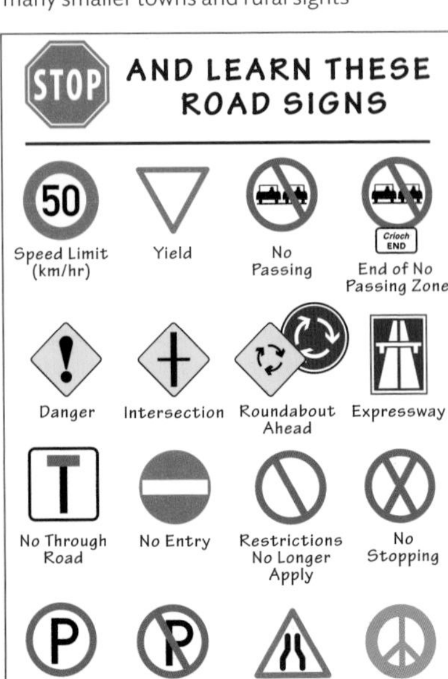

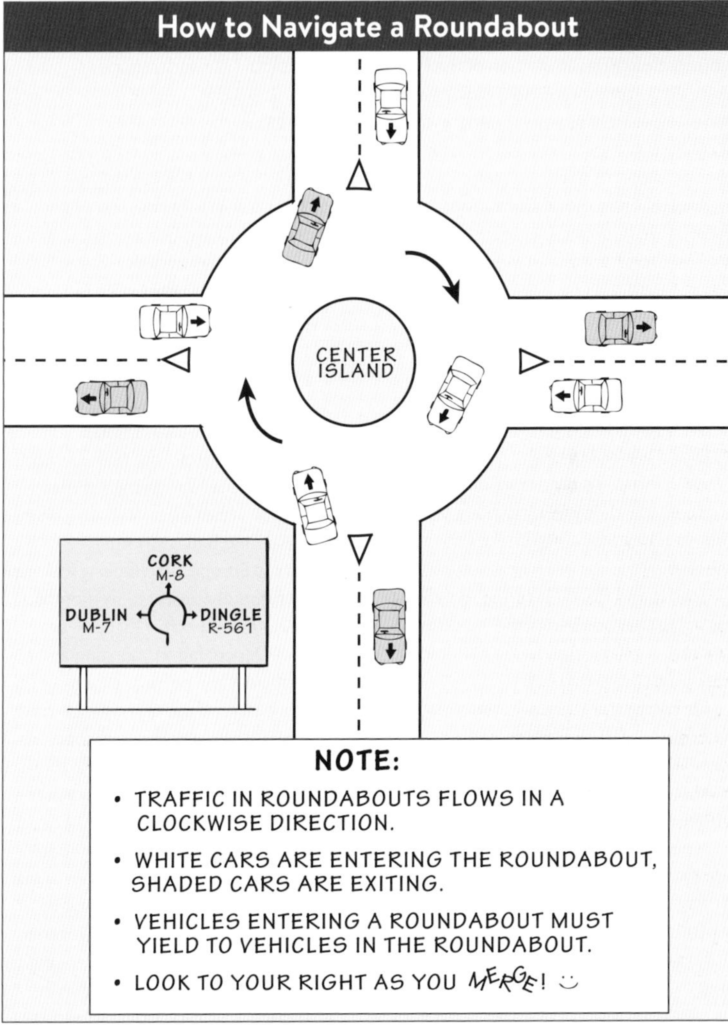

require driving on narrow country lanes. An Irish Automobile Association membership comes with most rentals (www.theaa.ie). Understand its towing and emergency road-service benefits.

Road Rules: Driving in Ireland is basically wonderful—once you remember to stay on the left and have mastered the roundabouts. The traffic in a roundabout has the right-of-way; entering traffic yields (look to your right as you merge). It helps to remember that the driver is always in the center of the road. As you approach bigger roundabouts, look for instructions on the pavement that indicate which lane to be in for your destination.

Be aware of typical European road rules; for example, many countries require headlights to be turned on at all times, and you're not allowed to turn left on a red light unless a sign or signal specifically authorizes it. Ask your car-rental company about these rules, or check the "International Travel" section of the US State Department website (www.travel.state.gov, search for your country in the "Learn About Your Destination" box, then click "Travel and Transportation").

Speed Limits, Road Conditions, and Fuel: In the Republic, the speed limit is in kilometers per hour, unleaded costs about €1.40/liter ($6.25/gallon), and the roads can be bumpy, narrow, and winding. In Northern Ireland, the speed limit is in miles per hour, unleaded costs about £1.30/liter ($7.30/gallon), and roads are better maintained.

Diesel fuel pumps (which are usually green in the US) are black in Ireland. Mixing them up while fueling is a sure way to ruin your day. Insurance doesn't cover this mistake.

Traffic and Road Hazards: Avoid driving in big cities; use ring roads to skirt the congestion. Real-time traffic conditions are updated on www.aa.ie.

On narrow rural roads, pull over against a hedgerow and blink your headlights to signal faster drivers to pass. Expect a slow tractor, a flock of sheep, and a one-lane bridge to lurk around blind turns. Honk when approaching blind corners to alert approaching drivers. Buses have the right of way.

Tolls: Many rental-car companies automatically charge for an eFlow pass that electronically pays the toll for Dublin's M50 motorway—ask (see www.eflow.ie). Toll motorways are usually blue on maps and are shown with the letter "M" followed by the route number (toll prices and map: www.tii.ie/roads-tolling).

Parking: One yellow line marked on the pavement means no parking Monday through Saturday during business hours. Double yellow lines mean no parking at any time. Broken yellow lines mean short stops are OK. For street parking, signs along the street indicate whether an area uses pay-and-display (machines have a blue circle with white letter *P*) or parking-disks (sold at nearby shops).

Flights

To compare flight costs and times, begin with an online travel search engine: Kayak is the top site for flights to and within Europe, easy-to-use Google Flights has price alerts, and Skyscanner includes many inexpensive flights within Europe. To avoid unpleasant surprises, before you book be sure to read the small print about refunds, changes, and the costs for "extras" such as reserving a seat, checking a bag, or printing a boarding pass.

Ireland's Airports: Four major airports are planted in the four corners of the island: Dublin (east), Cork (south), Shannon (west), and Belfast (north).

Flights to Europe: Start looking for international flights about four to six months before your trip, especially for peak-season travel. Depending on your itinerary, it can be efficient and no more expensive to fly into one city and out of another. If your flight requires a connection in Europe, see my hints on navigating Europe's top hub airports at RickSteves.com/hub-airports.

Flights Within Europe: Flying between European cities is surprisingly affordable. Before buying a long-distance train or bus ticket, check the cost of a flight on one of Europe's airlines, whether a major carrier or a no-frills outfit like EasyJet, Aer Lingus, Flybe, and Ryanair. For flights within Ireland, try Aer Arann, a regional subsidiary of Aer Lingus. Be aware that flying with a discount airline can have drawbacks, such as minimal customer service and time-consuming treks to secondary airports.

Flying to the US and Canada: Because security is extra tight for flights to the US, be sure to give yourself plenty of time at the airport. Charge your electronic devices before you board in case security checks require you to turn them on (see www.tsa.gov for the latest rules).

Resources from Rick Steves

Begin Your Trip at RickSteves.com

My mobile-friendly **website** is *the* place to explore Europe in preparation for your trip. You'll find thousands of fun articles, videos, and radio interviews; a wealth of money-saving tips for planning your dream trip; travel news dispatches; a video library of my travel talks; my travel blog; tips on finding the right rail pass for your itinerary and budget; and my latest guidebook updates (RickSteves.com/update).

Our **Travel Forum** is a well-groomed collection of message boards where our travel-savvy community answers questions and shares personal travel experiences—and our well-traveled staff chimes in when they can be helpful.

Our **online Travel Store** offers bags and accessories that I've designed to help you travel smarter and lighter. These include my popular carry-on bags (which I live out of four months a year), money belts, totes, toiletries kits, adapters, guidebooks, and planning maps.

Rick Steves' Tours, Guidebooks, TV Shows, and More

Small Group Tours: We offer more than 40 itineraries reaching the best destinations in this book...and beyond. You'll enjoy both great guides and a fun bunch of travel partners. For all the details, visit RickSteves.com/tours or call us at 425/608-4217.

Books: This book is just one of many in my series on European travel, which includes country and city guidebooks, Snapshots (excerpted chapters from bigger guides), Pocket Guides (full-color little books on big cities), and my budget-travel skills handbook, *Rick Steves Europe Through the Back Door.* A complete list of my titles appears near the end of this book.

TV Shows and Travel Talks: My public television series, *Rick Steves' Europe,* covers Europe with more than 100 half-hour episodes (watch full episodes at my website). My free online video library, Rick Steves Classroom Europe, offers a searchable database of short video clips on European history and culture. And, to raise your travel I.Q., check out the video versions of our popular classes (covering most European countries as well as travel skills).

Radio: My weekly public radio show, *Travel with Rick Steves,* features interviews with travel experts from around the world. It airs on 400 public radio stations across the US. A complete archive of programs is available on my website.

Audio Tours on My Free App: I've produced dozens of free, self-guided audio tours of the top sights in Europe. For those tours and other audio content, get my free Rick Steves Audio Europe app, an extensive online library organized by destination. For more on the app, see page 27.

Podcasts: You can enjoy my travel content via several free podcasts, including my radio show, clips from my public television show, my audio tours, and my travel classes.

HOLIDAYS AND FESTIVALS

This list includes select festivals in major cities, plus national holidays observed throughout Ireland (when many sights and banks close). Before planning a trip around a festival, verify the dates with the festival website, TI sites (www.discoverireland.ie and www.discovernorthernireland.com), or RickSteves.com.

Jan 1	New Year's Day
Late Jan	Temple Bar Trad, Dublin (Irish music and culture festival, http://templebartrad.com)
March 17	St. Patrick's Day (5-day festival in Dublin, www.stpatricksday.ie)
March or April	Easter weekend, including Easter Monday
Early May	Labor Day, Ireland; Early May Bank Holiday (first Mon), UK
Late May	Fleadh Nua, Ennis (www.fleadhnua.com)
Late May	Spring Bank Holiday (last Mon), UK
Early June	June Bank Holiday (first Mon), Ireland
Mid-June	Bloomsday, Dublin (James Joyce festival, www.jamesjoyce.ie)
Late June	Patrún Festival, Kilronan (*currach* boat races)
Late June	St. John's Eve Bonfire Night (Kilronan)
July 12	Battle of the Boyne anniversary, Northern Ireland
Mid- to Late July	Galway Arts Festival
Late July/Early Aug	Galway Horse Races (www.galwayraces.com)
Early Aug	August Bank Holiday (first Mon), Ireland
Early Aug	Dingle Horse Races (www.dingleraces.ie)
Early-Mid-Aug	Dingle Regatta (boat races)
Early-Mid-Aug	Puck Fair, Killorglin, Kerry ("Ireland's Oldest Fair" and drink-fest, www.puckfair.ie)
Early-Mid-Aug	Féile an Phobail, West Belfast (Irish cultural festival, www.feilebelfast.com)
Mid-Aug	Fleadh Cheoil, Drogheda (traditional music festival, www.fleadhcheoil.ie)
Late Aug	Summer Bank Holiday (last Mon), UK
Late Aug	Rose of Tralee International Festival, Tralee (http://roseoftralee.ie)
Late Aug/Early Sept	Blessing of the Boats, Dingle (maritime festival)
Mid-Sept/Late Oct	Galway Races (www.galwayraces.com)
Late Sept	Galway Oyster Festival (4 days, www.galwayoysterfest.com)
Late Sept/Early Oct	Dingle Food Festival (www.dinglefood.com)
Late Oct	October Bank Holiday (last Mon), Ireland
Dec 25	Christmas
Dec 26	St. Stephen's Day, Ireland; Boxing Day, UK

CONVERSIONS AND CLIMATE

Numbers and Stumblers

- In Europe, dates appear as day/month/year, so Christmas 2022 is 25/12/22.
- What Americans call the second floor of a building is the first floor in Europe.
- On escalators and moving sidewalks, Europeans keep the left "lane" open for passing. Keep to the right.

Metric Conversions

Both the Republic of Ireland and Northern Ireland use the metric system (except for driving signage in Northern Ireland). Weight and volume are typically calculated in metric: A kilogram is 2.2 pounds, and a liter is about a quart. The weight of a person is measured by "stone" (one stone equals 14 pounds). Temperatures are generally given in both Celsius and Fahrenheit.

On the road, signs in the Republic of Ireland show distances and speed limits in kilometers and kilometers per hour, while Northern Ireland uses miles and miles per hour.

Clothing Sizes

Women: For pants and dresses, add 4 (US 10 = UK 14). For blouses and sweaters, add 2. For shoes, subtract 2.5 (US size 8 = UK size 5.5)

Men: For clothing, US and UK sizes are the same. For shoes, subtract about 0.5 (US size 9 = UK size 8.5)

Children: Clothing is sized similarly to the US. UK kids' shoe sizes are about one size smaller (US size 6 = UK size 5).

Ireland's Climate

First line, average daily high; second line, average daily low; third line, average days without rain. For more detailed weather statistics for destinations in this book (as well as the rest of the world), check www.wunderground.com.

Dublin

J	F	M	A	M	J	J	A	S	O	N	D
46°	47°	51°	55°	60°	65°	67°	67°	63°	57°	51°	47°
34°	35°	37°	39°	43°	48°	52°	51°	48°	43°	39°	37°
18	18	21	19	21	19	18	19	18	20	18	17

Packing Checklist

Whether you're traveling for five days or five weeks, you won't need more than this. Pack light to enjoy the sweet freedom of true mobility.

Clothing

- ❑ 5 shirts: long- & short-sleeve
- ❑ 2 pairs pants (or skirts/capris)
- ❑ 1 pair shorts
- ❑ 5 pairs underwear & socks
- ❑ 1 pair walking shoes
- ❑ Sweater or warm layer
- ❑ Rainproof jacket with hood
- ❑ Tie, scarf, belt, and/or hat
- ❑ Swimsuit
- ❑ Sleepwear/loungewear

Money

- ❑ Debit card(s)
- ❑ Credit card(s)
- ❑ Hard cash (US $100-200)
- ❑ Money belt

Documents

- ❑ Passport
- ❑ Tickets & confirmations: flights, hotels, trains, rail pass, car rental, sight entries
- ❑ Driver's license
- ❑ Student ID, hostel card, etc.
- ❑ Photocopies of important documents
- ❑ Insurance details
- ❑ Guidebooks & maps

Toiletries Kit

- ❑ Basics: soap, shampoo, toothbrush, toothpaste, floss, deodorant, sunscreen, brush/comb, etc.
- ❑ Medicines & vitamins
- ❑ First-aid kit
- ❑ Glasses/contacts/sunglasses
- ❑ Sewing kit
- ❑ Packet of tissues (for WC)
- ❑ Earplugs

Electronics

- ❑ Mobile phone
- ❑ Camera & related gear
- ❑ Tablet/ebook reader/laptop
- ❑ Headphones/earbuds
- ❑ Chargers & batteries
- ❑ Phone car charger & mount (or GPS device)
- ❑ Plug adapters

Miscellaneous

- ❑ Daypack
- ❑ Sealable plastic baggies
- ❑ Laundry supplies: soap, laundry bag, clothesline, spot remover
- ❑ Small umbrella
- ❑ Travel alarm/watch
- ❑ Notepad & pen
- ❑ Journal

Optional Extras

- ❑ Second pair of shoes (flip-flops, sandals, tennis shoes, boots)
- ❑ Travel hairdryer
- ❑ Picnic supplies
- ❑ Water bottle
- ❑ Fold-up tote bag
- ❑ Small flashlight
- ❑ Mini binoculars
- ❑ Small towel or washcloth
- ❑ Inflatable pillow/neck rest
- ❑ Tiny lock
- ❑ Address list (to mail postcards)
- ❑ Extra passport photos

INDEX

C

P

Q

R

MAP INDEX

Start your trip at

Our website enhances this book and turns

Explore Europe

At ricksteves.com you can browse through thousands of articles, videos, photos and radio interviews, plus find a wealth of money-saving travel tips for planning your dream trip. And with our mobile-friendly website, you can easily access all this great travel information anywhere you go.

TV Shows

Preview the places you'll visit by watching entire half-hour episodes of *Rick Steves' Europe* (choose from all 100 shows) on-demand, for free.

ricksteves.com

your travel dreams into affordable reality

Radio Interviews

Enjoy ready access to Rick's vast library of radio interviews covering travel tips and cultural insights that relate specifically to your Europe travel plans.

Travel Forums

Learn, ask, share! Our online community of savvy travelers is a great resource for first-time travelers to Europe, as well as seasoned pros.

Travel News

Subscribe to our free Travel News e-newsletter, and get monthly updates from Rick on what's happening in Europe.

Classroom Europe

Check out our free resource for educators with 400+ short video clips from the *Rick Steves' Europe* TV show.

Audio Europe™

Rick's Free Travel App

Get your FREE Rick Steves Audio Europe™ app to enjoy...

- Dozens of self-guided tours of Europe's top museums, sights and historic walks
- Hundreds of tracks filled with cultural insights and sightseeing tips from Rick's radio interviews
- All organized into handy geographic playlists
- For Apple and Android

With Rick whispering in your ear, Europe gets even better.

Find out more at ricksteves.com

Rick Steves has

Experience maximum Europe

Save time and energy

This guidebook is your independent-travel toolkit. But for all it delivers, it's still up to you to devote the time and energy it takes to manage the preparation and logistics that are essential for a happy trip. If that's a hassle, there's a solution.

Rick Steves Tours

A Rick Steves tour takes you to Europe's most

great tours, too!

with minimum stress

interesting places with great guides and small groups of 28 or less. We follow Rick's favorite itineraries, ride in comfy buses, stay in family-run hotels, and bring you intimately close to the Europe you've traveled so far to see. Most importantly, we take away the logistical headaches so you can focus on the fun.

Join the fun

This year we'll take 33,000 free-spirited travelers—nearly half of them repeat customers—along with us on four dozen different itineraries, from Ireland to Italy to Athens.

Is a Rick Steves tour the right fit for your travel dreams? Find out at ricksteves.com, where you can also request Rick's latest tour catalog.

Europe is best experienced with happy travel partners. We hope you can join us.

See our itineraries at ricksteves.com

A Guide for Every Trip

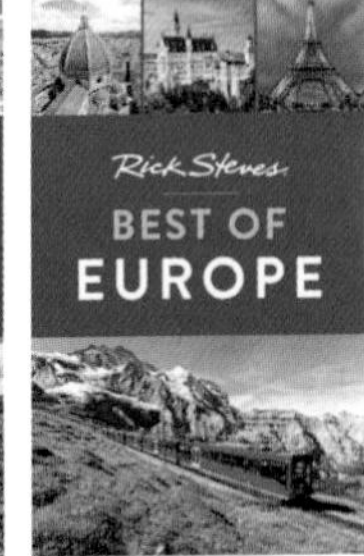

BEST OF GUIDES

Full color easy-to-scan format, focusing on Europe's most popular destinations and sights

Best of England
Best of Europe
Best of France
Best of Germany
Best of Ireland
Best of Italy
Best of Scotland
Best of Spain

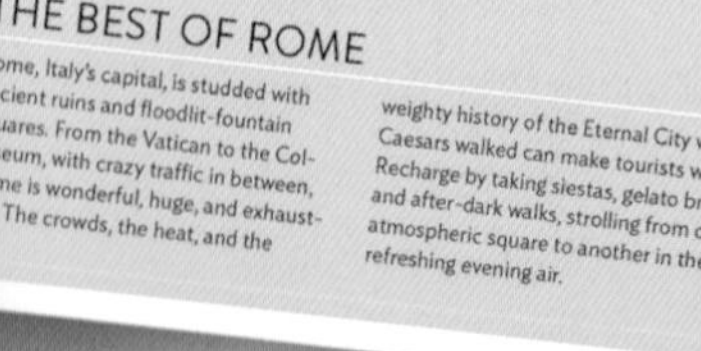

THE BEST OF ROME

ome, Italy's capital, is studded with cient ruins and floodlit-fountain uares. From the Vatican to the Colseum, with crazy traffic in between, ne is wonderful, huge, and exhaust- The crowds, the heat, and the weighty history of the Eternal City where Caesars walked can make tourists wilt. Recharge by taking siestas, gelato breaks, and after-dark walks, strolling from one atmospheric square to another in the refreshing evening air.

COMPREHENSIVE GUIDES

City, country, and regional guides with detailed coverage for a multi-week trip exploring the most iconic sights and venturing off the beaten track

Amsterdam & the Netherlands
Barcelona
Belgium: Bruges, Brussels, Antwerp & Ghent
Berlin
Budapest
Croatia & Slovenia
Eastern Europe
England
Florence & Tuscany
France
Germany
Great Britain
Greece: Athens & the Peloponnese
Iceland
Ireland
Istanbul
Italy
London
Paris
Portugal
Prague & the Czech Republic
Provence & the French Riviera
Rome
Scandinavia
Scotland
Sicily
Spain
Switzerland
Venice
Vienna, Salzburg & Tirol